XENA: THEIR COURAGE
CHANGED OUR WORLD

25th Anniversary Edition

AUSXIP

MARY D. BROOKS
(MARYD)

AUSXIP PUBLISHING
www.ausxippublishing.com

Xena: Their Courage Changed Our World
First Edition: September 04, 2020

Editing: Rosa Alonso
Cover Design: Linda "Calli" Callaghan
Cover Illustration: Lucia Nobrega
Interior Design / Typesetting: Mary D. Brooks / AUSXIP Publishing

eBook: 978-0-6485709-9-8
Paperback: 978-0-6481042-7-8
Hardback: 978-0-6481042-5-4

AUSXIP Publishing
Sydney, Australia
www.ausxippublishing.com

TABLE OF CONTENTS

PART 4: THE MIGHTY QUILL – BARDS OF THE XENAVERSE

PART 5: THE MIGHTY QUILL – FROM XENA FANFIC TO PUBLISHED AUTHORS

AUSXIP Publishing Newsletter

Subscribe to our newsletters to be the first to hear about our latest news, upcoming releases and giveaways.

https://newsletter.ausxippublishing.com

DEDICATION

To Susan "Xero" Podd

*If not for your persistent and stubborn refusal to accept that
I didn't want to get hooked on another TV show
twenty-four years ago... I would be a sane woman today.*

Thank you!

Sanity is highly overrated.

ACKNOWLEDGMENTS

It's been an enormous honor and a privilege to create, produce, and publish this incredible book! It has literally taken an Amazon Village to bring it to fruition. Thank you to all the contributors who gave of their time, talent, and enthusiasm to make that little idea that swirled around my head in late 2015 come into being. It has been the most challenging project I've ever undertaken and one of the most rewarding. I have quite a few people to thank in the production of this book...

Rosa Alonso – What can I say other thank you mate! You are indefatigable. Nothing is ever too big or too problematic that it can't be done. Thank you for tackling this massive body of work from multiple contributors without breaking a sweat. You deserve a warehouse of Tim Tams and a trip on The Ghan... *No hay suficiente chocolate en el mundo!*

Ann Sund – "I have an idea" is my battle cry, and what comes back is positivity all the way. I am blessed for having met you and having you as a dear mate. You are always with me every step of the way. Bless you.

Ian Pitt – Thank you for all your help and for making this book all the more incredible. You're a dear mate. It would not be the same without your help. Thank you for your friendship and support.

Lucia Nobrega – It was a life-changing day in 1999 when we first connected. Thank you, mate! You inspire me and encourage me every step of the way. I value your friendship in ways too numerous to mention. *Muito obrigado!*

Michele vanRoosendael – Thank you for being so generous with your artistic talents, beta reading and for your friendship.

Jay Tuma – Thank you for all your hard work and beta reading. You're a star! Battle on!

Last but not least, thank you to Universal Studios, Renaissance Pictures, and the *Xena: Warrior Princess* cast and crew. If not for all of you, the Xenaverse would not exist, lives would not have changed so dramatically, and this book would never have been created. Serendipity

BATTLE ON!

PART 1

A WORLD IN NEED OF HEROES

Chapter One

Evolution of a Fandom and Nerdy Sequoias

by MaryD

A SEQUOIA TREE starts its life as a tiny seed. It grows into the tallest tree imaginable—it has been measured at 115.55 meters or 379.1 feet. Yes, that is interesting, but it's not why you picked up this book. Why am I writing about giant sequoias?

Our world needs heroes (and at the writing of this introduction, our heroes are scientists, doctors, nurses, and front line staff in the fight against the dreaded COVID-19). Twenty-five years ago, our world was less complex (although not less lethal). Our thoughts were not on self-isolation and avoiding catching the coronavirus du jour. People were trying to make the best of it when troubles would befall them. We needed an escape from the many issues occupying our minds, from our world, even for a little while.

We were looking for a hero; escapism in the form of a television show. That weekly hour-long respite transported us back to Ancient Greece to a time of ancient gods, warlords and kings, when the land was in turmoil and cried out for heroes. We found them—they were Xena and Gabrielle, a Mighty Princess, and her Amazon Bard. Their power and passion gave birth to an extraordinary fandom, the Xenaverse. It was a show that changed lives in unimaginable ways. It set off a firestorm of the generosity of spirit, creativity, inclusiveness, and so much more.

Now, back to my sequoia tree. My ideas start off as a tiny seed and explode into giant sequoias. I gave up long ago the notion that I can ignore the little ideas fermenting in my noggin. It never works, so I surrender to these ideas and see where they lead. That's how the plan for a book about Xena's 25th anniversary began its life. On December 15, 2015, my website, Australian Xena Information Page (also known as AUSXIP) celebrated its 19th anniversary. In internet years, that was like being as old as Methuselah.

Coming up to AUSXIP's 20th year in 2016, why not write a book about the history of AUSXIP and the Xenaverse? It sounded like a great idea to me. I could go back into the AUSXIP archives to conduct research since it is a veritable time capsule of the Xenaverse. AUSXIP was born only eight months after the birth of the Xenaverse.

Between December 2015 and April 2016, that idea morphed into something far more significant. I was at the Xenite Retreat at Lake Hughes, and I gave voice to the idea for the book to Kym Taborn (creator of Whoosh!). Kym and I were chatting and figured this was the right time to let this idea spring forth. "Would you be keen on writing about Whoosh! and how it impacted the Xenaverse in a book I'm going to put together for the twenty-fifth anniversary?" I saw her eyes light up. She said, "Yes! Tell me more." The little sequoia seed had been given a growth hormone, and it went BOOM!

During the rest of 2016 and 2017, the plan started to grow. Getting the Xenaverse involved in this epic adventure wasn't hard. I pitched the idea of various chapters to people I have known for two decades, and the positive response just added to my excitement. My beloved editor, Rosa Alonso, and my dear friend Ann Sund came on board the speeding train, and there was no stopping it.

I announced the plans for the book to the Xenaverse, and the overwhelming support that came back made me more than a little emotional. Having received Universal's approval, it was the start of an epic project, and the biggest challenge I have ever undertaken. No pressure, right?

With sixty-eight chapters written by fifty-seven authors (plus a chapter written by *Xena: Warrior Princess* Executive Producer and Writer, Steven L. Sears) about the Xenaverse we love, seventy-one Xenites writing about how Xena changed their lives and we showcase artists and videographers, photographers and webmasters! I wanted this book to have the ENTIRE Xenaverse involved – a literal Amazon Village and, oh boy, I got exactly what I wanted! We have a book dedicated to this creative, incredible fanbase! This is the story of the evolution of a tiny fandom, flying by the seat of its nerdy pants. *Xena: Warrior Princess* was embraced in all its glory by people from all over the world. The message of the Greater Good became our battle cry, and we became a major force for good.

This extraordinary Xenaverse is a close-knit group, we are fiercely protective of each other and our Xena cast/crew. We circle the wagons when needed and provide a level of protectiveness not seen in any other fandom. The Xenaverse is unique in its approach from all other fandoms.

Both AUSXIP and the Xenaverse were born at the birth of the internet. We had no roadmap on how to run an online fandom. We WROTE the rules and set the roadmap for all other fandoms to follow.

We are the Xenaverse. This is our story. Celebrate the rich tapestry that is the Xenaverse, a diverse, inclusive group from all over the world, that has flourished for twenty-five years—the sequoia of fandom.

Chapter Two

The New World Order – How We Accidentally
Invented the Rules for Fandom

by Lee Winter

IT'S SO FUNNY now, looking back. We thought we were just watching a show, not starting a revolution. But break out the shiny chakrams, ugly green tops, and oozing subtext, because *Xena's* fans found themselves at ground zero for the collision of television, fandoms, and the internet. The growth in on-line fan communities alone was nothing less than spectacular, due to the fact the internet had only been widely popular for about a year when *Xena* began airing in 1995. With *Xena*, we witnessed the huge growth of lesbian fan fiction and a resultant boom in published lesfic novels. We saw the rise of dedicated fan forum boards, fan websites, and art, not to mention thousands of real-life romances forged in the heat of internet friendships.

Viewers, especially queer ones, discovered a powerful unifying cause (not to mention a seriously adorable one) and a way to connect with each other in ways that never used to be possible.

Critically, most of this, if not all, blew up to Herculean heights, because of one groundbreaking thing in an unassuming little show about a warrior and her BFF: subtext—deliberate, honest-to-goodness, put-there-on-purpose subtext between two women.

Well. That was unexpected.

What followed next, and how fans responded in vast numbers, rewrote the rules, and accepted wisdom of modern television in a way that has, arguably, rippled throughout fandom communities and Hollywood ever since.

Of course, back then, we didn't know any of this. We didn't even know whether two plucky women from (a multitude of) ancient times, who so many of us had hitched our barrows to, would get through the entire show without being paired off to random blokes. Because of this, for much of its run, subtext-loving fans existed on a cocktail of hope, joy, and fear.

No, we didn't know anything, but, boy, were we in for one hell of a surprise.

AY-YI-YI — A New World Order

There was a time when the only way you could meet a show's fans was to attend a convention—if you were lucky enough to be into a show big enough to hold cons. And even if you were, it was extra difficult if you were a queer fan in a sea of all that fierce, prevailing heterosexuality.

More than once in the late eighties, I witnessed a nervous soul at a *Star Trek* convention pluck up their courage and ask a respectful gay question, only to be dismissed or laughed at, amid a hail of audience boos. In that era, raising "uncomfortable" character sexuality topics of beloved acting stars was considered rude by many straight fans.

And then along came *Xena*. This larger-than-life warrior princess arrived fully formed as a lesbian icon. With her butch strut, low voice, fighting prowess, and knee-high leather boots, she was only one handful of glitter short of her own Sydney Mardi Gras float. Throw in a bard of bedroll-sharing, doe-eyed propensities, and, well, it's not hard to see why the ladies who love ladies, grabbed the popcorn.

The snowball effect from that teasing, charming, on-screen dynamic cannot be understated. Nor can its impact given just how different the show was. Throwing *Xena* into the world for the first time was like letting loose a unicorn in a paddock of dusty sheep and expecting no one to notice.

Oh, yep, we noticed.

Xena became a giant beacon. It inspired and brought together an enormous, easily accessible, tribe of fans who became the world's first large-scale, female-dominated fandom in the internet age.

For queer fans, suddenly, here was a fun place to discover people from all walks of life who were just as enthusiastic about these two women getting together romantically. That's why *Xena* was much more than just another fantasy hero show. For its LGBTQA+ followers, it was also a rallying point, a signpost to find like-minded people, and pretty importantly, a safe way to do so, no matter where you were from.

Having said all that, let's not overlook a really big thing. For all *Xena*'s powerful importance to marginalized people, it was also really, *really* fun.

There were the fifty-seven ways that Xena drawled "Gab-ri-elle," her slow-mo hair-washing, iconic eyebrow arching, and woman-of-few-words one-liners. There was Gabrielle's doofus hilarity—from her henbane highs, soap-sitting smirks, and snickers about fisting a fish to incensed outbursts about Xena's bathroom habits (*"You used my scrolls?!"*). And above all, there was love. So much love.

No wonder the world tuned into it in droves. Here was a fun show, oozing feel-good heart squishiness on the regular, that was also subversive to the point of downright revolutionary.

When Tech Reinvented Fandoms

The early-to-mid nineties internet was a hellscape of shockingly bad design, from pervasive clunky graphics, tinny, midi music files that auto-played until your ears bled, and multiple flashing, bouncing GIFS. This was also a new world open to users to explore and develop their own pages for the first time…or ruin other people's eyeballs, as they saw fit.

From the ashes of this gimmicky, garish hell were born some bold new concepts that we still use in part today. Many *Xena* fans got to play guinea pigs on the cutting edge of that latest technology.

We were witness to the first subscription, interactive emails, where hundreds of fans added their thoughts to the bottom of an ever-growing "CC-All" email-without-end. It was like a hypnotic precursor to today's bottomless social-media feed.

There were also fan fiction sites springing up everywhere, housing thousands of fan stories, as well as exhaustive collections of theses-like papers on ancient Greek times. Whoosh! excelled at these, and explored everything from hygiene for nomadic warrior women to the food Xena and Gabrielle would have eaten (spoiler alert: everything from nettles and eels to purple orchids).

But the biggest development, which attracted thousands, was the rise in popularity of forum boards. Those at *Xena* fan sites tackled everything from Ares's cool leather pants, and side-eying Joxer, to the supreme gayness (or otherwise) of our leading ladies.

All these tech developments, harnessed by mega-fans such as Mary D. Brooks, aka MaryD, webmistress at the Australian Xena Information Page (AUSXIP), meant that *Xena* was opened up to us in a whole new way. So many delighted fans came, saw, and plundered with glee.

So, Who Were The *Xena* Fans?

MaryD reports that the average *Xena* fans were women in their mid-thirties and that visitors to her AUSXIP website were more gay than straight.

"*The average Xena fan would have been around 35 to 55 at the time,*" she says. "*We are now much older, of course. We're all Amazon Elders now.*"

For many, this was their first fandom and also their first experience of "shipping" together an on-screen pair of characters.

Interestingly, they were, by and large, a pretty polite bunch of people. Indeed, with all the flame-wars that surround TV shows these days, as fans argue fiercely for their pairings or denigrate rival pairings, *Xena* seems like a peaceful oasis from a different era.

While things could and did get testy between fan camps, it was nothing like today. There was also very little launching of inflammatory hate at writers or show-runners, despite some dodgy plots being enough to drive fans to hit the mead hard. Why?

Well, it wasn't entirely just because the internet was young, or that trolls had yet to learn how to scorch a village, or that social media had yet to be born. There seemed to be something else afoot.

In the Talking Xena corner of the Xenaverse, and quite likely elsewhere, there were unwritten rules fans adopted. Thou shalt not anger show-runners or writers, nor diss straight fans and their on-screen couples.

Any transgressors regularly got called out and policed by fans. Mutual respect was demanded, even if it wasn't always achieved, and this made *Xena* one of the genuinely nicest shows to be a fan of.

But why did fans react like this?

No Scaring The (Straight) Horses

Just because there was subtext inserted into *Xena* didn't mean mainstream viewers automatically noticed it, or if it was pointed out, believed it. Maybe you could understand their confusion. Up until *Xena*, pretty much every mainstream TV show was for, by, and about straight people. So much so that, back in season two, all subtext was coded like a dog whistle for only those adept at noticing.

While there was a constant debate between fans of "are-they or aren't-they," those desperately hoping for the subtext to become the main text had one almighty fear: it'd all be snatched away at any moment.

Hollywood wasn't exactly subtle in espousing the view that lesbians were a tiny minority with limited pulling power. As a result, fans who wanted Xena and Gabrielle to become a real couple, not just a nudgy-winky one, were determined to not upset the applecart.

Softly, softly was everywhere. There were the *Xena* reviews worded in ways to ensure they didn't alienate straight viewers when discussing subtext. Fan interactions with *Xena* bosses were all about hopeful *pleas,* not strident *demands.* After all, that way, there be dragons.

Basically, we were well aware that *Xena*'s show-runners were being pressured to "straighten up" *Xena*. We didn't imagine it either.

In August 2000, *Xena*'s executive producer Rob Tapert, looking back on the run of the show to that point, gave a revealing interview with Titan's *Xena: Warrior Princess*—The Official Magazine.

He cited two popular, subtext-drenched episodes, "The Quest," with its Xena/Autolycus body-swap kiss with Gabrielle, and "A Day In The Life," which was about as romantic as two besties could get without including a U-Haul and a rescue puppy.

"We had a famous episode a long time ago, 'The Quest,' which was our highest-rated episode, and after that, we started to go downhill (in ratings)," Tapert said. "Then there was 'A Day in the Life,' which was the girls in the hot tub together playing 'hide the soap.' After that, our executives put a great deal of pressure on us to stop, to not go down that road because it could only lead to ruin."

We were always only too well aware that *Xena* was it. When the show first played up the subtext, it was before Ellen DeGeneres's bold gay declaration, and Tara and Willow hadn't fallen in love on *Buffy* yet. And this was just after the lesbian kisses on *Roseanne* and *LA Law,* which attracted a vicious backlash.

So for queer subtext-pining fans, we had *Xena* or nothing, and the fear was incredibly strong we'd lose even that, but what helped many of us through the nerve-wracking times were our loud, wonderful, and numerous straight allies.

Straight Allies Came Through

In the early days of *Xena*, various forum boards sprung up, which attracted tens of thousands of comments. Subtext, naturally, was a hot, hot topic.

Often at AUSXIP's popular forum board, Talking Xena, they would get, quite regularly, people wading in, heatedly telling the subtext fans they were delusional. They weren't trolls either. They really meant it—if they couldn't see what we were talking about, we were obviously imagining it.

It was demoralizing, but we were used to it. Besides, what could you do? Fight every adamant, vitriolic straight fan? That was just how things were on forum boards in those days.

But with *Xena*, something changed. I watched one day as MaryD waded in at Talking Xena and told a lesbian fan, who'd been told she was seeing things, "No, you're not delusional; I'm a straight woman, and I can see it."

I had never heard this before. Ever. A straight forum board admin supporting the gay fans? Like…in public?

As time went on, MaryD started doing this over and over, day in, day out. She laughs about it now, but it was a really big deal for fans.

"*I stepped in and stomped on people,*" MaryD recalls. "*I was used as the heavy artillery! If I stepped in, you knew something was going down.*"

Talking Xena and MaryD made it clear that insulting any *Xena* pairing, even if it wasn't part of show canon, was unacceptable. Ground rules were established about how on-line fans should conduct themselves when "shipping" fictional couples. The different ships/mutual respect approach, which includes same-sex pairings, is the gold standard these days on forum boards. While it seems obvious now, Talking Xena was among the first to explicitly lay down the law that the views of all fans, *regardless of sexuality,* should be treated with respect. And they actually enforced it.

This came as a shock to the vocal minority of straight *Xena* fans who expected the usual status quo to apply, where their views had always mattered more. These indignant voices were not to be confused with the polite, "I don't see the subtext, but you do" straight fans who always disagreed respectfully.

Rapidly, most of the entitled crowd got the hint. Some stayed and became respectful; others left.

For those of us at Talking Xena watching this go down in real-time, it was like a brave new world. Those simple actions felt incredible to marginalized fans resigned to being metaphorically (or actually) booed for just speaking up. It was mind-blowing.

As the weeks turned into months and then years, we discovered that the number of straight, supportive, subtext-loving allies we had in the Xenaverse was huge. Having these fans also chiming in, declaring, "Hey, leave the lesbians alone. I see it too; they're good", was not just powerful. It was glorious.

For a young, closeted lesbian like me, it meant everything.

The More Things Change…

As far as things have come since Xena first slid on those leather boots, many things stay the same.

The LGBTQA+ fans still hold their collective breaths over TV characters they pray might be queer. There are more characters like us that we can watch now, many more. But we're still the same: we still exhale in relief when a potential straight love expresses no interest in our gaydar-pinging character. We still desperately hope they don't get killed off, either.

None of this has changed with time. We're still at the whim of Hollywood. LGBTQA+ viewers are still not a primary thought. We're still often dismissed as barely worth catering to, and sometimes, that disrespect still leaks out into scripts and star/fan interactions.

So say what you will about *Xena* and our younger selves begging so politely for more, with rainbow sprinkles on top, but *Xena* never treated us like dirt for it. Yes, they often laughed (at first) at the cheeky subtext and the devoted, invested fans looking so hopeful, but despite that enormous studio pressure, they also never told us it was impossible.

They never flat-out mocked the fans for the dream or made us feel stupid for supporting the pairings we liked, and they never shut and bolted the door on gay content. That's a lesson some shows today could learn. It shouldn't be the case, but this is so true: *Xena's* openness to LGBTQA+ fans was groundbreaking.

Onwards And Upwards

Looking back, I wonder what we'd tell our younger selves about what lay ahead.

For me, when I first started watching *Xena,* I was in my mid-twenties, closeted, alone, and fearful of straight backlash if my secret was known. Those awful, mocking convention experiences in the eighties cut deep.

Xena brought together straight allies and gay people in a way that had never come before. That was simply astonishing. It was a huge boost for the confidence. The allies helped, the show helped, all of it was uplifting.

So what would I tell my younger self, watching the show on the fumes of joy, hope, and fear? That it'd be okay in the end?

It wasn't really, though, was it, given Xena died. And yet it also *was* okay, too, because, by the time Xena sacrificed herself in some ridiculous forced plot point, we were united and strong as a fandom. We had grown as fans and people. We had found our voices with regard to how LGBTQA+ characters get treated in the media. It was the start of the pushback.

Now we've seen the world change many times over, and the rise of queer characters in numbers and strength. We've seen same-sex ships come to be acknowledged or celebrated on TV show fan forums without all that entrenched homophobia that came before.

We've also seen more gay characters killed off, again and again, too. And we've had our wins. But here's a crucial thing: we've also seen younger fans counter-striking, turning their numbers into their favor, and coming up with their own events, such as Clexacon.

The queer and subtext-loving fans, once invisible, are seen and heard now. It's a cosmic shift, for example, to see a *Batwoman* TV series, which has its first out and proud lesbian lead character, along with a queer lead actress in Ruby Rose. This would have been unimaginable to me back in the day.

I like to think that all those *Xena* fans of every stripe, uniting and rising and gaining in confidence and coming into their own, were one small, but valuable step on that journey forward. We're part of history now.

Of course, none of us could have predicted any of this back then. None of us understood the power of the events that would unfold on some schlocky, crazy, dramatic, inspiring show shot on the edge of the world. People in the middle of change rarely understand what they're witnessing.

But that's how it happened, at least from my perspective—how *Xena* accidentally started a new world order and wrote the rulebook on fandom.

***

Lee Winter is an Australian award-winning lesbian fiction author who spent her Xena years hanging out in cyberspace with MaryD, delighting in the subtext, and watching most of the show through quivering fingers. Lee Winter's Official Site http://www.leewinterauthor.com

Chapter Three

I Am Not A Xena Fan

by Steven L. Sears

I AM NOT A *XENA* fan. There. I said it. I mean… "Get a life, will you, people? For crying out loud, it's just a TV show!"

For those who don't know where that quote came from and are, right now, reassessing everything you thought you knew about me, it's from a fairly popular segment of Saturday Night Live aired in December of 1986. In that segment, William Shatner (played by the amazingly versatile actor, William Shatner, playing himself) attends a "Trekkers" convention. The *Star Trek* fans are portrayed in the stereotypical geeky style of the 1980s, all wearing Trek shirts, fake Vulcan ears, and excitedly talking amongst each other of their merchandising finds. Shatner comes onto the stage to answer a few questions, and the questions are, let's say, very detailed and specific. One question referenced the safe in the Captain's cabin, "What was the combination?" Eventually, Shatner is so dismayed by the questions that he just explodes with the above quote.

Of course, the skit was done as comedy and was meant to poke gentle fun at the fans. At least I, as a Classic *Star Trek* fan, saw it that way. When it first aired, I had just started my career as a writer two years before. I was finishing up with my first series, *Riptide*, and my then-writing partner, Burt, and I were moving on to *The A-Team*. Back then, there were "fanzines," written by fans, which were sent out on mailing lists for fans of a particular series. Once a month, I would get one of these (yes, I subscribed), and I would read the letters the fans submitted where they talked about the various episodes. Some of them had fan fiction, where the fans would spin their stories for each other. But, pretty much, that was it.

The internet changed all that. Instead of seeking out fanzines and waiting for the postal mail, people only had to go on-line and do a search for their favorite TV series and, bam! There it was. Chatrooms! Bulletin boards! All dedicated to YOUR favorite TV series! And even better, there were other people just like you! Fans with the same love and passion you had! Instead of getting a fanzine once a month to connect with your peeps, you only had to log on, and instantly you were part of a community. A LARGE community! In real-time!

I think that was the turning point for me. That's where my story of how *Xena* changed my life really began.

Now you might think *Xena* must have changed my life the moment I started working on the show. Well, yes and no. Most fans out there who know of me don't really know where I came from. To them, it's assumed I sprung out of Zeus's forehead like Athena just as *Xena* began. I never existed before *Xena*, or so it seemed. Truth is, I already had a very long career on several TV series. As I already mentioned, *The A-Team* and *Riptide*, but also *Hardcastle & McCormick*, *Stingray*, *Highwayman*, *Walker – Texas Ranger*, *Raven*, *Swamp Thing*, and many, many others. When I started on *Xena*, it was just another series in a long history of work. By itself, it wasn't going to change my life any more than any of the other series had. I enjoyed all of them, put 150% of myself into the work, got paid, and moved on when that job was over.

But… that wasn't going to be the case with *Xena*.

Now, if you remember, *Xena* first appeared in 1995. I say "if you remember" because we have many fans now who weren't even born in 1995! So, for you old-timers, you remember that the internet also exploded in the mid-nineties. CompuServe was on its way out (God, remember CompuServe?), and AOL was becoming the major social network site. It was there, on AOL, that I first encountered the growing *Xena* insurgency…

So it was that one day, out of curiosity, I put the word "Xena" into the search bar of AOL just to see what came up. Much to my surprise, a chat room was listed. Now, the obvious question was, "Do I go into that room?" I was, after all, one of the writers and producers of the series. I make no pretense of being any kind of celebrity, but I was sure that my association with the show would create some kind of discussion, at least. And if I did go into the room, should I disguise myself? Just lurk and listen? Truth is, I'm not fond of lying about things, and I knew that it was likely someone would ask me what I thought of the show and how I started watching it. So I decided I would not keep my identity a secret but would set some personal rules. The first one being if the group wanted to talk about story ideas they wanted to see, I would voluntarily bow out of the room. As a producer of the show, it would have presented problems for me to hear these ideas, both legally and ethically. Second, if I, Steven L. Sears, became the topic of conversation, I would, again, voluntarily bow out. That wasn't because I didn't want people talking about me; it was because I didn't want to interfere with the free flow of conversation. So, not knowing what to expect, I went in.

Now, I can't actually recall how that first chat room meeting went. Perhaps someone who was in that room is reading this and can remember or kept a log. In any event, I do know the chat room was set up by a young girl named Laura, who was very excited about this new heroine named *Xena*. And, of course, when they realized who I was, there were LOTS of questions. Some I answered, some I couldn't answer, some answers I just teased about. I can't remember what my handle was in that first chat, but I was known later as Tyldus. Or, as some called me (because of my tendency to tease about upcoming plots), Tyldus the Torturer.

One thing I do remember is that I enjoyed the people there. Even the ones critical of the show. I enjoyed listening to them and interacting with them. They weren't just geeks and nerds (which would have been awesome just in itself); they were real people with real lives and real thoughts. I think most of all, it felt familiar to me. In my years of working in television on different shows, I had forgotten that I was also a fan at one time. I already mentioned Classic *Star Trek*, but also *The Time Tunnel* and other mostly sci-fi series. This was more of a homecoming than I expected.

Soon, other websites dedicated to the show appeared. WHOOSH, Tom's *Xena* Page, AUSXIP, and others. More places for fans to interact, more chat rooms, and fan fiction! I was both bemused and happy watching it unfold. Of course, this was all on-line. I didn't know what any of these people were like in person, and they certainly didn't know much about me except what I told them or they could find on-line (which, at that time, was sparse). The next step would be to actually meet some of these *Xena* fans in the flesh.

That opportunity came when people started organizing *Xena* Fests. Yes, yes, we did have conventions, but before the conventions, there were the *Xena* Fests. Several fans would meet up at a restaurant, watch videos of the episodes, and generally have a great time. I found out when and where one was to be held and I decided I would go. I've forgotten where it was, though I have a photo of all of us somewhere. Believe it or not, I was nervous about showing up. I didn't want to just sweep in and announce myself like some arrogant egomaniac. But, again, I wasn't going to hide who I was. So I sat at a nearby table and listened in. It was wonderful, just watching the fans chat and get excited about the episodes. Then the moment happened. One of the fans, sitting nearby, introduced himself. His name was Clayton, aka "Lord Nelson" on-line. Then he asked who I was. "Steven L. Sears," I replied. "Oh, hi, Stev—oh!" was his response. He knew. Soon, they all knew. One thing about fans; they read the credits.

Just as it happened in the chatroom, I got a lot of questions, a lot of praise, a lot of opinions, and we all had a great time. I found myself becoming very comfortable; these were really fun people to hang with. Oh, and for the first time, I found myself signing a lot of things; napkins, notepaper and assorted objects, as well as people asking for a photo with me. It was strange, and I still haven't quite gotten used to it. But if it made people happy, not a problem.

Next came the official conventions. Creation Entertainment ran the *Xena* conventions for twenty years. I think I only missed one in all that time. But, again, I had to set down some rules for myself. I'm not one to put myself on a pedestal and stay backstage. I'm a geek and I want to be amongst my peeps! I intended to spend my time out in the crowd, talking to people and, I don't know, just being me. I was advised that it might be a mistake, as I would be mobbed, I wouldn't have any freedom, the fans can be so demanding, etc. etc.. Well, that might be true for the actors and actresses as they were the main draw, but I wasn't worried about it. And you know what? I was right. Not to say that I didn't get my share of attention, especially from the con virgins, but as many of you now know, I went from "OMG! It's Steven Sears!" to "Oh, hey, Steve" very quickly. Which is the way I prefer it.

So how did this affect my working on the show? Not as much as you would think in some areas, but probably more than you would in others. The studio was a bit nervous at first since there had been some problems with staff interaction with fans on other shows, but they quickly saw that I was handling it well. And as other members of our staff started interacting with fans (granted, not on the scale I was), the studio saw that we were avoiding the pitfalls while, at the same time, making the show more popular by being accessible. Of course, it helped that we had actresses and actors who respected fandom (and still do). Even Rob Tapert, who was hesitant at first over my dealings with the fans, would ask me, "So, did they like it?" after certain episodes.

I was also gaining a reputation as "the convention guy" among the staff. Aside from *Xena* conventions, I appeared at many other fan-oriented cons around the country. Remember the *Hercules* episode that was set in modern-day, where Kevin Sorbo was missing, and the production staff was going crazy? The actors in *Hercules* played the roles of their staff. Bruce Campbell played Rob Tapert, Hudson Leick played Liz Friedman, and so on. Well, that was originally discussed as a *Xena* episode. In that one, the actors were still going to play the *Xena* staff, except for me. I was going to play myself… on a speakerphone. The running gag was that I was always at a convention partying with the fans, so you only heard my voice. We didn't get past the discussion stages on it when the concept was moved over to the *Hercules* staff for their episode.

And so it went, interacting with the fans on-line, meeting them in person at conventions, and trying to answer all the emails they were sending me. All the while, still a working writer and producer, trying to do my part to produce a TV series. Just as I had done for all my past series.

But here's the thing; I am not a *Xena* fan. I can't be. I was a part of it; I was on the other side of the camera; it was more than just a TV show to watch once a week and talk about with friends. You saw the final product; I was a part of all the effort involved in creating it. That included intense story meetings, late nights working, weekends gone because of emergency rewrites, occasional disputes and arguments between us (not surprising with creative people; as I've said many times, we were like a dysfunctional family); and dealing with unexpected setbacks. Remember when Lucy fractured her pelvis as a result of a stunt gone bad? That was a horrible day, and our first concern was about Lucy and her well-being, but I think the way we then responded to the crisis in our storyline was an amazing example of everyone coming together in an emergency.

So, you see, there is no way I can ever watch the series from the fan's point of view just as I can't really watch any TV series or film as a pure audience; I know too much about the process.

"But wait!" you say (Go ahead, say it), "Aren't you proud of your work? Don't you love watching it in reruns?" The answer is yes. And no.

Yes, because I am always proud of my work. When I take on a writing assignment or start writing something for myself, I put as much of my creativity into it as possible. I wish you could see into my mind during the creative process. Mostly because it would be easier to explain it. But I travel to all these different worlds, with my best friends (my characters), to have amazing adventures! And not just the adventure you eventually see on the TV. I travel many different paths during my drafts. Some things work, some don't, some choices are hard choices that you just have faith in, but I have to try them all, in my mind and on the page. For every 60-page script of mine, I probably wrote 700 pages of material to get there. Which is the "no" in my answer. Aside from what I have to watch during the production process, I rarely ever watch my work after that. I can't; I know all the paths I could have taken and I'll always want to do one more rewrite! Just to tweak it or try something else! Watching my own work makes me cringe, seriously. Those of you who are creatives understand this; the work is never done even when it's done.

But back to the original question and premise of this book: How did *Xena* change my life? In short, it didn't.

The *Xena* fans did.

As I went through the history I described, the most amazing thing happened. I was making friends. Not that I was desperate for them, but some of these fans became actual friends long after the series ended. We hang out at times, have dinner, go to events, parks, and museums together. On occasion, I've had the honor of watching these friends cement their love for each other in matrimony. And, yes, yes, I dated three or four women who were fans of the show. Let's acknowledge that elephant in the room and get it over with. I have fond memories of all of them and I hope they feel the same.

As a result, I began to see my own work through the eyes of the fans. I realized that my words, my stories, had an impact on them. It wasn't just entertainment for many; it was a calling. For some, a siren call to the power within themselves that they had denied. For others, a calling to help those who couldn't help themselves.

I remember the time a *Xena* fan pulled me aside at a convention just to tell me that her identifying with our show allowed her the strength to pull away from an abusive relationship and seek her own path of love. I told her the strength was always in her, but that, perhaps, she just needed a mirror to see it. Whatever it was, she said, it was there, in the message from *Xena*. I had others send me emails about similar situations. I try not to break down crying when I read these messages; for the pain that they went through but also joy for the happiness they found.

The willingness of our fans to find those uplifting messages, apply them to their own lives, and share them with others humbles me.

Which brings me to the other thing about *Xena* fans that changed my life: charity. I have never seen a more charitable and caring group than our *Xena* fans. Yes, some fandoms come close, but for a TV show that has been off the air for almost twenty years, to have a fandom this strong with this much of a commitment to the "Greater Good," is absolutely mind-blowing.

There are the times when I watched our actors on stage, talking to the fans, and they mentioned a charity close to their heart. The money started flowing in. Giving became such a staple of the *Xena* activities; from the conventions to the *Xena* Fests, MaryD's AUSXIP Charity Auctions for The Starship Foundation (Lucy Lawless) and The House of Bards (Renée O'Connor), Adrienne Wilkinson's charity dinners, Hudson's dresses being auctioned off, Brittney's bras on the bidding block, Lucy's devotion to Starship, Renée's devotion to children and the arts, and to the amazing Xenite Retreat that Penny and Kat Cavanaugh run each year. I could keep going on and still not mention everyone. The fans always respond. It's amazing.

To put it in perspective, by estimates, the *Xena* fandom has been directly responsible for twenty-four to twenty-eight million dollars of charity. That averages out to about one million dollars a year SINCE THE SERIES BEGAN!!!

Holy Centaur Poop!

It is, by far, the one thing about having worked on *Xena* that I am most proud of. A series that I was honored and blessed to have worked on has, through you, the fans, truly made a difference in the world.

Thank you all for letting me be a part of that.

***

Steven L. Sears Official Site
http://www.stevenlsears.com/

Chapter Four

When The Xena Horde Gathers – Official Xena Conventions

by MaryD

THE TERM "THE XENA HORDE" was invented by Steven L. Sears, and it harkened back to the *Xena* Season 2 Episode 20: "The Price." The Horde in "The Price" was not as nice as the Xenite Horde!

One of my favorite things to do before a *Xena* convention begins is to sit in the lobby of the convention hotel, and people watch. It's like a dance. One group of Xenites is hanging out in the lobby when the doors slide apart, and a weary traveler dragging their suitcase wanders in. They are tired from a long trip, and they look like they are about to drop to the floor (if they are from Australia, it's a 14-17 hour flight). All they want is to go to the check-in desk, get organized, and then go for a drink and a feed.

Then the transformation happens.

I watch the group of Xenites, then I watch the new arrival, and I don't have time to count because the lobby fills with SCREAMS. This is a glorious sound of genuine affection between people who haven't seen each other for a year or many years or never. There is something special about witnessing the coming together of friends who are as close as family. That's what the Xenaverse is—a family. A family we choose to be in. *Xena* conventions are our version of the family get-togethers.

This scene is repeated many times over, and I never get tired of seeing it play out in front of me.

How did all this come about? I'm glad you asked because I'm going to take you back to 1997 and the birth of the official *Xena* conventions by Creation Entertainment.

When you have a hit show like *Xena: Warrior Princess*, there is a natural inclination for fans to want to see and speak to the cast, producers, and writers. Like other franchises (and in particular *Star Trek*), conventions were a way of connecting fans and the shows they loved. Fans always had a way of connecting (long before the internet) via small groups and then larger groups organized by fans or the studio.

Xenites are spread far and wide in all corners of the world, and while the internet connects us in the digital world, it lacked the physical connection that fans craved.

In January 1997, Creation Entertainment took on the role of bringing the *Xena* cast to the fans. That convention also marked the turning point for AUSXIP to morph in the monster it would become. More about that later.

Lucy Lawless was going to be presented to the Xenaverse and Xenites FLOCKED to Burbank, California, for the very first official *Xena* convention. Xenites were eager to see Lucy, not just because she was Xena, but also because she had been recovering from an accident. Lucy was injured on the Jay Leno Show, which happened on October 08, 1996. Lucy was involved in a skit that had gone wrong. She fell from a horse after the animal lost its footing during the taping of a comedy skit. She was taken to the hospital, and NBC & MCA TV sent out a press release the next day to say that she had suffered pelvic fractures and was out of commission for a while. The fans were eager to see Lucy and give her all the love and support the Xenaverse could muster (which was considerable).

Also on the guest list were Ted Raimi (Joxer), Hudson Leick (Callisto), and Steven Sears. It was on that day that my initial plan for AUSXIP went out the window. Maureen McGowan sent me photos from the convention, AND she became the first Xenite contributor to the site. That opened the floodgates when MsMoo (don't you love that moniker?), Quest, Tina, and Cathy sent me their convention reports! All of these photos and convention reports are archived on AUSXIP Xena Conventions:
http://www.ausxip.com/conventions/97burbank/index.html

It wasn't until 2001 when I attended my first convention with Xenites present (not my first official *Xena* convention, which would happen in 2003). My first introduction to the physical Xenaverse was when I attended Dragoncon in Atlanta. It was then that I finally understood what others thought of AUSXIP (yes, clueless is my middle name), and I found my tribe in person rather than just on the web. I was overwhelmed by the love.

Creation Entertainment went on to hold their annual officially sanctioned *Xena* conventions, which brought us together every year since 1997 (see the end of this chapter for a full list).

Our conventions were always memorable, whether it was meeting people we had only spoken to online, catching up with friends we hadn't seen in a year, or find our soulmate among the thousands that attended the conventions. Then there are the moments that will never be forgotten—Lucy & Renée jumping out of a cake for the 10th Anniversary convention, Renee wearing her BGSB outfit at a Photo Op, and having everyone in raptures or the shocking news about Kevin Smith passing away that devastated all of us. There are so many memories.

Kevin Tod Smith

One heartbreaking convention was held on February 7-9, 2002. We lost our beloved Kevin Smith (Ares) in a shocking accident in China. Kevin had been in China to film a new movie. He fell down some scaffolding after the day's shooting had ended. He would never recover. The news of his death hit us hard. The Xenaverse webmasters such as myself, Debbie Cassetta from Sword & Staff, Kym Taborn of Whoosh! and others arranged to announce Kevin's passing at the same time.

It wasn't the first time the *Xena* webmasters collaborated, but this was our saddest moment. For those who were attending the convention, the news rippled through them, and they initially thought it wasn't true, but once they reached their seats, the devastating news became real. We pay tribute to Kevin in our memorial to our fallen friends, In Part 11: "The Xenite Memorial" with *Chapter 64: Our Fallen God of War: In Memory Of Kevin Tod Smith.*

Renée O'Connor

In 2009, Renée produced a film called *Words Unspoken*. The film blurb is "A man and his estranged sister battle against each other, their father, and ultimately themselves, as they look back on their childhood trauma, seeking forgiveness and ultimate freedom." What was so compelling about this film was the subject matter and the reaction to it from Xenites gathered at the 2009 *Xena* convention (the 14th Anniversary convention) on Sunday, February 01, 2009.

I was in attendance at this convention and had also watched the film. It was a powerful film about childhood trauma, such as abuse. The film moved me and made me think. What happened after the movie ended is what would stay in my mind long after the convention ended. There was a discussion about the film afterward with Renée asking the fans what they thought. It must have been a profound moment for Renée to see the reaction the film got. Depending on their experiences growing up (or the present), the fans were split. Did the son forgive the father for the abuse he suffered and wished to give his father his last wish, or did the father perpetrate a continuation of the abuse by forcing the son to break the law?

Half the audience was adamant that it was forgiveness, the other half saw it as a continuation of the abuse. I sat back and listened to impassioned opinions from those who had suffered abuse and how the movie affected them. It made me well up. I glanced over at Renée, who was standing in front of the crowd, and realized that for any creative person to get such a response, it was manna from heaven. This moment in convention history is one of my all-time favorites because of the emotional, passionate debate and support for Renee.

Lucy Lawless and Renee O'Connor Know Their Fans

Lucy and Renee know how to connect with the fans. When they are in front of Xenites, they are playful, sometimes serious and often goofy. Photo Ops are another way Lucy and Renee give Xenites a thrill. There's a Photo Op of Lucy with some fans holding a sword and giving that patented *Xena* stare that had the Xenaverse in raptures and demanding a Xena Reboot. I'm quite sure if Lucy wore her Xena leathers at a Photo Op, the organizers would need to call 911. Lucy hasn't worn her Xena outfit...yet. Maybe for the 25th Anniversary Convention.

Renee just needs to rock up to a Photo Op wearing one of her Gabrielle outfits and the Xenites will be hyperventilating. One year, Renee got dressed up for her Photo Op in her iconic BGSB (Bilious Green Sports Bra). Now, of course, there were differing opinions about which outfit was her best but everyone knew the BGSB outfit was one of the best. It was a fan hit (and one that I truly love because it's my favorite Gabrielle outfit).

Or the time Lucy and Renee jumped out of a birthday cake (10th Anniversary convention) wearing matching Go-Go outfits. It was and outfit similar to the one Renee wore (as Gabrielle) during the episode "Lyre Lyre Hearts of Fire." The decibel level reached in the convention hall was incredible! If sound could lift a convention roof, then it would have been blown all the way to LAX. I didn't think it could get louder UNTIL the 20th Anniversary convention during Katherine Fugate's play. I was roped in for that by Katherine days earlier and decided, last con, might as well start and end my theatre career at a Xena Con. I was the scene changer/cardboard carrier. What could possibly go wrong? I nearly collided with Renee on stage and almost went headlong into a piano trying to get off the stage. I 'deftly' executed one of those roadrunner maneuvers and stopped short of smashing into it just in time! That was memorable for a nanosecond and quickly forgotten because of what followed.

I was watching the play from the sidelines (and relieved my part was over and that I could retire from my 'acting' career without face planting on the stage). I was enjoying the play and knew what was going to happen, but not what Lucy did to Renee. Lucy sent the fans into meltdown. Lucy took Renee in her arms, then dipped and kissed. The decibel levels easily outdid the levels for the Go-Go entrance and it shook the foundations of the Burbank Marriott Convention Center.

Friendships, Love and Marriage

Those conventions saw many friendships form, quite a few marriages (official and unofficial, depending on where in the world you were) and a whole lot of fun. It was also the place where people felt safe to come out, be themselves, act the goof, and just have a great time. It was a joyous time to be with friends and just relax. You were in the company of like-minded souls.

At the time of writing this chapter, Creation Entertainment has announced that they have pushed back their Salute to Xena: The 25th Anniversary Convention, which was going to be held on August 28-30, 2020. It's now going to be held on April 16-18, 2021 due to COVID-19 and the restrictions this has caused around the world. In April 2021, we will once again see Lucy Lawless, Renée O'Connor, Steven Sears, and other guests join us in our gathering of our Xenite family. We long to see the *Xena* cast, but we are not going just for them. We are going to celebrate twenty-five / twenty-six years of the Xenaverse and party with our family.

When it's time for the Xena Horde to gather again, I will sit in the lobby, and people watch. Try it, and you will find your heart swell, and a smile will crease your face as you watch old friends hug each other, and new friendships blossom. It's a joy to watch.

The link below is from AUSXIP's Convention Page which lists conventions held from 1997 to 2020 and subpages for each of them:
http://ausxip.com/conventions/conlist.html

PART 2

XENA WEBMASTERS – DIGITAL NEW FRONTIERS

Logomancy Xena   Tom's Xena Page

AUSXIP   Sword & Staff   Whoosh!

Xenaville   The Xenaversity of Minnesota

Merwolf   Calli's Creations

Michelle's Xena Library

The Xena Scrolls   The Royal Academy of Bards:

Lunacy's Reviews   The Athenaeum   Loyal to Xena

Xena Movie Campaign

Subtext Virtual Season

Chapter Five

Universal's Ultimate Gift to the Xenaverse

by MaryD

WHEN I JOINED the Xenaverse in December 1996, there were a handful of sites dedicated to *Xena: Warrior Princess*. The big guns were Whoosh!, Tom's Xena Page, Logomancy, Warrior Princess, and a couple of others. Tom's Xena Page was the all-rounder. There was fan fiction, artwork, screen captures of episodes, message boards, magazine article scans, and various other *Xena* related material.

They were giant copyright violations that you could spot from space.

Yet, the copyright holders, Universal and Renaissance Pictures, did not do anything to stop the webmasters from creating these tributes to *Xena*. They didn't send their army of lawyers to send 'cease and desist' emails, nor did anyone get their site shut down. Why?

To answer that question, I must go back to the dawn of the internet (the early to mid-1990s).

Websites are ubiquitous in the 21st century. We do a web search using our favorite search engine for the show we love, the actors, and up to date news, and we don't spend a lot of time thinking about the process. If we are fans of a particular show, we find their social media accounts and then their site. We immerse ourselves in everything related to the show.

That wasn't always the case. For TV Shows such as *Star Trek*, there were no websites pre-1990s. There were physical meetups and fanzines (fan-produced magazines), conventions, and other ways for fans to interact in local groups.

Then along came the dawn of a new age. It was primitive by today's standards, but it allowed us to congregate on Fidonet (Usenet – the precursor to Facebook/Twitter). That's where I had my digital foray into fandom. The *Star Trek: DS9*, *Star Trek: The Next Generation* and *Babylon 5* Fidonet groups.

It was mainly a text-based web in the early 1990s. Websites were being built by fans to show love for their favorite show. I taught myself how to code html (the language that webpages are built on) and created my first website. The site was focused on *Babylon 5*'s power couple John Sheridan and Delenn and called it *The Australian John and Delenn Information Page*. I also had a *Star Trek* page called *The Australian Star Trek Information Page*. It was just one page with news and my fan fiction that had been published in various issues of Outpost by Orion Press (a fan-produced magazine – the dead tree kind). That was it.

It was then that something extraordinary happened that changed everything. Computer monitors and graphics improved. Computers began to get easier to use, the text-based browsers gave way to graphic interfaces. This was a significant change because it opened computing to the masses, especially for those who didn't have any knowledge of Unix or text-based interfaces.

The dawn of a new age brought about the explosion of web pages because WYSIWYG (/ˈwɪziwɪg/ WIZ-ee-wig) stands for What You See Is What You Get, and it became the norm. WYSIWYG is a system where the software allows content to be edited without messing with code. With that ability, creating web sites became easier and let more people create websites without the need to learn how to code.

How did the studios respond to this new medium? There were two ways they could have reacted to this explosion of sites: encourage the web sites to showcase the show and get free publicity, or discourage the fans and try to shut them down. What did Universal do with this new medium and their hit show *Xena: Warrior Princess*?

Universal Studios was smart. They learned from the mistakes of other studios who didn't understand the new medium. Universal allowed *Xena* webmasters as much freedom as possible; that's not to say they didn't keep an eye on us. We were allowed to create everything our hearts wanted with the peace of mind that it had the unwritten permission of the copyright owners.

Websites had the disclaimer:

"This site is a not for profit site for the show Xena: Warrior Princess. Xena: Warrior Princess is the copyright property of MCA/Universal and Renaissance Pictures. No copyright infringement is intended, and images/video/characters for published fan fiction used are for non-commercial use."

Fan fiction had the disclaimer:

"Disclaimers: Xena: Warrior Princess, Xena, Gabrielle, and other Xena characters are the sole property of MCA/Universal and Renaissance Pictures. No copyright infringement was intended in writing this story. This story cannot be sold or used for profit in any way. Copies of this story may be made for private use only and must include all disclaimers and copyrights."

We attributed and thanked the copyright holders for allowing us the use of their characters, images, and artwork. That satisfied Universal, and everyone was happy.

That is not to say that fans did not cross the red line Universal had set:

we must not sell copyrighted material such as artwork. I know of a couple of incidents when Universal took exception and went after webmasters and artists. This was EXTREMELY rare.

There were instances when Universal would step in and ask for something to be taken down, and the smart webmaster would quickly comply. Having a good relationship with Universal would allow everyone to create their sites in peace.

Could Universal have enforced their copyright and banned Xenites from expressing the love for their show? Of course, it would have been their right as the copyright holders. Would it have made a difference to the fandom if Universal chose to go down that route?

The explosion of creativity that this fandom has produced would have been extinguished if Universal had not allowed us this freedom. The deep well of creativity may not have existed in the way that it blossomed over the last twenty-five years.

I started the *Australian Xena Information Page* as a way to express my love for this new show. All I wanted was to create art from the episodes (episode montages). Without Universal's unwritten permission for fans to have complete freedom to express their love, AUSXIP would not have existed, nor would the other sites in the Xenaverse in the way they were created. They would survive, but they would be bland and utterly pointless.

AUSXIP was and is one giant copyright violation that could have been taken down by Universal at any time in the last twenty-four years. Universal chose not to. Win/Win for everyone UNLESS I overstepped the unwritten rules that Universal had set for the Xenaverse.

What a difference it would have made to this fandom if we had not been able to express our love of the show with our fan fiction, artwork, or (later) video. What a difference it would have made if Universal had exercised its copyright.

I was reminded again of Universal's gift to the Xenaverse in 2010. I received an email from a studio about a site I had created, and they asked me not to post screen captures. This site was populated with screen captures, news, and official episode stills as per AUSXIP policy with the appropriate copyright attribution.

AUSXIP policy for EVERY site in the AUSXIP Network was and still is that it must be respectful of the actors and TV shows. It must be positive and not step over that line in any way through images and/or articles. This new studio didn't know about these rules; there was no reason they should know about them. AUSXIP was just another web site in a sea of millions of sites, and they had no inkling of the history of the website. All they wanted to do was protect their copyright. The studio had ZERO experience with fandom. The Studio took the attitude of stomping on ALL creativity. I had to pass this demand on to the

AUSXIP Talking Xena forum, which the moderators and the members thought was unreasonable. Still, AUSXIP Talking Xena was under the same rules as the rest of the AUSXIP sites. So they complied with those rules.

The Studio placed a blanket ban on all sites for this new show (and there were quite a few). Some of those sites ignored them and others abided by their rules. Did that stop the fans from posting screen captures? Of course it didn't. I felt that the studio shot themselves in the foot with that decision because they would, later on, relax those rules, but the damage had been done. There wasn't the level of creativity in the fandom as there was in *Xena*. Their decision did not stop people from posting anything they wanted, and the studio lost the battle.

Why didn't that studio take Universal's route? Maybe it was because they were a new(ish) company and did not have experience with fandoms. It wasn't a battle that they would ever be able to win, not these days. Maybe they could have achieved it back in 1995, but not today.

Universal could have taken the same route, but they didn't, and that led to a vibrant and robust fanbase. Universal's decision paved the way for the success of *Xena: Warrior Princess* as a television hit show and an energetic fanbase that has lasted for twenty-five years.

Was Universal's choice to turn a blind eye to the copyright violations the right choice? I know it was, but it was also the smart choice.

You need a lot of money to publicize a product or a show. Studios allocate an X amount to publicity, but it also needs bums on seats to watch the show. Allowing the fandom to express their love is the cheapest option, and word of mouth is the best publicity you can have without spending a fortune. There were level, smart heads at Universal and Renaissance Pictures who knew what they were doing and got the results they wanted. Other than Star Wars & *Star Trek*, what other fandom has not only lasted but grown for twenty-five years?

A great many of the sites that were born during Xena's six-season run have now disappeared. Lost to the Xenaverse (and the Wayback Machine that wasn't able to archive them). Of course, some have remained (and have been archived with other sites to keep them online). Here is a small list of sites that are still on-line (although some of them have not been active for many years):

Active

- AUSXIP (Australian Xena Information Page) ausxip.com/xena
- Calli's Creations: calliscreations.com
- Hercules and Xena The Legendary Wikia
  hercules-xena.fandom.com/wiki/Xena

- Loyal to Xena: loyaltoxena.com
- Melissa Good Fanfic Site: merwolf.com
- The Royal Academy of Bards: www.academyofbards.org
- The Xenaversity of Minnesota: xenaversity.tripod.com/
- WHOOSH! whoosh.org
- Xenaville: xenaville.com

Retired But Still On-line

- Logomancy Xena: klio.net/XENA
- Lunacy Reviews: lunacyreviews.com
- Sword & Staff: sword-and-staff.com
- Taiko's Xena & Gabrielle Page: xenite.net
- The Athenaeum: xenafiction.net
- The Xena Scrolls: thexenascrolls.homestead.com
- Tom's Xena Page: xenafan.com
- Warrior Princess Nerd Zoe: warriorprincessnerd.com
- Xandrella: xandrella.com

On behalf of all *Xena* webmasters, thank you to Universal / MCA and Renaissance Pictures for allowing us to flourish and build a creatively rich Xenaverse. Your willingness to allow us to express ourselves through our art and fan fiction is what helped make this show and this fandom legendary.

Chapter Six

AUSXIP (Australian Xena Information Page) – Evolution of a Xena Fan Site

by MaryD

I HAVE THIS strange system in regards to television shows. I give them six months and see if they survive or if my interest wanes. That happens even if the show had grabbed my attention from the first episode. I gave *Xena: Warrior Princess* six months to see if I kept watching, or I tuned out to find something else. So, how did we get to this point? There are moments in our lives when we are at a crossroads—do we take one road, or do we take the other? We may know we are at a crossroads, or we may be blissfully oblivious to it. In 1996, I was completely unaware of the change that was about to happen (blissful I was not, but that is why AUSXIP was born).

My life then was quite a shambles dominated by an abusive marriage and by my attempts at surviving it without going totally off the rails. It was not an easy task, but I found ways to distract myself and aid in my mental wellbeing. I discovered that teaching myself how to code websites and master Photoshop was challenging and exciting (I get super focused, and the rest of the world does not exist). By teaching myself these new skills, I was challenged, and that occupied my mind, and doing something creative brought me joy. When someone or something brings you joy, continue doing it…if it's legal (of course) and does no harm.

Fandom has always been this weird animal for me. I liked the community and the shared love of TV shows (mine were Star Trek and Babylon 5). I had never met any of my online friends, but that didn't matter. I'm an introvert, so meeting people wasn't high on the list. I was a prolific fan fiction writer for Star Trek: Deep Space Nine and The Next Generation and had eleven of my ST: DS9 stories published in print by the OUTPOST fanzine, which was the precursor to online fan fiction archives. I also participated (with a great deal of fun and craziness) on the Fidonet bulletin boards (the Twitter / Facebook of its time) in the ST: DS9 message board. My goodness, that was so much fun. I also put my website building to good use and created my first ever website, called "The John and Delenn Information Page." That site was going to be the first in a long list of sites I would build.

In September 1996, my friend Xero (also known as Susan Podd to her parents and the IRS), who I had known for a long time, told me about a new show she had fallen in love with called *Xena: Warrior Princess.* Xero thought I would be interested in the show because it featured a strong female character, just like my Star Trek and Babylon 5 heroes: Tasha Yar (TNG), Major Kira (DSN), and Delenn (Babylon 5). I'm drawn to female characters who are strong, resilient, and courageous. Xero thought that Xena was precisely the show I would fall in love with. I wasn't so sure.

Xero's stubborn refusal to let my "I'm watching too many shows to be involved in another fandom" protestations became my saving grace. She didn't give up and kept at me until I relented in October 1996, when I agreed to watch this sword and sandals show just to stop her persistent emails! The show just didn't appeal to me (yes, I hadn't watched any episodes, but then I was determined not to like it).

Now, how would I watch a show that wasn't on Australian television? Easy peasy with a little help from a friend in the United States and the state-of-the-art multi-region Video Cassette Recorder (VCR). Geeks rule!

Back in the stone age, when we taped television shows on videotape (NTSC for Americans and PAL format for Australians—this will play a part, so that's why I'm making a distinction), Xero sent me two episodes: "The Titans" and "The Prodigal."

Let me just say that if you ever want to get someone interested in *Xena: Warrior Princess*, DO NOT make these two episodes to your prospective convert. To appreciate these episodes, you need the backstory of who Xena is and what is Gabrielle's relationship, etc. I didn't have that connection, and they bored me. This was not going to end well for Xero's crusade.

I told Xero I wouldn't watch this show even if they paid me! It's okay to laugh at my stupidity. You would think that Xero would give up, right? Wrong. She persisted. Not only that, but other friends got involved in urging me to watch. When the universe is giving you messages, just take the time to listen.

Fast forward to December 1996. I walked by a newsagent, and there I spotted the Australian TV Week magazine with Xena on the cover in all her glory, breastplate, sword and all, walking through some long grass. That was the first official image I had seen. It's funny how you remember stuff that seems so inconsequential at the time. I called Xena a "Wonder Woman ripoff" and mocked those shoulder guards and everything about it. I thought the actress was cute but trying too hard to look like Wonder Woman. As you can see, I was DETERMINED to hate this show and everything about it.

That magazine cover signaled the arrival of the Warrior Princess to Australian television. I picked up the magazine for my friend because I knew it would interest her, and she had persevered in her Quest to get me to love the show she thought was worthy of my attention.

Wouldn't you know it, it just happened that Xero didn't have "Sins of the Past" (Season 1, Episode 1) on videotape, and could I please tape it for her? At the time, it didn't occur to me that it was a ruse to get me to give the show another chance. Sneaky Xero.

Determined not to disappoint my friend if I taped Friends instead of Xena, I sat down and made sure I got the right show. It was a warm evening (this is where the 'what were you doing and how you felt' moment comes into it), and I was trying to fix my computer. The show started, the music soared, and I was satisfied that I was taping the right thing. I fully intended to turn off the television and do my work for reasons that I still don't know why I didn't do that. I kept the tv on as background noise while I worked.

I looked up from tinkering with the laptop to see Xena burying her weapons, and I remember thinking, 'what an odd thing to do.' I kept watching and tried to figure out why this woman was getting rid of her sword and her metal frisbee. I had not seen the Warrior Princess trilogy on Hercules: The Legendary Journeys for this scenario to make any sense. Nothing about this show made sense to me (The Titans, The Prodigal, and now Sins of the Past).

Then something happened that would change my life forever.

There was Xena in her underwear, a long petticoat thing called a 'shift' came out of the bushes to defend some village women that were being confronted by a bunch of surly-looking soldiers. With no armor to protect her, no sword or frisbee, it was her show of strength and courage that captured my attention. In those few minutes, my indifference blossomed into instant love.

I can tell you the EXACT moment AUSXIP was born. Xena had been knocked down, and she was trying to find a way to fight, but without her weapons, she was outnumbered and defenseless (or so I thought). I was now intrigued as to how she was going to get out of the mess she was in. Xena fumbled around for the weapons that had been buried (conveniently Xena buried them in the spot where they could easily be found a short time later after she got knocked to the ground), and having found them, Xena rose like a phoenix brandishing her sword and a devilish grin on her face. She's faced off Draco's deputy, and she laughed. It's difficult to describe without seeing the scene, but Lucy Lawless got me with that little laugh. Who knew it would be so easy to convert me to the Xenaverse with a giggle. Maybe Xero should have shown me that one minute of footage instead of me having to wade through The Titans and The Prodigal.

When you watch Xena at that moment, it becomes crystal clear that Xena was going to enjoy beating the soldiers; it was going to give her pleasure to pound them into the dirt. Xena wasn't a helpless woman lost in the woods, but a warrior and was about to spank them into next week! That moment was when AUSXIP was born. It's that little laugh that had me hooked. POP! Mary is now paying attention; I do remember smiling and leaning forward, my computer long forgotten. I'm not quite sure why that laugh made such an impact; maybe it was because of the totally crazy scenario where a woman in her underwear brandishing a sword against a well-armed opponent was just so incongruous.

Whatever it was, I wanted to create something from that show. By the time we got halfway through the episode, the artwork had started forming in my head. I've come to realize that when an idea is implanted in my mind, nothing will shift it unless I do something about it.

That was December 14, 1996. I reasoned I didn't have time to immerse myself in another show. I didn't have time to create a new website. When you really want to talk yourself out of doing something, you can find reasons, but I'm not very good at talking myself out of my ideas.

When the episode finished, the first thing I did was email Xero. I may have said, "You were right," and maybe also, "I'm creating a site."

The second thing I did was go online. There had to be a fandom based around this show. I fired up the browser (does anyone remember Netscape Navigator?) and went in search. The first site I found was Tom's Xena Page, the second one was Whoosh!, and the third one was Logomancy. These are three incredible sites and served as my introduction to the fledgling fandom known as the Xenaverse.

My idea for a site grew, but I didn't want to recreate the wheel. Tom's Xena Page was the AUSXIP of the Day – it had everything a Xena fan would wish for: screencaps, news, fan fiction. I didn't want to make something that would take away from Tom's site, but to create my own niche within the Xenaverse.

What could I do that was unique in this fandom? I looked at all three sites and found something that no one else was doing. There were no Xena episode montages (collages) being created. There were a couple of Xena montages of one or two images but not the type I had wanted to create. That was going to be my niche, so I started to create the episode art that very night.

With my new art, I would need a new site. The new baby needed a name. I toyed with two options: DOWN UNDER XENA or AUSTRALIAN XENA INFORMATION PAGE. I chose to plagiarize myself and rip off my Australian John and Delenn Information Page name.

Why didn't I choose Down Under Xena? You are laughing at reading that, aren't you? I know you are. DUX was a catchy acronym, but I'm glad I didn't go that route because of what I now know of the Xenaverse…yep, you know.

My mission was to create a site to showcase my artwork, add a little bit of Xena info with an Australian slant, plus a little bit of Lucy and Renée info all on ONE page. Don't laugh. It was doable because that's what the John and

Delenn Information Page was. That started my journey into the Xenaverse, but my goal of having just one page with bits of information and art, lasted less than a month. So much has happened over the last twenty-three years.

Here are some of the highlights.

1996: I Find My Tribe

I uploaded the site on December 15, 1996, and I introduced myself to the Xenaverse by going and joining the mailing list known as 'The Xenaverse.' I was received warmly, and one of the first messages of 'Welcome to the Xenaverse' was from Tom Simpson of Tom's Xena Page. I was chuffed at the friendly nature and acceptance. I even remember what my first question in the Xenaverse was: "Who is Callisto?" That question was met with friendly banter and "Oh, no spoilers for you!' type responses. It was charming, and it felt right. I had found my tribe.

1997: Becoming Part of the Fabric of the Xenaverse.

I quickly became part of the Xenaverse. I volunteered to be a fanfic editor for Tom's Xena Page. In April 1997, I came up with the idea to create fan fiction awards and pitched it to Tom, who agreed (bless him). What a world of incredible fiction! Lots of fun. The Eddies (The Editor's Choice Awards) were born on Tom's Fan Fiction section. So much fan fiction to devour!

The show was heading into its second season, and I had a lot to catch up on. Xero, who must have been giddy with delight, sent me the COMPLETE Season 1 on videotape (and surprise, surprise, Episode 1 was on that tape… sneaky Xero). Because of the number of times that video had been copied, the color would turn green or gray or blue. I did not care at all because I had twenty-one episodes to watch to catch up. What a giddy ride!

1997: Well That Idea Didn't Last Long…

On January 11-12, 1997, Creation Entertainment held its first official Xena convention, and that signaled the start of AUSXIP's transition from a niche site to something not envisioned less than a month earlier. The first fan to contribute to AUSXIP was Maureen McGowan. She sent me photos of Lucy Lawless at the convention. That was followed by a convention report by Quest, and two more reports by Tina and Cathy. The genie was out of the bottle, and there was no going back. These three fans were the first to contribute to my site. You can find the convention page with the images and the reports here:

http://www.ausxip.com/conventions/97burbank/index.html

This was the beginning of what AUSXIP was going to be. As much as I wanted to create just a little niche in the fandom, the Xenaverse had other ideas. After realizing that I just didn't have the time to devote to Tom's fanfic section and the ever-increasing demands of my own site, I made the decision to concentrate on AUSXIP. Tom was a gracious fellow and a good friend who understood my choice.

I concentrated on AUSXIP from an Australian point of view, giving a different angle on the news and having a fan fiction section that was by invitation only. I introduced the XIPPY Awards – AUSXIP's Fan Fiction Awards. That one-page site became a whole lot bigger.

1997: Media Attention

AUSXIP gets some attention from Cinescape Magazine, July/August 1997... *Since there seem to be hundreds of Xena-Oriented websites to choose from, we've decided to make your search a little easier by compiling a list of some of the more resourceful Xena Sites. http://www.xenite.simplenet.com (AUSXIP before getting a domain). This excellent Xena: Warrior Princess information page is packed with easy-to-read episode, character and actor guides. The site also boasts sound files, episode clips, a graphics gallery, and fan fiction, in addition to a cool section where transcripts to Xena articles from newspapers, talk shows, and mags have been compiled.*

1998: First Contact with Xena Cast / Crew

Exciting stuff happened around April 1998… Steven L. Sears emailed me surprising me his email and the message. He sent me a photo of Chris Manheim, the Executive Story Editor for *Xena*, and a note to say she LOVED (capitals were used) my montages. To prove it, Chris was photographed with a row of my episode montages. To take it another notch…Steven ALSO loved my art. Yeah, that's how you make a fan very happy. Little did I know that Steven was going to become a friend, and years later, he would be writing a chapter for this book. Life is funny sometimes.

1999: Time For An Upgrade

The demise of simplenet.com brought upon some major changes. It was time to get serious and buy a domain name. On July 20, 1999, I purchased AUSXIP.COM. I should have also bought AUSPIX.com because people like to switch XIP and PIX around! I have received quite a few emails asking where the site had disappeared to because they couldn't reach it, and my response is a question. How did you spell it? Do a

2001: A Safe Haven for Xenites

AUSXIP Talking Xena message board was born to find a safe place to chat about Xena after the Official Net Forum closed. The rules were simple:

be polite, don't disparage other fans who 'ship' differently (i.e., Joxer/Ares, Gabrielle/Joxer), and hate against LGBTQA+ members was forbidden. Gay or Straight, didn't matter to me; just be a good netizen of AUSXIP Talking Xena. I discuss the formation of AUSXIP Talking Xena in Part 6: The Social Xenaverse in *Chapter 35: AUSXIP Talking Xena - A Safe Haven for Xenites.*

August 2001: I Meet My Tribe

I decided to travel to the US to meet the friends I had made. It was my first US trip. Up to this point, I hadn't met any other Xenites except online. It was an unbelievable introduction. It was also the first time I truly understood what AUSXIP meant to other people. It wasn't just my site anymore, but it belonged to the Xenaverse.

August 2001: Big Surprise... Don't Annoy Xenites!

2001 was the year that I found out that sudden change and the Xenaverse are not compatible. Changing a site's design without alerting its many visitors will lead to heartache; for the webmaster. While I was on my US tour, Mesh was looking after AUSXIP. She asked me if she could redesign the site. I was feeling adventurous (I was traveling to another country THOUSANDS of miles from home), and I said sure, go for it. Yikes.

I forgot one tiny thing. I forgot to take into account the visitors to the site. Up to this point, I didn't really understand how essential AUSXIP was to other people. I had never met any of the other fans in person to get that impression. We were in for a shock at how vehemently Xenites reacted by the unexpected (for them) change. I was surprised and inundated with a lot of upset emails from people. Xenites were emailing Mesh to demand I return the site to its original design, and how dare she change the layout while I'm away and then emailing me begging me to intervene. We both learned a lesson from that experience. An abrupt change like a site design was jarring. I decided that it would be the last time something that drastic would happen to the site design, and in the future, the design would evolve into what I wanted it to be rather than present it all at once.

April 2003: AUSXIP Splits Into Three

A massive change for AUSXIP. I split AUSXIP into three websites in April. The main AUSXIP site, which was Xena, and the AUSXIP Lucy Lawless http://lucylawless.info (that would later change to http://lucylawless.net in 2012) and AUSXIP Renée O'Connor (http://reneeoconnor.info). Those three sites became the core of the AUSXIP Network. Many more sites were to follow but at the core, AUSXIP will always sites related to Xena and the cast.

December 2007: AUSXIP Gets Its Own Dedicated Server

Having AUSXIP on it's own dedicated server gave me the opportunity to do so much more than shared hosting would allow. In December 2007, I moved the site to its own server. Things were getting serious. That extra power and space on the server allowed me to host larger image/video files and expand without worrying about running out of space. Today, AUSXIP sits on a server with terabytes of space and more bandwidth than I could ever use.

July/September 2004: AUSXIP Absorbs Other Xena Sites

I was asked to take care of other Xena sites and to absorb them into AUSXIP. July 2004 - Forevaxena is incorporated into AUSXIP - Forevaxena was run by Cindy Tingley. September 2004 - Judi's Creations merges with AUSXIP - Judi's Creations was run by Carol Stephens.

December 2006: AUSXIP Greater Good Is Created

AUSXIP was about to turn ten years old, and I wanted to celebrate this event by doing something that was core to Xena's message—the Greater Good. It was a massive undertaking and, although I had run a small charity auction before to raise money for Hurricane Katrina relief, this was going to be different. Read how we created AUSXIP Greater Good Charity Auctions in *Chapter 51: AUSXIP Greater Good: Together We Have Made a Difference.*

2008: We Honor Our Fallen - The Xenite Memorial

AUSXIP absorbed part of the NutBread Brigade Website Xenite Tribute Page. In April 2008 Becky Calvert passed away and the Xenite Memorial was without a home. Becky created The Xenite Memorial to remember and honor the fans who had passed away, and I took over the task of keeping a permanent record of the friends we have lost over the years. The Xenite Memorial can be found here: http://ausxip.com/xenitememorial. I discuss more The Xenite Memorial in Part 11: *Chapter 62 - Becky Calvert's Legacy - The Xenite Memorial* and the full list can be found in *Chapter 65: The Xenite Memorial – Our Fallen Warriors.*

April 2008: Major New AUSXIP Fan Site - Adrienne Wilkinson!

I created a new site dedicated to Adrienne Wilkinson. Adrienne would later approve this site to become the Official Adrienne Wilkinson Fan Site: http://adriennewilkinson.net

March 2015: AUSXIP Publishing is born!

In March 2015, I decided to open the doors to my own publishing company, AUSXIP Publishing. As Lucy Lawless likes to say, "*Do something scary, the payoff is awesome*'. Boy was that scary! More about my transition from published author to owner and publisher in Part 7: Because of Xena and *Chapter 40 - Doing Something Scary - AUSXIP Publishing is Born.*

2020 & Beyond: What's Next For AUSXIP?

That was one very long six month trial period, right? Twenty-four years later and AUSXIP is still alive and thriving. I started AUSXIP to save my sanity. It has done that and so much more. Yes, the site is a lot of work because I always find new ways to improve the design and presentation. Once I'm satisfied with a design, it may stay that way for years, or it might change again next month (slowly slowly). I have this unquenchable desire to improve all aspects of the site and along the way to improve my skills. The friendships and the sheer joy I've received from the Xenaverse is the reason for AUSXIP's existence for twenty-four years. No other fandom can come close to what the Xenaverse has meant to me.

How long will AUSXIP stay online? I have the attention of a flea when it comes to TV shows. Once the interest fades, it's gone forever. Xena, surprisingly, has never entered that black hole. To my absolute surprise, my interest in Xena has never waived, and maintaining AUSXIP is as strong as it ever was.

AUSXIP has evolved over the years to encompass other shows with strong female characters, but the core is still the Xenaverse. It will always be the Xenaverse. I review the decision to keep it alive every year, and every year I ask myself: do I still want to spend time working on this monster of a site I have created? The answer for the last twenty-four years has been: YES. Will it ever go quietly into that good night? Of course, it will, at some point. Nothing stays the same; time moves on, life changes. For the moment, AUSXIP will continue its original mission.

In 2021, AUSXIP will celebrate twenty-five years online. That's a quarter of a century of something that has given me so much joy. AUSXIP achieved the one goal it had in the beginning: to occupy my mind and create beautiful art.

Mission accomplished.

I know it has given me more than what I anticipated or wished for. It saved my life, but I also gained thousands of new friends, new experiences, a worldwide family, new skills, and a whole lot more.

How do you calculate what that is worth? You can't.

It's priceless.

INTERNATIONAL ASSOCIATION OF XENA STUDIES

Chapter Seven

Whoosh!
A Memoir of a Rabid Fan

by Kym Taborn

WHY I BECAME A RABID FAN

What initially attracted me to *Xena: Warrior Princess* was that it involved a woman who was not waiting around to be rescued or accompanied by a man. What kept me watching was the slow evolution of a complicated relationship between two women. Before *Xena: Warrior Princess*, you hardly ever saw on TV or the movies women with more than a bare hint of an internal life. With the arrival of *Xena: Warrior Princess,* you were rewarded with a real-time unfolding of how female relationships form, grow, evolve, and change. At the time, I was intrigued. Later, I realized I was experiencing the overturn of an old oppressive archetype and the rise of something that really was going to change the world.

When I was watching *Xena: Warrior Princess* for the first time, I started a dialogue in my mind. "This is silly. No woman could do that!" I told myself. Please, remember this was before our current time's presentation of strong women on TV and the movies. Nowadays, women are always fighting back and often giving just as good as they get. In fact, it now feels strange and retro to see a woman being harassed and her not at least trying to fight back (see Depiction of Women below for more on this thought). But, even though this was the 90s, I stepped back and realized that in the male versions, no human could really do that either. It was the hero archetype I was watching. It's supposed to be larger than life. Then I understood what was really going on.

I had been socialized not to question the privilege of men to participate in the fantasy hero archetype. And yet, here I was questioning the same privilege for women. My culture had embedded in me the concept that men had the power to transcend reality, whereas women did not. The greatest power a human being has is their ability to transcend reality, and here I was, denying that to those of my same-sex. Pretty messed up. And with the advent of *Xena: Warrior Princess*, I was witnessing our society being gifted with an alternative to the whimpering damsel in distress. Whether by design or luck, the creators of *Xena: Warrior Princess* infected our world with a new model of what a woman could be in popular culture, to the point where watching damsels in distress felt antiquated and frustrating, and dare I say, unrealistic?

True, Xena was not the first female kick-ass popular icon. In the movies, there was Ellen Ripley and Sarah Connor. But then, to make it palatable to the conditioned audience, these women had to evolve from stereotypical women in distress to the eventual hero, usually within the last fifteen minutes or so of the film. Xena came to the world fully formed, already full of agency and power. On TV, there was Wonder Woman and Charlie's Angels. Still, Wonder Woman was caught up with superpowers, and Charlie's Angels looked like they would snap like toothpicks in a real fight. When you saw Xena ride up on a horse, she looked like she'd be able to give as good as she got. *Xena: Warrior Princess* was a delivery system of a new female warrior paradigm that was impossible to stop and infected popular culture in a way it had never been infected before.

At the time of Xena's arrival, there were very few characterizations of adult women pursuing mature relationships on television. Where you could find such characterizations, they would tell you there was a relationship. Still, they rarely, if ever, showed you the relationship form throughout time. If you watch *Xena: Warrior Princess* over its six seasons, you will see in as close to real-time as episodic TV could muster in the 1990s, the beginning, middle, and end of a relationship between two women. It develops slowly over time, like in real life. Episodic TV before and during the time of *Xena: Warrior Princess* rarely dedicated so much time and character development in portraying the evolution of a relationship between two women. Regardless of how you choose to characterize the specific nature of the relationship (and remember, these are fictional people, not real people; they are ultimately reflections of the viewer), it is clear that there is a strong bond between them—they are indeed soulmates, and why they are together is self-evident. Why? Because the audience experiences it with the characters almost in real-time. Even more so for the audience that existed before DVD collections and binge viewing. They had to wait no less than a week to a quarter of a year between episodes. A season a year. Six years. Six years of viewing these friends of yours as they discover that they are better people together than apart. That they have chosen to (mostly) remain together and support one another through thick and thin. It was a powerful emotional experience to go through. And who wouldn't want to have a soulmate/friend/lover/fill-in-the-blank like Xena or Gabrielle?

I became a rabid fan of this show because of the interweaving of complex aspects that were cultivated and nurtured by the creators and producers of the show either by design or accident. My opinions are based entirely upon my personal and subjective experiences with the show, too many discussions with both fellow fans and production staff of the show, and my flirt with fandom. In the day, I edited multiple *Xena: Warrior Princess* on-line publications, ran the

Whoosh.org website and produced features for the Anchor Bay DVDs from Season 3 on. I have been active in *Xena* fandom for longer than I care to admit.

What inspired people to devote thousands of hours to writing fanfiction? To creating intricate music videos? To drop everything on a moment's notice to fly cross-country for the chance sighting of a cast or crew member on a talk show or the stage? To work incessantly on keeping websites and mailing lists up to date with the latest buzz? To spend years searching the web to find out anything about the show? Learning English so you would have a purer relationship with the show? Or today, decades after the last episode aired, to attend local gatherings, perhaps a 25th Anniversary convention, or even a Xenite Retreat in the middle of a forest to visit old friends? People come from all over the world to attend these events. Almost twenty years after the show ended. So, what was the attraction?

In alphabetical order, I will share with you an attempt to explain what attracted me to *Xena: Warrior Princess,* a TV show that I devoted over a decade of discretionary time to, and to the somewhat chagrin of family and friends. Please, be kind as I visit my past and revisit some of the power, the passion, and the danger of my Xena fandom experiences and observations. At the same time, I try not to cause post-traumatic stress or undue enthusiasm to carry me away.

ACTION/FANTASY

Action-adventure

From over the top martial arts to fighting mythic creatures, lots of fighting and quests can be found in *Xena: Warrior Princess.* From the very beginning, the Hong Kong martial arts/wuxia tradition is continued in the show. Fighting on heads, kicking while twirling around a staff, running up a wall and back-flipping, using items conveniently located nearby as a weapon. If *Xena: Warrior Princess* is anything, it is an action show with great adventures. Xena meets with the ancient gods of not just Greece, but India, Scandinavia, and pagan lands. She travels to many lands, including Egypt and China, and meets all types of people, historical and fictional. You are always meeting historical personalities in a new light: Julius Caesar, Homer, Ulysses, Lao Tzu, Boadicea, Genghis Khan, and the like.

Fantasy

Xena: Warrior Princess homages the Chinese Wuxia fantasy tradition as well. Xena is on her path of redemption and explores the challenge of finding the greater good. She has supernatural tendencies that she uses to fight for the good and to remove oppressors. Xena is also unstuck in time – she meets people separated in real life by hundreds or thousands of years. The show never attempts to be historically accurate or even politically correct.

The fantasy influence was incestuous at times. "The Debt Part 1" paid homage to a scene from the movie *A Chinese Ghost Story*, which was a tribute scene from Sam Raimi's *Evil Dead* movies. Sam Raimi was an executor producer of *Xena: Warrior Princess*. Type in "Xena Hong Kong Connections" into a web browser, and you will be entertained for hours.

ATMOSPHERE

New Zealand

Filming in New Zealand, pre-Lord of the Rings, allowed the natural settings to stand out. It was a landscape we had not seen before. It was green and verdant, vivid, and gorgeous, and always raining—new places to look at, which was very refreshing. There was no other show on at the time which matched the visual appeal of the show.

Multicultural

The show shamelessly stole from all cultures–you'd see African, European, Polynesian, and Asian influences, and that'd be just one scene! And it went further, the cast was multicultural too. We saw perhaps every actor in New Zealand at least a couple of times.

Anachronistic

When the heck was this happening? Thank goodness it was fantasy, or you'd get whiplash figuring out when in history Xena was at the moment. Xena would be hanging out with Helen of Troy (1200 BCE) in one episode, and then Homer (850 BCE) would pop up in another. Did I tell you she dated Julius Caesar (44 BCE) and met Beowulf (550 CE), and fought some Samurai warriors (1000 CE)? And the biggest anachronism of all? How they talked. It was a Kiwi/SoCal surfer dude twang at times, but most pulled it off as a generic US accent.

CASTING

The show had fantastic luck in casting. Can you imagine someone different than Lucy Lawless for Xena? And Renée O'Connor for Gabrielle? Their chemistry fueled a lot of fan fiction. And what about Hudson Leick as Callisto? She nailed it when Xena took over Callisto's body. Leick pulled it off, making Callisto full of pathos and depth instead of a mere caricature. A young Karl Urban and Kevin Smith added nuances to their roles.

CULTURE

Her Courage Will Change the World

Xena is recognized the world over. Her archetype is understood by millions who have never seen the show. She has taken on global pop culture and won. The show has been the topic of many dissertations, theses, and other academic output.

The effect of *Xena* infiltrated other TV shows and movies. The creators of *Buffy the Vampire Slayer, Dark Angel, Alias, Kill Bill, Battlestar Galactica, Agent Carter,* and *Supernatural,* to name a few, have all credited *Xena: Warrior Princess* with making specific characters or premises possible for them. The show's appetite for serialized episodes influenced subsequent shows to become more serialized.

And did I mention that for a while, there was a dwarf planet temporarily called Xena (eventually named Eris) with a moon called Gabrielle (eventually called Dysnomia)? Turns out the astronomer who discovered them was a big *Xena* fan. And this happened four years after the show had ended. How many other TV shows characters get dwarf planets named after them, albeit temporarily, four years after the show has ended?

Fan Fiction Influences
– Slash Becomes Primary, Uber, And Mainstream Lesbian Romance

Almost at once, the audience picked up on the Xena archetype. This was a new representation of womanhood in the media. Like people stranded in a desert for a long time, they lapped up the show in droves. Some felt that their energy could not be contained and felt cheated by only having the show for forty-four minutes once a week. They began to write fan fiction. It attracted a spectrum of writers who had written before to some who had never considered it, but for this show.

The quality was all over the map, but it did not matter. The audience was desperate for more *Xena*. And they got it. In multitude. Published authors caught the bug and wrote fan fiction. Fan fiction writers from other fandoms joined in. Some used their *Xena* fan fiction experience to become published authors.

And, as is want in all fandom fan fiction, there was a healthy amount of slash fiction in *Xena* fan fiction. Slash fiction started in *Star Trek* fandom, where fan fiction writers started exploring a romantic and sexual relationship between Kirk and Spock. They notated it as Kirk/Spock. That evolved into two names separated by a slash indicating a romantic or sexual relationship between the two names. And that led to it being called "slash" fiction. Slash fiction can be found in all fan fiction, but it tends to be a small percentage of the fan output.

Slash fiction being a mature fan fiction genre by the time *Xena* started, was employed from day one, especially between Xena/Gabrielle. It was also called "alt fiction," in that it was an alternative to the mainstream fan fiction show that riffed off the storylines that the show was broadcasting. This type of alt or slash fiction went hand in hand with the emerging idea that Xena and Gabrielle were in the process of forming a romantic relationship. This observation was called the "subtext," and it was being discussed on-line as early as the third episode.

There was such tremendous backlash about the nascent alt fiction and interpreting the subtext of the show (called by the fans "The Shipping Wars" due to a disagreement about the nature of Xena and Gabrielle's relationship), that many authors and fans of the Xena/Gabrielle pairing created private mailing lists so they could work on, discuss, and enjoy the alt fan fiction in peace. These private areas allowed fan fiction writers to experiment, find editors, and get feedback on their work. It was a nursery for creating new genres of *Xena* fan fiction and for honing the skills of writers who would become quite good and some even becoming professionals.

It was in one of these private areas that something amazing happened. It was after the episode "The Xena Scrolls" aired. The show highlighted two new characters, Janice Covington and Mel Pappas. They were Gabrielle and Xena reincarnated in 1940s Egypt. Within days and weeks, the fan fiction community started writing not just fan fiction about Janice and Mel, but they took this idea of reincarnation and created a playing field where time and space did not matter, but that Xena and Gabrielle would always find each other. When I started seeing these fan fictions pop up on a private list I was on, I got very excited. The idea still excites me. I saw *Xena* fan fiction that did not have Xena or Gabrielle or anyone else on the show as characters and did not take place at all with the time and place of the show, and yet is was clearly *Xena* fan fiction. And it scratched an itch that those that read *Xena* fan fiction had.

A little background on me and the word uber. I was a music major in college. I studied under a music professor who had been taught by a student of the musicologist Heinrich Schenker. Then when I studied music in grad school, I worked under another professor who had also been taught by a student of Schenker. Schenker developed an obscure form of analysis. As you can surmise, I became familiar with that technique. It's a rather obtuse and complicated method. Still, a small part of it can be summarized as reducing tonal music to its Ursatz, its essence, that consists of Ur tones. Once a piece has been reduced to its Ur tones, then one can test its integrity by creating a new piece using Uber tones. If your Ursatz was in the ballpark, then your result should be another piece in the same style as the analyzed piece.

When I saw these types of stories being written, I recalled the relationship between Ur and Uber tones in Schenkerian analysis. I considered Xena and Gabrielle as the UrXena and UrGabrielle, and these characters from this new type of genre to be the UberXena and UberGabrielle. Please, note this observation became modified after the Alti episodes when it became clear that Xena and Gabrielle in the TV show were ubers and not the Urs. UrXena and UrGabrielle apparently are lost in time, appearing way before the show takes place. That means, of course, there are definitely some prehistoric UberXenas and UberGabrielles out there. It is likely the UrXena and UrGabrielle might have been two proteins floating around the primordial ooze looking for a hook-up and inadvertently starting life as we know it. I'm just saying it could happen.

Others picked up on my usage, and the genre finally had a name: Uber Fan Fiction.

Eventually, Uber fan fiction was matching mainstream *Xena* fan fiction in numbers. The subtext eventually became maintext in *Xena* fandom. The subtext interpretation of Xena and Gabrielle's relationship won the shipping wars. The subtexters came out of their private areas triumphant.

Meanwhile, Uberfiction was picked up by mainstream lesbian romantic fiction, re-invigorating it, and leading to a renaissance that resulted in many new authors and printing houses. It got to the point where uberXenas and uberGabrielles were all over the pages of fiction being consumed by an audience that was none the wiser.

DEPICTION OF WOMEN

Earlier above, I mentioned that now it feels strange and retro to see a woman being attacked or threatened and her not at least trying to fight back. That is in part because of *Xena: Warrior Princess*. Sure, you had Sarah Connor and Ellen Ripley taking names and kicking ass, but those were movies – a couple of hours every so many years...or decades! Xena came into your home every week for six years. That's a lot of subliminal messaging. It did the trick. All women benefit from living in a post-Xena world because now we have cultural permission to fight back, to be assumed to be able to defend ourselves, to stand up for ourselves and others, and to be strong. Take, for example, the story of the knight in shining armor and the damsel in distress. These archetypes hardly make any sense anymore unless in a fairy-tale type way. These archetypes populated the vast majority of TV shows and movies before *Xena: Warrior Princess*. They morphed into allowing the sexes to change in the paradigm. A woman could save a man just as plausibly a man could save a man. *Xena: Warrior Princess* got the culture to consider that women are not by nature, the weaker sex. It broke the lock on a door, which, while sadly still needs to be fully opened, others following have opened up further and further.

The show provided not only a female lead as its hero but also a female sidekick, whose story turned out to be a classic hero's journey.

And Xena had female adversaries who were her equals in most ways: Callisto, Velasca, and Alti, for example, and allies such as Ephiny, Lao Ma, and Brunhilda. You don't find that many fully realized female-centered action-oriented story zones even today. *Xena: Warrior Princess* was an anomaly in the 1990s, and would still have stuck out like a sore thumb if it had existed today.

DUMB LUCK

The show was syndicated and was not under any micro-managing from a network. The kids were given the keys to a candy store, and this is what came from it. At times one hand did not see what the other hand was doing. But, luckily, it all worked out. The writers were given more freedom. Decisions could be made on the set. Many people were given latitude that generally they wouldn't have had. What we got was something new and fresh and not seen before. It was not weighed down by expectations, by tradition, by habit. It was die-cast and then ran with. Sometimes things were done because they were deemed cool, not whether it made any sense or not. Sometimes it didn't work so well, but when it did work, it was terrific. The show could have been a colossal failure. But it wasn't. The planets aligned when by luck the right staff and the right actors were allowed to enter the candy store.

FANDOM

Diversity

Xena: Warrior Princess was a wild mishmash of cultural influences with a breezy approach that invited theatrical styles ranging from slapstick to melodrama, from fantasy to high drama, and threw in a couple of musicals (*Xena: Warrior Princess* was the first genre TV show to do a completely musical episode, now common for genre shows to do), while also laying the foundations for dramatic explorations of redemption, multiculturalism, aggression, and humanity. Fans flocked to this inclusive fantasy world where many of the present-day prejudices were ignored, where Hong Kong wuxia moves were common-place, and where the laws of physics often took detours. The audience was young and old, male and female, straight and gay, and of all races. I found the *Xena* fandom to be one of the most refreshingly diverse fandoms. True, when modern audiences watch the show, they cannot ignore that the show was white-centric, but for its time is was very multicultural. It showed interracial relationships, had black and non-white actors play traditional white roles, used Asian actors to play Asian roles, and even had a transgender actor play a transgender character.

Generosity

Whenever Xenites gather, a charity event is not far behind. Since day one, the Xenaverse fans have been active in charitable giving. From Debbie Cassetta's Sword and Staff to MaryD's AUSXIP Greater Good current day charity auctions (you are reading a book where the royalties will be donated to charity). And not just charities. When a Xenite is in need, often, another Xenite arrives to help out. The Xenaverse is riddled with a generosity of time, money, and spirit.

The Internet

Xena: Warrior Princess arrived at a time that the world was just beginning its love affair with the web. It was the tenth episode, "Hooves and Harlots," when the URL to the official website was first provided at the end of an episode. That one event gave all the budding *Xena* fans a place to meet and interact with other fans. Before the web, fans could organize and mobilize, but it took a lot of work and was mostly centralized in urban hubs. It took the internet to globalize the fandom and make fans all around the world join in their love of *Xena*. Before you knew it, even before the official merchandise train could get out of the station, fans were putting on their own conventions and gatherings, crafting jewelry and art, writing fan fiction and magazines, publishing websites to share fan news and fan output, and creating one of the most potent and vibrant global fandoms ever seen. And this was the engine that made Xena a cult figure and gave her a permanent spot in popular culture.

Cross-fertilization

The *Xena: Warrior Princess* producers, writers, and staff also have been one of the most open productions to fan interaction and contributions. Since day one, members of the staff and rank fandom intermixed on the early forums, mailing lists, and websites.

One of my earliest memories of how powerful that bond was, was the night of October 8, 1996.

In the second issue of the Journal of the International Association of *Xena* Studies (more on that later), I wrote the following editorial about what happened on October 8, 1996.

I am still in recovery over the events of Tuesday, October 8, 1996. That was the date of the fateful Tonight Show with Jay Leno taping. For those who have not heard, around 3pm of that day, Lucy Lawless fell from a horse during the taping of a pre-recorded skit. Around fifty fans were waiting in line to enter the studio when it happened. Several of the fans actually viewed the accident. I was one of the unlucky ones who viewed a portion of it. We were not informed of the severity of the accident until during the show, when Jay Leno made his announcement about Ms. Lawless' condition. Although we saw the ambulance take Ms. Lawless away, we were assured by the NBC employees that Ms. Lawless was okay, the hospital check-in was for insurance reasons, and that they anticipated that she would be back in time for the show. I assume they informed us because they feared that a significant part of their audience would leave. As we later found out, Ms. Lawless had sustained several fractures in her pelvis and would be hospitalized for at least a week.

In spite of the accident, the post-taping party was still held across the street at The Acapulco restaurant. The party was attended by concerned members of the

XENA: WARRIOR PRINCESS production staff, including Robert Tapert and R.J. Stewart. It was wonderful to have met these interesting people; however, the circumstances shaded a dark cloud over the proceedings.

Nonetheless, it was a very exciting, if not a sobering, experience. I wish the gathering would have been devoted to celebrating yet another successful media interview for Ms. Lawless, instead of being a watch over her health. I felt guilty about the fact that I enjoyed the evening so much. I got to meet and talk with both Mr. Tapert and Mr. Stewart, two of the creative minds behind XWP. As with my previous opportunity to converse with Steven Sears, I gained much insight into the show, not to mention heard some cleverly stated clues as to the coming season.

Most importantly, I discovered that Mr. Tapert was aware of Whoosh, actually had read it, and that he...gasp...approved of it. Talk about putting the heat on. If trying to meet the needs of thousands of unforgiving Xena fans is tough, now we want to try to live up to the creators' spirit and professionalism. We will try and we want to succeed.

This could have never happened had there not been a concerted effort to rally the fans together for the taping and for the party afterward. The gathering was quite a logistic feat, and I want to thank Carolyn (Xenatized) for conceiving it, executing it, and seeing it through. My words can never convey my appreciation adequately for her sacrifices.

And this was not an anomaly. The producers and staff of the show were always open to meeting with the fans. Even after Lucy Lawless' accident, the creators of the show still found time to meet with the fans, many of whom had traveled cross-country or over oceans to be there. And this was 1996. The second episode of the second season had just been released in some markets, and there were fifty people at the show and for a post-show gathering with the producers and staff all organized through the internet fandom.

The cross-fertilization continued. Fans who flew out to New Zealand were invited to the set. Fan-created website Whoosh.org was mentioned in an episode. fan fiction writer Missy Good was asked to write two of the episodes. Staff members would respond to fan concerns in mailing lists and on websites.

No other show had such an open-door policy with its fans. It was all possible because of the internet.

HUMOR

From slapstick to dramedy, from camp to parody, *Xena: Warrior Princess* could be hilarious. There are the exaggerated sound effects (parodied by the show itself many times). There's comic situations. There's meta-humor where the show literally folds in upon itself. There's the teasing of fandom. There's the witty banter. The humor can be situational, verbal, or physical, but it is there in every episode, even in the high dramas and even if it is only the whoosh of a head turn or a chakram throw.

For a show that was not highbrow entertainment, it had some intense drama going on, and it covered that dense core with a sweet sheath of humor. I found it one of the most hilarious shows I had ever seen. The witty quips, the odd winks at the bizarre situations the characters would find themselves in, and even the sarcastic or silly disclaimers in the show's credits. I personally did not like the slapstick, but it was in there too. No sudden movement was not possible without a sound effect, and the complicated physics of baby tossing or chakram tossing never escaped them.

Xena: Warrior Princess was one of the first shows to frequently break the fourth wall, making fun of its fanbase and its own existence as a show in creative ways. There were shows where purported fans were characters and there seemed to be innuendo and internet fandom inside jokes in every episode starting midway the first season.

MORALITY PLAYS

What *Star Trek* was in the 60s, *Xena: Warrior Princess* was in the 90s. Both shows artfully discussed current events in a way that was not as threatening otherwise. Just in the first two seasons, *XWP* used the mythological backgrounds to shed new light on age-old debates: What it would have been like had Helen of Troy been given agency ("Beware Greeks Bearing Gifts," 112); the interplay of religious intolerance and tolerance and a re-telling of Abraham's sacrifice of Isaac/Ishmael ("Altared States," 119); cartoon violence vs realistic violence ("Is There a Doctor in the House," 124); logical results of social systems based upon the premise of us versus them ("The Price," 220); interracial relationships without making it a plot point of the episode ("The Path Not Taken," 105); and the morality of pacifism (a whole bunch of episodes - we had to go through the agony with Gabrielle, episode by episode by episode!).

MUSIC

Haunting! Striking! Bulgarian folk music! Joseph LoDuca's Emmy-winning music kept the whole mishmash of a show together. It provided the emotional foundation that allowed the show to carry off the big drama arcs while peppering other shows with slapstick and broad humor. The music is gorgeous and introduced American pop culture to the joys of Bulgarian folk music. It is hard to get the music out of your head, especially the theme music.

REDEMPTION

Hidden within *Xena: Warrior Princess* is a gripping drama about the nature of redemption. Even though it could have arguably been a series-wide Macguffin in the show, Xena's path to redemption is compelling and complete.

STORIES

The Salon on-line article *What We Owe Xena* stated that *Xena: Warrior Princess* was "*the product of spontaneous evolution more than intelligent design.*" This show could have gone sideways at any time. Look at its contemporaries: *Highlander, Forever Knight, Sinbad, Relic Hunter, Poltergeist, The Cape, Jules Verne, Tarzan, Earth: Final Contact.* Not to dis these shows, but they were second-tier shows, disposable for their times. *Xena* could have been that. Many people thought *Xena: Warrior Princess* was disposable for her time as well. But as time went on, more and more people noticed something more was going on. Xena entered the culture as an icon for a woman with agency. That image became more acceptable slowly through the aughts. Now, you cannot have an action-adventure show without someone playing a "Xena" - a woman who can take care of herself filled with more agency than most (male) writers know what to do with.

Robert Tapert's wish to make a woman the hero of an action-adventure show without changing the tropes because it is a woman laid the foundation. His hiring of writers and producers such Liz Friedman allowed the writers room and production team to look a little different than before. Staff writers such as R.J. Stewart and Steven L. Sears, among others, lifted the series above their peer shows. The show was able to pull off a long slow burn of profound drama interspersed with slapstick, craziness, and post-modernism that no other show could pull off, including its sister show, *Hercules: The Legendary Journeys.*

XENA AND GABRIELLE

Well, did they or didn't they?

The subtext crowd of fandom was there from the beginning. Using the internet only encouraged it. Soon, the subtexters became the maintexters. The queer reading of the show won. I remember watching the first-time fanfics being released within hours of the show being aired in the large markets. That repeated itself for six years! Some had Xena and Gabrielle confessing their love in the "Sins of the Past" fanfic; some were feverishly writing about their first time after "Friend in Need Part 2." The show played the subtext close to the vest. That is why it was so easy to create plausible first-time fanfics after every single episode. So much first-time fan fiction was produced that it became its own major genre of *Xena* fan fiction. The show kind of resolved the issue of are they or aren't they when it revealed Xena and Gabrielle to be soulmates who had and would eternally reincarnate as a couple. They could reincarnate into male or female bodies, and some were shown to be sexual relationships and some were not. Yet, where the sexual relationship was implied in the episode, Xena and Gabrielle had reincarnated into a male and female married couple. The show was a child of its times and it wanted to stay in business, so they skirted the subtext in canon by these types of semantics. That frustrated some but delighted others. Many of the fans were grateful to have the subtext not burned and buried and drowned their sorrows in the subtext fan fiction.

Because of this situation, for many viewers, the Xena/Gabrielle relationship became a role-model. Xena and Gabrielle's relationship represented something on the screen the viewers had not seen portrayed so positively before. Two women in a supportive relationship that was not judged to be wrong. These two women were obviously together and they were not openly harassed because they were together, either socially or institutionally. *Xena: Warrior Princess*, although flawed, became a crucial place for lesbians to see themselves in a positive and socially accepting way.

This might not be the best place for it, but it needs to be addressed, as it did involve Xena, Gabrielle, and their fans. Things were going well with this flirt with subtext in the show's canon until a section of fandom found the death of Xena to be too much. The fandom had had schisms before, for example after Gabrielle's rape by Dahak in "The Deliverer," and after the extended Gab-drag in "The Bitter Suite," but Xena's death and beheading devastated an area of fandom who had strong emotional ties to Xena and Gabrielle's relationship. Positive queer representation on TV was scarce if there at all. Xena and Gabrielle represented to many fans what a healthy, loving, sustaining, and natural relationship looked like. The power of representation should not be taken lightly. I was in a mixed-race family, and I went through the process of where you never saw mixed-race families on TV to now, where you see it quite a bit more.

Such representation stands out and is very life-affirming when it is seen. *Xena: Warrior Princess* was on during a time you rarely had two women put on screen together for fear that people would think they were lesbians. Here were two women in a nurturing relationship who were treated as fully functional and valuable members of their community and culture. They did not have to be in a closet, or hide that they were together, or put up with institutional or societal repression and abuse, or even micro-aggressions. It was very powerful to see Xena and Gabrielle together. And then they kill Xena and if that wasn't enough, they chop off her head. As you can imagine, that did not go down too well. It's been about twenty years since that happened. There are still a lot of fans who cannot re-watch *Xena* without Xena's treatment in the final episode coloring their enjoyment. The new fans don't seem to be as traumatized, perhaps because they have so much more representation in the media than they did in the turn of the 20th century.

Women as hero and sidekick and the inversion of it being all about Gabrielle after all.

The subtext aside, and it is difficult to put it aside, the show pulled off, showing a woman as a hero. She was not over feminized or under feminized. She was not a parody, nor were they apologetic that she was a strong woman. She did not care about breaking a nail or what some guy thought of her. They did not tell us what she was; they showed us what she was.

I cannot over-emphasize how great it was to see this. You never saw women with an agency on TV; you saw only caricatures, which were housewives/girlfriends, plot points, or victims. But on *Xena*, you saw a woman as the lead in a hero action-adventure show, and her sidekick was...another woman. The other woman starts out goofy, but she has agency too! You see over time (not told, but shown), how these two women become friends, perhaps something more, and create a family in front of your eyes. Regardless of which team you are on, you cannot deny that Xena and Gabrielle are indeed soulmates and that they are the best they can be when they are together. Yes, I said two women were doing that. On TV. On a top-rated show. In the 1990s. Let that sink in.

Then the show ends, and you realize, yes, you did see Xena play out her redemption storyline. Xena's name is in the name of the show you watched, but the show really was Gabrielle's origin story, how she became a hero. Had Joseph Campbell lived to see that, I have no doubt he'd be jumping up and down, saying, "Gabrielle just finished her hero's journey!"

AND MORE?

Give me more time and I know I can list more pages of why I became a rabid fan and allowed the show to become a part of my life. The show has, for many people, given them an excuse to talk about the many things that can be found in the Xenaverse. Through fan interaction on the internet, I was able to join a community of diverse people who, although attracted to this show for their own unique reasons, are able to find unity in the concepts of the sanctity of human relationships, equal rights for women, the intrinsic human need for redemption, and the constant challenge of working towards the greater good. Not to mention the forever debates of are they or aren't they and WTF was "Friend in Need."

THE FRUITS OF BEING A RABID FAN

And now we come to Whoosh.org

"Fifty issues is a fantastic achievement if I do say so myself. Over these fifty months, WHOOSH has grown from a private conceit of mine to an endeavor that has been shared with hundreds of thousands of people. Many of these people feel just as passionate and close to the project as I ever have. It is both humbling and highly gratifying to know that this bizarre interest of mine has positively affected so many people and has added to the enjoyment and education of more people than I could have ever imagined a mere four years ago. I wanted to open up the celebration of this 50th issue by inviting all the past contributors to let us know what they are up to now and how they look at this past four years of fandom. Unfortunately, there were a lot of unusable addresses, but there were also many who did agree to share with us their thoughts, feelings, opinions, and assessments of what participating in fandom meant to them. I have added them here.

At first, I fretted over how to present these memoirs. I went through different drafts and charts and layouts, until finally I just decided to present these mini-essays in the order I worked on them. Some are long, some are short, some concentrate on specifics, some concentrate on generalities. They all speak of the multi-faceted fan experience. As a whole, they are an incredible collection of self-reflective living histories. Some are happy, some are sad, some are neutral. Some have left the experience, some are just revving up, and others are just seeing where it takes them."

Editor introduction to "Whoosh Contributors Ponder Fandom" Journal of the International Association of Xena Studies, Issue 50.
http://whoosh.org/issue50/contributors50.html

The Journal of the International Association of Xena Studies made it to 102 issues before I stopped editing one of the deepest rabbit holes I have ever gone down. I would have loved to have included a quote from the 100th issue, but there was no 100th issue. JIAXS dropped monthly from issue 1 through 99, which dropped March 1, 2005. The 100th issue should have dropped April 2005, but on April 1st my husband of eighteen years passed away unexpectedly. It took the wind from my sails. I did not at first realize my energy to keep the site going was gone. I decided to take a break, thinking I would get my wind back. Six months later, issue 101 was released. And then, 102 came out three months later. And I knew by then, the energy was gone. But 102 issues is still nothing to dismiss.

As my editor introduction above testified, I was impressed by a fandom that would give out of the goodness of its heart so much. Fans of *Xena: Warrior Princess* were so taken by the show, that they had to express it. Some by writing fan fiction, some by making jewelry or artwork, some by creating music videos, and some, much to my benefit and luck, wanted to write about the show – how it affected them, how they saw it in terms of art and literature, how they felt it fit into culture and popular culture. We got fans who were professional writers, people who were amateurs, some who never wrote non-fiction before or thereafter, and some were inspired to start careers in journalism. All because of a knuckled-headed show.

It was September 1995. I was channel surfing, looking for entertainment. And there it was. "Dreamworker." I had heard a little about *Xena: Warrior Princess*, but it looked silly and I was not a fan of fantasy, so I passed over it when it started airing. But here it was on TV. Airing now. I was bored. So I watched it. And then my life completely changed.

A little background. Early 1990s I started a BBS called Resistance is Futile and published a primarily on-line Star Trek parody newsletter by the same name. At the time I was thinking of starting another newsletter and I tried a few fandoms (Babylon 5, Mystery Science Theater 3000, etc.), but nothing jelled for me. I also felt like I had just missed the barnstorming days of Star Trek fandom. I was ripe for doing something in a fandom, but I did not know what or for who yet.

I watched "Dreamworker." I though this very silly stuff, but amusing. Then the infection started to spread. I had my epiphany about thinking it was silly that a woman could do what Xena did, and yet I was not as judge-y when a man did it. That got me thinking. The next week I sought out another episode. Something somewhere started speaking to me. I jumped onto the web. I wanted to know everything I could about this show. I started a database of references to the show in newspapers and magazines. The database grew and grew. I used it to refer to things while discussing the show with others on-line. Some people asked me for copies. Soon I was supplying people media references to *Xena: Warrior Princess*. Then it hit me, I could make a newsletter out of this material. Xena fandom had great potential, so I thought I would not be wasting my time devoting time to such a huge project. The gamble was not only whether the Xena fans would be interested in reading essentially old news about the show, but whether they wanted to read commentary about it as well. I discovered that not only was there a demand for it, but that I eventually could not keep up with it. Xena Media Review (XMR) was born in March 1996. It was the first regular Xena fan magazine to be published not associated with a fan club and it may have been the first Xena publication to be produced by any group in any media. XMR started out weekly and then went bi-weekly, then monthly. It lasted for 30 issues until April 1997. It was superseded by This Week in Xena News (TWXN) which lasted until 1999.

Writing the XMR commentaries made me think about the show, how it was made, and how it was affecting our culture. I loved reading stuff like that when people posted their observations on line. Other than what I was writing myself and reading from a few people, I did not see much fan non-fiction about the show. I realized if I wanted to see more, I'd probably have to do something about it myself. I decided to start doing the leg work to see if a non-fiction fanzine would be feasible. First I needed a website to anchor it to. I went to Betsy Book and used her as a sounding board. She offered me space on her website and the International Association of Xena Studies was born May 1996. Tom Simpson designed the website graphics, Tricia Murphy designed the website, and the Whoosh website went up on June 1, 1996. The monthly Journal of the IAXS would not go live until September 16, 1996, under the unveiling of the web URL of Whoosh.org.

Before going to law school, I was in a doctoral program. I had always seen myself as being an academic when I grew up, but law school pointed me in another direction. By the time I was pondering creating Whoosh.org, I was already in a non-academic career. However, I thought it would be amusing to call the sponsoring organization The International Association of Xena Studies. And then it flowed naturally that there would not be a monthly fanzine but an academic journal attached to it. In keeping with the academic conceit, I took out all contractions in the articles (because really, I have a strange sense of humor and I thought it was hilarious) and numbered each paragraph, so that quoting the articles would be easily referenced. But one thing I was adamant about– anyone could contribute. I did have editors edit each article, but I did not reject any articles. Some articles did not make it into the journal proper, but they were printed in either XMR or TWXN. I wanted to provide a soapbox for any fan who felt passionate enough to spend time on a topic that moved them. Subsequent fandoms that copied the Whoosh model were more exclusive in their editorial policies. Whoosh.org was always inclusive. I always tried to find a place for any fan who wanted to express themselves.

In my planning for the journal, I was not confident that I would get enough submissions without writing many of the articles myself, so I banked articles for the first three issues and committed myself to writing articles for at least a year. The journal would come out monthly. I would open up the submissions to whoever wanted to write about *Xena: Warrior Princess*. I did not appreciate how compelled people would be to write journal articles. I stopped writing articles for the most part after the third issue. The website traffic became very heavy to where eventually we were getting massive amounts of visitors and getting more visitors than the official websites. I had around fifty volunteers at any given time helping me with the site. We not only did the journal articles, but we had our correspondents also cover conventions and gatherings, update an episode guide, maintain a gossip column (who can forget Laura Sue Dean?), and did as many reviews as we could. I could feel something major was happening culturally and *Xena:*

Warrior Princess was a part of it. We tried to capture the Xena experience and put it in a bottle called Whoosh.org.

Whoosh had contributors who were in their early teens and others in their 70s. I tried to keep Whoosh as neutral as I could and even published an all-Joxer issue. The letters to the editor, many articles, and the episode guide wound up representing unfettered fandom reactions to the show. Even with Whoosh defunct since 2005, it is a museum for Xena and internet fandom, a moment of time captured in amber for the future to see an aspect of Xena fandom that might not be apparent in the future.

Whoosh has been cited in academic studies and magazines and newspapers. Whoosh even appeared in the episode "Soul Possession." The opening has Barbara Binder of Whoosh asking a question at a press conference.

Because of my work on Whoosh, I was asked to help produce extras for the Anchor Bay *Xena: Warrior Princess* DVD releases third season on, including the 10th anniversary collection. I not only had an opportunity to do a documentary on the episodes "The Sacrifice, Parts 1 & 2," but also featurettes on the Hong Kong influence on the show and an in depth look into Aphrodite. Because of the interviews I did, I was able to locate some director cuts from some of the episodes and we were able to provide deleted scenes on the DVDs. I remember that it took hours of watching and rewinding to identify the scenes. I was truly insane back then.

Not a bad return for devoting a decade of my life to an intensive hobby. My family humored me. They were not rabid fans, but they often enjoyed the show with me, and we had many a conversation about the deeper aspects of Xenamania. I dragged some of my prior friends into the Xena rabbit hole with me, and they still talk to me. Many people sacrificed for that darned website which had no choice in the matter, but they supported me and my obsession. It is humbling and also a source of pride to know I have shared something with the world that might not have existed if I had not been crazy enough to do it. And they liked it. They really liked it.

Whoosh.org would not be possible without the generosity and kindness of past Board of Directors (in alphabetical order): Betsy Book, Cynthia Ward Cooper, Beth Gaynor, Tricia K. Heintz (Murphy), Stacey Robillard, Bret Rudnick, and Diane Silver; and the following staff members (in alphabetical order): Sue Barnes, Bongo Bear, Beboman, Debbie Cassetta, Eric Chor, Christi Clogston, C.R., Adrienne Dandy, LC Dimarco, Cathy Duszynski, Jill T, Dybka, Sally Dye, Darise Error, Dyann Esparza, Utah Fan, Anita Firebaugh, Fillipa Morgan Flasheart, Lady Jane Gray, Jan Thimo Grundmann, Vanessa Hoy, Jeff Jenkins, Carol Johnston, Christine Kearns, Erin Keefer, Dianne Kelly, Michael Klossner, August Krickel, Laryssa, Lyris, Dinah Malone, Loretta Miller, Tory Moore, Bat

Morda, Marian Murdoch (Samuels), Catherine O'Grady, Cathy P, Holly M. Paddock, Jacquie Propps, Elizabeth "Missy" Ragona, ChelSierra Renly, Marissa Robillard-Meli, Debbie Roche, Lesa S, Joanna Sandsmark, Adriane Saunders, Liz Sheppard, Kent Simmons, Tom Simpson, Bonnie Tryonoveich, Serge Allen Walters, Debbie White, Faith A. Williamson, Lydia Woods, and Xorys.

AFTERTHOUGHTS

The impact of *Xena: Warrior Princess* is immense. It has entered the culture to where people who never watched *Xena* know exactly what Xena represents and amazingly enough, why Gabrielle is so important to her. It has rippled not just through fandom, but through academia and mainstream culture. It has influenced many other subsequent TV shows and even literature.

Running the Whoosh.org website over a decade with only volunteer help turned out to be a master class in management and leadership. In my day job, I began to use the skills I gained, keeping a website current with up to a hundred thousand visitors per day. It eventually led me to management and leadership training. I would not have my current career without the lessons learned while active in *Xena* fandom.

I am honored to have been a member of the fan community and to have been there to watch it begin, grow, and mature. And it still lives. In a few months from writing this, I will be attending the 5th Xenite Retreat in Southern California. Four months after that, I will be attending the 25th Anniversary Xena Creation Convention in Los Angeles. I interact almost daily on Facebook with friends forged in the heat of *Xena* fandom. Even though I do not have the spirit to revive Whoosh.org, I cannot escape the show or its hard-core nutballs. I am humbled by the selfless work of many generous and clever souls who helped create and maintain Whoosh.org. It is a monument to *Xena* fandom and a place where you can re-live the agony and ecstasy that *Xena* fandom offered millions of people back in the day.

***

About Kym Masera Taborn

She became a rabid Xena fan in September 1995 after accidentally watching an episode of Xena: Warrior Princess. The disease forced her, over the next decade, to publish fanzines and create the website Whoosh.org (named after the sound of a chakram on a cold night), to give a name to Uber fan fiction, to hang out at Xena fan events, and to produce features for the Anchor Bay DVD sets. She currently is an attorney, works for the federal government, and is obsessed with leadership studies, an area of interest she discovered as a collateral benefit of her adventures in Xena fandom.

Chapter Eight

The Xenaversity of Minnesota (XOM)

by James Gottfried (Mr. Jamester)

WE HAD NO IDEA...

I remember looking out across the living room at the dozen or so people that I had never met before, not knowing that just being here with them all that day was totally going to change my life. We had no idea that over the next twenty years, we would step out into our community and become a force for a greater good. We had no idea that for the next two decades, we would spend our next twenty 4th of July weekends throwing commemorative themed parties. We had no idea that we would travel coast to coast just to meet these incredible performers that we had only known on TV, and be face to face, smile to smile, hug to hug with them. We had no idea that the bonds we started creating that day would give us friends for life. And we most certainly had no idea that our family would grow tenfold as we met hundreds and hundreds of other fellow fans like ourselves. Yes, we had no idea that *Xena: Warrior Princess* was going to forever alter our destinies.

In March 1998, Beverly was surfing the internet and found herself engrossed in the on-line Xenaverse! Realizing how important (and fun!) it is to have face to face interactions with people, she put feelers out to see if there was any interest in starting up a fan club for the television series *Xena* in the Twin Cities. Liz, Jono, Robin, and Sara responded with a resounding yes, and the Xenaversity of Minnesota was born. We first met in Minneapolis on April 20, 1998, with five people. Our membership immediately grew from 5 to 22. We voted in regents, deans, treasurer, and the website www.xenaversity.com was born with me at the helm. The rest is her-story. It's true what they say: *Xena: Warrior Princess* fans are the nicest people you'll ever meet.

Being a member meant you were a XOMbie (with a Z) with X.O.M. standing for Xenaversity of Minnesota – basically a Minnesota Xenite. It was amazing how fast we grew locally and internationally with members in England, Ireland, Scotland, Italy, Brazil, Germany, Greece, Canada, Singapore, and even New Zealand. Anyone could join, and they received a membership card, certificate, access to monthly meetings, newsletters, participation in club committees, episode viewings, local events, show and tell, greater good functions, and more! Our mission was inviting and inclusive: the Xenaversity of Minnesota was a fan club devoted to the television series *Xena: Warrior Princess*. Located in Minneapolis/St. Paul, our purpose was to meet monthly to share our enthusiasm for *X:WP*, to encourage and support each other in our fun fascination of all things Xena, to be a clearinghouse of information about the Xenaverse in the Twin Cities and beyond, and to help new or potential fans better understand *X:WP*.

A Day In The Life Of A Xombie

Our get-togethers started out as monthly meetings at our homes and at the local library. Eventually, it grew to include many other social events such as Hamline Fanfest, participating in the Twin Cities Pride Parade on a self-made *Xena* float with themes such as Amazons to Tartarus to the Gods of Olympus (we won the Grand Marshal Award twice). We built a community with other sci-fi groups like the Klingons, who we challenged in laser tag. We hosted outdoor picnics, went tubing, went to drive-ins, played mini-golf, road-tripped to Chicago to see Xena Live 1 and 2, went horseback riding, visited the Renaissance Festival, hosted Halloween parties, and summer Xenabrations! And what kind of fan club doesn't do *Xena* episode marathons with themes like Mighty Aphrodite Nighty and Alti-mate Alti-Thon? We celebrated our anniversary every year with fun concepts like the Golden Chakram Awards, Regent Survivor, Lucky 7, and even a murder mystery dinner where we all played an alternate version of *Xena* characters played out to an original script "Xena, the 9th Life", my first attempt at a murder mystery script!

The Xenaversity got some media attention as well! Various articles were written about our club in local Twin Cities newspapers like the Star Tribune and the Pioneer Press. We also had TV coverage on the local WCCO channel, the Cherry Hill New Jersey TV station, and a radio interview filmed at the Mall of America on Ruth Koscielak Radio Show. A New Zealand radio show even contacted us for a 15-minute interview that aired in New Zealand! We were very excited for this attention, as it brought even more fellow fans into the fold! Probably our biggest media event ever was being on the television show Fanatical. This show focused on extreme fans of different sci-fi genres, and of course, we were the focus of the *Xena* episode. The story itself revolved around one of our members, Karen, who was sharing her coming out story and finding family within the Xenaversity group. Many members were interviewed as we showed off costumes, memorabilia, and the overall love we had for the show and each other.

The Greater Good And The Chakram Banner

The members of the Xenaversity wanted to emulate the greater good that Xena and Gabrielle always practiced, so we decided to write some of that into our own story. Over the first decade, we got involved in many other different organizations such as Adopt a Family, the Mitten Tree, Second Harvest Food Drive, the Caring Tree, toy distribution, soup kitchens, KTCA Phone Pledge Drive, and Habitat for Humanity. We volunteered for the annual Twin Cities Human Rights Campaign dinner. We even adopted a brick at the local zoo that has our name on it.

Two of our favorite projects for the greater good were Adopt A Highway and the Linus Foundation. For several years we adopted a highway, which required us to clean that stretch of road several times a year. All decked out in our orange vests, we proudly stood with our highway sign at the end of the day with our countless bags of trash! And once we learned how to make fleece blankets, we got together multiple times over the holidays to make them, then donated them to the Linus Foundation. It was never for kudos nor for a pat on the back. It was simply to do our part and pay it forward and hope that others would follow suit!

Earlier, we referred to things that we had NO IDEA that would ever happen. The story of the purple chakram banner was definitely one of those that took on a life of its very own. The banner began simply as a prop. Three Xenaversity members, Lizzy, Matt, and I, got together one afternoon and painted a purple sheet with the famous *Xena* symbol. The plan was to hang it from our cabana at a local sci-fi convention to attract attention to our *Xena* party room. It worked very well, and we used it at several events after that for the same reason.

Then the idea evolved. This was something a bit unusual; why not get it signed by a few of the stars we would meet at conventions? And so the banner took flight and was brought around the U.S. by different members to be signed by a handful of *Xena* celebrities, twenty-six to be precise. Then another idea was formed. Why not try to make the banner the most autographed item in fandom? The problem was just how to do this and what we were going to do with the banner once it was signed. The club decided to use any and all contacts we could find to get the banner signed and then auction it off for charity. Not only did we want to have actors' and actresses' autographs, but also cast, crew, writers, directors, and anyone who had their hand in the making of *Xena*!

With the help of some very kind people at Creation Entertainment, we were able to get the banner down to New Zealand and on to the *Xena* set during the final weeks of filming for the series. We also took a chance and included several disposable cameras in the hopes they'd take photos too. It took about a month or so to get it back, and when it showed up, there were so many autographs that we could hardly count them all. And to add "totally" to "totally tubular," the cameras were full of photos of each of the cast and crew autographing the banner–including LUCY and RENÉE!

The autographed chakram banner was complete. It had 191 autographs in total. We brought the banner to a Xena convention in Burbank, hosted by Creation Entertainment, where Gary himself brought us on stage and auctioned off the banner. At first, the bids were at a couple thousand dollars (already higher than we ever expected), but then suddenly, the bidding flew off the charts! As it raised a thousand, and another thousand, we stood on stage with tears in our eyes and pride in our hearts. The banner finally sold for $13,000! We were completely in shock. The generosity of *Xena* fans was overwhelming! We presented the banner and a book of the photos from New Zealand to the winner and walked on air for the rest of the day. When we returned home, we donated the money to two local charities here in the Twin Cities: The Family Support Network and People Serving People. Our proudest moment was coming together to create something unique and personal and using it to raise money to help others—the total definition of "for the greater good."

Connnnnnnnnnnnn!!!

So where can a bunch of *Xena* fans fit in with other fantastical sci-fi fans, meet stars from all the shows and movies, and walk around in cosplay? Well – conventions, of course! Our band of merry members attended countless conventions over the years. We were always excited to meet the stars but equally excited to meet existing and new Xenite friends, thus expanding our *Xena* family!

Some of the Xenaversity members were lucky to work with Creation Entertainment behind the scenes to help celebrities acclimate to each new city and acclimate to *Xena* fandom. My son Cory and I were lucky enough to be the first to greet and escort Adrienne Wilkinson and Meg Foster at their first Xena convention in Cherry Hill. Teresa and Theresa will never forget walking backstage and finding Hudson Leick waiting there to greet them! Karen will never forget getting to escort Vicky Pratt and Alexandra Tydings around the charity breakfast. And Kathy and Angie will never forget bumping into Lucy Lawless while trying to find a bathroom in a bar!

What is con without cosplay? I don't want to know. Being Cupid at conventions allowed me to kiss the hand of many beautiful actresses, and even the lips of Claire Stansfield! Xenaversity members constantly amazed me with their ability to make amazing costumes! Todd made an emperor Caesar costume from scratch. Karen created a beautiful Marquessa costume that was too real to believe! Angie dressed up as the Collector and looked like she had walked right off of the Simpsons! Cory dressed up as Lucifer and Teresa dressed up as the Daring Dragoon.

Conventions were also a great place to share *Xena* themed music videos. One of our first members, Matt, introduced us to videos he had made for *Xena*, which sparked interest in several other members to create videos of their own. Together we created over 60 videos which were shown by Creation at many conventions – often to introduce a celebrity on stage! We took the video editing one step further and created three Xena Silent Movies: Curse of the Furious Femmes, Legend of the Shamrock, and Soul Sucker of Japa. All debuted at Xena conventions! The process of scriptwriting, footage selection, and video editing was probably the most memorable part of all.

While going to conventions in other cities was great, one convention we loved being a part of was called CONvergence. We made our first appearance at this con during its debut year thanks to Dayna's invitation. In a nutshell, this convention was a melting pot for every sci-fi genre and everyone would host a three-day room party-themed out to the max that all attendees could visit. Over the past twenty years, we've participated in almost every one of them with themes such as Clash of the Wonder Women, Aphrodite's Temple, Xtreme Game of Thrones, ParadoXena, Greek Geek Idol, Chakram Asylum, and even Xena for President! It was a great way to connect with other fandoms locally, promote *Xena* and the Xenaversity, debut new costumes, and basically have fun!

The Breakfast Of Charity Champions

There have been dozens of charity breakfasts put on by Anita Ellis through Creation Entertainment at the Xena conventions across the nation. The very first one was in Cherry Hill, New Jersey, August of 1999. I was lucky enough to meet and assist Anita with putting together her first breakfast. The first celebrities to donate their time were Bruce Campbell, Claire Stansfield, Robert Trevor, and Jacqueline Kim. From there, the breakfasts grew in popularity and the name and generosity of Anita Ellis was known by every *Xena* fan! The concept of her breakfast evolved, and she started to have not only the celebrities but also her students speak about how the scholarships had helped them. She made the breakfasts memorable events for the celebrities and the fans.

All the money raised from these breakfasts went to the James W. Ellis Jr. Scholarship. It was established in October 1997 by Anita Ellis to honor the memory of her father, James W. Ellis, who died from cancer. This is an endowed scholarship awarded to one or more returning Hofstra University students, or parents of students, who have cancer or is in cancer remission to ease one or more of the burdens of the student.

Of course many of the stars had donated their time for the charity breakfasts. One, in particular, stood out because of her complete endorsement of this charity and of Anita: HUDSON LEICK! Not only did Hudson donate her time for the charity breakfasts, but she also donated outfits and other items to auction off that raised thousands! The Xenaversity and several other Xenites have had the pleasure to work with Anita and Hudson on these breakfasts to help raise money for a very worthy cause. When you have a friend in Anita you have a friend for life.

The Bitter And Suite Of It

The *Xena* series went out on a limb and produced two musical episodes: "The Bitter Suite" and "Lyre, Lyre." "The Bitter Suite" was incredible not only because the sets and the costumes were boldly colorful, not only because it was the culmination of a heavy story arc between Xena and Gabrielle, but because it was SINGING, real live singing from Lucy, Kevin, and Ted themselves! The songs, good or bad, were stuck in our heads forever.

We thought to ourselves, we have many skills within our club. We should produce our very own stage version of the Bitter Suite! And with that, we didn't waste another second. We put together a cast, assigned a director, chose a cinematographer and a choreographer, assigned a prop and costumer designer, invited a stage manager, found a place to rehearse, and enlisted musical tutors too! And almost every role was a member of the club!

We showed a demo of our performance at a local Xenafest at Hamline University where a couple months later, April 29, 2000, we filmed the performance and added special effects! Then we performed in front of a live audience on May 7, at All Gods Children Church. We placed an ad in the local paper inviting people for free and we had many family and friends in attendance as well.

We had so much fun performing in front of people that we did it again at MarsCon on May 13. The performance had everything: Lisa as an amazing Lucy lookalike, Cory, my son, played Solan, a melt into me moment with me playing Ares, fun musical banter between the villagers and the warriors, a naked Gabrielle, and even a mighty Joxer!

It's Not Goodbye; It's See Ya Later!

Twenty years is a long time; members have come and gone, there have been fewer and fewer conventions, and *Xena* never got renewed or got a movie. But that doesn't change the fact that we had no idea that a beautiful blue-eyed brunette, who made an appearance on *Hercules* in 1995, would change our lives in so many dramatic and amazing ways. We not only watched the show, but we were there alongside them on their journey together from gauntlets to goddesses, from demons to demigods, from haircuts to spinal injuries, and through life and death (a couple times). There are new fans every day. Through them, through us, Xena and Gabrielle will live on forever!

In a time of sitcoms, syndicated shows, and cancellations,
TV in turmoil cried out for a hero.
She was Xena, a mighty princess forged in late-night television.
The chakram...the subtext...the continuity issues...
Her fandom will change the world!

A Dedication

These people are no longer with us, but their inspiration and light will burn in the halls of the Xenaversity forever. Bonnie Glander was one of our first members who taught us how to fight like a warrior. The beloved Kevin Smith, who played Ares, taught us that a sexy smirk can get you basically anything. Alexis Arquette played Caligula and she taught us to be our true selves. Karen Nielsen, a mother of one of our members, Angie, taught us that no matter how old you are, it's perfectly fine to be a self-proclaimed lover of all things Sci-Fi. We love and miss you all.

HUNUA FALLS, NEW ZEALAND

Chapter Nine

Loyal to Xena –
The Xena Film Locations Site

by Martine De Grauw & Karin Oosterveen

THEY ALWAYS SAY THAT time flies when you are having fun. And time has flown, and we had fun and still have fun. Let me tell you a little story about how my website came to life, what it did for the Xenaverse, and where Lady Faith led us. Since I was a little girl, I, Martine, was always interested in a country far away down the map. It was a country that everyone frequently forgot about in Geography exams. But not I. No, I consistently scored 100% because I knew that New Zealand was that tiny piece of land on the map, just to the southeast of Australia. Even today, people still think I live in Australia. Not so, I live in New Zealand, aka *Xena* land, with my lovely wife, Karin.

I was always convinced that there were some hidden gems in New Zealand in acting, movies, and television. I didn't know then how close to the truth I was. Time went on, and when I was eighteen years old, I had all the information I needed to move over to New Zealand. But I didn't. I couldn't leave my mum behind. What would my life have been if I had done so? Would I have ended up working on *Xena*? I have always been interested in the film industry and curious about the magic behind the camera, but I never followed that route. In my time (that sounds old and I am only fifty-seven young today and behaving like a teenager) there wasn't much of an option; nobody knew a lot about where I could get education or training. I was and still am a creative person, but not even my mom, who was super creative, could tell me where to go to follow that road. However, the hunger for filming and drawing is still there. So, who knows what would have become of me if I had moved over at eighteen?

As one *Xena* character said, "When you put your mind to it, anything is possible." And so it was. Thanks to *Xena*, I met my lovely wife, Karin Oosterveen, fell madly in love, and got married. We spent our honeymoon in New Zealand. We had a delightful experience visiting the *Xena* film locations, and it was so beautiful that we wanted to share this with all the *Xena* fans. I've been a Xenite from the start of the show, but I only created my first website in 2006. Until today, I do keep that date in a footnote on my website. A few years earlier, in 1996, the internet was born and my first search entry was "Xena," and what a world I discovered. I did find it so exciting to read and look at other fans' websites and wanted to contribute as well and have my own website: www.lotolux.com. I started with general information and *Xena* con information and pictures. I lost that website due to the wrong registration by the person I hosted it with. I started up a new one: www.loyaltoxena.com. This time I wanted it to be a little different.

It all began after our first visit to New Zealand, and it's still going on. We started by documenting the best-known film locations with as much detail as possible. As I said, I have always been interested in how they work magic behind the cameras. Well, looking for and discovering the film spots, visiting them and investigating them, taught us how amazingly film editors put the shots together to give us the impression that the action was filmed at one place when, in fact, it was filmed at several locations. That was an exciting discovery and something we wanted to share with the *Xena* fans. I was also able to get my first domain name back. The idea is to put everything under www.loyaltoxena.com

Some film locations are small, others are not easily accessible, and some are on private property. Once we had seen these places, we were amazed.

Most of the film locations are in West Auckland. We were lucky we were granted access to some film locations on private property. Today, unfortunately, that is no longer possible. However, there are still a lot of places open for visiting, and there is a lot to see.

The goal of our website was to share our experience and show you those magical *Xena* places and what it is like to walk in the footsteps of our heroes. We also added some great places to visit in New Zealand and tried to show how adventurous and beautiful New Zealand is. It became a small travel guide.

What we never expected to happen is that after twenty-five years, people still look us up. A lot of *Xena* fans have finally found their way down to *Xena* land, and they contact us with regards to the *Xena* film locations. We happily try to assist them wherever and whenever possible. We have already guided some *Xena* fans and *Xena* friends around and it gives us such a happy feeling when we see how they enjoy walking in the footsteps of Xena and Gabrielle.

Xena is and will always remain a magic word here in New Zealand. After twenty-five years, when I have to provide my email address, which is xenafan4ever@gmail.com, people immediately identify it with *Xena: Warrior Princess,* and this has led us to great experiences and to meeting great people. Once it led us to a helicopter flight with one of the pilots who worked on the show taking air shots, and we were treated to an extra-long flight above some great filming spots.

But there is still one dream we would like to achieve. We tried it once but had to stop as our New Zealand partners pulled out. We still have it in our minds—a *Xena* convention in New Zealand, *Xena* Con NZ. We have the ideas, we have the places, we have the New Zealand guests. Ladies and gentlemen, we can do the first *Xena* convention in New Zealand. It would be different, exclusive, adventurous, and Kiwi style. We would love to make this happen one day.

Discovering and walking on the *Xena* film locations has brought back the child in me. I do get excited, but when I saw for the first time the *Xena* beach coming into sight, well, I can assure you that was more than being thrilled and excited. Let us tell you now about the film locations we discovered.

BETHELLS BEACH – A MAGIC STAR

For our first visit to New Zealand, we had booked our stay at Bethells Beach Cottages. We were picked up at the airport, and as we were driven across the Waitakere Ranges, we were surrounded by nature. We saw the unique New Zealand hills, where we expected some hobbits to appear any second. At one moment, I noticed that particular *Xena* rock we always see in the intro to each episode. I got a bit excited and still could not believe I had spotted it. As the road curved, the rock played hide and seek with me all the time. And then I saw the other rock on the other side. "Yes, hmmm, oh, I mean, no..." I started missing pieces of the conversation in the car. Then we arrived at our cottage and got treated to a unique view of Bethells Beach, aka *Xena* beach. Do I have to tell you how excited we were? The list of all the episodes and scenes filmed here just rushed through our minds. We were shown a private track to go down to the beach.

I was sure that we'd find the Little Problem rock and then Callisto's cave. We started walking down the track and... yes.. SPOT ON! The Little Problem rock was in front of us. And of course, we climbed it. How amazing it was to feel those *Xena* vibes… Then we walked further to Callisto's cave. All the little rocks in front of the entrance were still there as we knew them from the episodes. Today they are all gone. Twenty-five years have affected the landscape. We left the Little Problem rock behind us and walked across the beach to where Xena was crucified. Funny to see the coast guard hut that is a blooper in many scenes. The second beach connects to O'Neill Beach, where we went across the dunes.

Let me give you a helpful tip. Black sand is hot. It is volcanic and has metal particles in it. Always wear shoes!

Bethells Beach is a popular place for Westies (West Aucklanders). Te Henga has something magical. Even after all these years, you feel Xena was there. It is a place I surely would miss if I ever needed to relocate here in New Zealand. Te Henga, *Xena* Beach, gives out that relaxed and zen feeling. Some episodes filmed here are Ulysses, Return of Callisto, Little Problems, Miss Amphipolis, Motherhood, Tsunami, Ten Little Warlords, Bitter Suite, Destiny, To Helicon and Back. Website link: http://loyaltoxena.com/bethellsbeach.html

O'NEILL BEACH

This is a small beach. There are never many visitors there. Therefore, this was a perfect film location. Here Odin visited Xena when she lost her memory. This is the place where Xena walked into the water dressed in her white gown. Before I forget to tell you, use sunscreen. Hiking on Bethells Beach and O'Neill Beach takes a few hours altogether, and the sun is tricky. Don't do what I did, or you will end up sunburnt as I did.

O'Neill is where the gods stood when blasting Xena, Gabrielle, and little Eve down the cliff. Some episodes filmed here are Return of the Valkyrie, Looking Death in the Eye. Website link: http://loyaltoxena.com/oneillbay.html

WAINAMU LAKE AND DUNES

Let the child come out when you go to Wainamu Lake and its dunes. There is no way to resist it, believe me. The dunes connect Wainamu Lake and the Tasmanian Sea. The way to get around the whole place is to start walking over the dunes to the lake, do a tour of the lake, and from there go back via the Wainamu stream. You will pass a lot of filming spots here. When we first walked on the dunes, we were amazed by how big and beautiful they are. Then I tried to run, and I can assure you that black sand is tough to run on.

Oh boy, Xena and the Amazons must have been in great physical shape to do that. The further we went, the more excited we got, knowing that somewhere ahead, the lake was waiting for us. And then we walked over the last dune and, oh man, what a great view we had.

There was THE lake. It's precisely the same view as in the episodes. We got excited when we stood at the shore, ready to jump in. It was a super great, funny, and crazy feeling to dive and swim where Xena had. Where else can you do this? We often come back to this place as do all the locals, as it is a great place to be. After our swim, we walked around the lake and passed a lot of other spots that were used on *Xena* and *Hercules*.

Once back at the swimming spot, we followed the Wainamu stream. It led us to great *Xena* film locations. Everywhere we looked, we saw the scenes happening. The dunes have that mystic aura around them and the lake gives you that mysterious feeling. What does it hide? Tartarus? The Elysian Fields? One thing for sure, it works like a magnet, and we are drawn to it every time we visit. It is another place I would miss if I needed to go live in another part of New Zealand. The West has something special about it.

Some episodes filmed here are Chariots of War, Callisto, Mortal Beloved, Return of Callisto, The Deliverer, Bitter Suite, Fins, Femmes and Gems, Sacrifice I, Adventures in the Sin Trade I, Purity, Eternal Bonds, To Helicon and Back, Seeds of Faith. Website link: http://loyaltoxena.com/wainamu.html

WATERFALLS

There are some very nice waterfalls that have been filming locations. Let's talk about some of the best known on the show. There are hiking trails that lead to all the falls. In some of the lakes, you can even go for a swim.

HUNUA FALLS

One of the waterfalls you can get very close to and which is a regular hiking place for a lot of New Zealanders. One episode filmed here is Altared States. Website link: http://loyaltoxena.com/hunua.html

KAREKARE FALLS

This is a nice hike. It takes longer than you would think, in and out of the bushes. Some episodes filmed here are *The Furies, Warrior – Priestess – Tramp*. Website link: http://loyaltoxena.com/karekare.html

HUKA FALLS

This is one big fall full of force. The water rumbles on the way down. It is a beautiful example of the power of mother nature. One episode filmed here is *The Abyss*. Website link: http://loyaltoxena.com/huka.html

OKIRITOTO FALLS

Where do they find these places to film? We have often wondered about this. There are so many beautiful waterfalls in New Zealand. This one is well hidden on private property, but it is accessible. You can take a dive if you don't mind the cold water. We admire the actors/actresses who did this take after take. Some episodes filmed here are *Many Happy Returns* and *Kindred Spirits*. Website link: http://loyaltoxena.com/okiritotofalls.html

PIHA

The Lion Rock is well known for some general views, but there weren't any scenes filmed there. Website link: http://loyaltoxena.com/piha.html

LAKE PANORAMA – XENA RULES

This area has changed a lot since they filmed there. At the time of the *Xena* show, there was one big lake with a lot of land around it. Today, the lake is surrounded by brand new houses. Still, some film spots can still be found. There is a *Xena* park as well. Some episodes filmed here are Most of season 1 and 2 – *The Dirty Half Dozen – A Good Day*. Website link: http://loyaltoxena.com/lakepanorama.html

THE TREE

One of my favorite places. It is on private property. We were lucky to get in touch with the owners and were granted and guided to THE tree. You know that magic tree from *Motherhood* where Xena prays to Eli.
Website link: http://loyaltoxena.com/TheTree.html

MURIWAI BEACH - WOODHILL FOREST - MAORI BEACH

On top of Muriwai Beach, they filmed the dive in the Bitter Suite. Maori beach is a tiny beach, but one of my favorite spots. It has something magical. Think about Xena, Gabrielle and little Eve being blown by the gods down the cliff. This was filmed on top of O'Neill beach, but the scenes after the fall were filmed at Maori Beach. Watching the scene, you would think it is all one place. A true masterpiece of putting scenes and sceneries together. Some episodes filmed here are *Looking Death in the Eye*, *The Bitter Suite*
Website link: http://loyaltoxena.com/xenatour.html

BETHELLS BEACH (TE HENGA), NEW ZEALAND

BETHELLS BEACH (TE HENGA), NEW ZEALAND

MURIWAI BEACH, NEW ZEALAND

PART 3
CHANGING THEIR WORLD
THROUGH THEIR ART

Chapter Ten

When the Muse Lights a Fire –
Xena Episode Montages

by MaryD

www.ausxip.com/marydart

SINCE THE DAWN OF time, humans have wanted to draw or paint what they saw. Our creative brains were crying out for the way and the means to express our innermost thoughts and passion. To our ancestors, this meant carving wood or making paint from the earth and painting rock walls. Creativity is sparked by love. You need to be passionate about what you see; it has to make you feel and drive you to create.

In the early days of fandom, we did this by using the medium of a pencil or watercolor to draw our favorite characters. There was no digital way of expressing our passion.

In 1988, a small company created software for the new age—the computer age. That software was called Display, and then it got changed to ImagePro. You will more than likely know it as Adobe Photoshop. Those were heady days as Photoshop entered the internet age and gave artists a new way to create their art.

For me, it started in 1993 when a friend sent me some art he had created in Photoshop. I looked at it and marveled at the power of the software. It inspired me. The price was steep, but I was determined to get my hands on this program (or PROGRAMME if you live in Australia, N.Z., or the U.K.).

I saw the potential of this fantastic software and was excited at the possibilities. I created *Star Trek* montages (a montage is a series of images set out on the canvas to tell a story). It wasn't easy, but passion overcomes doubt (at least for me). Photoshop in the early days was hard to learn and navigate, but once you got the hang of it, it was EXTRAORDINARY.

Then along came *Xena* and that fateful day in December 1996. My world changed forever. Where there is a TV Show, there is a fandom. I wanted to join in the fun and be a part of that community. I was involved in *Star Trek: The Next Generation* (ST:TNG), *Star Trek: Deep Space Nine* (ST:DS9) and *Babylon 5* (B5). My preferred moniker in my online fandom world was 'MaryD' so I stuck with that name when I went on-line to search for the fandom for *Xena: Warrior Princess*. I found Tom's Xena Site and discovered the fandom was called the "*Xenaverse*". I found what I was looking for!

With fandom found, I marveled at all the goodies, and then went in search of for more websites. I found *Whoosh!* and *Logomancy Xena* (the FIRST Xena site on the web), I also found Warrior Princess and a few others. Want I wanted to find was the type of art that I had in mine for the site I wanted to create. I wanted something different and not to recreate the wheel. What about art?

There were some, mostly hand-drawn, but not the type I wanted to create. I was going to make *Xena* montages. I believe (judging by what I had seen on-line – and I could be wrong if they were being done offline) that I was the first to create *Xena* episode montages. The montages would set out to tell the story of the individual *Xena* episode using screen captures.

I had found my tribe and my little niche in the Xenaverse. I created AUSXIP to house the artworks, and it was just going to be my art and a little bit of *Xena* news from Australia. That is all (the P in AUSXIP stands for PAGE. One page with lots of art). The best-laid plans of mice and Xenites often go askew… (apologies to Robert Burns for bastardizing his poem "The Mouse"). The Fates were laughing at me. The idea for a one-page site lasted less than a month when everything changed once again, but that's for another chapter (see the section *AUSXIP Twenty Four Years of Evolution of a Xena Fan Site*).

It was challenging to convey what the story was about in a handful of images, but then they do say a picture is worth a thousand words, right? My goal was to create an overall vision of the episode with five or six images. It was exhilarating to stare at the screen and try and come up with those perfect images. Early on, it would take me two to three hours to get the pictures, arrange them to tell the story, and then finalize / upload.

It wasn't until I attended Photoshop World, a three-day conference for photography and Photoshop, that creating my montages became so much easier. I sat in on a Scott Kelby panel on creating montages. For those that don't know, Scott Kelby is a Photoshop God (he is the Lucy Lawless equivalent in the Xenaverse). I fully intended to take notes, but I was left with my mouth agape; while he was joking with the audience, he was creating a montage. Took him TEN minutes what would have taken me two hours!

I was still thinking about that presentation when I went to McDonald's for lunch, which was near the conference venue. To my surprise, I saw Scotty Kelby come in with a friend. They sat down at the table near to me. Now for those that don't know me, I'm an introvert, and going up to strangers to talk is not what I do. Unless you're Scott Kelby. My desire to tell him how much I loved his presentation and the value I got from it, won over my aversion to chats with strangers. I had the good sense not to interrupt his lunch, but

I stalled in leaving until he was finished. Once he was ready to go, I found the opportunity. He was an absolute delight to talk to, and he gave me a few more tips about creating my art, which I vowed to try the minute I got back to my hotel.

My artwork improved with what I learned from Scott Kelby. All it took was flying 19 hours from Sydney to Miami, a thirty-minute panel with a Photoshop God, and a trip to McDonald's for a one-on-one chat. Priceless.

Now back to my art. What about screen captures? They were tiny, and our videotapes were atrociously bad due to multiple copies of the same tape, etc., but we persevered. The fans volunteered to create screen captures for those that didn't know how. Logomancy, Tom's Xena Page and of course AUSXIP.

AUSXIP's screencapper was Judi Marr, who did an AMAZING job of screen grabbing episodes. I posted the screencaps on the day they were shown and sometimes before they were shown. Yes, we were naughty by doing that, and I still wonder why Universal just didn't slap us for what we were doing.

Universal's relaxed attitude gave us all the freedom to create without worrying if they would shut us down. Bless their cotton socks. AUSXIP and my art were and still are, giant copyright violations you can spot from space. Universal did not take a heavy hand with any of the Xenaverse artists (with the caveat that you couldn't sell your art with the copyrighted images). Their unique approach to letting fans express their love for the show allowed me free rein to do and create what I wanted. What more do you want as an artist? Universal's attitude helped build AUSXIP and pushed my creative boundaries. Win/Win.

These days the studios release high-resolution episode stills, but that did not occur in 1995. We had images from magazines and screen captures. The scans from magazines were constrained by the power of the scanner, the person scanning, and the modem speed.

Of course, as the series progressed, Creation Entertainment created the Official Xena Photo Club – a series of eight high-resolution images from various episodes or from one particular episode with a commentary sheet about each image from the episode written by the Fan Club President, Sharon Delaney. We were thrilled to get high-resolution images.

In addition to the talented artists, we also have talented video storytellers! They blended music and images/video to create a tribute to the show we love. It takes an exceptional talent to create these artworks that tell a story within a story. You need passion, a desire to express yourself, and the means to do so, and you have the Xenaverse artist. The following chapters and interviews with artists will give you a good idea of how this creative fandom blossomed.

Chapter Eleven

Introducing Little Xena & Gabrielle to the Xenaverse – Interview with Lucia Nobrega

by MaryD

lucia.ausxip.com

IT WAS AUGUST 1999, AND I received an email that would set in motion the formation of a friendship that has spanned twenty years. That email was from Lucia Nobrega. I didn't know the name, but I would find a kindred spirit and a dear friend in her. Lucia is the creator of the adorable and much loved comic strip "Little Xena and Gabrielle." On August 29, 1999, I added Lucia to the growing Xenaverse artist page with her Little Xena and Gabrielle art, and the Xenaverse fell in love!

Lucia and I are going to tag-team this chapter because of her limited English, so we are doing a Q&A.

Lucia, Tell us a little about yourself and your background.
My name is Lúcia da Ascenção de Nóbrega, Lúcia Nóbrega for short, also Lootcha as a nickname. I am a comic book writer for children publications in my country, Brazil, where, by the way, I was born from a Portuguese family. I started as a pencil artist in Mauricio de Sousa Produções, a well-known artist in Brazil, kind of our own Disney. There, I learned everything about comic books and established myself as a writer, but a writer that could draw.

After three years, I left the studio and spent the next six years drawing educational toys. After that, I was contracted by the most prominent publishing company of Brazil, which had Disney rights (Editora Abril) to write comic books, mainly Brazilian comics, and sometimes Mickey and Donald as well. From that time on, comic books became my life. I received some awards along the way, including Best Comic Book Writer for 1995 by fellow artists of São Paulo, my hometown.

When did you discover Xena and join the Xenaverse?
I discovered Xena when I accidentally found a T.V. channel and saw this big, beautiful woman warrior beating ten bandits. I remember I laughed because I thought that was impossible, so I didn't take it seriously, but in the end, I was not laughing anymore; I was, in fact, intrigued by her and her companion. I

thought that there could be something more between them. Since that day, I followed the series and had an incredible time.

Of course, just seeing the girls on T.V. wasn't enough, so I searched for information about the series everywhere. Eventually, I found MaryD's AUSXIP, and it was such a joy to see so much information and pictures. I couldn't believe it! To make things better, I found tons of fan fiction stories and devoured many of them.

Lucia, what was it about the show that got your creative juices flowing?

I was very inspired by that colorful universe that came to me. I wanted to make something to celebrate Xena and be part of her world, the Xenaverse! Then it occurred to me—why don't I transform Xena into a little girl and turn that universe into a children's universe? Also, it made sense for me to bring her to my world of comic books that I knew so well.

I created a site for Little Xena, but it didn't work. I didn't have enough knowledge to even upload the artworks. I was really frustrated, but then I saw AUSXIP's art pages for fans, and I wrote to MaryD in my poor English and asked her to put my Little Xena on her art page. The next day I received the email message that changed my life forever—Mary liked the girls and asked for more. From that day on, I made my entrance in the Xenaverse and gained a new friend.

Oh, I remember that day when Little Xena and Gabrielle popped up in my inbox! I took one look at them, and I fell in love. I was absolutely sure that Lucia's Little Girls were going to be a massive hit in the Xenaverse! I couldn't say 'yes' fast enough. So, Lucia, how much did Universal's relaxed attitude about the fans using their copyrighted material help in creating Little Xena and Gabrielle and, of course, all the other incredible art you have since created?

I saw how free people were to work with the series material by using pictures and videos. For me, it was difficult to even follow on T.V. because Xena was on season 3 at the time, but only in season 1 here in Brazil. If Universal had not been so liberal with Xena, it would have been impossible for me to follow the series and make sure the jokes for my Little Xena comic strips were up to date with the Xenaverse.

Without Universal's relaxed attitude, I wouldn't have been so creative in the making of the illustrations for the Subtext Virtual Season. Knowing that I could use a large number of pictures freely was a blessing. Those illustrations were a real challenge for me because, up until then, my work had been all about writing and making art for children, so it was a significant change, and I loved it!

I also have to add that Lucia took on the creative role of drawing my own fictional characters (Eva and Zoe from my Intertwined Souls Series). Lucia, what would you consider to be the best Xena art that you have created?

My favorite artwork is the "Campfire scene" with Little Xena sharpening her sword and Little Gabby writing on parchment by the fire. I am not a perfectionist; I don't look for perfection, but I like to believe my art has a soul and that it is what people see.

I've always loved that piece! They have been enjoyed by thousands of fans all over the world. What's your favorite quote about creating art?
My favorite quote about art is from an American artist whose name I forgot: "You find your style when you can't do it any other way."

Thank you, Lucia, for the interview and all the fantastic art you have created over the years. You can find Lucia's Official Little Xena & Gabrielle comic strips here: https://ausxip.com/lucia/littlexena-english/

***

Lucia has also created her own series called The Little Runaways. AUSXIP Publishing's imprint AUSXIP Kids will publish the comic strips in English and Portuguese. The Little Runaways series tells the story of a group of research animals that flee a research center in search of great adventures.
https://www.facebook.com/bichoixos
More information on her AUSXIP Publishing author page:
http://ausxippublishing.com/authors/lucia-nobrega/

Chapter Twelve

Art, Cosplay, and the Xenaverse

by Deborah Abbott

I WAS A CHILD of the 70s, raised on shows like *Wonder Woman, Charlie's Angels, The Bionic Woman*, and *Cat-woman*. Although the Felis didn't have her own show at the time, she appeared on the television show *Batman*. These were all strong, powerful role models for a young girl. I loved self-sufficient female role models, but my first crush was the character Batman played by Adam West, and to this day, I still have that crush on Batman. I spent my Saturdays as a child walking to the drug store around the block to look at the art comics of Batman and art magazines of "Mad Magazine" and anything Frazetta, who painted many strong warrior women. I was also a fan of Robert E. Howard's "The Sword Woman" long before *Xena* came along. She was very much like Xena, but a redhead.

"The Warrior Princess" (*Hercules: The Legendary Journeys, Season 1 Episode 9*) was Xena's first appearance on T.V. and it was on a show I was occasionally watching called *Hercules*. The year was 1995, and I was an animator at a studio called Heart of Texas Productions in Austin, Texas. Heart of Texas freelanced for the larger animation studios in Los Angeles, and I was currently working on one of the big films. Let me paint a picture for you with my words as to how this went down.

I heard my co-worker yell from the next room. "Deb! You, dark-haired spawn of a woman, you are on T.V. Get over here and look at this!" I rubbed my hard-working, burning eyes, and put down my drawing pencil. I believe I was drawing some Bugs Bunny art for the film "Space Jam" at the time. My co-worker yelled for me again, "This woman on T.V. looks just like you; come take a look!'"

I picked up my speed to the T.V.; this was a time before we all had computers in our phones. I replied, "Where is this goddess that imitates me and my image?" I was joking, of course; what I actually said is, "Really, you think so?" I didn't see the resemblance, but it was very much a compliment to be compared to Lucy Lawless's flawless looks.

I felt this warrior of a woman, Xena, was different than anything currently on T.V. She was strong and confident. She had watchful eyes as if she were always thinking about her next Machiavellian move. She was a woman, yes, but she was like a lion, a giant cat hunting for its prey. I put aside my animation drawings for the day and watched the rest of the show. The episode was about Xena, a power-hungry princess who outlined a plan to kill Hercules (Kevin Sorbo) and wields Hercules's friend Iolaus (Michael Hurst), to ambush him. Soon after the character Xena was shown on *Hercules*, she earned her very own show, *Xena: Warrior Princess,* on September 4, 1995, created by Robert Tapert. I will never forget the intro, "In a time of ancient gods, warlords and kings, a land in turmoil cried out for a hero. She was Xena, a mighty princess forged in the heat of battle. The power, the passion, the danger. Her courage will change the world." To me, this show felt like the words in a Robert E. Howard book had come to life in images, but instead of Howard's, it was the words of Robert Tapert. Xena was a sword-swinging, chakram-tossing woman. I was hooked, along with millions of other people in 1995. Let me put my pen down; I feel a song inspired by these memories...

This is a story about me, Deb A.
I started watching Xena back in the day.
Backflips, front flips, high jumps, kick-ass, high action-packed jump flips.
If you want to see a gal doing anything,
stand back, Wonder Woman, this princess has a dynamic, awesome,
majestic, super-duper power-ring.
If she throws it in the air,
villains beware.
It will cut through anything while leaving a blur,
ricocheting right back to her.
This gal is no ham,
she knows how to slam.
Ares and all evildoers don't stand a chance;
when they charge at her, she can stand still and put them in a trance.
Her beauty is like no other.
When you lay your eyes on her, your heart will flutter.
Strolling minstrel Gabriel at her side,
she carries around a long wooden stick with pride.
A bard by day and a guard by night,
she has the gift of insight.
She follows Xena around the land,
and always makes a great big stand.

Xena on her horse, watching like a hawk.
Gabby on foot, walks and talks.
The two traveling along,
until the next conflict, together, always staying strong.

So, back to my story, my love for *Xena* started years ago on the first day the character aired, and I became a faithful viewer of the show every week. In 1997, Halloween was right around the corner, and I began to collect materials to make a Wonder Woman costume for Halloween festivities when my fellow animator friends at my job at the time suggested I make a Xena costume instead. They all had seen *Xena* on T.V. and said I looked just like the character. I was inspired and went to the store to collect black leather, belts, pipe putty, plastic bowls, wire, and other materials I needed to mold this majestic costume. That's how all this business started my interest in *Xena: Warrior Princess*.

Little did I know, *Xena* was about to change my world. I wore the costume to the 55th World Science Fiction Convention (World-con), at the Marriott Reverent, Riverwalk, held on August 28-September 1,1997. I parked in the garage across from the event and stood motionless as I looked down at the street from the third floor. The sky was gloomy, as the sun was hidden by rotating multitudes of clouds which fought their way out as a surging wind made its way from the heavens to bring forth light.

A swift spark flickered as I drew steel from my sheath from upon my waist and gripped my sword in my right hand. Strange new confidence flooded my soul as I handled a chakram, which was now in my other hand, and it was as if an old friend had come home. I found myself neither afraid nor shy. I paraded myself down the street in true warrior form as people yelled out of their car windows, "Xena: Warrior Princess!" and then they did the battle cry, "Yeieieieieieieiei!" I did a battle cry back and it was glorious. I began my entrance into the convention room dressed in leather from head to toe, and I heard vows and hoots behind me. Standing tall, armed with a sword and chakram, heads turned, and the costume was a grand success. There was a table set up at the con representing the show *Xena*, and the workers stopped me for photos. "By The Gods, are you Lucy?" one worker asked. "Are you her?" another worker spoke. "What do you think?" I asked. "Look at my eyes; they are green, while hers are ice blue."

The first worker shook her head. "You look a great deal like her, and your costume helps the illusion. A chakram too". The second worker added, "You resemble Xena for sure; the way you marched in here with confidence, as if on a field of battle. And there is something similar in your features… the set of your jaw. I might add the leatherwork is spectacular". They concluded that I should go to an official *Xena* convention because I would be appreciated there. They also informed me that Lucy would be appearing in one of my favorite plays on Broadway, in New York, starring as Rizzo, the bad girl in "Grease," later in September. A *Xena/Hercules* convention was also happening in Valley Forge, Pennsylvania on October 4-5, so I booked my tickets and was off to see the play and go to a *Xena* convention.

Ahead of the play, there was a dance/hula hoop contest on stage before the show started. I was volunteered to go up by an usher, which I did. I noticed some actors from "Grease" who were already dressed in their costumes and pointed at me from behind the curtain and whispered to each other. I wondered what it was all about. The play was exceptional, and Lucy was a phenomenal Rizzo. After the play, we were allowed to meet the actors outside. When I met Lucy, she took a picture with me and then turned to her security guard and said, "Is this the woman the others were telling me looks like me?" I laughed so hard inside; I was tickled to hear this. Xena herself was told that I look like her, how about that?

My next journey was my first *Xena* convention in Valley Forge. I spent an extra day going on historic event explorations. Valley Forge marks the spot of the six-month encampment of General George Washington's Continental Army in the winter of 1777-1778, a major turning point in the American Revolutionary War. After seeing the sights, I put on my warrior-leather gear and made my way into the convention halls.

This convention was a bit different than the San Antonio experience because there were actual fans of the show dressed in *Xena* character costumes. As I stepped inside, I was surrounded by people asking for photos. I was also surrounded by other people dressed as Xena, exchanging tips on how the costumes were made. Security asked us to stand outside the doors to take pictures because we were too much of a distraction from the stage where the actors from the show were answering questions. As I began to step out of the room, I was abruptly stopped by a devilish, hair-raising cry of horror coming from a dark-lit stage. Before I understood what was going on, a tall blonde stood in a chiseled gold dress and reached out to me to join her on stage. At this instant, I knew terror and almost dropped my tightly gripped sword. It was Xena's archenemy, Callisto, played by Hudson Leick, who had seen me and called me up on stage to be next to her. The room was silent, and the eyes of everyone were on me as I slowly turned to face the origin of the ear-piercing sound.

My panic had overcome me senseless, but somehow, I knew that I must do this and convinced myself to join her on stage. At this time, I have forgotten what she said while I was on stage, but it was something like, "You aren't afraid of me, are you, Xena? I won't bite!" Before I understood what was happening, a well-defined, thin arm embraced me for a photo. I left the stage with a half-developed rendition of a battle cry, not knowing what had just taken place.

Later in the day, I entered my first costume contest, where about twelve others dressed as Xena and a few Gabrielles competed with various skits. We all won some picture stills of the actors from the *Xena* set and a shirt. The other Xenas told me about an official *Xena* convention on January 18, 1998, in Burbank, California, the *Hercules and Xena* convention at the Hilton. They told me I should attend and I said I'd be there.

I had time to regroup and revamp my costume a bit. This was a very large event that I would be attending with lots of stars from the show, including Lucy Lawless.

When I rolled up at this convention, it was another ball game; the experience was like Mardi Gras in the sense that there were tons of people in costumes, dressed as all sorts of characters from the show. I felt in my element as costumes go. I was hoping that Lucy would be dressed in her Xena outfit but she was in a simple yellow, purple, green and black striped long sleeve top and mini skirt, but still charming.

She shared many personal stories about the behind scenes of the show and talked a bit about how the show was made. I made lots of long-lasting friends at this convention who I am still friends with to this day. The famous Xena twins, Virginia and Lourdes Sanchez, Nina Knapp, Zeta, and Richard Chandler, come to mind. Richard and I have recently been working on a few books together. I can't forget the one and only MaryD, who I am very appreciative of, asking me to write my story in this book. Soon after this Xena convention, I was asked to be featured in Nikki Stafford's book, Lucy Lawless and Renée O'Connor: Warrior Stars of Xena. I was also invited to be a Xena look-a-like in the 1998 Toy Fair in New York to promote the Breyer Horse Argo at their booth. I can't forget riding the subway and being stopped by N.Y. cops to snap a picture with me.

I met Rob Tapert for the first time and Lucy again on January 20, 1998, at the NATPE convention in New Orleans. Heart of Texas had a booth, and I was there promoting new, in-house animated shows we were pitching. Unfortunately, the shows were not picked up, and soon after the animation industry shifted to computers, so lots of hand drawing animators were out of work, and I was one of them.

I shifted my attention to acting, and in Texas the work was limited. In 1999, Breyer Fest asked if I would be a look-a-like as Xena to sign the boxes of the Xena horse, Argo. I signed the boxes writing, "Battle On! Xena." In 1999, I was flown to Chicago to be on a show called *Jenny Jones,* and the episode was called "Celebrity Fakes." The show gave me a horse to ride in on and Jenny had me create a *Xena* skit to act with the workers on her show. When I flew home, I was called in by a casting director to be in the movie "Miss Congeniality" as a featured actor playing Miss District of Columbia. Soon after that, I was cast as a featured spy mom in "Spy Kids 2." I continued to act in films and learned to make and produce small films of my own.

I continued to frequent the annual *Xena* conventions in California, being on stage and being honored by hundreds of *Xena* fans while doing short skits in the many costumes that I made as one of many joys at the *Xena* conventions. I met Wendy Woody, a fellow Texan, who had the same passion for film-making as I did and also lived in Texas. We became filmmakers together and made *Xena* fan films that played at the *Xena* conventions. We experienced a trip to New Zealand, where we were Xena and Gabrielle for a local New Zealand T.V. show called *The Holmes Program.*

The production had us ride a chariot on Bethells Beach to promote chariot rides with the *Xena* show stunt doubles. I was on a chariot with Caesar, and Wendy was on one with Xena. Wendy and I were able to watch Lucy in the play "*The Vagina Monologues*" and meet Lucy after the production. It was a memorable experience. Wendy and I had a conversation with her about New Zealand and where to go while we were there and about her baby, who was in her belly at the time.

The first *Xena* film we made together was "*True Love Never Dies,*" a spoof on "*A Christmas Carol.*" I played Xena, and Wendy played the short-haired Gabrielle, and Robin Hines played the long-haired first version of Gabrielle. Robin was later cast as Lucy's student in a T.V. movie with Lucy Lawless called "Vampire Bats." I remember shooting "True Love Never Dies" with Robin. The famous scene when Gabrielle's eyes open to stare up at Xena's as she begs to travel with her for the first time... It was a wonderfully strange experience. Robin thrust forth her hand in mine, and our fingers fastened quickly as she swung up behind me, and we both rumbled off down the path on Argo. Thus, our journey in *Xena* fan-filmmaking began.

I made many Xena costumes—the traditional leather costume, the Empress, Cleopatra Xena, Chains Xena, Meg, Xena as a man, Gabrielle, and many more. I guess my favorite was the traditional leather one because it was the first one I created and the one the character wore the most on the show. If I had to pick a second favorite, it would be the Empress, although the headpiece was not comfortable. The man from "Many Happy Returns" was fun because no one knew who I was, and, believe it or not, people did not recognize me with blonde hair as Gabrielle.

There are so many memories and stories that I am leaving out because there is not enough space to cover everything; that is how big a part *Xena* plays is in my life. Xena is still inspiring my life today, keeping me strong. Xena is a character who is a strong, powerful woman who can conquer any problem or situation that comes her way.

That is the reason I watched the show and those are the qualities I kept deep in my heart. Today I am still holding the show in a place in my heart, and it helps me with some of the conflicts that I battle myself. "Her courage will change the world" was in the intro, and it's so true. Courage can change the world. We all need the courage to believe in ourselves.

We need the courage to create the dreams we have inside of us and make our dreams a reality. We can all be Xena in the fact that if you just believe and follow through and stay loyal to yourself and trust in yourself, anything is possible.

Chapter Thirteen

Interviews with Artists –
Changing Their World Through Art

by MaryD

I HAD THE PLEASURE of sending out interview questions to some well-known Xenaverse artists about their process in creating their art. It's a tiny sample of the talented Xenaverse pool of artists. I hope you enjoy their responses. This fandom unleashed passionate creativity.

I'm grateful to the following artists who participated in these interviews.

XENA

ANOTHER TIME. ANOTHER PLACE

Linda "Calli" Callaghan

calliscreations.com

Tell us a little about yourself?

I'm a Kiwi and live in New Zealand's South Island. I am now retired and enjoying life.

When did you discover Xena and join the Xenaverse?

Xena wasn't shown in N.Z. straight away, so we had to wait. When it was finally shown, I thought I would just watch an episode to see how our local girl got on. One episode led onto another, and by then I was pretty well hooked. So I guess I joined the Xenaverse in 2000. I purchased my first computer back in 1999. It was a little H.P. 14 desktop (space saver) computer, and a friend's son gave me a copy of Photoshop, and he showed me the basics, so I played around making birthday and Christmas cards (as you do) and that was about it.

I then searched the internet for anything Star Trek or Xena related and found AUSXIP and thought I had better bookmark the site just in case I couldn't find it again (silly me). I was pretty green about the internet and dial up was slow. Anyway, I started to do some montages of Xena and Gabrielle just for fun, and I got more proficient at using Photoshop. Later I discovered fan fiction, and I started doing some fanfic covers as well. This led to doing book covers for some overseas publishing companies.

What was it about the show that got your creative juices going?

I just loved the show, really. It was escapism. It made me laugh; it made me cry. Plus, it was a story about the relationship between two strong women, and I saw them as soul mates. The availability and use of the images allowed my creative side to flourish.

How did Universal's relaxed copyright rules help in creating your art?

It really was the best thing, and I am so grateful that we could download and use the images, plus the ones that other Xenites would upload as well. It allowed the Xenaverse to grow, and the fandom just got bigger and bigger, and I was happy to be part of it. I started my own website, CallisCreations, back in 2000.

What do you consider your best art?

To choose one favorite is really hard, so two favorites would be

Xena graphic:
calliscreations.com/wallpapers/wallpaperxwp2013.html

My favorite Uber:
calliscreations.com/wallpapers/wallpapertimeandplace.html

What's your favorite quote about creating art?

KISS - Keep it simple stupid.

Manip by Carpe Chakram

Carpe Chakram (Sandra Sue Serf)

www.Carpechakram.com

Tell us a little about yourself?

I was born in the little town of Cumberland, Maryland, USA in 1946. I taught high school for forty-two years in the suburbs of Washington D.C and then I moved back home when I retired.

When did you discover Xena and join the Xenaverse?

I was watching Entertainment Tonight back in the 90s, and Liz Friedman was doing an interview on lesbians in current T.V. shows. Then they showed the kiss from "The Quest" and…Yowsa-Wowsa ! Later that year, I found some tapes at yard sales, and then, when I finally got high speed internet, I was on my way!

What was it about the show that got your creative juices going?

The story lines, and the filming on a shoestring budget. You never knew what you were going to get from week to week. The hand-held cameras and the varying of the camera speed added class. Of course, the scenery and the music didn't hurt! As far as creative juices go, there were so many hand-held close-up scenes of the actors… This gave the show a completely new look, and great screen grabs.

How did Universal's relaxed copyright rules help in creating your art?

Well, I can't draw worth a hoot, but I can "manipulate." I'm very thankful that the PTB seemed to want their show to live on by not raising a fuss over us using screen grabs.

What do you consider your best art?

https://bit.ly/37MYaep (Link goes to Facebook - see art on page 114)

What's your favorite quote about creating art?

"In art, the hand can never execute anything higher than the heart can imagine."
Ralph Waldo Emerson

Klippart

www.deviantart.com/artbyklipp

Tell us a little about yourself?

I am a WOC (Woman of Color) fan from Canada that loves the show. I used to sketch when I was younger but dropped it later on in life. When digital art came along, I took to it right away. I'm very introverted and enjoy watching Xena, movies, and other T.V. shows. Xena's greater good message resonated with me, and I like to use my social media to cover issues going on in our world.

When did you discover *Xena* and join the Xenaverse?

When Season 2 aired. So, I guess that would be in 1996. I joined the Xenaverse fandom in 2008, when I joined YouTube.

What was it about the show that got your creative juices going?

I wanted to create a background for my YouTube channel back in the good ol' days when YouTube had more personalization. Xena was my favorite show, so I wanted the background to be of her. And THAT'S how I first started with digital art.

How did Universal's relaxed copyright rules help in creating your art?

Universal never flagged artwork. I felt safe creating it and posting it. I appreciate that they generously allowed us our fanart. They didn't have to do that. I think they know that fan creations actually help promote the show. It's sort of symbiotic.

What do you consider your best art?

This is one of my digital drawings. It took longer than usual as it was both of Xena and Gabrielle, and I'm really proud of the way it came out. I was trying some new things and thought this digital art came out pretty cool looking.
www.deviantart.com/artbyklipp/art/Melinda-Pappas-and-Janice-Covington-771291609

I don't know if this counts as it's not a Xena digital drawing. I love the way this came out. Right down to the hair and fingernails and shirt. Everything just worked out beautifully.

www.deviantart.com/artbyklipp/art/Gabrielle-Xena-Double-Exposure-616396723

I don't know if this counts as it's not a Xena digital drawing. I love the way this came out. Right down to the hair and fingernails and shirt. Everything just worked out beautifully.

https://www.deviantart.com/artbyklipp/art/Lucy-Lawless-as-Punk-Rock-Girl-from-Spider-man-773285141

I still use this as my Facebook header. I love the way the light, shadows, and fog gave it such a dark goth look.

www.deviantart.com/artbyklipp/art/Xena-Badass-Warrior-Princess-336117208

What's your favorite quote about creating art?

Well, on my Zazzle account, I have:

"Create, don't hate!" Don't know if that counts? Also, I like: "Do your own thing. Be original." I have that in my Twitter banner.

Judi Marr

www.ausxip.com/judiscreations/

Tell us a little about yourself

I am retired and not doing much at the moment, just like everyone else.

When did you discover Xena and join the Xenaverse?

I discovered Xena in 1998 while I was waiting for a feed (I had a big dish at the time and could see programs as they got downloaded for airing on the networks) of Lois and Clark. Xena used to come down before LnC. I caught the end of an episode one day and made a point the next week to catch it from the beginning. I was hooked. I had just found out I had R.A. and was very limited in what I could do and was very lucky to find the Xenaverse. I still have very good friends I made in those early days of the show.

What was it about the show that got your creative juices going?

I actually never considered myself creative, like Linda, Lucia, or MaryD. I just was fortunate enough to find a graphic program I was comfortable with and just played around. I was a bit surprised when others seemed to enjoy what I had done.

How did Universal's relaxed copyright rules help in creating your art?

It was very helpful as I used to do screengrabs for MaryD and we never had a problem posting those. I used to get the show a week early so we were actually spoiling the show every week.

What do you consider your best art?

My favorite was a montage I made using art from my friend Lucia, and it was the creations she did for our Virtual Subtext Season.

https://bit.ly/2Lsa43b (directs to AUSXIP Subtext Virtual Season Site)

Arkie Ring

www.arkiemalarkey.tumblr.com
www.facebook.com/arkiemalar

Tell us a little about yourself?

I'm pretty happy with the nerd life. I like T.V., comics, movies, video games, bright colors, magic, and spooky monsters. I live around Chicago, Illinois and spend a lot more time than I should be thinking about dragons and Xena instead of the real world.

When did you discover *Xena* and join the Xenaverse?

I remember watching Xena when it was on T.V. I think my first episode was "Destiny" in season 2, so that would have been around 1996. I didn't actually get addicted to it until about 2002/2003. Then I slowly started finding Xena YouTube videos and making on-line friends who liked Xena too. I don't think I officially joined the Xenaverse until I went to my first con in 2009.

What was it about the show that got your creative juices going?

A bunch of things! I think the look of the show is super special and I haven't seen stuff like it anywhere else. It's really easy to pick out of a crowd. The sets, costumes, and actors all have reeeeeally amazing looks. Because T.V. has changed so much since the 90s, it doesn't really seem like anything will be able to look like Xena again. I also like how creative the whole world is, from the writing to the characters to the mythology that they threw a Xena shaped monkey wrench into. Because of that, I love being able to be part of that world in any way I can!

How did Universal's relaxed attitude help in your creation?

It's really nice that Xena was able to become anything it wanted, which made it so different from other shows. If Universal hadn't given it all the freedom to do that, who knows what we would've ended up with.

What do you consider your best art?

I'm not really sure... I think I always get a little more attached to the newest thing

I make than the older things, partly because I notice style changes I made more in the older stuff. But something I'm pretty proud of right now is a cartoony picture based off of the Athens City Academy of Preforming Bards episode and a little comic strip about Gabrielle counting the seconds in Xena's pinch. The stuff with stories in it mostly.

https://www.facebook.com/arkiemalarkey/

What's your favorite quote about creating art?

I think it would be "Get out of your own way." I think that's really useful because a lot of the time I can overthink what I'm trying to do and I lose whatever got me excited in the first place.

Publishers note: Arkie Ring will soon have his first children's illustrated novel called A Kid's Guide to Monsters published by AUSXIP Publishing's imprint AUSXIP Kids. For more information go to: www.ausxippublishing.com

LAWLESS

RIZZO REDUX
saul trabal   12/1/2012

Saul Trabal

www.deviantart.com/2112st/gallery/
www.trabalcreations.com/index.html

Tell us a little about yourself?

I'm fifty-four years old and I live in northern New Jersey, in the New York City area. I'm an illustrator, writer, and photographer.

When did you discover *Xena* and join the Xenaverse?

In 1995. The very first episode I saw was "Dreamworker."

What was it about the show that got your creative juices going?

Well, I've always done creative stuff—writing and drawing. Being creative is a drug. My very first bit of writing was a fanfic novel that I wrote in the 1980s based on a Japanese animated T.V. show. It took five years, five drafts, written on three different typewriters: manual, electric and semi-word processor in that order. All the drafts combined totaled 1,600 pages! So yeah, I'm quite obsessive when it comes to getting my work just right. I take what I do as an artist very seriously.

I've drawn quite a number of Lucy portraits. Lucy Lawless is a striking woman. So, I first started working on some early pieces in the 1990s. I then went through a five-year period where I didn't draw anything—from 1999 to 2004. From 2004 on, I did an occasional Lucy piece every other year, the final one being in early 2019. I've also drawn a number of Xena cast members, including people behind the scenes. I've drawn Rob Tapert twice, as well as Steven L. Sears. or me, it isn't about doing a photo-realistic representation of a person. That is incredibly boring to me. If I'm going to go through all that trouble, why not just take a photo? Photo-realistic pieces are too "paint by the numbers" for me and hold no appeal. So, early on, I set about doing expressionist works in color. What medium do I create in? Digital, line art, and Prismacolor pencils. I currently work on 90-pound, hot press paper. I do some tweaking of the brightness/contrasts in Photoshop if need be.

What do you consider your best art?

Oh, I don't have a "best art." I'm never satisfied as an artist. I'm always looking to improve; I'm always trying to do something different.

What's your favorite quote about creating art?

I have two I go by. The first is from bassist Geddy Lee, of my favorite band Rush: "You have to be willing to fail in public if you really want to achieve any kind of growth as an artist." The second is from my favorite writer, the late Harlan Ellison: "Art is SUPPOSED to be hard. Art is SUPPOSED to be demanding. That's how I look at it."

Michele vanRoosendael

www.MyArtisticMind.com

Tell us a little about yourself?

My name is Michele vanRoosendael and I am a tattoo artist by trade. I have been drawing since I could hold a pencil and am a very passionate Xenite. I was raised in Hollywood, CA. I do any and all kinds of art. I love digital hand drawings, sculpting and painting but will always favor charcoal pencil drawing. Something about it seems classic and personal. It's my go-to.

When did you discover Xena and join the Xenaverse?

I watched Xena: Warrior Princess on television since the day it first aired. I immediately fell in love with the characters and storyline. I've only recently discovered the Xenaverse in 2018 and of all the fandoms out there, and I have to say that Xena fandom is full of the most amazing people I've ever met! Very dedicated and loyal to Xena and each other. Feels like family.

What was it about the show that got your creative juices going?

The depth of the characters. The back story of them is what piqued my interest in my Xena art. There are so many ways to draw the emotion of a character. Whether it's a facial expression or a simple pose, no words are needed most times to describe a drawing. It's infinite to me; so much can be done with Xena artwork.

How did Universal's relaxed attitude help in your creation?

It left many doors open for the creative mind and that is what it's all about.

What do you consider your best art?

Any of my art that can make someone smile or think of a time in their lives that brings good memories I think I'd consider that my best art. I try to give my best every time I draw or paint anything; I put so much of myself into each piece I create.

What's your favorite quote about creating art?

"Art is not what you see, but what you make others see." Edgar Degas

Publishers note: Michele vanRoosendael will soon have her first novel Dragon Doodles and Common Sense Care published by AUSXIP Publishing's imprint AUSXIP Kids. For more information go to:

ausxippublishing.com/authors/michele-vanroosendael/

Hayriye Makas Uygun

www.instagram.com/hayriye_art?igshid=bxynelp5c3zd

Tell us a little about yourself?

I live in a coastal city in Turkey. I'm married and I have a daughter and a son. I own a kindergarten and I'm a manager there. I love drawing and writing, and theatre, and kids. I am actively involved in activities involving women's and children's rights, climate change, and minorities.

When did you discover Xena and join the Xenaverse?

I first discovered Xena in 1996. It was when the internet was slow and Yahoo was more popular than Google. Then I joined Xena chats via AUSXIP and Microsoft chat, but I was too young and my English wasn't good enough. I also had to deal with the negativity in my life. It was impossible for me to be an active fan as a young person from Turkey, but I was a Xenite in my own circle from the beginning.

What was it about the show that got your creative juices going?

I find it tempting to reflect on Xena's glory and the magic of Xena and Gabrielle's relationship. It's kind of relaxing, like therapy. I try to add something from myself instead of just reproducing photos from the show. This is very enjoyable. I'm kind of obsessed with drawing them!

How did Universal's relaxed attitude help in your creation?

It helped me to feel free to create and to implement great ideas. I thank them.

What do you consider your best art?

https://www.instagram.com/p/B7bfG9qjoGs/?igshid=182i2rav2a0q8

Chapter Fourteen

Videographers & Links –
Changing Their World Through Video

by MaryD

THE XENAVERSE HAS been blessed with a deep pool of talented people and one of the ways this talent has been brought to the surface is through video in the form of music videos.

Videos are crafted from episode segments set to music. As part of the Artists section of the book, I called on the videographers to submit their work to be a part of the book. These are just a small sample of the massive body of Xena music videos. Here are the submitted videos, their creators and a link to view the video on the *Official Xena: Their Courage Changed Our World* site.

- Regina Alexander
- Vanessa Bailley
- Martine De Grauw
- DJWP
- James Gottfried
- Lynne Krause
- Jordan
- Kate Mendes and Anna Urbano
- Pooka
- Danielle Shamir
- Karin Oosterveen
- Vlamme

Regina Alexander

http://xena25years.ausxip.com/video/artist/regina-alexander/

- Spend My Time Loving You
- This Time – Xena/Ares/Caesar
- Wind Beneath My Wings – Xena & Gabrielle
- Xena Pumps It Up

DJWP

http://xena25years.ausxip.com/video/artist/djwp/

- Gladiator

Martine De Grauw

http://xena25years.ausxip.com/video/artist/martine-de-grauw/

- Best Friends Forever
- The Best
- Girls Just Wanna Have Fun

James Gottfried

http://xena25years.ausxip.com/video/artist/james-gottfried/

- Wind Beneath My Wings - Xena and Gabrielle
- This Time - Xena/Ares/Caesar
- Cupid Soldier of Love
- I Am A Warrior
- Spend My Life Loving You
- I Like The Way You Move
- In The End - The Many Deaths of Xena
- Callisto Vs. Alti - Queens of Evil
- Xena Pumps It Up

Lynne Krause

http://xena25years.ausxip.com/video/artist/lynne-krause/

- Because I Knew You
- Darkness is Only The Absence of Light
- Love Changes Everything
- Piece of Me

- Something To Believe In
- Soulmates: Twin Flames
- We Go On

Jordan

http://xena25years.ausxip.com/video/artist/jordan/

- Beautiful

Kate Mendes and Anna Urbano

http://xena25years.ausxip.com/video/artist/kate-mendes-and-anna-urbano

- This Is My Soulmate

Karin Oosterveen

http://xena25years.ausxip.com/video/artist/karin-oosterveen/

- Everything and More

Pooka

http://xena25years.ausxip.com/video/artist/pooka/

- At Last (Etta James)

Danielle Shamir

http://xena25years.ausxip.com/video/artist/danielle-shamir/

- From Darkness To Light

Vlamme

http://xena25years.ausxip.com/video/artist/vlamme/

- Destined Soulmates – Tribute
- Fearless – One Against An Army – Tribute

PART 4

THE MIGHTY QUILL –
BARDS OF THE XENAVERSE

Calli

Chapter Fifteen

A Fic by Any Other Name

by Linda Crist

FAN FICTION HAS been around since William Shakespeare penned plays such as *Romeo and Juliet* and *Othello*, which were based upon other existing fictional works of his time. Before *Xena: Warrior Princess* and the internet, the most well-known fan fiction based upon a television show began in the world of *Star Trek* in the 1960s, when fanzines containing fan fiction stories were printed on mimeograph machines and distributed via snail mail or in person at conventions and other fan gatherings. One of the most popular genres of *Trek* fan fiction was Kirk/Spock Slash—stories that depicted Captain Kirk and Mister Spock as lovers.

As the access to the internet became widespread, fan fiction began to be posted on-line and quickly took off. Today, you can find fan fiction for almost any television show, movie, book, or video game you can name. *Xena* fan fiction, however, was arguably the first to become well organized on-line, is perhaps the most prolific in terms of volume of available stories, and in many ways defined how nearly all fan fiction is written and categorized today. Like the early days of *Star Trek* fan fiction, *Xena* fan fiction played and still plays an important role in keeping the fandom alive, and also like *Trek*, one of the most popular *Xena* fan fic genres, Alternative/Subber, portrays Xena and Gabrielle as lovers.

In addition to Alternative/Subber, there are several other genres of fan fiction to explore, including some genres that are unique to *Xena*. Besides Alternative/Subber, there is General/Classic, Shipper, Gabrielle/Joxer, Conqueror, Alternate Universe, Clone Fic, Post-FIN, Virtual Seasons, Crossover/Multi-Fandom, Mel and Janice, and Uber. In this chapter, we will review the different genres of *Xena* fan fiction that were and are still being written by *Xena* fan fiction writers, who are often referred to as bards in honor of the show's own bard, Gabrielle.

Genres of *Xena: Warrior Princess* Fan Fiction

General/Classic:

The General/Classic genre is fiction based upon the timeline of the *Xena* television series and generally follows series canon. These stories were some of the first to appear on-line and formed the foundation for the other genres of *Xena* fan fiction that quickly began to emerge as the show progressed. These stories may take Xena and Gabrielle on adventures in addition to the storylines of the series, may explore what happens between the episodes of the series, or may embellish upon episodes within the series, but they do not stray too far from the time frames and character arcs established on the television show. Like the TV series, these stories may contain subtextual references to Xena and Gabrielle's relationship, hinting that they may be more than "just friends," but these stories do not focus on romance, they do not cross the line into what has come to be known in the Xenaverse as "maintext," and they do not contain detailed love scenes.

Alternative/Subber:

Alternative/Subber stories more or less follow the definition of General/Classic stories above, with one primary difference: in this genre, Xena and Gabrielle are depicted as lovers or are on their way to becoming lovers. It is by far the most voluminous category of *Xena* fan fiction. References to "Subbers" is unique to *Xena* fan fiction and was established early in the fandom as a way of referring to fans who believe Xena and Gabrielle are in a physically intimate relationship. The term "Subber" comes from the subtext within the show itself, in which nearly every episode suggests in some way, blatantly or subtly, that Xena and Gabrielle's relationship could be romantic in nature.

These stories take that subtext to the next level—maintext, and nearly always have a primary focus on a romantic/sexual relationship between the two characters. How that relationship is played out varies greatly from story to story, with some bards choosing to fade to black when our dynamic duo enter the bedroom, while others describe their love-making in graphic detail, and still, others fall somewhere in between these two ends of the spectrum. No matter the level of detail to the sex scenes, in these stories, it is crystal clear that Xena and Gabrielle are in an intimate, usually loving relationship.

Within this category is a subcategory of stories known as "First Time" stories, in which a primary element of the story describes how Xena and Gabrielle come to make love for the first time. In addition to Alternative/Subber being a stand-alone genre of *Xena* fan fiction, it can also overlay nearly all of the other genres, except for General/Classic, Shipper (Xena/Ares), and Gabrielle/Joxer.

Shipper and Gabrielle/Joxer:

In modern fan fiction, to "ship" two characters from a television show, movie, or another medium, is to see the two characters as being in a relationship, whether or not that relationship is canon. The term "ship" comes from the last syllable of the word "relationship." When *Xena* fan fiction was first posted on-line, during the time the television series was in its original run, the term "Shipper" meant something more specific and referred to fans who saw Xena as being in a relationship with Ares, the God of War. This term distinguished "Shippers," fans of the Xena/Ares relationship, from "Subbers," fans of the Xena/Gabrielle relationship.

Shipper fic is fan fiction that depicts Xena as being in a sexual/romantic relationship with Ares. Similarly, Gabrielle/Joxer fic is stories that depict Gabrielle as being in a sexual/romantic relationship with Joxer. In the show's heyday, there was frequent, sometimes friendly but often contentious, banter in on-line forums between Subbers, Shippers, and Gabrielle/Joxer fans, and it made for lively panel discussions at fan gatherings such as DragonCon.

Conqueror Fic:

There is a two-episode arc in the fourth season of *Hercules: The Legendary Journeys* ("Armageddon Now," parts 1 and 2) that presents an alternative timeline in which, along with a primary plot focused on Callisto, there is a sub-plot in which Xena never met Hercules, remains evil, and has risen to conquer and rule Corinth. In the second of the two episodes, Gabrielle is a rebel and is brought before Xena for speaking out against Xena's rule, and Xena orders that she be crucified and her legs broken. There is a little more to the Xena sub-plot, but the one brief scene of Xena crucifying Gabrielle gave birth to an entire genre of fan fiction unique to the *Xena* fandom—Conqueror fic.

These stories vary greatly, as the canon on which they are based leaves wide room for expansion. The only fairly uniform elements of the stories are that Xena is the ruler over kingdoms that vary in size from story to story, and Gabrielle is usually either her slave or in some other service-related position. Background on the two characters in Conqueror fic sometimes loosely, but not completely, follows established canon. Some bards combine elements of the two Hercules episodes with elements from the second season *Xena* episode "Remember Nothing," which shows what would have happened if Xena had never became a warlord, never met Hercules, and therefore never saved Gabrielle from Draco's slavers.

In Conqueror stories, Xena's level of ruthlessness varies along a broad scale from extremely brutal dictator to a more benevolent, seasoned ruler. In nearly all of these stories, Xena and Gabrielle eventually become involved sexually, and often fall in love, with Gabrielle being the one who takes on fully the job of reforming Xena, rather than Hercules being the catalyst prior to Gabrielle.

There is also a small sub-genre in this category in which Gabrielle is depicted as the Conqueror and Xena's role varies even more greatly, including but not limited to gladiator, slave, commander of Gabrielle's army, and sometimes her reformed self who meets Gabrielle later in life than canon timeline. In some of these stories, it is Xena who reforms Gabrielle. The Conqueror genre as a whole is really a sub-genre of Alternate Universe fiction.

Alternate Universe:

Stories in the Alternate Universe genre are about Xena and Gabrielle, but they deviate from series canon, placing them in a partially or entirely alternate universe from the one established on the television show. These stories may or may not fully or partially follow background canon for the characters, and their personalities are generally the same as on the show, but the TV series plotline is abandoned. In some stories, for example, Gabrielle is an Amazon princess or queen when she first meets Xena.

In some stories, they are based somewhere other than ancient Greece. Some stories may even place them in modern times, but they are still Xena and Gabrielle (rather than Uber characters). These stories may or may not depict Xena and Gabrielle in a romantic relationship, and some of the stories may have them in relationships with other characters from the show, such as Ephiny or Lao Ma.

The two *Hercules* episodes and the *Xena* "Remember Nothing" episode mentioned in the Conqueror fic section, as well as the sixth season *Xena* episode "When Fates Collide," are examples of the *Xena* franchise's own efforts at telling Alternate Universe stories.

Clone Fic:

Clone Fic is a genre unique to *Xena*. The stories are based upon the sixth season *Xena* episode, "Send in the Clones," which ends with two Xena and Gabrielle clones bearing the memories of the original Xena and Gabrielle, riding off in the back of a taxi together, presumably somewhere in the twenty-first century United States.

These stories depict the adventures of the clones after the episode ends. This genre is very closely related to Alternate Universe fiction, except that the two main characters are clones rather than the original copies of Xena and Gabrielle.

Post FIN:

Post FIN is a genre very specific to *Xena*, relatively narrow in focus, and falls roughly into two categories. The smaller category is comprised of stories about Gabrielle going on alone after Xena's death in the series finale, "A Friend in Need part 2." The larger category within this genre is also sometimes referred to as "Fix FIN" fic, because the stories focus on bringing Xena back to life after "A Friend in Need."

The stories nearly always follow series canon and most depict Xena and Gabrielle as being in a romantic relationship, which was basically canon at that point. The two-part series finale is full of romantic imagery and dialogue with regard to Xena and Gabrielle, but even before then, the subtext had gradually given way to maintext. Rob Tapert, Lucy Lawless, and Renée O'Connor all stated in separate interviews that Xena and Gabrielle's relationship was a romantic one by the time the show ended. Post FIN fic may vary significantly in the length of time it takes to bring Xena back to life, or the method used to do so, but the vast majority of the stories portray a heartbroken, often angry, Gabrielle fighting to bring her lover, Xena, back from the dead, so they can carry on together and get a happy ending.

Virtual Seasons:

After the show ended, a handful of fan fiction on-line virtual series were written that picked up where the show left off. Among these were *The Messenger* series, which focused on the life of Xena's daughter, Eve, after the death of Xena; the *Xena Shipper Seasons*, which focused on Xena coming back to life and having a relationship with Ares; and the *Subtext Virtual Season*. The latter is perhaps the most well-known and long-running.

In its two-episode premiere, Xena comes back to life, and the series carries on for seasons seven through ten. It follows TV show canon and firmly establishes Xena and Gabrielle as a romantic couple. It picks up where the series ended, and each episode is written in an expanded script format, taking the elements of a traditional television show script, and adding descriptive narrative beyond what is usually contained in a script intended for TV. Original artwork and screencaps from the show are used to illustrate these script-format stories. The series was a collaborative effort among several prominent Xenaverse bards, artists, and webmasters, and even includes one script of an unfilmed episode from the show, "Fallen," which was written by *Xena* bard and sixth season episodic writer, Melissa Good, and crediting the script's story idea to *Xena* Executive Producer Rob Tapert. You can read more about *Xena Subtext Virtual Season* later on in this chapter.

Crossover/Multi-Fandom:

Crossover/Multi-fandom stories include the characters of Xena and Gabrielle as well as characters from one or more other television shows, movies, or other media, and in some cases the stories include original characters. Crossover stories usually mix only a few fandoms, while multi-fandom stories usually mix several shows. How Xena and Gabrielle are featured in these stories depends upon many factors. A story's time period may be the present-day or some other time period. It may be set in Xena's world, or it may be set in the world of some other fandom, and Xena and Gabrielle somehow find themselves in that world. Xena and Gabrielle may be the primary characters, or they may be supporting characters in a story that focuses on characters from another fandom. These stories may or may not follow *Xena* canon, and may or may not depict Xena and Gabrielle as lovers. Sometimes these types of stories explore what would happen if characters from different fandoms were to meet and become involved sexually or romantically.

Mel and Janice:

The Mel and Janice genre is unique to *Xena*. The stories are based upon the second season episode, "The Xena Scrolls," in which the character Melinda "Mel" Pappas is a descendant of Xena and the character Janice Covington is a descendant of Gabrielle. In the episode, Janice is a 1940s Indiana Jones-like archeologist on a dig for Gabrielle's buried Xena scrolls, and Melinda Pappas is an ancient linguistics scholar. At the end of the episode, after surviving an encounter with Ares, the two agree to team up for further adventures. Mel and Janice fan fiction stories are based upon these two characters. They are basically a sub-genre of Uber fiction, except that they are based upon series canon from the one episode. These stories usually depict Mel and Janice as being in a romantic relationship.

Uber:

Uber stories feature characters that generally bear the Xena and Gabrielle archetypes. One character, the "Uber Xena," is usually tall with dark hair and blue eyes and is more aggressive and cynical, and the other character, the "Uber Gabrielle," is usually short with blonde or red hair and green eyes and is more peaceful and optimistic. On rare occasions, Uber Xena and Uber Gabrielle may switch personalities from the TV series archetypes. Uber characters are given different names from Xena and Gabrielle. They are sometimes, but not always, understood to be the reincarnated souls of Xena and Gabrielle. These stories may be set in any time period in history, with the majority taking place in modern times. The characters sometimes have backgrounds similar to Xena and Gabrielle, but adjusted to fit the story's setting.

Once the show's producers brought forth the idea of these reincarnated uber characters, it was only a matter of time before *Xena* bards followed their lead. It is generally accepted that the very first Uber Xena and Gabrielle story was "Toward the Sunset," a western written by a bard who went by the on-line pen name of Della Street. In "Toward the Sunset," tall dark-haired outlaw Jess meets and eventually falls in love with petite blonde school marm Mattie. The Uber fiction genre opened up a whole new world for *Xena* fan fiction writers. While there were hundreds of fan fiction stories written about Xena and Gabrielle, those stories had mostly pre-established characters and settings, and only the plots were partially or completely original. It was refreshing and challenging for *Xena* bards to write Uber stories. While the two main characters' personalities might be fully or partially pre-established, the bards had the freedom to create completely original names, backstories, settings, and plots.

Uber stories nearly always feature two female characters who become lovers or are already established as lovers at the beginning of the story. Over time, Uber fiction became more and more original and eventually opened up publishing opportunities for some Xenaverse bards, which will be covered in the next article.

Chapter Sixteen

Brave New Worlds

by Denise Byrd

I NEVER PLANNED to become a writer, not even as a hobby. I loved reading from the time I was old enough to do so, but I never thought about writing as something to do beyond school assignments; it was never a goal for me to achieve. I just sort of fell into it.

Back in the early days of the *Xena* fandom, there was a massive amount of fan fiction around, and new stuff was being produced every day. Honestly, there was so much out there that if you couldn't find something to your liking, you just weren't looking hard enough. I can't say I didn't like some of what was out there—I had several authors that I followed and from whom I anticipated regular updates.

It wasn't until 2000 that I started writing, and it wasn't because I was unhappy with what I was reading. I had long since learned how to utilize the delete key and the backspace button. No, my problem was I got hit with the idea that just wouldn't go away... because of a three day discussion on a mailing list. It was about a woman crushing on her oblivious straight friend. I don't know what happened with them, but that extended conversation was long enough for the idea to germinate and turn into what eventually became *A Valiant Heart*.

The story that I wrote actually bears no resemblance to its origin, but it was also never supposed to be more than a one-and-done shot. There is every possibility that if *Xena* had not ended as poorly as it did, Miranda Valiant would have remained dead at the end of *A Valiant Heart*. But I saw what FiN did, not just to the fandom as a whole but to people individually, and I decided there was absolutely no reason to inflict more unhappiness on the world. So, the Storyteller's Cardinal Rule was born—*No matter what happens in the story itself, it must have a happy ever after ending.*

That became my downfall. My one-shot became a seven-story series, and from there, there was simply no looking back. To date, I have written seventeen original novels, twenty-one original shorts stories, twenty-seven fan fiction stories in seven fandoms, plus a number of multi-fandom crossover stories that all tie into my Xena and Gabrielle *Blood Bond universe.*

Even though I started writing Uber as opposed to genuine fan fiction, it's still very much fandom based. If you read the *Valiant Series,* you can find many references to Xena and Gabrielle as they were given to us in the television show. It was just easier to write my own characters in a setting of my choosing because I could overlook any YAXIs (Yet Another *Xena* Inconsistency) that the show was infamous for producing.

I have been exceptionally lucky in finding beta readers with whom I can work that have stuck with me for a long time. Phil has been with me from the first, and Mac came along not too long after. I had a third beta, Jeanne, but she had to quit when she went back to school.

Phil and Mac know what to look for in my writing—dropped words and letters; *correct* words instead of *close* words because I couldn't think of the *right* word. Mac knows what questions to ask when something needs clarifying; if she asks, it means I skipped something pertinent that will probably be important later. They've never really made suggestions or demand that something be put into a story, but they're both willing to talk to me to help me out when I sometimes get stuck. That may not sound like much, but it makes a huge difference for me. I trust them to have my back to help me put out the best story that I can, and after hundreds of thousands of words, that's important. I am continually thankful for them and their hard work on my behalf.

On top of that, Phil serves as my primary researcher, because I truly *hate* research… like, I don't actually research *anything* (except character names). For much of my writing, it doesn't really matter; I can just sit down and write. It's all fiction… all make-believe… and when you're building your own world or stepping away from the real one, you can use your imagination and do magic. But for something like *Blood Bond,* which is a massive historical epic that weaved actual historical events into a Xena and Gabrielle narrative that was ultimately a FiN fix, I needed to use real dates and incidents that could conceivably have been affected by either Xena or Gabrielle but wouldn't change history on a larger scale.

For that one story alone, Phil ended up bookmarking 143 sites to take us on an accurate historical journey. So I am eternally grateful that Phil not only beta reads for me, but that she also does all kinds of research as well. All that extra work she does makes for a much better, richer story.

I cringe now when I go back and reread my early work. Not because I don't think the story is there, because it is, but because of word choices and descriptors. Honestly, I'm not sure why I thought using blue-eyed/dark-haired/warrior was a better choice than simply calling the character by her given name, particularly when I deliberately chose each name with care to fit the character. But even so, I am proud of the stories I've told. They're good stories.

Funny thing about choosing character names… I always used a baby name site to research the meaning and origin of the names I was looking for. Most times, that didn't matter, but I still went and checked because I wanted the names to mean something. However, if you are a woman of childbearing age that has already proven herself fertile, it might not be a shrewd idea to leave the baby name page up and walk away from the computer… even for a minute. It is liable to give someone the wrong idea… just saying.

I made *that* mistake when I was preparing to write *Most Cherished Dreams*, another story into which I sort of stumbled. I was sitting at the computer, and the television was on in another room… just enough to be background noise while I was working. A commercial came on, telling about a new special on the Bermuda Triangle. I don't remember the commercial anymore or even what channel it was on, but it sparked the idea for *Most Cherished Dreams*. That is probably the most controversial story I've ever written, simply because of the time travel aspect. I have had readers legitimately want to argue the nuances of time travel rules and laws with me. I just shake my head and remind them that it is a fictional story and time travel is a fictional device; therefore, rules don't apply.

I have found that, as a writer, I cannot let what other people think or feel about my work affect me. I write first and foremost for me because I find joy in it, and while I am certainly pleased when people enjoy my writing, if I allow how people respond to change the way I am writing a story, it's no longer my story to tell.

Don't get me wrong; I do enjoy hearing from folks and talking to them about things I've written, especially when they have questions that make me think or realize something I hadn't noticed. In *Made For You*, one character actually ends up in a timeline that allows her to be the only thing she chose to do/be in the other timelines she was in. I didn't even realize that until a reader pointed it out to me, because not everything is planned out in my world. Actually, almost nothing is planned when I write. I have a beginning and an ending, and if the story is novel or epic length, there are usually two or three salient points that need to be made somewhere in the middle. Otherwise, I tend to fly by the seat of my pants.

But I also love hearing from readers when something has touched them personally. That has happened a few times, but the one story it happened the most with was *Guardian Angel*… maybe because of the supernatural themes involved. There's a tale behind the origin of this novel too. I was dusting and talking to Phil on the phone, and we were talking about someone or other being in the closet for the sake of their career. The story blossomed from that conversation and ran away with me after that.

Interesting note—when I wrote *Guardian Angel*, my visual of the two political protagonists was not what I described in the story. The brunette was shorter and had brown eyes, and the blonde was taller and had blue eyes. But I know that many on-line readers automatically change the written description to the archetype they grew used to, that of Xena and Gabrielle. I was okay changing my visual to suit the reader in this case. It made it a little more interesting to have the two sets of characters share that particular characteristic. I already had a start written for the Angels, and they were based on Xena and Gabrielle. But that particular story has not actually reached fruition yet.

I have a number of unfinished stories: ten story starts and five WiPs right now. Some starts only have a sentence or two; some have a paragraph; still others have several paragraphs or even a page. They're ideas that I've had at one time or another that simply wouldn't leave me alone. I write down enough so I have some clue as to what the story should be if and when I ever decide to pick it up again. But at least putting the story down on paper means it is out of my head, and I appreciate whatever peace and quiet I can manage to give my two brain cells, Pink & Fluffy. The WiPs are stories that, for one reason or another, I have difficulty writing, so they only get worked on sporadically.

There are also short stories that I would love to be able to make into longer, novel length stories. Not all of them *could* be, not all of them *should* be, and some of them will *never* be because I don't like them. But there are a few -*Aftermath*, *Blind Date*, *Coming of Age*, *Don't Take the Girl* and *Made For You*, especially- that I think I could probably turn into a pretty decent epic if I would just sit down and write them. The problem there for me is twofold. The first is that I have so many ideas of things that want to be written… see above… and there are always new ideas to consider. The other is because I'm afraid writing would become like work for me then. I don't write and rewrite and edit. I write, send to my betas, make the necessary corrections, and move on. I don't go back and revisit and rewrite; once I'm done with the corrections, I'm done; I move along with the story. So I'm honestly not certain that I could go back in and pull things apart, insert new pieces, rewrite old bits… Partly because I write very linearly. The way it reads in the story is the way it was written, even the flashbacks, unless it was like what happened with *Valiant*. I literally did a cut and paste to give readers a place to pick up from because it was months between installments. The *Valiant Series* is just one very long story told through a succession of novels, but not many people want a book that is fourteen hundred or so (1400+) pages long. Those are usually doorstops!

My only other series, *Favors of Fortune*, is much the same—six novels that run sequentially to tell a single epic tale. The first five are strong stories but I need to either go back to the last story and add to it or write one more story for the series. *Caught in the Storm* got hijacked by Aphrodite, so I never told the story I intended. I was exhausted long before I reached the end, so the characters never received the fair treatment or ending they deserved.

Then there is *Drifter*. I don't remember what brought the story about except that I wanted to write a western because it was one of the few genres I hadn't attempted. Except for the language barrier that caused no small amount of frustration, this one was one of the easiest stories for me to write. A sequel will likely never get written unless I move to a deserted island that has running water and electricity but no internet by which to be distracted. I left them in a happy place where it would be fairly easy to pick up where I left off, but there is also no problem if they never get written again, because again… *happy place*.

I do have one story I would really like to see the end of: *Franklyn & Rhodes*. It's probably one of the more unique novels I've written because each novella is a stand-alone tale. The only thing tying the stories together is the building in which they are housed, the building at Franklyn & Rhodes. My hold up here is also twofold. The first is that this is the first story for which I never had an ending because of the way it is structured as stand-alone works. The second is that I try to make all my chapters fairly even in length, and chapter length in my early stuff is ten pages. I would have to retrain my brain back to ten pages, and that is a daunting prospect but not an impossible one. When I figure out how to end it, I'll worry about the chapter length issue. *Franklyn & Rhodes* is one of the stories that I think might do well as a mini-series, partly because the self-contained stories lend themselves to that sort of treatment.

As for the rest of my original stories, I think seeing any of them brought to life would be a pretty cool prospect. I'm not really sure how well it would work though, because I know what I could see when I wrote them. I'm not certain any kind of treatment beyond the pages of a book would do justice to what I have already seen, not because I am some kind of fantastic writer, but because I'm fairly sure that I couldn't completely convey with words everything that my mind's eye could see. However, since the likelihood of something like that ever happening is slim to less than-none, it's a fun little thing to contemplate.

The fan fiction, however, is rife with all sorts of visual treatment possibilities because there are so many to choose from. In the *Blood Bond* multi-fandom universe, there are twenty-nine fandoms in a single story—*A Diva's Demise*. This story was a lot of fun and required a 4'x8' whiteboard for me to keep up with everyone involved. I would love to see this brought to life, if only so I could see some of the actresses involved pull double or triple duty because they have multiple characters in the story. *A Diva's Demise*, *Brave New World*, and *Blood Bond* are my favorite fanfic stories that I've written, although I'm happy with all the fanfic I've written outside of *Xena*. I've only written individual stories for those fandoms I've actually seen: *Birds of Prey, Facts of Life, Law & Order: SVU, Popular, Stargate: SG1,* and *Wonder Woman*. There are some good stories there, and I feel like I have done those shows and characters justice.

Brave New World stems from the Xenaverse that the show gave us, though that was accidental. I wanted to write a Wonder Woman story (well before the movie came out), and it managed to weave itself around the ending the show gave us. It wasn't my intention, but it made for a good story. I have a story start for a sequel to this story. It's called *Darkest Dawn* and starts out with one of the main characters dead and the other seeking vengeance. You can see why I'm hesitant to write it.

Xena was a lot harder for me to write. I felt like Missy Good gave the characters a better story than the show, and it was difficult not to want to write from her characters rather than the show's. I did manage a few short stories for challenges and invitationals, but it wasn't until I started a Halloween story called *Blood Bond* that I finally seemed to find my groove writing Xena and Gabrielle. Having them as immortal Bacchae means I could put them somewhere other than the ancient world, and I like that. I like having them around in modern times; it allows me a lot more freedom in my stories with them. It allows them to interact with characters in other fandoms as well as whatever historical icons would work, and that makes it more fun and interesting for me as a writer.

Fan fiction brought me into the *Xena* fandom as much as the show did; it encouraged me to tell the stories I wanted to tell. Though it took me a couple years and a few original stories first, I've found a way to tell fan fiction stories that make me happy. The fact that I can add in a number of other shows and fandoms is just icing on the cake.

I don't know if I'll ever publish beyond the internet, but as long as I have stories to tell, I'll keep on writing and sharing them with folks.

Denise's *Xena* fan fiction Page
www.academyofbards.org/authors/d.html

Chapter Seventeen

Forever Changed –
One Bard's Journey Into Fanfic

by Iseqween

A DARK-HAIRED WOMAN *on horseback descends from the mist. Clad in a revealing leather outfit, she wears armor and carries a sword. Looks kind of somber, tough even. Seems alone, in no hurry to be anywhere in particular, except maybe away from visions she's having of violence and flames – herself as the cause.*

She strips off her fighting gear, is burying it in the dirt, but sees bad guys bullying villagers, about to strike a defiant young redhead. The woman leaps, kicks, spins to the rescue. After, she rides away dressed again in her warrior duds.

The redhead secretly follows and talks her way into saving the warrior from a stoning by kinfolk. Some action and a few chats later, the two set off together, in no hurry to be anywhere in particular – except "where there'll be trouble."

I doubt I'll ever tire of revisiting those scenes from the *Xena: Warrior Princess* premier episode "Sins Of The Past." So intriguing. A perfect embodiment of the creativity, humor, angst, and surprising relationships that would follow. In hindsight, I realize what captured my imagination most was the mystery in the two main characters simply roaming about, engaging life – or death — wherever it presented itself. "Where to next?" our girls wondered at the beginning of the series finale "A Friend In Need." Indeed. Endeavoring to answer that drove my continuing obsession with the show and ultimately my journey as fanfic bard.

Water Soft and Raging

I love exploring philosophical issues, the yin/yang conundrums so wonderfully dramatized in *XWP*'s third season "The Debt." I got my first real taste in "Return Of Callisto." Our "hero" calmly watching her nemesis sink in quicksand absolutely stunned me. I realized the show was about a lot more than the female warrior who initially got my attention. RoC sucked me in like the helplessly sinking Callie.

A few months after *XWP*'s launch, I decided to get AOL, ostensibly to modernize my consulting business. I'd seen the web reference at the end of episodes and figured it could be a fun route to investigating the internet. Talk about meandering… Oh, my. I discovered chat rooms, entertainment articles, fan clubs. And Tom's Fan Fiction site. Rebekah's revered "All Through the Night" (Part I of "Nor the Battle to the Strong," originally posted in 1996) and Flynn's 1996 "This Day" particularly touched me. I began devouring stories anywhere I could find them, impressed by their power to add such richness to a show I didn't think could get much better.

I started doing ep reviews and posting them on the Chakram list (as IfeRae). In 1999, "Ides Of March" moved me to write first-person, in-the-moment reflections – one from Gabrielle's perspective, the other from Xena's. I titled the pair, "So Close." The Chakram moderator rejected this submission, indicating the forum did not accept fiction. I was shocked, as I had never intended to write fanfic, nor considered my review as such.

I had also joined a *XWP* writers' list. A member encouraged me to send "So Close" to the AUSXIP Bard's Corner. I blame MaryD for accepting the darned thing and planting the seed to consciously try doing a "real" story. I submitted the first, "Under Other Circumstances" as a lark, fully expecting it to be my last. That was in January 2000. By 2011, I had posted 90.

I didn't know about fanfic, but figured it centered around particular productions. I set out to replicate *XWP* as much as possible. Nearly all my stories are "classics," in that they take off on events portrayed in the series. Even the post-finale, clone and somewhat "uber" ones stay close to the original characters. I have no desire to try my hand at fiction beyond that.

I am a journalist at heart and by training. I observe and report. I try mightily to stay true to the show's spirit, personality, and themes. I love how *XWP* covered nearly every genre, often in the same ep. Likewise, I tried to make my stories a blend of heart, serious chats, action/adventure, and playful banter. The TV version is my bible. I can't pretend whatever I saw or heard didn't happen, just because it differs from what I might've preferred. I have all the DVDs and still occasionally watch an episode when the spirit hits me. My fanfic served as extensions or new versions enabling me to continue enjoying *XWP*.

Initially, the episodes themselves generated ideas for me—filling in the gaps, delving into the ambiguities, imagining what was going on between the lines or in the characters' heads. Debates on Chakram also generated ideas. The series finale both saddened and inspired me, more so than if X&G had strolled together happily into the sun. It compelled me to envision how to resurrect them for further adventures. It freed me to go beyond what I'd seen on TV in terms of X&G–their relationship, maturing, adapting to new challenges, being with friends and family for extended periods.

Interestingly, the end also fueled my curiosity about the beginning, but through a retrospective lens. Though one of my least favorite, the first season ended up generating nearly twice as many stories as any other. So much seemed to happen instantaneously between two women portrayed as night and day. Why did their improbable friendship feel so natural? What did they see in or need from each other? How, with so much unexplained and despite the contradictions, did they make it work?

I began to picture Gabrielle airily ruminating about some topic, with the taciturn Xena, out of respect, taking her companion seriously, giving painfully honest answers. Gabrielle's innocent, usually nonjudgmental responses often mitigated Xena's angst, like chipping away at the crust and showing what lay underneath as not so hopeless after all. Over time, walking along or during fireside chats, I could visualize them gradually seeing the world differently through each other's eyes.

I found myself also exploring the world around me from a fresh perspective—the woods, my martial arts class, two senior citizens sailing a boat, young people arguing about who's right, wondering, "Ooo, could I use that for a story?" *XWP* dealt with issues and settings that could happen anywhere, to anyone at some point in their lives. It's been years since I penned fanfic, yet I still see story ideas, "noodling" what might occur between Point A and Z, using *XWP* as the medium.

The Path Taken

Novelist Stephen King reputedly said he started most of his books with "What if?" That question propelled my stories as well, except I wanted the answers to come mostly from X&G. I have definite impressions of them, based on the wonderfully confident and nuanced performances I viewed. I control the "What if" that starts the ball rolling with commitment to honoring the actors' interpretations and creating new scenarios true to the show's themes.

The characters dictate how everything develops. I disagree or get impatient with them sometimes, but they always get their way. I do tweak quite a bit, often based on feedback from a long-time beta reader. I focus on fiddling with dialogue or gestures, as I prefer the characters communicate for themselves, rather than using a lot of exposition.

The beginning can be somewhat stressful. I have a particular "What if" in mind, but not necessarily a clue about how it could play out. Somewhere in the middle, I start to see the end. I feel confident enough about the foundation I laid for the characters' journey. I get excited because I'm curious about where they may take me.

I typically write sections (about five pages) patterned after the show's use of commercial breaks or fade outs for scene transitions or to build momentary suspense. I stop after a section, often with little idea of what comes next. I usually write at night and go to bed anticipating what might be revealed the following day. I enjoy most feeling less and less like it's about what I already know, and more about discovering something new as the characters take more control.

When dealing with philosophical issues, I sometimes get bogged down in making things too complicated and heavy. That usually means I haven't paid enough attention to the heart of it. I ask the characters why or whether what I've written is important to them, rather than an excuse for me to go off on my own tangent. They may have a little chat about it in the story, or another character/situation may pop up to keep the flow going in a way that takes me out of my quandary. If I'm actually imposing on them something that just doesn't fit, I cut it and move on.

There's such a wealth of great *XWP* fanfic in so many genres. Each bard has a unique motivation for writing. Mine was gaining insight into the little things that add to our sense of purpose, that help us make decisions about what we do, why, how, and with whom. I enjoy writing for characters both like and unlike myself. Putting them in situations I might find personally uncomfortable. Respecting their viewpoints. Trying to understand what makes them tick.

As an example, I'm very much a Xena girl–action, butt-kicking, more so than smelling roses, huggy-feely. I used to fast-forward through Gabrielle scenes. Forcing myself to "be" Gabrielle led me to appreciate her strengths, why the series (and Xena) would have suffered without her. I believe living the conundrums, conflicts, contradictions of her evolution led me to be more empathetic, more sensitive as a person, more fascinated by how these contrasting people could be traveling the same road while seemingly headed in opposite directions – "two wandering souls [who] lost themselves in each other and found their way," as I put it in my "Friends In Need" vignette, "What Stories Are For."

"Teach Me"

While writing this piece, it struck me how much I identified with *XWP*'s portrayal of the main characters' constant quest for knowledge. We witness that in real time with Gabrielle as she matured. While flashbacks show Xena's attraction to mentors who made the warrior presented initially in "Sins Of The Past," we also see Gabrielle's influence on the hero Xena became.

Once I made the decision to go public, I pictured connecting with a particular audience who shared my (and the show's) fondness for word play, droll humor, irony and allowing partakers room to add what suits them. Because I liked to let the characters dictate what happened, I honestly didn't have a feel for whether a story rambled, made sense, got tangled up too much in my tendency to be verbose or overanalyze. That's where feedback made all the difference.

I was very fortunate to join a writers' list made up of the very people I hoped my stories would touch. I could post drafts for private or shared comments, make revisions before sending off to a fiction site. The reactions, discussions and different styles made me a better human as well as a better bard. I believe it helped give my characters more depth. A script writer on the list helped me make my dialogue briefer, more conversational, to better match the TV version. I lucked up on an invaluable beta reader whose appreciation and honesty helped me hone nearly all my stories for nearly ten years.

I wrote mainly for my own enjoyment, but, oh, did I beam at my first reader response! I saved it and the many others I received. I was devastated when a computer crash obliterated emails from my first three years of barding. Somebody asked what feedback does for you. Yes, I want to know how to write something better. It's nice when people enjoy a story, but what's really fascinating to me is when they find all this stuff I didn't even know was there.

Given the overall intent of my fanfic, I'm particularly gratified by feedback that compares it to "watching an unaired episode," "true to how I would picture the characters," "putting me right there with them," "actually hearing Xena's velvety voice." Others appreciated possible explanations for what they didn't see enough of in aired episodes, such as "showing the small steps, the slow progression from acquaintance to friendship, and what that means to both of them."

Tackling post-finale and Golden Girls subjects led to some of my most popular stories. Wrote one person, "When I read your stuff, Xena and Gabrielle become more than television characters or even fictional characters at all. They are REAL, two extraordinary women continuing their journey through the years after the show, but growing up too, talking things out, working together, knowing each other too well, yet always learning."

My biggest surprise came from comments about my portrayal of «the relationship.» As I alluded to earlier, what attracted me first was the enigmatic warrior dedicating herself to righting wrongs. It took me a while to appreciate Gabrielle, let alone the subtext. Other bards helped open my eyes through illuminating conversations and their own fanfic. This added a new dimension, more layers for me in terms of the heart of the show. I felt a greater warmth for and between the two heroes, which I believe infused my portrayal of them.

Mind you, I liked the diverse interpretations people had of them as friends, companions, soulmates, sexual partners. I generally tried to maintain similar ambiguity in my stories during the original run of the show, based on what I perceived the *Xena* staff to be showing (or not showing) at the time. But by the end of the fourth season, when I posted my first pieces, I had already come to view them as a joined couple, which I totally embraced in my post-finale stories (though none depicted explicit "exchange of bodily fluids" scenes). I considered my ep-based stories "gen" (especially those centered on the first season), yet many readers categorized them, or said they felt, "alt." Apparently the romance came through and, judging from emails I received, enhanced the bond between the characters regardless of the label applied.

Them Bones

When asked which of my stories is the favorite, I acknowledge I like a few equally for different reasons. I'm particularly satisfied with my vignettes, many of which give the viewpoints of minor characters (e.g., Minya, Salmoneus, Tataka, even Argo). The Academy of Bards' 50-word fiction exercise presented a great challenge. "Seasons" was a series of fifty-worders where I tried to capture the essence of each year of eps. I like the precision required of these shorter pieces.

On an intellectual level, "When Xena Was Callisto" explores a concept that has always intrigued me–justice. In the show, Xena was formally tried for crimes she didn't commit. "When Xena" examines what justice might mean from a lot of different viewpoints and is ripe with the irony indicative of *XWP*.

"Fifty Winters Ago" was the true launch of what my long-time beta reader fondly referred to as the "geezer" series. It became the framework for portraying X&G in their later stages and giving them unique opportunities to re-experience what made them or what they did in the past. *XWP*'s many mature fans ultimately motivated me to make that the second largest category of my work.

In terms of pure writing, "My Dance With the Devil" uses a sort of poetic format to review highlights of *XWP* through the 6th Season "Heart Of Darkness." It was very different for this analytical person. I feel good about the way I could use the sensuality of that ep to convey – in one reader's words – "many layers of meaning."

"What Stories Are For," my sentimental favorite, is actually one of the few I set out to do for someone other than myself. Though I was okay with "A Friend In Need," I came to empathize with fans who had a deeply negative reaction. I could understand those who felt it unfair to Gabrielle, who had to endure a terribly painful goodbye to the physical Xena. I wanted to leave those fans with a possible scenario of how Gabrielle might've resolved Xena's death in *AFIN*. It ended up allowing me another chance to grieve the finality of the show, at the same time reminding myself and others our girls could always live on through our imaginations.

Legacy

Writing this piece has certainly jogged my pitiful memory. Upon reading my first draft, I realized I hadn't paid tribute to three bards who passed on, leaving indelible impressions. One, Cousin Liz, created the beautiful Soulmates site. She hosted my stories, in many cases adding graphic designs that enhanced and made them complete. Thankfully, I saved most of those visually imprinted with her spirit.

Rebekah did more than serve as my most memorable introduction to fanfic. Her work set a standard for so many bards. Beyond her craft, she conveyed a deep appreciation for the characters, their mutual love, their on-going quest to become closer. I kept a printed version of "All Through the Night" for a more physical closeness, to literally touch her words and appreciate the spirit made manifest of someone I never got to know otherwise.

I met PD Wonder through her bright, articulate on-line conversations with my bard group. We learned she had a brain tumor and would be absent for treatment. The eventual surgery took a huge toll on her memory and language skills. As part of her therapy, family said we should continue our communication with her. I figured on sending a couple "Miss you; here's what I thought about the latest *XWP* episode; get well soon" messages. Instead, our correspondence spanned nearly every day for about a year, across continents and a virtual lifetime of emotions.

I hadn't anticipated PD would be struggling with the alphabet itself. She put letters together to approximate words I didn't always get, then asked if they meant what she intended. Through a long, tortuous process, we talked (as she called it) in an invented, frequently imprecise shorthand. We "lafed," expressed anger, frustration, joy and eventually pride at our hard won accomplishments. She'd lost the filters to edit what she said, which produced the purest form of honesty I've ever encountered–true as well as coming from an innocent place. When she asked, "How you?", I laid bare my soul.

Despite her situation and poor prognosis, PD maintained her courage, thoughtfulness, determination and see-good outlook when she died a couple weeks before the *XWP* finale. I wrote "The Ghost of A Smile" with her in mind, to work through sadness to renewal for both losses. Gabrielle asks

Xena's spirit tough questions about her decision to stay dead, forcing the warrior into rare self-analysis and leading to acceptance they could always be together in many ways. I saw the triumph in PD's "how I do" approach to cards dealt her. I couldn't help but likewise find triumph in the series end, especially X&G's enduring bond, or forever in my own life and work.

There are so many other reasons I may be searching the rest of my existence for the words to convey this *XWP* journey's meaning to me. What I know now? Self-discovery. The framework to express my creativity in a way that satisfies *me*. Learning from and being inspired by strangers around the world, some of whom became wonderful friends. Being motivated to experience technology, new media, activities, and trips I probably wouldn't have otherwise. Feeling I have companion spirits whom I can call upon whenever or however I want.

I do regret missing out on the original *XWP* fanfic movement–engaging in the discussions, learning from the pioneers, being able to share more than this one bard's journey. I am so honored MaryD nevertheless included me in her 25th *XWP* anniversary celebration. I am so grateful she gave me the platform for sharing my love of *XWP*, my outlet for creating a fantasy world where characters can sometimes spend time questioning (or reliving) previous decisions, in the process helping me gain insights into my own motivations. Her phenomenal, enduring dedication has kept alive so much of what we cherish, for both long-time and new devotees.

I'm reminded of the third episode, "Dreamworker," which concludes with Xena's throwing a rock in the lake. Gabrielle observes that the rippling water will eventually become calm again. Xena responds, "But the stone's still under there. It's now part of the lake. It might look as it did before, but it's forever changed." How amazing IseQween will be part of the Xenaverse for years to come, in cyberspace or somebody's collection of stories. Still me, forever changed.

You can find Iseqween's Xena Fan Fiction here:
http://www.ausxip.com/fanfiction/iseqween/index.html

Chapter Eighteen

Their Journeys Continue –
Subtext Virtual Season

by Denise Byrd & Carol Stephens

ASK ANYONE WHO was a Xenite in 2001 - not just the Hard Core Nut Balls - and 99 out of 100 of them will agree - Xena ended badly. Even The Powers That Be have stated as much… in hindsight.

That's not a criticism - it's a statement of fact. The outcry at the time was overwhelmingly negative, and to this day continues to be a point of controversy throughout the fandom. In fairness to TPTB (The Powers That Be), it wasn't supposed to be the end. They had planned to make 5 follow-up movies that would have resolved a number of issues… not the least of which was leaving Gabrielle alone because of Xena's death. However, a myriad of unfortunate circumstances ended that possibility before it became a reality, but what it did do - fortunately - was spawn a plethora of creativity within the fandom. Fanfiction exploded with a profusion of 'Fix-it' fics, and the fandom itself created several virtual seasons - one that followed Eve's journey; one that paired Xena and Ares; one that kept to the precepts of the show that allowed Xena and Gabrielle to be 'just friends'; and one that proved out Lucy Lawless' statement, "They were *married*, man!"

The Subtext Virtual Season was the very first virtual season to make an appearance. It led the way for all the others that followed - not just in the Xena fandom, but in every fandom that has come after. The SVS was the brainchild of the late Sue Beck (Sword-n-Quill). Sue had a firm idea of what she wanted to do, and how she wanted to accomplish it, but she knew it was going to take a village to bring it to fruition. So she came to a small group of Xenite friends in August 2001 - almost the exact moment the second part of 'Friend in Need' finished airing - asking if we couldn't give Xena and Gabrielle a better ending than the show had. Given the fiercely negative reaction the entire fandom had to the series ending, it was no wonder most were anxious to jump on board and rectify what we saw as a grievous wrong. It was agreed to at the very beginning that *this* virtual season would make clear what the show never could… that Xena and Gabrielle were lovers.

When Sue originally suggested the idea, there were 2 caveats upon which she insisted. One was that the first two episodes were absolutely going to fix 'Friend in Need'. Xena was going to be brought back to life. The other was that we were going to be clear that Xena and Gabrielle were lovers - subtext was going to become main text. Other than that, this was an entirely new collaborative project that would set the standard for all that came after, and storylines were wide open. Anything was possible... except another unhappy ending.

The SVS started out with three of the best-known writers in the Xenaverse: Sue Beck, Melissa (Missy) Good, and TNovan (Morgan L. Sams); and three of the 'Verse's top artists: MaryD, Linda (Calli) Callaghan, and Lucia Nobrega. The rest of the team was made up of three others: Judi Marr did screen grabs; Denise Byrd served as director, and Carol Stephens was the producer. Eventually, three more writers - Denise Byrd, Trish Kocialski, and Linda Crist - were added to the staff. We were fortunate in that several volunteers stepped up to do translations into 5 other languages over the course of our 4 years. Some of those translators were: Spanish (Shibeti, Elenis, Lysia, Ana P. Alonso, Cris, Inma, Montse, Xhogun); Italian (Scanto, Harry); Portuguese (Chris Burle); French (Katell); German (Beatrice, Bonnie, Michaela & Sabine).

It should be pointed out here that the small group of women that undertook this rather daunting task of creating the Subtext Virtual Season were scattered around the globe - Australia, New Zealand, Brazil, and 2 of the 4 time zones of the continental United States. Logistically, it could very easily have been a nightmare; instead, it became a challenge to which we adapted and overcame, but not without a lot of time and effort.

Our first challenge was to actually become a cohesive team, because there were a lot of strong personalities within this group of women. But we knew that was the only way we would be successful. So when Sue brought her original idea to the table, we sat down and hammered out a few rules to make it as pleasant an experience as possible for everyone involved. We agreed that everyone had to participate - no one could be a part of the project unless they were contributing in some way. For some, their role was already laid out. The writers knew they were expected to turn out full, four-act episodes, the same length as would be expected if the series was to go to film. The artists - MaryD and Calli - were responsible for the cover art of each episode, and they had the freedom between them to decide who worked on each episode. Lucia always commented on the places she wanted to contribute drawings, and Judi filled in the spaces between with screen grabs she manipulated to fit the scene. That only left Carol and Denise, and we were left to handle the mechanics of producing an on-line virtual season, which included the setting of the schedule. Most of the rest of the production aspects fell to Carol as the producer, as it was a very involved, physical process.

Everyone was expected to offer comments and criticism and ask questions to help make the stories something that would have been worthy of becoming an actual episode.

Courtesy was required… even when things got heated, and they sometimes did. This was a very passionate group, after all. But we found ways to talk to each other; to offer constructive criticism without attacking; to laugh together; to support one another. Most of us are still friends today, and we have many fond memories of this era of our lives.

Our last rule could have been considered an aspect of courtesy. Still, we made it separate to emphasize its importance to everyone. Timeliness - sticking to the schedule - was a necessity. That was probably the most difficult challenge to maintain because this was a side gig for everyone - something we did because we *wanted* to, not because it was a *requirement*. We all still had real-life, grown-up responsibilities to take care of - homes, jobs, families - and the SVS took up a *lot* of time. So we knew we had to keep to our schedule as much as possible. Sometimes, that required more than a little juggling on the SVS front.

When we had our few rules in place, the first thing we did was set up the schedule. In hindsight, we were a tad ambitious where that was concerned, but in our defense, we really didn't have the first clue going into this the work it was going to take to be successful. Besides, we were anxious to get our product out to the readers. If you were around then, you probably remember the heartache and turmoil that was swirling through the fandom right after the series ending aired. If you weren't… count yourself lucky, because it was an ugly time in Xenaverse history. This was worse than the Rift of Season 3. For a brief time, this series - that had changed so much for so many - had caused the fandom to revolt, and it was in danger of imploding on itself. Had that happened, there is a very good likelihood that it would never have recovered. So we pushed *hard* to get our continued vision out to the public, so they could have a positive hope for Xena again.

Once everyone was on board as part of the team, we formed a work list and did just that - We went to work! Fortunately, when Sue presented her case for a virtual season, she already had a solid story for the first two-part script. Our writers started offering up ideas for other episodes, and we began slotting things into the schedule. Each episode took the entire team 6 weeks to complete and the whole season was produced over a 9 month period

Everything depended on everything else to get done. Once a writer's idea got approved, they would begin the writing process - which meant turning in a beat sheet so we had an idea of what the story was about; how it would be broken down into acts; who was involved beyond Xena and Gabrielle; and what the denouement would be. This was important because it allowed us to create a timeline where the stories could feed into one another, if only loosely. And it gave the artists an idea of who they needed to search for inclusion in all the visual graphics. The cover artists would decide who was going to do the front page graphic for the episode, and they would go to work.

Unless a writer was stuck on a particular plot point, the list usually didn't see anything until an act was complete. Only then did they send their work to the list for commentary. Sometimes there was a lot; others there was just a little, but once they got the okay from the list, they would move on to the next act. Meanwhile, Judi had started her great hunt for the right screen grabs. When you consider that she had over 100 episodes to look through - sometimes frame by frame - you begin to get an idea of just how long and involved of a process that was.

After the first week or so, there was never just one story going on at a time. Usually, there were three - one for each writer - something that, for several reasons, didn't change when we added more writers to the mix. Three stories at a time is a lot to juggle with all the different things going on - especially for those that worked on every episode - and adding more writers to the team was done to alleviate some of the pressure the writers felt having to produce so much written content so quickly. No matter how gifted or creative you are, that kind of burden and expectation can cause burnout, and no one wanted that.

The stories were at different stages in their evolution, of course, and we kept tabs on their process keep us on schedule. The graphic artists would send their ideas for the front page art… most of which would morph significantly from the original idea to the final product. It was probably 15-25 hours of work per episode, and many, many, *many* manipulations and layers of Photoshop.

Ideas for other episodes were offered as they occurred to someone - kept in mind as the writing was progressing, but not too deeply discussed until a writer was free to pursue a new story. Everyone was encouraged to offer story ideas. Not all ideas got used, but everything was discussed and weighed as a possibility.

Depending on the writer, the initial writing process could take between 2-48 hours, mostly due to the research or rewrites involved. Fortunately, they generally never had to do a full rewrite on anything; it was mostly just tweaks of things… some of which could be solved with a single sentence or two, and many times that was handled during the editing process. When a writer was done with their episode, they usually had a few days off to take a deep breath and consider how they wanted to write their next piece. This was the time that Lucia chose the illustrations she wanted to draw, and Judi figured out what places needed screen grabs. Lucia averaged 4-5 pieces of art per episode, and these took her approximately 15 hours per illustration. We never expected her to do so many - we never hoped for more than 2-3… max - but she was determined, and we were certainly not going to say no.

Judi, on the other hand, spent 15-25 hours searching for the absolutely perfect screen grab to place in many of the spaces throughout the story to help the audience visualize the scene. Many of these grabs she had to manipulate to fit the situation, but she had a knack for finding the right expressions to fit whatever emotion was being conveyed.

Meanwhile, as soon as an episode was completed and sent to the list, Carol would format the story into what was our production standard - work that took about 8-10 hours by itself - and then she would forward the formatted piece to Denise. Denise's main job was editing. So she would go line by line, correcting grammar and punctuation, asking for clarification from the writer if something was missing or unclear, adding the occasional word or eliminating others. All in all, it was a four to six-hour process of meticulous work. Then she and Carol would get on the phone for 3-4 hours and go through the entire story again… line by line.

Carol, by far, had the most labor-intensive piece of the puzzle. She averaged 40 hours of work per episode, simply creating the visual aspect into what it was. Aside from the initial formatting and the hours spent of the phone with Denise doing cleanup, she spent 3-4 hours on the phone with Judi as well, carefully placing each screen grab in its precise location. Space had to be left for Lucia's illustrations and those were placed later… much closer to the actual release date. There was the presentation that had to be done for each of the reading formats the SVS was offered in, and each of those required 6 hours each. She maintained contact with the translators and posted those episodes as they were turned in. Originally, the SVS was hosted on its own site. When it came to an end, it was incorporated into MaryD's AUSXIP website, where it remains archived today.

The SVS picked up where the show left off and produced almost sixty episodes! This was a fantastic experience to be a part of, and the work was actually read by series producer Rob Tapert. This had never been done before to such an extent, and even today remains unmatched. It is something we all look back on with pride to this day.

Chapter Nineteen

Subtext Virtual Season Guide – Seasons 7 to 10

by MaryD

svs.ausxip.com

Season 7: http://svs.ausxip.com/s7_epguide.htm

#701 - October 31, 2001 | A Friend Indeed - Part 1

The seventh season of *Xena: Warrior Princess* opens with Gabrielle in Egypt trying to help Queen Zenobia defend her land from an evil force intent on destroying it.

http://svs.ausxip.com/season7/en_s7e01/s7-e01-teaser.htm

#702 - November 7, 2001 | A Friend Indeed - Part 2

Xena has joined forces with Lucifer, who is intent on destroying Egypt and Gabrielle's worst fears may be realized as she is forced to face the possibility of going against an enemy she can't fight.

http://svs.ausxip.com/season7/en_s7e02/s7-e02-teaser.htm

#703 - November 14, 2001 | Choices

While trying to deal with the aftermath of Japa and Egypt, Xena and Gabrielle find themselves defending a village from an angry god and religious zealots bent on making a sacrifice.

http://svs.ausxip.com/season7/en_s7e03/s7-e03-teaser.htm

#704 - November 21, 2001 | It's All in the Mind

During a morning time spat, Gabrielle expresses a wish and Aphrodite grants it. Or does she? Sometimes there's truth in the saying "Be careful what you wish for; you just might get it."

http://svs.ausxip.com/season7/en_s7e04/s7-e04-teaser.htm

#705 - November 28, 2001 | For Want of an Herb

When a plague spreads through Greece, Xena and Gabrielle must travel to the deepest jungle in a desperate attempt to find the cure.

http://svs.ausxip.com/season7/en_s7e05/s7-e05-teaser.htm

#706 - December 5, 2001 | War's Children

When Xena and Gabrielle encounter some friends in big trouble, they jump to the rescue. Trouble is, it seems they're not wanted, and now they have to risk their lives to find out why.

http://svs.ausxip.com/season7/en_s7e06/s7-e06-teaser.htm

#707 - January 16, 2002 | Divided We Fall

Xena and Gabrielle investigate an abandoned temple that holds a secret that could change their lives forever.

http://svs.ausxip.com/season7/en_s7e07/s7-e07-teaser.htm

#708 - January 23, 2002 | Dreams of the Heart

In a place where life, love, and honor were lost, Gabrielle must find a part of her soul she thinks long gone to save the fortune of a family that claims her as their own.

http://svs.ausxip.com/season7/en_s7e08/s7-e08-teaser.htm

#709 - February 6, 2002 | Sins of the Father

Someone is looking for Xena and Gabrielle. Can they help this old friend out of a tight spot?

http://svs.ausxip.com/season7/en_s7e09/s7-e09-teaser.htm

#710 - February 13, 2002 | Happily Never After

Taking a shortcut away from trouble, Xena and Gabrielle find themselves locked up and tied down as they try to help a hapless couple navigate love - and taxes!

http://svs.ausxip.com/season7/en_s7e10/s7-e10-teaser.htm

#711 - February 14, 2002 | Crossroads

While escorting a lost group of Hestian Virgins to their temple in Thebes, Gabrielle tells a story to help pass the time.

http://svs.ausxip.com/season7/en_s7e11/s7-e11-teaser.htm

#712 - March 20, 2002 | Been a Wonderful Life

After keeping a small village from being destroyed, Xena and Gabrielle take a moment to wonder how their lives might have been different if they had been separated years ago.

http://svs.ausxip.com/season7/en_s7e12/s7-e12-teaser.htm

#713 - March 27, 2002 | Picture Perfect

Journeying to the wedding of the daughter of an old friend, Xena finds herself unexpectedly the center of attention in a race to salvage the wedding and prevent a war!

http://svs.ausxip.com/season7/en_s7e13/s7-e13-teaser.htm

#714 - April 10, 2002 | Roman Holiday

Journeying across Roman territory, Xena and Gabrielle are doing their best to avoid meeting any Romans - until they discover a friend who wasn't nearly as lucky. Will they be able to disguise themselves long enough to help out?

http://svs.ausxip.com/season7/en_s7e14/s7-e14-teaser.htm

#715 - April 17, 2002 | Beau & Arrow

Xena and Gabrielle suddenly find themselves taking care of six young Amazons out on their Rite of Passage, but definitely out of their element.

http://svs.ausxip.com/season7/en_s7e15/s7-e15-teaser.htm

#716 - May 8, 2002 | Prelude (Amazon Arc - Part 1)

After returning to the nation, Gabrielle finds herself once again serving as queen to troubled Amazons.

http://svs.ausxip.com/season7/en_s7e16/s7-e16-teaser.htm

#717 - May 15, 2002 | Not Even Death (Amazon Arc - Part 2)

Caught between Amazon squabbles and an old promise, Xena and Gabrielle find answers in a surprising discovery inside their own hearts.

http://svs.ausxip.com/season7/en_s7e17/s7-e17-teaser.htm

#718 - May 22, 2002 | Promised Land (Amazon Arc - Part 3)

Xena, Gabrielle, and the Amazons fight storms, pirates, and threats of mutiny in order to get to the Promised Land.

http://svs.ausxip.com/season7/en_s7e18/s7-e18-teaser.htm

#719 - May 29, 2002 | Season Finale - Fallen

Justice takes on new meaning as Xena finds herself faced with a legacy she can no longer outrun and a choice that might bring both her and Gabrielle truly full circle.

http://svs.ausxip.com/season7/en_s7e19/s7-e19-teaser.htm

Season 8: http://svs.ausxip.com/s8_epguide.htm

#801 - October 30, 2002 | Virtual Reality
The eighth season of *Xena: Warrior Princess* opens with Xena and Gabrielle looking for a bath and winding up with a lot more than they bargained for.
http://svs.ausxip.com/season8/en_s8e01/s8-e01-teaser.htm

#802 - November 6, 2002 | Final Options
In their quest to retrieve the chakram, Xena and Gabrielle must make a hard choice.
http://svs.ausxip.com/season8/en_s8e02/s8-e02-teaser.htm

#803 - November 13, 2002 | A Muse in the Hand - Part 1
Xena and Gabrielle finally meet Sappho, but what will the meeting with the Tenth Muse cost the Bard and the Warrior?
http://svs.ausxip.com/season8/en_s8e03/s8-e03-teaser.htm

#804 - December 4, 2002 | A Muse in the Hand - Part 2
There's a killer on the loose. Can Xena find him before someone else gets hurt?
http://svs.ausxip.com/season8/en_s8e04/s8-e04-teaser.htm

#805 - December 11, 2002 | My Brother's Keeper
Xena has an opportunity to catch up with a bit of her own past - unfortunately, the past definitely wants to outrace her.
http://svs.ausxip.com/season8/en_s8e05/s8-e05-teaser.htm

#806 - December 18, 2002 | A Funny Thing Happened on the Way to Poteidaia
Is Xena really getting old? A solstice gift tells her the answer.
http://svs.ausxip.com/season8/en_s8e06/s8-e06-teaser.htm

#807 - January 15, 2003 | Cloning Around
Alive and well in 21st century Los Angeles, it hasn't taken Xena and Gabrielle long to figure out the future is a far more difficult place to live than the past.
http://svs.ausxip.com/season8/en_s8e07/s8-e07-teaser.htm

#808 - January 22, 2003 | Magic in the Air
Gabrielle has been kidnapped. Xena must work with a clan of forest dwelling creatures to get her back.
http://svs.ausxip.com/season8/en_s8e08/s8-e08-teaser.htm

#809 - January 29, 2003 | A Queen Thing
Xena and Gabrielle find an academic argument coming back to haunt them as they agree to help a town with a very odd request.
http://svs.ausxip.com/season8/en_s8e09/s8-e09-teaser.htm

#810 - February 5, 2003 | My Fair Dite
In an effort to help Aphrodite deal with the death of her brother, Xena and Gabrielle invite her along on an adventure.
http://svs.ausxip.com/season8/en_s8e10/s8-e10-teaser.htm

#811 - March 19, 2003 | Behind the Scenes of the SVS
Let us show you what it takes to put together the Subtext Virtual Season Episodes.
http://svs.ausxip.com/season8/en_s8e11/s8-e11-teaser.htm

#812 - April 2, 2003 | Life's Little Challenges
Hoping for a night of simple peace, Xena and Gabrielle find themselves in mortal danger trying to defend a remote town instead.
http://svs.ausxip.com/season8/en_s8e12/s8-e12-teaser.htm

#813 - April 9, 2003 | In Your Eyes
While meeting up with some old friends who have a problem only they can solve, both Xena and Gabrielle learn the truth in the old adage "be careful what you wish for."
http://svs.ausxip.com/season8/en_s8e13/s8-e13-teaser.htm

#814 - April 16, 2003 | Season Finale - Echoes
On yet another routine heroic adventure, Xena and Gabrielle unexpectedly find themselves facing their literal worst nightmares.
http://svs.ausxip.com/season8/en_s8e14/s8-e14-teaser.htm

Season 9: http://svs.ausxip.com/s9_epguide.htm

#901 - October 29, 2003 | Who Watches the Watcher - Part 1
While minding their own business and trying to get a little rest from the road, Xena and Gabrielle discover a religious cult doing its best to ruin their fun and everyone else's - but the simple problem soon becomes far more complicated than they ever imagined.
http://svs.ausxip.com/season9/en_s9e01/s9e01-teaser.htm

#902 - November 5, 2003 | Who Watches the Watcher - Part 2

Xena and Gabrielle track down the source of a religious farce spreading across the countryside, only to find a shocking kernel of truth at its core.

http://svs.ausxip.com/season9/en_s9e02/s9e02-teaser.htm

#903 - November 12, 2003 | Roots

After their recent trials, Xena decides she wants to visit Amphipolis. Unfortunately, it doesn't want to visit with her. Can Xena and Gabrielle exorcise some of the ghosts of Xena's past?

http://svs.ausxip.com/season9/en_s9e03/s9e03-teaser.htm

#904 - December 3, 2003 | Horsefeathers

Xena and Gabrielle work to save one of the last godly creatures, which leads them to yet another encounter with Aphrodite.

http://svs.ausxip.com/season9/en_s9e04/s9e04-teaser.htm

#905 - December 10, 2003 | Yo Ho Ho

On a quest for a warm room and a soft bed, Xena and Gabrielle make a slight detour to roam the seven seas as pirates.

http://svs.ausxip.com/season9/en_s9e05/s9e05-teaser.htm

#906 - December 17, 2003| X Marks the Spot - Part 1

A scavenger hunt brings a different prize than Xena and Gabrielle expected.

http://svs.ausxip.com/season9/en_s9e06/s9e06-teaser.htm

#907 - January 14, 2004 | X Marks the Spot - Part 2

Xena helps her counterpart find the hidden truth while she tries to return to Argos.

http://svs.ausxip.com/season9/en_s9e07/s9e07-teaser.htm

#908 - January 21, 2004 | Candlemarks

Gabrielle receives a set of strange, secretive scrolls. Is she hiding something from Xena?

http://svs.ausxip.com/season9/en_s9e08/s9e08-teaser.htm

#909 - January 28, 2004 | BardCage

Xena and Gabrielle find themselves assisting an old friend when a problem comes up that could cancel his son's wedding.

http://svs.ausxip.com/season9/en_s9e09/s9e09-teaser.htm

#910 - February 18, 2004 | Pompeii - Part 1
As often happens with their vacations, Xena and Gabrielle pick the exact wrong time to visit the lovely Pompeii.
http://svs.ausxip.com/season9/en_s9e10/s9e10-teaser.htm

#911 - February 25, 2004 | Pompeii - Part 2
As often happens with their vacations, Xena and Gabrielle pick the exact wrong time to visit the lovely Pompeii.
http://svs.ausxip.com/season9/en_s9e11/s9e11-teaser.htm

#912 - March 3, 2004 | Water, Water Everywhere
A shipwreck leads to deeper trouble than Xena and Gabrielle could ever possibly have imagined.
http://svs.ausxip.com/season9/en_s9e12/s9e12-teaser.htm

#913 - April 7, 2004 | From Joyous to Grimm
Xena and Gabrielle learn the old adage: "Never take candy from strangers."
http://svs.ausxip.com/season9/en_s9e13/s9e13-teaser.htm

#914 - April 14, 2004 | Poke
Xena and Gabrielle find themselves in a small village surrounded by some interesting people.
http://svs.ausxip.com/season9/en_s9e14/s9e14-teaser.htm

#915 - April 21, 2004 | Season Finale - Deserting the Past
As Xena and Gabrielle finally look towards the future, they find their past hasn't quite given up its hold on them yet.
http://svs.ausxip.com/season9/en_s9e15/s9e15-teaser.htm

Season 10:
http://svs.ausxip.com/s10_epguide.htm

#1001 - October 31, 2004 | The Xenthurian Legend
Sometimes the smallest of actions can come back to haunt you, with the greatest of consequences, as Xena and Gabrielle will learn on an unexpected trip to Camelot. The round table may never be the same once it has a taste of the Warrior Princess and the Battling Bard.
http://svs.ausxip.com/season10/s10e01/s10e01_teaser.htm

#1002 - November 7, 2004 | Demons in the Dark

A town is in trouble and Xena and Gabrielle are there to help. But all isn't as it seems at first glance.

http://svs.ausxip.com/season10/s10e02/s10e02_teaser.htm

#1003 - November 14, 2004 | A Sister's Love

The bond of love between sisters is very strong. Can Xena and Gabrielle help this bond survive death?

http://svs.ausxip.com/season10/s10e03/s10e03_teaser.htm

#1004 - November 21, 2004 | Hero Worship, On the Rocks

Xena and Gabrielle run into a little problem and end up having to prove that sometimes heroes really are born, not made.

http://svs.ausxip.com/season10/s10e04/s10e04_teaser.htm

#1005 - January 30, 2005 | The Gift

Travel back in time with Xena as we find out how she came to receive one of her most precious possessions.

http://svs.ausxip.com/season10/s10e05/s10e05_teaser.htm

#1006 - February 6, 2005 | Life in Paradise

Tara's daughter has married and run off with her husband. Is there trouble in paradise? Only Xena and Gabrielle know for sure.

http://svs.ausxip.com/season10/s10e06/s10e06_teaser.htm

#1007 - February 13, 2005 | Season Finale - Ocean of Fire

In the loneliest of times, Xena finds friendship and hope in most unexpected ways.

http://svs.ausxip.com/season10/s10e07/s10e07_teaser.htm

Chapter Twenty

AUSXIP XIPPY Awards & Fanfic Reviews

by MaryD

www.ausxip.com/xippy/index.php

THERE WAS A great deal of fan fiction deserving of praise in the Xenaverse. The following stories have been awarded the AUSXIP XIPPY Award for outstanding fiction. The stories are sorted as GEN, ALT or UBER. More about the fanfic genres in *Chapter 15: A Fic By Any Other Name* by Linda Crist. All links to the stories are online and available to download.

GEN STORIES:
The General/Classic genre is fiction based upon the timeline of the *Xena* television series and generally follows series canon.

ALT FICTION:
Alternative/Subber stories more or less follow the definition of General/ Classic stories above, with one primary difference: in this genre, Xena and Gabrielle are depicted as lovers or are on their way to becoming lovers.

UBER:
I have included Conqueror and Janice & Mel fiction in the Uber category. Uber stories feature characters that generally bear the Xena and Gabrielle archetypes. One character, the "Uber Xena," is usually tall with dark hair and blue eyes and is more aggressive and cynical, and the other character, the "Uber Gabrielle," is usually short with blonde or red hair and green eyes and is more peaceful and optimistic.

GEN STORIES

A Best Friend's Magic by Advocate
This is a Little Xe & Gab story (I love those), and the magic of being young and innocent where believing in the tooth fairy is all that matters. A beautiful short story by one of my favorite bards.
ausxip.com/fanfic11/best_friends_magic.html

A Prayer for You by Lariel
This is a very touching short story and it tugs at your heartstrings of love lost Very moving and you will need a tissue or two. Very well written.
http://www.ausxip.com/fanfiction/a/aprayerforyou.html

Bardic Theories by Karen Dunn
This is a total riot - I loved it! Gabrielle has a theory and when you mix Gabrielle's theories, and the Goddess of Chaos...you get one very ticked off and whipped Warrior Princess. Great writing.
https://www.ausxip.com/fanfic9/bardicthoeries.html

Case of the Missing Snowman (The) by Claire Withercross
This is a story about friendship and about giving. Little Xena and Little Gabrielle share their friendship in this beautiful story about a snowman.
http://ausxip.com/fanfic12/case_of_the_missing_snowmen.htm

Harder Please by Silk
This is funny. It's a short piece that is just too good and saying any more will ruin it. Let's just say - go and read it!
http://ausxip.com/fanfiction/h/harderplease.html

Healers Choice by Maggie
This story is a total riot. I couldn't stop grinning after finishing it. One of the gals is afflicted with a sore tooth - I won't spoil it as to who it is - but it's a real joy to watch Maggie weave this tale. Excellent read.
http://ausxip.com/fanfic/healers.html

The Huns by Eimajj
The Huns are on the move across Greece, and soon they will reach the Amazon lands. Xena and Gabrielle set out to stop them. Xena infiltrates the Huns and becomes the leading general. The Amazons meanwhile think that the power has gone to Xena's head, and they set out to kill her when they start the battle.
http://xenafan.com/fiction/content2/thehuns.html

In My Life by WarriorNutcase
This story combines one of my favorite songs with the aftermath of Sacrifice - Part 2. A beautifully written piece about a friend's love and her inability to accept the death of Gabrielle. Xena has a plan, and nothing will stop her in getting Gabrielle back.
http://www.academyofbards.org/fanfic/w/warrriornut_life.html

Mother's Plea (A) by Eimajj

This story is a sequel to The Contest. Xena and Gabrielle are back in Amphipolis with Xena's mother. This is a beautifully written hurt/comfort tale where the bard tries to get her warrior back on her feet.

http://ausxip.com/fanfiction/a/amother.html

Nor the Battle to the Strong: Part 1 - All Through the Night by Rebekah

I've wanted to give this story a XIPPY since I started them. I am so thrilled to see this absolute CLASSIC of a Xena story. This story, ladies and gentlemen, was one of the first I had read on-line, and I fell in love with Xena fanfic. It's a hurt/comfort tale that is superb and well written!

https://www.ausxip.com/fanfiction/t/thruthenight.htm

Xena and Gabrielle Little Adventures by Lucia

I don't often give a XIPPY to cartoons, but I think this series by Lucia tells a story. Lucia's work gives me a good feeling about two little children who are best friends and together, they try and get out mischief or get into it. Little Gabrielle has a thing for eating too much, liking Mr Potato Head a bit too much and gluing Xena's chakram together. Little Xena likes to pout and tries to get Gabrielle out of trouble! A very good series drawn by a very talented artist.

http://ausxip.com/xandg/index.html

Yeah, With a Really Big Sword by Temora

This is a wonderfully written story between the episodes God Fearing Child and Eternal Bonds. Xena, Eve and Gabrielle go to Potidaea to visit with her folks, but there is big trouble brewing. Very good characterization of Gabrielle and Xena. Excellent writing by this new bard.

http://ausxip.com/fanfic10/yeahreallybigsword.html

ALT FICTION

A Bard's Faith by L. Fox

This is a follow up to L. Fox's story Cage of Elysis. Ares hatches a plan to get Gabrielle away from Xena but he doesn't realize how much they mean to each other or maybe he does! An old friend returns and the story is beautifully written.

http://www.ausxip.com/fanfiction/f/faith1.html

Afterglow by T. Novan

What can you say about this...don't read this at work. Xena and Gabrielle in their bedrolls. A little steamy.

http://ausxip.com/fanfic11/afterglow.html

Appetite by Vivian Darkbloom

Appetite is a post fin fic story in a cell - two people held together on different paths and different hopes. Great story and made me sad a little.

http://www.ausxip.com/fanfic21/appetite.htm

After Thoughts by BJ O'Donnell

This short story is from Gabrielle's POV. It's set after a battle and the love she has for a certain black-haired warrior princess. Beautiful.

http://ausxip.com/fanfiction/a/afterthoughts.html

A Nitwit Guide For Alt Fanfic Collaborators by Silk & TZ

Ever wonder what goes on when two bards collaborate on a story? This is a hilarious "fly on the wall" story as we follow the bardly path.

http://ausxip.com/fanfiction/a/anitwit.html

A Once And Future Journey by Temora

This story is set after the events of FIN #2 - Xena has died and Gabrielle has sailed off to right wrongs. She is befriended by a young woman who tells her "you can't leave me here". You've got to take me with you. Teach me everything you know. I could be very useful to you…" A beautifully written story of Gabrielle alone but with her soulmate.

http://ausxip.com/fanfic15/a_once_and_future_journey.htm

Attention Shoppers by Lawlsfan

I really enjoyed this tale - A Warrior Princess, her warrior bard and shopping… mix them up for some fun and 3 dinars for a hog! There's also a spare Centaur running around here.

http://www.ausxip.com/fanfiction/a/attentionshoppers.html

A Queen's Sacrifice by BL Miller

This story is not for everyone - it's a tale about violence and how two people who love each deal with it. BL Miller has written a very well thought out and thought-provoking story that will tug at the heartstrings and have you teary. It's a story of love and sacrifice. An excellent story .

http://ausxip.com/fanfiction/aqueen1.html

Arguing on the Ides by Jade

This tickled my funny bone and I need a good laugh. I don't think I'll be seeing this episode the same way again even though it's my favorite. "I love you, Xena" takes on a whole new meaning.

http://www.xenafan.com/fiction/content5/jadecb_ides.html

A Woman Called Alika by M. Parnell

In a strange turn of events, Xena loses her memory and ends up with a family who are determined to make her a wife for their son, whilst Gabrielle is trying to find her. The story is very dark and reveals a strange way of living by the people who live in The Vale. M. Parnell has created another great story with this tale.
http://ausxip.com/fanfiction/a/alika1.html

Because You Loved Me by Katelin B

This is a sorrowful tale of the aging Amazon Queen saying farewell to her consort. Xena's final words via a scroll got to me. It's beautifully written. Set to the lyrics of the Celine Dion song "Because You Loved Me." Have a box of Kleenex handy.
http://www.ausxip.com/fanfic2/because.htm

Back Trouble by Della Street

I love Della Street's work and this little tale is just too cute for words. Poor Xena has hurt her back. Just when she and Gabrielle were finding out what everyone out there in subtext land already knew! She is under orders to stay put in bed by the Amazon healer. Doing this is a tough job—a cute story.
http://www.altfic.com/subtextfic/Xena/della/backtrouble.htm

Bargain Hunting by Della Street

This is one of the funniest stories I have read. Xena goes to see a slave owner about a slave…a blond, green-eyed slave that is rather excitable! I won't say anymore because it's got to be read to be appreciated. A lighter side to Xena: Warrior Princess.
http://www.altfic.com/subtextfic/Xena/della/bargainhunting.htm

Between a Breath and a Heartbeat by Bel-wah

This is set between the time Xena after she hits Gabrielle with the chakram and before she convinces Aphrodite to take her to Mount Olympus to confront the gods. A moment in time where Xena realizes that till the end, she is a warrior and will fight to the end for those she loves.
http://ausxip.com/fanfic9/betweenabreath.html

Beyond Sex by Della Street

Well, this little story will lift your spirits! Our gals are beyond sex or so Mr. Tapert and Co tell us. So Gabrielle tells Xena that their relationship goes beyond sex and they don't need it. Well Xena has other ideas!
http://www.altfic.com/subtextfic/Xena/della/beyondsex.htm

Blessing in Disguise by Lady Catherine

A first-time story that starts off with Xena reverting back to her warlord persona to protect Gabrielle from a warlord from her past. A little on the brutal side for Gabrielle as she endures some rough treatment but realizes that Xena is only trying to protect her. Very nicely written.

http://www.academyofbards.org/amazontrails/xena/blessing.htm

Blind Faith Restored by Zzelami

Way back in the second season there was an episode called Blind Faith - Xena is blinded in a fight and Gabrielle is taken to be the queen of a dead king. It was a fantastic episode reminiscent of many fanfic stories. The ending I thought needed something and Zzelami produced what I thought was the perfect ending to this episode. It's funny but yet very tender and the love that Xena and Gabrielle share shone through.

http://ausxip.com/fanfiction/b/blindfaith.html

Blind Faith Revisited by Mikki Hibbens

This story is set after one of my favorite episodes, Blind Faith. Mikki does an excellent job in showing the love Xena and Gabrielle share. An excellent read and a follow up to a beautiful episode.

http://www.academyofbards.org/fanfic/m/mikki_blindfaith.html

Blood Bond by D

This is an incredible epic love story - set after the events of FIN. It's the story of a quest, of longing, of a desire to find Xena and Xena's quest to find Gabrielle. A magnificent story, well written that will keep you riveted to your seat (or in my case with my airline seatbelt fastened securely and the chair in the reclining position). We follow Gabrielle's journey as well as Xena's as they try and reunite. D has interwoven history throughout this story, which for me as a history nut was incredible. Sit back and enjoy; this is a looooong story but worth it!

http://www.ausxip.com/fanfiction/bard-d/blood-bond1.htm

Bonding of Souls: Homeward Bound by CN Winters

This is the first part of a series called Bonding of Souls, which carries over from Changes of Heart by CN. In Homeward Bound, Eve wants to go back to the Amazons and face justice for all the wrongs she's done. Gabrielle convinces tells her about the greater good. A very nice start to a series that will be running parallel to the episodes as they screen.

http://ausxip.com/fanfic12/bos-homeward.html

Bonding of Souls: Down Home by CN Winters

This is a funny piece set after Old Ares - Xena and Gabrielle talk where Gab's hands were while they were sleeping in one bed with Ares. Adorable.

http://ausxip.com/fanfic13/down_home.html

The Broken Thread by Ella Quince

I was really moved by this tale. This is the story of Xena getting ready for battle when a stranger walks into her camp. A stranger who is also very familiar. They join forces to prevent death.

http://ausxip.com/fanfiction/t/thread.html

The Breaking by Redhawk

I would recommend you get a hanky or two and then settle back and read this fantastic follow up to Redhawk's Only One and Oktoberfest. Xena, the immortal, is once again faced with a loss so shattering that the world would soon see a return of the Destroyer of Nations. If not for Rickie, Xena would be lost.

www.academyofbards.org/redhawk_infinity/infinity/breaking/one.htm

Champions by Kamouraskan

I absolutely loved this - it had one of my favorite wacky characters - Valaska (not as a god) in it and a great story dealing with Gabrielle as Queen of the Amazons. You can't go wrong with a story about Amazons, Xena's past and Gabrielle's decision about accepting the mask. Excellent storytelling.

http://ausxip.com/fanfiction/c/champions.html

Changes of Heart Series by CN Winters

This series hasn't been completed yet but it's very interesting and very well written. It picks up from where Motherhood left off and it hits home with issues that, as yet, haven't been dealt with on the show. Gabrielle and Xena need to talk and deal with the problems they have managed to get themselves into. A great read.

http://www.ausxip.com/bards_w.php#Changes_of_Heart_Series

The Conqueror Series - Tale One - Journey's End by LJ Maas

I'm not big on the Ruler of the Known World but LJ converted me. This is unbelievably good. Xena is Lord, Conqueror of Greece, but she is almost forty-five years old when she meets the slave, Gabrielle. The little slave girl turns the hardened warrior's life upside down. EXCELLENT storytelling .

http://www.ausxip.com/fanfiction/conqueror/journeys_end1.html

The Conqueror Series - Tale Two - The Petal of the Rose by LJ Maas

The much-anticipated sequel to Journey's End. I love this conqueror and her soon to be Queen. The arrival of Solan, Xena's son, brings new problems for the Lord Conqueror and the now free slave. This is one of the best stories set in the Conqueror genre that I've read. Don't miss this one.

http://www.ausxip.com/fanfiction/conqueror/rose1.html

The Conqueror's Stone by DJWP

I wasn't a big Conqueror story kind of gal and very few conqueror stories really interested me but when DJWP wrote this absolutely fantastic piece, I was overjoyed. It's a brilliant piece It's a Xena and Conqueror story rolled into one. That is OUR present Xena and the Conqueror. Very interesting.

http://www.ausxip.com/fanfic14/stone1.htm

Creative License by Ella Quince

A bard's stories about a mighty warrior princess is spread throughout the land but there is a slight problem - the warlord Xena isn't at all like the stories! A fascinating look at what it might have been if a bard had made up stories about a hero that would change the world with her courage.

http://www.ausxip.com/fanfiction/o/oldpromise.html

Crossing the Fire by Linda Crist

Gabrielle ponders what went wrong in her relationship with Xena as she watches her warrior play with baby Eve. Xena also wonders what happened and with a little help from the Goddess of Love, a mystery is solved. Xena and Gabrielle finally have that talk about what went wrong in their relationship. This is a beautifully written story. This easily goes into my favorite story folder.

http://ausxip.com/fanfic12/crossingthefire.html

Dark Comes The Morning by Melissa Good

This is truly an epic tale and I mean EPIC. Melissa Good weaves a tale of a danger to Greece from a mysterious medallion worn by a warlord intent on capturing Greece and the Warrior Princess. All the characters that many Missy Good fans have come to enjoy reading about are back in this novel and get set for one final bloody battle for the greater good! An excellent story. Well worth the time and effort.

http://ausxip.com/fanfiction/d/morning1.html

Darkness Falls by Melissa Good
The rift in the series between Xena and Gabrielle was traumatic enough and I was dreading reading fanfic about it. Still, Missy came through with my favorite post-rift story that I have read so many times. She dealt with the issues that Xena and Gabrielle endured and crafted it into one of my all-time favorites. Darkness Falls is about that journey back from Tartarus that Xena and Gabrielle took -- a look into a relationship that withstood the angst and the bitterness. An exceptional story.
http://ausxip.com/fanfiction/d/dark1.html

Deal of a Lifetime (The) by T. Novan
This is number ten in the Legends Legacy series by TN. Xena makes a deal with Ares to save the life of her granddaughter. Xena at her best - dealing with Ares.
http://ausxip.com/fanfiction/ll/legends10.html

Deborah by L. Fox
I love this time period and I love the subject matter. Xena and Gabrielle meet Deborah - a prophetess in the land of Israel. She was a woman of courage. Xena and Gabrielle get shipwrecked and the story unfolds from there when Xena's help is required. A beautifully written story by one of my favorite authors.
http://ausxip.com/fanfic5/Deborah.html

Denouement by Bel-wah
A story set just after the events of When Fates Collide - we read the thoughts of both Xena and Gabrielle. Beautifully written.
http://ausxip.com/fanfic14/denouement.html

Did You Know? by DS Bauden
It's been a long time since I read a first time story between Xena and Gabrielle and this one was entertaining, Xena is "stressed" and needs some relief. She goes to the nearest inn and finds a mysterious stranger who turns out to be Xena's greatest desire. Very well done.
http://ausxip.com/fanfic14/didyouknow.html

Divinity by Texbard (Linda Crist)
This is the sequel to Cleopatra 4AD. Xena and Gabrielle set sail for Lesbos where they spend time in relaxing and showing each other how much they love each other. It's written from Xena's point of view and I really enjoyed it.
http://ausxip.com/fanfic12/divinity.html

Do You Know by Lawlsfan

Tears welled up in my eyes after reading this. I'm not sure when I will get over that scene in Ides of March in the cell. I don't think there has been any other scene in the show that was as powerful. This story is from Gabrielle's point of view and it's tender, heart-rendering and just so moving. A Well written story.

http://www.ausxip.com/fanfiction/d/doyouknow.html

Echoes of the Battling Bard by Iseqween

This story takes place between the episodes When Fates Collide and Many Happy Returns. You have to read it very carefully because sometimes things are not as they seem. I enjoyed this a great deal.

http://ausxip.com/fanfic14/echoes_of_the_battling_bard.htm

Finding Peace by Murphy

This is a wonderful story set after the events of Ides of March where Gabrielle is feeling guilty about the men she has killed to save Xena. An old friend soon helps her realize a very important point.

http://www.academyofbards.org/fanfic/m/murphy_findingpeace.html

Foolish Notions by Kamouraskan

Set in the aftermath of Amphipolis Under Siege - Gabrielle gets the attention of the citizens of Amphipolis. A very moving short story and proves once again that although Gabrielle is now a warrior she can also be a bard and a support to her warrior.

http://ausxip.com/fanfiction/f/foolishnotions.html

Friend In Need - Part 3 by T. Novan

T. Novan finishes what Rob Tapert should have done (but didn't). This is how FIN should have ended. Gabrielle seeks to get Xena back and is willing to pay the ultimate price to do it, will Xena let her? This also features Xena and Gabrielle's descendants.

http://ausxip.com/tnovan/fin3.html

Gabrielle and Xena (Deceased) by Mark Annetts

I thoroughly enjoyed reading this Post FIN Fic story. It picks up from the time Gabrielle leaves Japa with Xena's ashes and takes them back home to Amphipolis. Armed with sacred scrolls and rituals to bring Xena back, it somehow doesn't happen the way she wanted and Xena is back on earth as a ghost. Enlisting the help of gods and former enemies is going to be tricky! Well written story.

http://ausxip.com/fanfic18/gabandxena1.html

Gift (The) by Lawlsfan

A hurt/comfort tale that brings back my favorite psycho - Callisto on Solstice Eve. A beautifully written story. Xena gets injured while looking for a gift for Gabrielle and Callisto goes a little mellow when she saves Xena's life as a gift to Gabrielle.

http://www.ausxip.com/fanfiction/g/thegift01.html

Gift of Family (The) by Susan A Rice

The story is set one year after FIN. Back to her family home, Gabrielle is alone and reminisces about the family she was born into and the family she had made with Xena. A visitor comes on Solstice eve with surprising results.

http://ausxip.com/fanfic18/gift_of_family.htm

Ghost of a Chance by DJWP

Wow, I absolutely LOVED this short story by one of my favorite bards. Xena and Gabrielle enter a deserted Castle on a stormy night. The only problem is, it's not deserted, and it's haunted. Gabrielle reaches out to this poor lost soul and Xena uses her own method to flush him out.

http://www.ausxip.com/fanfic12/GHOST.html

Happy Anniversary, Gabrielle & Happy Anniversary, Xena by LJ Maas

This is two stories by LJ Maas about Xena and Gabrielle wanting to give each other something special for their anniversary. Xena regrets not telling Gabrielle how she felt about her and she let Gabrielle slip away from her and marry Perdicus. Xena wants to be Gabrielle's first lover so she goes into the dreamscape to alter Gabrielle's memories. A very touching and well written short story. In Happy Anniversary, Xena, Gabrielle decides it's time to give her wife a special memory of her own and as usually happens when Gabrielle is involved, not everything goes according to plan.

Happy Anniversary, Gabrielle

http://ausxip.com/fanfic9/anniversary_gabrielle.html

Happy Anniversary, Xena

http://ausxip.com/fanfic9/anniversary_xena.html

Hardcore Nutcrackers by Nalysia

What a hoot this is. What if Xena and Gabrielle were really immortals. This short story cracked me up and I loved the pillow fight.

http://www.academyofbards.org/fanfic/n/nalysia_nutcrackers.html

Healer's Kiss (The) by Cath, Bard

The scenes in Ides of March in the cell stories have always made me tear up. It was one of the most difficult scenes I have witnessed on this show. This story takes place there and it shows how a love for a soulmate can be healing. Beautifully written. Highly recommended.

http://ausxip.com/fanfiction/h/healers_kiss.html

Hold Me By The Fire by T. Novan

This is a short story about the power of holding each other and what it means to both Xena and Gabrielle. Beautifully written and I expected nothing less from this talented bard. Beautiful.

http://ausxip.com/fanfic9/hold_me_by_the_fire.html

Holding On by Raine

Set just after the events of Motherhood, Xena and Gabrielle both feel like they are losing each other. It's a beautiful piece that I found very moving. I loved it. Raine crafts this short story quiet well. The proper ending to Motherhood.

http://ausxip.com/fanfic9/HoldingOn.html

Home Fires by Roo

This is a Mel and Janice story and it's set in Australia. This is a story about being true to who you are and what you feel. It's a very nicely written story.

http://ausxip.com/fanfiction/h/home_fires.html

Home From The Sea by Melissa Good

My favorite Uber couple return - Dar and Kerry - in this short Halloween story. Dar tells Kerry about the mansion that is near their condo. In true Missy fashion, this story is well written and thoroughly entertaining.

http://ausxip.com/fanfiction/mgood/dar-and-kerry/homefromthesea.html

How Thin The Veil by Bel-wah

Bel-wah is one of my favorite bards and she once again she delivers this stunning piece of work. We have a look into the mind of a Xena the warlord but with a twist. I won't ruin the story as it has a real twist at the end which I'm sure many won't expect. Another sterling performance by a bard who writes so beautifully.

http://ausxip.com/fanfiction/h/howthintheveil.html

I, Conqueror by SwordnQuil

Oh boy what a ride! I, Conqueror is a tale of Gabrielle waking up to find that she is not where she is supposed to be and her loving warrior is not the Xena she knows. She is faced with Xena, the Mighty Conqueror, with a heart that is black and merciless. SwordnQuil weaves a tale that has become one of my favorites. Sit back and enjoy a fantastic read from a very gifted bard.

http://www.ausxip.com/fanfiction/i/i_conqueror.html

The Joining by Kamouraskan

This is a Uber with a difference. Xena and Gabrielle are joined by their friends for their joining in the Amazon village. All their friends are there and two people that have a lot in common with the bard and her warrior. A very entertaining story mixed in with some time travel (I love those) and very good storytelling. A thoroughly good read.

http://www.ausxip.com/fanfiction/j/the_joining.html

Keystones in a Tapestry by Ambyrhawke Shadowsinger

This is set during the events of the Ides of March and the moments we didn't see during the episode and beyond it. It's beautifully written and I was rapt. A wonderful tale.

http://www.ausxip.com/fanfiction/k/keystones.html

Kindred Scrolls by Allan Plessinger

This is the missing scene from Kindred Spirits - I absolutely loved this. Xena finally realizes something about Gabrielle that she has been taking for granted. Excellent!

http://www.academyofbards.org/amazontrails/xena/kindredscrolls.htm

Legends Legacy - #13 - Cupid's Arrow by T. Novan

Every parent's worse nightmare - their child grows up and dates. What happens when Xena and Gabrielle's daughter, the new Queen of the Amazons, falls in love (with a little help from Cupid and a stray arrow)? A rollicking good story.

http://ausxip.com/fanfiction/ll/legends13.html

Little Gabrielle Learns to Read by Susan A. Rice

The characters are based on Lucia's Little Xena and Little Gabrielle comic strip. This story deals with Little Gabby learning how to read with the help of her older little warrior. Very cute.

http://ausxip.com/fanfiction/l/little_gabrielle_learns_to_read.html

Making Up by Jaden

This short story deals with events after Antony & Cleopatra - Gabrielle is giving Xena the silent treatment and Xena gets a little payback the Gabrielle way.

http://www.academyofbards.org/fanfic/j/jaden_makingup.html

The Marriage of Xena and Gabrielle by DJWP

This is a great tale for those romantics out there - Gabrielle is challenged for the Queenship of the Amazons but she can't have her champion unless she is her mate and well things are not what they seem when Xena asks Gabrielle to marry her. Ephiny is written so beautifully. A top read this one.

http://ausxip.com/fanfiction/m/marriage.html

Me, Myself and I by Annemaart

This is a riotous short story. We've seen Xena clones - Meg, Diana and Leah (Pwaise Hestia!) but we haven't seen THREE Warrior Princess all at once! Great read and an interesting story with Aphrodite doing her magic!

http://www.ausxip.com/fanfic14/me,_myself_and_i.htm

Mistress Of The Two Lands by L Fox

L. Fox has been one of my favorite writers and he has once again written another fantastic piece. Mistress of the Two Lands is set in Egypt thus combining my favorite duo and the land of mystery and Pharaohs. This story is so well written that I felt I was there watching instead of reading. Excellent stuff.

http://ausxip.com/fanfiction/m/mistress.html

Mother, May I Sleep with Thracians? A Musical Homage to Love, Redemption, and Gratuitous Violence"

I suggest you keep liquids away from the keyboard for this one. It's a FIN Parody and just so wickedly good.

http://ausxip.com/fanfiction/antonygirl/mothermay1.html

Motherhood Revisited, Again by Lena

Motherhood let a lot of people feeling like something wasn't said or resolved. Lena puts that right with this addition to the episode. Xena finally listens to Gabrielle about her feelings and her coldness during Xena's pregnancy.

http://ausxip.com/fanfic9/motherhoodrevist.html

My Cup of Tea by Deb

Xena and Gabrielle travel to a town that is full of musicians and talented people. Gabrielle has a plan - an inventive one to get Xena to admit her feelings for the bard.

http://ausxip.com/fanfic11/mycupoftea.html

My Dearest Friend by Rachel Hahn

Oh this is a tearjerker! Gabrielle is given a scroll by Eponin - the last letter

from Ephiny. Grab the tissues, get comfy and get set to get emotional.
http://www.ausxip.com/fanfic14/DearestFriend.html

Never by Grit Jahning

A short story set after the events of Friend In Need of a loving soulmate standing by her battling bard. Beautifully written.
http://www.ausxip.com/fanfic15/never.htm

Night Promise by Cath Bard

This is a very well written vignette of Gabrielle taking care of Eve. Set after the events of God Fearing Child. Very misty eyed after this tale.
http://www.ausxip.com/fanfic13/night_promise.htm

Nipple 1 to 5 by Archaeobard

This story just made me laugh and if not for anything else, it just deserves to be recognized as a good tonic! What can you say about a series that started off "innocently" enough. That crafty Gabrielle sure has a way about her.
Nipple I:
http://ausxip.com/fanfiction/n/nipple.html
Nipple II: The Re-Erection:
http://ausxip.com/fanfiction/n/nipple2.html
Nipple lll: Twin Peaks:
http://ausxip.com/fanfiction/n/nipple3.html
Nipple IV: Therein Lies the Nub:
http://ausxip.com/fanfiction/n/nipple4.html
Nipple V:
http://ausxip.com/fanfiction/n/nipple5.html

Origins by M. Parnell

Oh what an absolutely fantastic piece of fanfic this is - it's breathtaking in its storytelling. M. Parnell has woven a great story. This is a story about Xena finding her father and finding more than she bargained for, taking command and being the best leader she can be - but there are forces working against her, including the psychotic Callisto. This is a must-read. I can't praise it enough.
http://ausxip.com/fanfiction/o/origins.html

Raising Melosa Series (Complete Series) by T. Novan

There are 101 stories in this outstanding series. TN has created a whole new series within a series - if you can call it that. Raising Melosa is about Xena and Gabrielle who have decided to settle down with the Amazons

and Gabrielle has become their Queen. Melosa is their child - conceived in a most unusual way. This series is one of my favorites.
http://www.ausxip.com/fanfiction/rm/index.html

Remember, Never To Forget by Sinful

This new bard's first story is one that I found interesting and addictive. Her depictions of our favorite duo was so well written. Where have you been hiding, Sinful?! This is the story of Xena and Gabrielle going to the Amazon village, Xena then goes and gets herself captured. Her courage and her love for Gabrielle gives her the will to survive. It's a true epic - sit in your comfy chair and be prepared to be engrossed in a tale you won't want to set aside until finished. Excellent story.
http://ausxip.com/fanfiction/r/remembernever1.html

The Return of the Warrior by Lena

This is the fourth story in the series "Ares Gift" that follows Xena, Gabrielle and their daughter Arielle. In this story Xena protects her family. A hurt/comfort tale which is very well written.
http://ausxip.com/fanfiction/r/returnofthewarrior.html

Reunions by Sinful

What can I say about a story that blew me away...well, it blew me away. Sinful written a well-crafted story of what A Family Affair SHOULD have been. It's brilliant. We see the return of Hope and her offspring and deal with the Amazons and their anger towards Xena. A wonderful story.
http://ausxip.com/fanfiction/r/reunions1.html

Rising Sun by Erin Jennifer

Rising Sun is set after the events of Friend In Need - Part 1 and takes over the telling of Friend In Need Part 2 (the way it should have been done). It's a very moving storyline that gave me a great deal of satisfaction.
http://ausxip.com/fanfic15/rising_sun.htm

Saving Grace by FlyBigD

This is the second story in the "Plan D" series. Xena is attending University to be with Gabrielle and is called away in an emergency at the hospital. She never gets there. It's a story of Gabrielle's love for Xena and never giving up hope. A very touching story that will bring a smile to your face by the end of it.
http://ausxip.com/fanfiction/s/savinggrace.html

Soul Searching by T. Novan & Advocate

If you read only one Conqueror story this year - this has to be it. It's one of the best that I've seen deal with the ruler of the Known World. Xena, the Conqueror, is tired and goes out of her palace in search for some peace and quiet. She finds it in a small town of Potidaea where an innkeeper and a young boy capture her heart. I can't say it often enough, it's a fantastic read and well worth the time to read this long story. You won't be disappointed.

http://ausxip.com/fanfic12/soulsearching.html

The Stalker by Kelly Noble

This story is set after the events of Them Bones Them Bones. Someone is out to hurt Gabrielle and friends are not what they seem and an old foe returns. This is a very sensual piece and the love that the warrior has for her bard shines right through—an excellent story.

https://www.ausxip.com/fanfiction/s/stalker.html

Stitch in Time (A) by T. Novan

I don't think I have read anything like this before. Gabrielle goes to the future to change the past and alter events. It's a thought-provoking short story and VERY well written. I expect nothing less from T. Novan. He always comes up with innovative stories and this is one of them.

http://ausxip.com/tnovan/a_stitch_in_time.htm

Subtext Virtual Season Seven: Been A Wonderful Life by T. Novan

Every Xena and Gabrielle fan wonders what would have happened to them if they hadn't met each other. We had a glimpse of that in the episode Remember Nothing and the glimpse wasn't all that flash. This episode takes it another step forward - as they both wonder what life would have been like if they didn't have each other. They get a little help in seeing what it was like from a very old friend.

http://svs.ausxip.com/season7/en_s7e12/s7-e12-teaser.htm

Subtext Virtual Season Seven: Divided We Fall by Susanne Beck

Xena and Gabrielle investigate an abandoned temple that has very serious consequences for them both. I enjoyed this episode a great deal as it deals with a part of Xena that usually is just under the surface. This time it has resurfaced and no one is safe - not even Gabrielle.

http://svs.ausxip.com/season7/en_s7e07/s7-e07-teaser.htm

Subtext Virtual Season Seven: It's All in the Mind by T. Novan

I absolutely adore fanfic that makes me laugh out loud - it's a balm to the soul. This episode of the Virtual Subtext Season 7 is one of those that did make me feel good. Gabrielle wishes to know what goes on the head of a certain Warrior Princess (don't we all). She gets more than she bargained for. TN also throws in a couple of squirrels that I just found SO cute (yes, I admit I'm a squirrel nut - heh). A great story.

http://svs.ausxip.com/season7/en_s7e04/s7-e04-teaser.htm

Subtext Virtual Season Seven: Roman Holiday by Melissa Good

The subtext virtual season has picked up from where Season 6 ended with our heroes either dead or alone. Roman Holiday is the 14th episode and is a real stunner. Xena and Gabrielle have to go back to Rome to rescue a friend despite their feelings for the place. It's an excellent piece of writing and one that I would have loved to have seen on the screen.

http://svs.ausxip.com/season7/en_s7e14/s7-e14-teaser.htm

Teach Me Everything You Know by Lawlsfan

This is a real tear-jerker - it's the story of letting go and how one warrior outlives her soulmate and Queen of the Amazons. Very moving. Have a tissue or two handy.

http://www.ausxip.com/fanfiction/t/teachmeeverything.html

Tears and Diamonds: Goodbye to Love by Cath, Bard

This is just so moving. Gabrielle visits Aphrodite's temple before the Twilight begins. An extraordinary friendship exists between bard and the goddess of love.

http://www.ausxip.com/fanfic13/tearsanddiamonds.html

The Queen of My Heart by LJ Maas

This is the fourth story in the Queen series and it continues in the same excellent way that the other three have. It's up to Xena to stop Hera and get an elixir to save the Amazons while the rest of the gods are helpless to help. Has a very interesting twist at the end. Excellent storytelling.

http://www.ausxip.com/fanfic10/MyHeart.html

To Rest by Brigit M Morgan

Set long after the events of FIN, Gabrielle goes back to Amphipolis to keep a promise she made to Xena so many years before. The life of a warrior with a broken heart. It's a sad story but very well written.

http://www.ausxip.com/fanfic22/to_rest.htm

To Walk The Path of a Queen by LJ Maas

The Path of a Queen is the fifth installment in the Queen series and is the sequel to The Queen of My Heart. Xena and Gabrielle are with the Amazons. Gabrielle is Queen of the Amazons and pregnant with their first child. It's a very poignant tale that will tug at your heartstrings. Beautifully written story.

http://ausxip.com/fanfic12/queenpath.html

Towards Our Distant Rest by Zuke

This is very a different story but it goes back to what Gabrielle is best at. She is a warrior but she is also a gentle soul who has always wanted to help people. Towards Our Distant Rest showcases this side of Gabrielle and it's a beautiful story. Gabrielle helps a slain soldier reach his ultimate goal. An excellent story.

http://ausxip.com/fanfic22/towards_our_distant_rest.htm

Visiting Hours by Ella Quince

This story will make you smile. Ella weaves a tale of a Warrior Princess very much in trouble in a prison with only a few hours to go before she is executed. Gabrielle needs to get her out of there quick and well all Xena needs is a little motivation to get moving!

http://ausxip.com/fanfiction/v/visit.html

Walls and Hurdles by Kamouraskan

This is set just before the episode Looking Death in the Eye. Xena and Gabrielle have a few issues to discuss - something that has been missing in their lives since India. A nicely written story that has some humor and a great deal of drama. Excellent writing by this very talented bard. I also absolutely howled at the end with Eve but you have to read it to find out what it is!

http://ausxip.com/fanfic9/walls_and_hurdles.html

What You Can't See...by T. Novan

Xena is invisible and that causes all sorts of problems for the Warrior Princess, Gabrielle and Autolycus. Who did it and why? What will cure it? Three little words are needed. A very amusing short story..

http://ausxip.com/fanfic11/what_you_cant_see.html

When The Time Comes by Rose Corsaro

I absolutely LOVED this short story- just loved it. It's a story of a dream and the realization that good things will happen to the bard and her warrior. This is such a beautifully written story that will make you smile.

http://ausxip.com/fanfiction/corsaro/when_the_time_comes.htm

Wish Upon a Star by Murphy

This is a delightful short story into Gabrielle's thoughts as she records them in her journal. Beautifully written.

http://ausxip.com/fanfic11/wishuponastar.html

What are Little Girls Made Of? by DJWP

This story is priceless. Gives another meaning to Little Xena. Xena and Gabrielle are off on another adventure when a mad alchemist has plans for Xena. This leads to Gabrielle trying to find a way to make Xena her normal self. Very well written.

http://ausxip.com/fanfiction/w/whatare.html

What Mom Doesn't Know Won't Kill Her by FlyBigD

This is a very funny short story on what happens when the bard wants to get amorous and the Warrior Princess just doesn't want to "do it" with her mother around.

http://www.ausxip.com/fanfic13/what_mom.html

What Stories Are For by Iseqween

This is a moving short story based on Xena's death but done in such a way that it wasn't gruesome but in the arms of Gabrielle. Beautifully written.

http://ausxip.com//fanfic22/whatstoriesarefor.html

Who's Child by Kamouraskan

This is a delightful piece that deals with Xena and Gabrielle's daughter. It's sweet and very loving. The opening paragraphs made me laugh as many a parent would recognize.

http://ausxip.com/fanfiction/w/whochild.html

You've Got Scrolls by Advocate, Fanatic & T. Novan

What can I say to this? It has to be the funniest parody I've ever read. Gabrielle joins a secret Literary list (she can't say the name of it to anyone - it's a secret) where only Amazons or Amazon-like women can join. It's a total riot and I laughed myself silly. This is for anyone who has been on a mailing list - it's a hoot!

http://ausxip.com/fanfic12/scrolls.html

UBER

A Feast of All Souls by Joseph Connell

Redhawk created the genre of Xena - the immortal - and this installment of the series is one of the best and one of my favorite series. It picks up where Redhawk

left off - Xena coming back to Gabrielle after Callisto (still a God) kills the immortal Xena. Xena finds a way to return after many centuries. Yet, without a memory of her former life - this story reveals what happens. There is also an extreme danger to Gabrielle, who herself is an immortal and a Bacchae!
http://ausxip.com/fanfiction/a/afeast.html

The Agent by C. Paradee
C Paradee has written one of the best Uber stories in the Xenaverse with this tale. It's the story of Tony Viglioni an FBI undercover operative who wants out and wants to be an average FBI agent. She gets sent to help solve a series of murders - a murderer who doesn't leave any clues. There she meets Megan Donnovan and her priorities change dramatically as they search for the serial killer. An exciting read and well written.
http://ausxip.com/fanfiction/a/agent-cparadee.html

Alias Smith & Jones by Advocate & T. Novan
Once I stopped laughing so hard I had tears running down my cheeks, I decided to give this an award. It's one of the hysterical stories I have ever read. Delilah Foster & Dixie Wagner follow the great tradition of those tv preachers who swindle money from good Christian people. What they don't bank on is a visit from 'God' and his mama. They are soon turned from their bad ways and want to give away the money but it's not so easy.
http://www.ausxip.com/fanfic20/alias_smith_and_jones.htm

A Valiant Heart by D
This is the story of Randi Valiant (a marine) and Gwen (a storyteller). The story takes us through their lives as Randi goes off to war and Gwen wonders what might have been had she been honest about her feelings for the tall, dark-haired woman. Saying any more will spoil the story so sit back and enjoy a thoroughly well-written story.
http://ausxip.com/fanfic15/A%20Valiant%20Heart1.htm

The Battle by Wishes
The Battle is a kind of different story. Set in the future where people can be imprisoned for writing about the government (or maybe not in the future...). It's very dark and it's not for everyone. It is the story of Caroline who is a young technician who cares for the prisoners sent to a Medical facility. Elizabeth is her patient who undergoes genetic testing...to breed a better and stronger human. Wishes has given us a glimpse into a future world. An excellent read.
http://ausxip.com/fanfiction/b/battle.html

Before The Dawn of Time by BladeMast (aka Sword'n'Quill)
Okay I think this must be the first Uber in the whole wide universe. Puts another meaning to going BOOM. It's a delightful piece that had me just grinning.
http://ausxip.com/fanfiction/b/beforethedawn.html

Bloodlust by Protek
Set in the Series created by Redhawk. Xena is an immortal and Rickie is the reincarnated Gabrielle. This particular tale involves Xena's meeting with Vlad The Impaler of Count Dracula fame. If you love the Immortal Xena series then you will love this one!
http://www.academyofbards.org/redhawk_infinity/infinity/blood/lust1.htm

Blood Red Scream by Tragedy88
This story gripped me from the start with the story of two very unlikely people meeting, falling in love and discovering that danger lurks for both of them. Very well written.
http://www.ausxip.com/fanfiction/b/bloodredscream1.html

The Burning Candle by AH-Ladis
I absolutely adored this story. AH-Ladis has written a beautifully told story. It deals with Xena and Gabrielle in the land of Babylon. I don't want to give too much away but Xena is a child in a grown up body - the tender compassion and love that Gabrielle shows this child is so precious. They are captured and are to be sold as slaves and this is where their adventure begins.
http://ausxip.com/fanfiction/b/burningcandle.html

Burning Time by Sandakat
This is a tale of two old souls reuniting...it's a beautifully written story that got me involved and I couldn't put it down until I finished it. It's the story of Dr Rene Covington and Firefighter Dina Pakadios who ignite their own fire when they meet. As I said above a beautifully written story.
http://ausxip.com/fanfiction/b/burningtime.html

Chicago 5 AM by LN James
This piece of fanfic is intriguing and very well written. It's the story of an FBI agent and a private detective who team up to stop a slave market ring. I don't want to give too much away. It does contains scenes of drug taking and bondage but it doesn't dwell on these for very long. The main story deals with the relationship and how these two people meet and how it affects their lives.
http://ausxip.com/fanfiction/c/chicago1.html

Cold War by L. Fox

Set during the dark days of the cold war between the US and Russia this is a story of a young woman, Rachel Clark, is accused of being a spy. She is kidnapped and meets her Russian interrogator, Valenta Alekseyev, a woman efficient in her job and considered the best. Well written story and I want more!

http://ausxip.com/fanfiction/c/coldwar1.html

The Coward by Mark Annetts

Terry Farmer is a private investigator living alone and liking it until she meets Nikkoletta Takis, the daughter of shipping tycoon. Hired as her private bodyguard despite her misgivings, Farmer begins the long journey of falling in love and trying to protect Nikki in the process. A few surprises are in store for the tall, dark haired investigator on this journey. An Excellent read.

http://ausxip.com/fanfic18/coward.htm

Crimson Snow by Advocate

This is the sequel to Connections which first introduced Gumby (aka Claire) and Mandy (Amanda). Claire is a successful lawyer and Amanda is a psychologist. A normal vacation for these two is ruining by an ex client of Amanda's and then all hell breaks loose. A very well written story with characters that grow.

http://ausxip.com/fanfiction/c/crimson_snow.html

Dead Fall by Anne Azel

We were first introduced to Alberta in the Seasons series Spring Rains by Anne and I was sold on the character even if she did something that worried me! You have to read Spring Rains to see the first time we meet Alberta. Alberta goes back home and lands in an investigation of a crime that goes back a few years. It's a very good story with a flawed hero.

http://ausxip.com/fanfiction/d/deadfall.html

Dead Funny by Anne Azel

LOVE THIS! Anne brings back my favorite forensic pathologist Dr Alberta "Aliki" Patea with this very interesting story about a serial killer who targets tall, dark haired women. Alberta is reunited with Dawn and Mac and they make a decision about their future. Added to the mix is my other favorite Anne Azel couple, Robbie and Janet Williams with as surprise addition to Robbie's family. Excellent storytelling.

http://ausxip.com/fanfic9/deadfunny.html

The Deal by M. Ryan

I'm always fascinated how a bard can weave a story and snare you from the word go...well M. Ryan has done that and more. This is the story of Laura

"Kaz" Kazdan and Christine Hanson. These two meet and things literally explode. Where Chris is trouble surely follows as Kaz finds out. It's also a first time story which is rather sweet. It's not finished yet but if you want a good read and don't mind the wait...go for it! Highly recommended.
http://ausxip.com/fanfiction/d/deal1.html

English Encounters - The Final Story by Anne Azel
English Encounters is the final story in the Encounters Series. It brings together two couples, Gunnel and Jamie and Robbie and Janet to where the rift all started - Britannia. It's a very interesting and thoroughly engrossing story. A few twists and turns are added to the mix and you get one heck of a good read.
http://ausxip.com/fanfic10/ee1.html

Exposure by XWPFanatic, T Muir & T. Novan
This is a continuing series based on a look behind the scenes of news team. Two people come together - it's hate at first sight. Kelsey is a successful anchor woman ready for big things in the new biz and Harper is a hot shot, Harley driving, reporter with a lot of flair! Mix them together and you have one of the best teams since Xena and Gabrielle. I enjoyed this series from the first episode.
http://ausxip.com/exposure/episodes/episode1.html

Fields of Gray by Redcat
Fields of Gray is a poignant story sure to bring a tear to your eye. It's the story of Morgan and Piper and the love that binds these two women together as they face the ultimate test. A very moving piece by Redcat.
http://ausxip.com//fanfiction/redcat/fieldsofgrey.html

Flashpoint by ArdentTly
Flashpoint is the third story dealing with the firefighter Zeen Phipolis and her partner Abby Dean. This story is dark - it's about Zeen's loss of control after she is caught in a chemical fire and the struggles she goes through. Very moving.
http://ausxip.com/fanfiction/f/flashpoint.html

Forces of Evil by TrishK
This is a story from a new bard that has been hiding her talents. Two women meet in a sleepy little town. One is an ROTC Commander and the other a waitress. All is not what it seems. It's a riveting tale set against the backdrop of a sleepy little town where unbeknownst to the residents, a sinister plan is afoot! A very well written story that promises a lot and delivers. DO NOT MISS!
http://ausxip.com/fanfiction/f/foe1.html

Forgotten Way by Tragedy88

This is a really interesting story. The Uber Gabrielle lives on a farm, with two horses and no one else in a very bigoted town. Uber Xena is the loner who passes through town, where a set of circumstances gets Dusty (Uber X) to come to the farm. An interesting look at small town mentality and bigotry with an added twist of the farmhouse having it's own story to tell.
http://www.ausxip.com/fanfiction/f/forgotten_way.html

The Gravesbury Murders by Archeobard & Lariel

Do not have any liquids near your computer when you read this. This has to be one of the funniest stories I've read in a long time. Weeny Xena and her friend Amelia - who is a slightly obsessed Xena fan go on a murderous rampage all in the name of Xena Freedom! You just have to read this hilarious story written by two of the funniest bards I've ever met.
http://ausxip.com/fanfic9/gravesbury_murders.html

Gun Shy by Lorelei

Lori has woven a story that gripped from me the moment I read it. It's the story of a Police Officer who goes to the rescue of a rape victim and makes a huge impression on the victim's friend - enough for her to enlist in the police force herself! We follow the lives of Desiree "Dez" Reilly - the big copy with a heart of gold, a loner until she meets Jaylynn Savage.
http://ausxip.com/fanfiction/g/gunshy1.html

I Can't Do This Alone by Kamouraskan

A young woman loses all hope when her mate dies. Carrying their child she thinks of ending her life until an accident occurs and she is reunited with her love and is fortified for what is to come when she wakes. A very moving story.
http://ausxip.com/fanfiction/c/cantdothis.html

I Found My Heart in San Francisco - Book 1: Awakenings
by SX Meagher

This is a wonderful tale of two people who are totally opposite - both in upbringing and orientation coming together and developing a deep friendship that turns to love. It's the first book in a 'alphabet' series about the lives of Ryan O'Flaherty and Jamie Evans. An excellent read.
http://ausxip.com/fanfic9/foundmyheart1.html

I Found My Heart in San Francisco - Book 2: Beginnings
by SX Meagher

Book Two continues the story of Ryan O'Flaherty and Jamie Evans. The story picks up where Book 1 left off. Ryan and Jamie are training for the

AIDS bike ride and having to deal with their newly admitted love for each other. A very well paced novel, An excellent followed up to Book 1.
http://ausxip.com/fanfic9/book2a.html

I Found My Heart in San Francisco - Book 3: Disclosures by SX Meagher

Book 3 continues the story of Ryan O'Flaherty and Jamie Evans. Now committed to each other, they move into Jamie's house but problems await them when Ryan finds it hard to leave home and family. Jaime decides to tell her parents about their relationship which has some very interesting results. A great follow up. Get comfortable this is another long read.
http://ausxip.com/fanfic11/disclosures1.html

I Found My Heart in San Francisco Series Book 12: Lifeline by SX Meagher

This is an incredible sequel to the 11th book by Susan. Ryan and Jamie. In Book 11: Karma, Jamie and Ryan are involved in a car jacking that has terrifying results. Lifeline picks up from that and deals with the effects of the car jacking has on Jamie and in particular Ryan.
http://ausxip.com/fanfic17/lifeline.html

It's All In Your Point of View (#1 in the Perspectives Series) by Minerva

This is the first story in the Perspectives series about Cory Donovan and Taylor Wilson who work together. Taylor is Cory's new boss and the series starts off with their first meeting and getting to know other. Minerva does a very good job of making giving these characters some depth which I really enjoyed and led me to reading the next parts of the series. Excellent writing.
http://ausxip.com/fanfic9/yourpointofview.html

I Will Always Love You by Marcella Wiggins

This is the story of two women - one an FBI agent whose job is to protect the CEO of a major hospital from a stalker. Marcella has written a tale that had me captivated and on the edge of my laptop, wondering what was going on. Very well written and the ending has a nice little twist.
http://ausxip.com/fanfiction/i/iwillalwayslove.html

Last Night by Lariel

This had me crying at the end of it. Emily and Charlotte are two people who love each a great deal and it's a story of love reaching out. I don't want to spoil it by saying anymore. Have a tissue ready at the end.
http://www.ausxip.com/fanfiction/l/last_night.html

Light Fantastic (The) by LA Tucker

This is so well written and an interesting story. The characters are well developed. The author blends in the dramatic with a great comedic element that I found myself enjoying this story a great deal. It's a uber set in a small town. Chloe is a wonderfully written character with a quirkiness that I totally loved. Sara is the brooding, hurt actress that needs to trust. An excellent story.

http://www.ausxip.com/fanfic21/tlf1.html

London Blitz by Joseph Connell

This story continues the story of Xena who is an immortal (in the Highlander fashion) and Rickie (the reincarnated Gabrielle). Xena and Rickie travel to London unaware until it's too late that there people watching them and waiting to kill Xena. Descendants of a very close friend of Xena's when she was roaming the high seas of Greece play a prominent role. A very good story. EXCELLENT.

http://ausxip.com/fanfiction/l/london_blitz.html

Lost Soul Walking by DJWP

This is such a tear jerker that I couldn't stop myself from tearing up after reading it. Two souls destined to be together forever meet one another. Very moving. Excellent read. Have some tissues handy.

http://ausxip.com/fanfiction/l/lostsoulwalking.html

Love's Rendition by Tragedy88

This is an absolutely captivating story about a rich gallery owner and a struggling artist who meet and their lives are forever changes.

http://ausxip.com/fanfiction/l/loves_rendition1-9.html

Lucifer Rising by S. Bowers

My first Uber story and I was hooked. What a revelation it turned out to be. This story is packed with adventure, intrigue, love that knows no bounds and a good dose of mystery thrown in. This is the story of Jude Lucien, an ex DEA agent and Liz Gardener a nosey reporter.

http://ausxip.com/fanfiction/l/lucifer.html

Make A Wish by AH-Ladis

I had tears in my eyes reading this story - it was so emotional. Its a story about loss and recovery and the lengths a love will go in order to achieve what they set out to do. It's also a Uber and how a dying young woman helps a warrior who is hurting very deeply. Beautifully written and it packs a punch. Excellent work.

http://ausxip.com/fanfiction/m/makeawish.html

Meridio's Daughter by LJ Maas

Set on the island of Mykonos, Greece this is a tale of two very different people, one the only child of a wealthy Greek who is seeped in crime and the other is the boss' second in command. A very well written story.

http://www.ausxip.com/fanfiction/m/Meridio.html

My Protector by JC Wilder

It's very good to see this story back on the web. It's the story of Empress Sarika who must choose a mate and the dashing and beautiful Major Ramsay who is out of her time when she crash lands on earth thousands of years in the future! It had me riveted and it's a very good spin. I really enjoyed reading this story.

http://www.altfic.com/subtextfic/Xena/wilder/my_protector1.htm

Night and Day by JuneBug

This story is set in Sydney, Australia (yeay my home town) and it's set in a hospital. Two greats things going for it already! Junebug has written a beautifully crafted tale of two people set in the backdrop of a major Sydney hospital. I feel for these characters and I really enjoyed the characterizations. Go and have a read - I'm sure you will enjoy it as much as I did.

http://ausxip.com/fanfiction/n/nightandday1.html

None so Blind by LJ Maas

What an absolutely wonderful read! This is the story of Torrey and Taylor (or T'n'T..that gave me a chuckle) -- a story spanning 15 years! Its true when they say love is blind! The story goes back and forth which is most unusual but very entertaining.

https://www.ausxip.com/fanfiction/b/blind.html

Only One by Redhawk

I was overjoyed on reading this story. Xena is an immortal - in the grand tradition of Highlander. Being an immortal can be rather tiresome when you don't have your soulmate to be with you and Xena goes through the millennia without Gabrielle - who promised to come back to her - and she does in the form of Rickie - a street kid who witnesses the immortal in action! Highly recommended.

http://ausxip.com/fanficton/o/one1.html

Palomino Heart by FlyBigD

This is the latest installment of the Grace/Faith series. Gabrielle gives Xena a chance to rebuild her mighty Palomino Heart - her bike that was scrunched in Saving Grace. EXCELLENT sequel.

http://ausxip.com/fanfiction/p/palomino_heart.html

The Pappas Journals Part 1 and 2 by Elaine Sutherland

This story is not for everyone. It deals with Nazi Germany and the concentration camps. We near the end of the 20th century and we have witnessed (and in my case) read about the brutality of the concentration camps during WW2. Few people could witness the films from these camps and not be moved with the sheer animalistic brutality of the Nazis. Elaine takes us into the world of WW2 and for Melinda Pappas a close up view of the concentration camp. This story is so well written I felt like I was there. Be warned: Part 2 of The Pappas Journals may upset people but it's a must read.

Part 1: http://ausxip.com/fanfiction/p/pappas.html
Part 2: http://ausxip.com/fanfiction/p/pappas1.html

Redemption by Susanne Beck

This story is about two women - both in a place that heroes don't usually hear heroes come from - prison. We journey into their lives through the eyes of Angel. This story is full of the joy of love found in a place that is cold and harsh. Sue has weaved a story that captures you from the first paragraph and you want to know more about. I cannot recommend it highly enough.

http://ausxip.com/fanfiction/r/redemption.html

Retribution by Suzanne Beck (Sword'n'Quill)

Retribution is the sequel to one of my all time favorite Ubers, Redemption. It's the continuing story of Ice and Angel. It's set in the Canada where the pair have gone to avoid Ice's recapture. It's an extraordinary story written by a very talented bard. I thoroughly recommend it.

http://ausxip.com/fanfic9/retribution1.html

Resa by Journs

Wow! What an adventure this story turns out to be - starts off quietly until the events in the life of Resa turn everything upside down and inside out for the young college student Jennifer. She sets out to write a novel in order to graduate but gets more than she thought she would when she is invited to write the story of Resa - the ex leader of a gang with more troubles that she can handle!

http://ausxip.com/fanfiction/r/resa.html

Second Soul by Revan

Revan explores the idea of the soulmate in this tale about two doctors. The story goes into the idea what a soulmate is and whether we have the same soulmate at a certain age.

http://ausxip.com/fanfiction/s/secondsoul.html

Shadows of the Soul by Melissa Good

A Conqueror fanfic piece by Melissa Good...I never thought it was possible but there you go. I must say this is absolutely fantastic and leaves you wanting more from one of the best bards in the Xenaverse. The Conqueror of Missy's story is a bloodthirsty tyrant ruling over her conquered lands. Add a general who wants more than to lead her armies and see a closer inspection of her bedchamber, aides who conspire against her, slaves who riot and of course one slave in particular - the young Gabrielle whose heart is pure. Her loyalty to Xena is a turning point in the Conqueror's life. Excellent writing by one of my favorite bards.

http://www.ausxip.com/fanfic19/shadow1.html

Shattered Innocence by Tragedy88

Wonderful story that I found absolutely fascinating. It's a Uber story but with Uber Xena being an 18 year old in high school and Uber Gabrielle a few years younger. It's an excellent story.

http://www.ausxip.com/fanfiction/s/shattered_innocence.html

Somewhere in Time by Friction

What an absolute wonderful story - I've always liked time travel stories and this one has elements of this and elements of a good Xena and Gabrielle adventure. A thoroughly good read. Excellent storytelling.

http://ausxip.com/fanfiction/s/some1.html

Spring Rains by Anne Azel

This is the third in the Seasons series by Anne Azel and it's a very moving story. Robbie is arrested for the murder of her father whilst Janet has to deal with other issues that will may affect her relationship with Robbie. Sure to provide readers of the Seasons series with plenty to talk about.

http://ausxip.com/fanfiction/s/springrains.html

Storm Front by Bel-wah

The return of Captain Catherine Phillips and Rebecca Hanson sees them embroiled in international terrorism as an Orbis plane is bombed. Had me on the edge of my keyboard and I just barely prevented myself from going to the last section to see how it all ended! A thoroughly good read.

http://ausxip.com/fanfiction/s/storm_front.html

Stranger in the Your Eyes (The) by SwordnQuill

This is one of my favorite all time stories. I'm surprised I didn't give this a XIPPY a long time ago. My mistake. Xena is an immortal living a life

without her soulmate until one day she is protecting a young woman from the Mafia. A young woman that looks a lot like her Gabrielle. Awesome story. A very good read by one of my favorite authors.
http://ausxip.com/fanfiction/s/stranger1.html

Summer Heat by Anne Azel
Anne ends the Seasons series with this story and it's one of my favorites! Robbie & Janet Williams are back as well as Reb & Ryan and their dog Rufus. Someone is out to destroy Robbie's life. We also see the return of Alberta. The story has a nice little twist at the end which really surprised me. A very good read.
http://ausxip.com/fanfiction/s/summerheat1.html

Take Time Out by RJ
Take Time Out is the story of Jess, a basketball coach and Robin a teacher at the same University. Jess is worried what others think of her which prevents her from letting the woman that she loves get close.
http://ausxip.com/fanfiction/t/tt01.html

Take Two Tablets and Call Me in the Morning by L. Fox
This is a story set in Larissa, Greece. Janice goes in search of a kidnapped Mel and meet Zoe Lambros and Eva Haralambos. They help in trying to find Mel! (Eva and Zoe are my own characters and it's strange not having written them myself!) It's an interesting mix and very well written.
http://ausxip.com/fanfic11/tablets1.html

The Pocket Watch by Cheyne Curry
We all know the events of 9/11 and the devastating effect it had on thousands of lives. The Pocket Watch is one of the most moving pieces of fiction I have read in a long time. It tells the story of a courageous firefighter and the woman she believes may have died in the attacks on the World Trade Center. Beautifully written.
http://www.ausxip.com/fanfiction/cheyne/thepocketwatch.html

The Truth and Nothing But The Truth - Part 5
This is a series that has tickled my funny bone. What if Xena and Gabrielle existed and are immortal - and they work on the show called...Xena: Warrior Princess helping Lucy and Renée with their roles! This part deals with the final episodes of Season 5 so if you want to remain spoiler free - be warned.
http://ausxip.com/fanfiction/t/thetruthandnothingbut5.html

The Truth and Nothing But The Truth - Part 6

Xena goes online and taunts the Net forum - you know this is too funny. With the recent troll problem on the net forum with fruit loops running around, the Xenaverse really needs Xena. TN once again delivers a great addition to this series.

http://www.ausxip.com/fanfic12/thetruthandnothingbut6.html

Tropical Storm by Melissa Good

Missy has created two characters that are so believable that it's easy to forget they don't exist but in the mind of this talented writer. Paladar Roberts and Kerrison Stuart are two ordinary people in Miami, Florida who meet and although the path is rocky at first - it soon becomes apparent that Kerry Stuart has won the heart of this corporate shark!

http://www.ausxip.com/fanfiction/t/tropical1.html

True Colors by Karen Surtees & Pruferblue

This is such a great story! True Colors deals with a powerful CEO of a major corporation who returns to a small town to rebuild herself and in the end rebuilds the town as well. The Uber characters are very well written and handled with so much care. The Uber Xena was injured and is now a paraplegic and the Uber Gabrielle character is the local vet.

http://ausxip.com/fanfiction/t/truecolours.html

The Truth and Nothing But (Truth Series) by T. Novan

What would happen if Xena and Gabrielle really did/do exist? they would work on the show of course! This is a hilarious look at what might be. A very funny series.

http://ausxip.com/fanfiction/t/truthnothing.html

Truth Is Stranger Than Fiction by FlyBigD

This installment in the Plan D series is very timely. It deals with drink driving and how Grace tries to save the lives of 37 children whose bus was hit by a drunk driver. Drink driving is a crime and bloody stupid. I wish everyone who has ever been involved in something like this had a T around to convince them to stay around. A very well written addition to the Plan D series.

http://ausxip.com/fanfic9/truthisstranger.html

Untitled: The Story of Me by Advocate

This has to be one of the funniest stories I have read - it has a "straight" ex driving instructor, a very gay nurse out for revenge and two talking squirrels! LOL! This

is a truly great piece of work from a very talented writer. Simply wonderful.
http://ausxip.com/fanfiction/u/untitled1.html

White Trash Series by Vivian Darkbloom
This has to be one of the funniest series I have read. Had me laughing so hard. So far there are four stories in this series. This is the story of Zina a reformed petty criminal who is now a firefighter living in Chakram Creek and Gabrielle her lover. Gabrielle's boyfriend Purdy is settled with her sister Lilla and it gets crazier after that!
Love and Death in the Trailer Park
http://www.ausxip.com/fanfiction/l/loveanddeath.html
Ways To Be Wicked
http://www.ausxip.com/fanfiction/w/waystobewicked.html
Mayonnaise and it's Discontents
http://ausxip.com/fanfiction/m/mayonnaise.html
I've Been to Pocatello But I've Never Been to Me
http://www.ausxip.com/fanfiction/i/ivebeen.html

The XO by C. Paradee
A story about a soldier and a new officer trying to deal with their increasing attraction to each other despite the military being against it. This is an EXCELLENT story and one you don't want to miss.
http://ausxip.com/fanfic11/xo1.html

I hope you all enjoyed my reviews. Looking back on those, I am going to go re-read all of the great fanfic these bards had produced. Thank you to all the bards who shared their work with us over the last twenty-five years! Check out more quality fanfic on http://ausxip.com/fanfic.php

AUSXIP The Bard's Corner is now hosting audio fanfic by the Virgin Podcasters (Xenites who are producing audio versions of the fanfic we love). http://ausxip.com/fanfiction/audio/virginpodcasters

You can find more fantastic fan fiction on the following sites:

Lunacy Reviews: lunacyreviews.com

The Royal Academy of Bards: www.academyofbards.org/

Tom's Xena Page Fan Fiction: xenafan.com

The Athenaeum: xenafiction.net

The Pink Rabbit Consortium: www.altfic.com/subtextfic/rlxena.htm

Chapter Twenty-One

A Passion for Xena Fan Fiction

by Jay Tuma

IN 2012, I WAS LOOKING for groups on Facebook to try to find some more *Xena* fans to interact with. I had been offline for a couple years dealing with health issues. I found some groups, but none of them mentioned or dealt with fan fiction. As a reader of fan fiction, I wanted to talk about it and reread some of the older stuff I had enjoyed.

I decided to start a *Xena* fan fiction group and share links to the stories I liked and remembered. It started as an open group; anyone could see it, and anyone could see the posts. I promoted it in the *Xena* groups I was in at the time. I added people I knew and anyone that wanted to join. Back then, it was common practice to just add whoever wanted to join a group, though that has obviously changed.

I quickly found out that it was a bad idea. I ended up playing referee more than reading fan fiction, so I culled membership, and I made the group a closed one. I had to approve all members. I started checking the timelines of people that requested to join for signs of hate or prejudice against the LGBTQA+ community and spam accounts. Now they have questions to help weed out trouble makers or spam. Still, I am careful about adding people.

This group has been a safe place to discuss fan fiction, but also different aspects of the show. We have quizzes and giveaways, trivia contests, tons of fan art, and my occasional gushing about Renée O'Connor. People can post a request for cop stories or Amazon stories or westerns. They can also post something like, "I'm looking for the story that has an airplane crash" and get the answer from someone in the group. I get this type of private message regularly, and if I can't answer, we put it in the group for brainstorming. There are also frequent conversations about writing, canon information, and opinion discussions on the show. Recently, we tried to figure out exactly when Ares supposedly gave Xena her chakram.

Once I saw how busy the group was getting, I decided I needed a way to keep track of what stories were posted. I didn't want to post the same story twice in a week. So, I tried making a Word document list of the stories I posted. I'm not educated in computers or programs. Everything I know is from trial and error or from asking someone else how to do it. Word just wasn't as easy as I had hoped. At someone's suggestion, I tried a spreadsheet in Excel. Now I was onto something. I started with columns for Title and Author. Then I decided to add a column for Links so I didn't have to keep going to my bookmarks to find it. Everything grew from there.

Now there are columns for Title, Author, Who (character names), What (professions), Link, Icon (they tell you if there is sex or if it is an unfinished story, etc.), Category (Alt, Conqueror, Uber, etc.), Read (you can mark that you have read it), and Summary (I just recently started adding small descriptions of the story).

When I got requests for 'all the westerns you know about' or 'stories with lawyers and cops,' I decided to add pages for a few general topic requests like Amazons, Legal-Cop-PI, Sports, etc. I've also added a page to list fan fiction that went on to publication and websites where you can look for more fan fiction. This isn't an all fandom encompassing list; I stick with *Xena* and *Xena*-inspired stories. I rarely include crossovers unless they are very popular, like A Diva's Demise, which includes many fandoms.

The alphabetizing is really not what a librarian would do, but I needed to be able to find a story quickly. If I'm looking for the link to The Bluest Eyes in Texas, I go to 'The' not 'Bluest.' I know, I know, but it is set up that way and changing it after all these years would be a pain. A series is listed by the name of the first story in the series. A Warrior By Any Other Name is in 'A', and the rest of the series is in chronological order of the series.

I started filling in the background to highlight stories I thought others would enjoy. They are my favorites or ones that I reread often. Once I started finding more fan-made covers for stories, I decided to change the text color so readers would know there is a cover in the Photos section of the FB group. Of course, I also add the links for the story to those group posts too.

I feel I should explain one more thing. The first three pages, Title, Author, and Category, are all the same stories but just rearranged according to what page it is. The first page, Title, is the complete list. Everything is alphabetized by the Title. The second page, Author, is alphabetized by the Author's name. The third page, Category, is alphabetized by what Category the story falls into. Again, I needed to be able to easily find, say, a specific author. I put Mavis Applewater under Mavis, not Applewater.

The current *Xena* Master Fan Fic List is at 5,067 links. I add to it all the time, but I only upload new versions every month or so. The members are great at letting me know when a link no longer works or when they find a story I don't have on the XMFFL. It may seem large, but there are thousands of stories out there. Some of them have been lost with so many websites that used to host *Xena* fan fiction being lost. Long ago I started saving Word copies of every story on the list. If it is on there, I have a copy. There USED to be hundreds of sites and webrings. Now, there are very few. I still have a list of some stories I'm on the lookout for even to this day.

I encourage you to visit *Xena Fan Fic Chat*' group on Facebook and join us. Also, I'm always open to ideas to better the group and the list to make them easier and more informational. I want to thank all the members and bards that have helped me over the years and that continually participate in the group. You are my peeps and I love you to the ends of the Known World.

Links:
Xena Fan Fic Chat (Facebook):
https://www.facebook.com/groups/xenafanficchat

You can download the latest version of *Jay's Xena Master Fan Fic List:*
http://jayfanficlist.com/

Chapter Twenty-Two

Our Fallen Bards –
Their Extraordinary Legacy

by MaryD

IN THE LAST TWENTY-FOUR years, I have read thousands of stories and millions of words. Sometimes I can't remember what I did yesterday, but I will remember the stories that touched my soul. There are stories that stay with me, and re-reading them is like my happy place. That's a writer's gift to the world.

Writers have a way of making the written word come alive and take us to places where we have never been. We lose track of time and place—it becomes a blur as we feast on the words that have us enraptured. That is the mark of a great writer. You will have read in this section about the amazing contribution that writers (bards) have given the Xenaverse and how they have enriched our world.

There comes a moment when it's time to shuffle off this mortal coil (whether old age, sickness or accident) and at the end we are left with the good we have done in this life, and how we changed our particular corner of this incredible planet.

For the writer, it's their stories—those pieces of prose that materialized from nothing. It is the purest form of creation: creating something out of nothing. Our stories are our babies. What we are left with once the creator of that story passes away is their stories, their legacy.

The Xenaverse has been blessed with a tsunami of talent in the creative arena. We have artists, writers, videographers, and poets. This chapter pays tribute to some of the incredible writers of the Xenaverse who have left us—our Fallen Bards.

Susanne M. Beck (Sword'n'quill) – April 21, 2019

On March 01, 2019, Susanne M. Beck (aka Sue Beck) signed on to AUSXIP Publishing for me to republish her amazing Ice and Angel Series. This was something I knew her fans would love (I was one of those fans). Sue and I had known each other for over twenty years and I was excited by the prospect of publishing her series and for her stories to find a new audience that had not been exposed to Sue's incredible talent. Little did I know that on that early morning of April 7, 2019 I would speak to my friend for the last time. I was on-line and having a chat with Sue and we were joking around. I was due to leave Australia and wouldn't be catching up with her until I got back. On April 15, 2019, I was with a group of Seattle-based Xenites, and at the table was a dear friend of Sue's who reminded me of a prank someone had played on Sue. I was in stitches because that incident was one of the funniest pranks played on Sue. She was a good sport about the prank (an large inflatable penis was left on her doorstep). Less that six days later, Sue Beck would peacefully pass away in her sleep on April 21, 2019 at her home.

It was Sue's brother, Paul, who posted on Sue's Facebook page that his sister had passed away:

With great sorrow, I have to announce that my sister Suz Beck (Sue) passed away in her sleep over Easter Weekend. She was 55. Sue was a sister, a daughter, a mother of four amazing dogs, a passionate creative mentor and collaborator, a skilled and capable nurse and thoughtful, compassionate medical professional, an award winning writer, friend, activist in the gay community, and a human rights warrior putting herself in harm's way to help those she cared about and causes she believed in. She suffered from the results of that commitment several times severely but never wavered from her resolve or beliefs in humanity. She is survived by her parents, myself, and two amazing dogs, Whiskey and Gremlin, who have been placed with loving families already. She will be dearly missed. Please, reach out to me if you have any questions or anything you'd like to share. Her ashes will be spread in her "zen place," referenced in many of her books, the Wequaquet Lake in Cape Cod, later this summer. We will miss you, Sue, and as always, we love you. Xena, Star Trek and so many other characters will always have your heart and mind in them for so many people.

Thus ended the life of a woman with extraordinary talent, a sense of fun, and at times, just out and out hysterical. Sue left us an incredible legacy with her fiction.

Sue's Xena Fan Fiction Official Site
http://ausxip.com/fanfiction/swordnquill

Published Editions of the Ice & Angel Series can be found here:
http://ausxippublishing.com/authors/susanne-m-beck/

LJ Maas – October 29, 2005

Give a Man a Fish, and You Feed Him for a Day. Teach a Man To Fish and You Feed Him for a Lifetime is an unusual quote to place here, but there is a good reason.

On August 31, 2001, I found myself in Atlanta for DragonCon. LJ and I were rooming together. We were both published authors for Renaissance Alliance Publishing (now called Regal Crest), and we became fast friends. She was a gifted writer, down to earth, creative soul, and I was a newbie at this business with just one book. I'm not shy about asking for help if I'm on over my head. I was in over my head with one aspect of writing; writing love scenes. I'm a big fan of fading to black. I could not 'fade to black' for the next novel "Where Shadows Linger" because it called for a love scene. I knew who to call, and that was LJ Maas. Reading her love scenes was just beautiful. They didn't read like a how-to manual or worse. When I asked for her help, LJ didn't hesitate. Every writer has their own voice; it's as unique to them as fingerprints, and that's why you know instinctively who wrote something by their writer's voice.

It takes a gifted writer to turn off their voice and write like someone else. That was LJ. She merged her voice into mine. LJ wrote the scene, had me read it, study it, and learn from it. Then she deleted it and asked me to write the scene. LJ read it and made suggestions. That was a gift that I will forever treasure. LJ's gift was extraordinary, and she kept you enthralled by her words, characters, and stories.

I have so many stories of LJ's generosity and kindness towards her fellow authors. She made me a better writer; learning from her was a privilege and one that I treasure a great deal. LJ was also a gifted artist. She turned her attention to my characters and drew them, conjured them up from my descriptions, and they were pretty close to what I saw in my head. We lost LJ on October 29, 2005. You can find her incredible fiction here: http://ausxip.com/fanfiction/ljmaas

Rebekah Wright – October 29, 1999

In December 1996, when I stumbled into the Xenaverse, I went in search of *Xena* fan fiction. My other loves: *Star Trek: The Next Generation, Star Trek: Deep Space Nine* and *Babylon 5* had a wealth of fanfic written by talented fans. I thought the Xenaverse would be the same. The first story I read was a newly released fanfic by Rebekah. It was called "All Through The Night" (Later to be known as Nor The Battle to the Strong: All Through The Night Part 1).

This is my review of Rebekah's story when I awarded it a XIPPY Award:

I've wanted to give this story a XIPPY since I started them. I am so thrilled to see this absolute CLASSIC of a Xena story. This story, ladies and gentlemen, was one of the first I had read on-line, and I fell in love with Xena fanfic. It's a hurt/comfort tale that is so moving and so well written. I am so ecstatic to see it back on-line! Welcome back, Rebekah!

https://www.ausxip.com/fanfiction/t/thruthenight.htm

That was my first introduction to *Xena* Fanfic, and it BLEW ME AWAY. The caliber of writing was EXTRAORDINARY. Rebekah and I became friends in 1997, and it came as a complete shock when the news about her passing was announced. I wrote:

It is with great sadness that I announce that a friend and one of my favorite bards has passed away. Rebekah passed away on the 29th of October from a short illness. Becky had a great sense of humor——she was a down to earth woman. She was one of the first bards in the Xenaverse with her classic story Nor The Battle to The Strong: Part 1: All Through The Night. It was one of the truly great stories this fandom has produced. May you rest in peace, Rebekah. If you want to read her absolutely beautiful stories, they are still on-line at the Cave of Choirs website. The Cave of Choirs has now ceased to exist, but I have preserved Rebekah's work on AUSXIP.

These are just three of the bards we have lost, but if I wrote about them all, it would require more than a few chapters in this book. Below is a list and the dates these bards passed away – this is not a comprehensive list, just the names listed in the AUSXIP subsite "The Xenite Memorial."

1999
- Rebekah Wright – October 29, 1999
  www.ausxip.com/fanfiction/rebekah
- Kristian S. Fisher

2000
- Frances Spinella
  www.angelfire.com/az2/blackrage/

2001
- Tonya Muir – January 25, 2001
  www.ausxip.com/fanfiction/tonyamuir

2002
- Carolyn "Diamonddog" Cason - February 10, 2002

2005
- LJ Maas – October 29, 2005
  www.ausxip.com/fanfiction/ljmaas/

2006
- Linda (Lynka) – August 08, 2006
  www.academyofbards.org/amazontrails/
- Amy Goodwin (Leslaureat) – January 04, 2008
  http://xenafiction.net/scrolls/Leslaureate.html
- Atara – March 21, 2008
- Regina Ward – July 13, 2008

2010
- Cousin Liz (Liz Staub) – October 10, 2010
  www.academyofbards.org/cousinliz/

2011
- Cathy Liddicoat (CathBard) – March 20, 2011
  http://www.ausxip.com/fanfiction/cathbard

2014
- Dax (Patricia L. Givens) – February 09, 2014
  http://xenafiction.net/author_pages/patricialgivensdax.html

2015
- Nene Adams – October 03, 2015
  http://xenafiction.net/author_pages/neneadamsbardwynna.html

2018
- Baermer – September 04, 2018
  http://ausxip.com/fanfiction/baermer/

2019
- Susanne M. Beck (Sword'n'Quill) – April 21, 2019
  www.ausxip.com/fanfiction/swordnquill

Thank you bards for leaving us an extraordinary legacy.

Lest We Forget

PART 5

THE MIGHTY QUILL –
FROM XENA FANFIC TO PUBLISHED AUTHORS

Chapter Twenty-Three

Quill Them All – The Impact of Xena: Warrior Princess on Published Lesbian Fiction

by Linda Crist

IT'S DIFFICULT TO imagine today's world of published lesbian fiction absent the community of fan fiction readers and writers that grew out of the *Xena* fandom. Certainly, it would have evolved by now from where it was in the 1990s, but how it would have evolved without *Xena* we'll never know, for the two by history are mutually inseparable. Further, if not for *Xena*, many current lesbian fiction writers might never have seen their books in print, and some might never have written anything at all.

As the internet came into widespread use, in addition to *Xena* fan fiction, on-line writers also posted fan fiction for *Buffy the Vampire Slayer, The X-Files, Babylon 5, Star Trek: Voyager* and *Deep Space Nine, Stargate SG-1,* and other shows that aired around that time. When fan fiction first began to appear on-line, some showrunners initially thought to shut it down, viewing it as copyright infringement.

Meanwhile, *Xena* executive producer Rob Tapert and others on its production staff went on-line and were amazed at the fandom that had grown around their campy little television show, especially and surprisingly to them, the booming lesbian fan community. Their show, featuring two strong women facing the world without relying upon men, resonated with lesbians and the greater LGBTQA+ community, and the on-line fandom surrounding the show quickly became a safe haven for queer persons of all stripes.

Rather than viewing fan fiction as something bad, Tapert saw the benefit of allowing the fans to write, post, and discuss stories on-line. He understood that enabling the fandom to flourish freely on-line could only help in keeping fans interested in tuning into the show itself week after week and season after season. As other shows' producers saw the *Xena* fan fiction community growing along with it the show's viewership, they also took a more favorable stance toward fan fiction, paving the way for the current state of both on-line fan fiction and published lesbian fiction.

At the time *Xena* first aired, available lesbian fiction was somewhat limited. There were only a few publishers, the now-defunct Naiad Press being the largest at the time. Before the internet, lesbians and bisexual women usually obtained their reading material in one of three ways. If you were fortunate enough to live in a city with a queer or feminist book store, you could buy some books in person. In more progressive cities, the public library was an option for some. The most popular method of obtaining lesbian novels prior to the internet was Naiad's snail mail catalog, or by ordering from book lists that could be found at the end of all Naiad novels. Readers checked off the books they wanted and mailed the list to Naiad, along with a paper check for payment. For some LGBTQA+ persons, if it was not safe to be out where they lived, the risk of being outed by the banker, the postman, or the librarian eliminated even the few options there were at that time.

Accessibility issues aside, and with nothing but the greatest respect for Naiad's legacy and contribution to lesbian fiction, it is true that most twentieth-century lesbian novels were relatively short and formulaic in nature. For lesbian fiction readers, the internet changed everything. Not only could they access *Xena* fan fiction from the privacy of their own homes, but it also provided hours of free reading. While quality was sometimes lacking, the quantity was seemingly endless. Readers could go to dozens of websites such as *Tom's Page, The Athenaeum, Shadowfen, Lynka, ForevaXena, The Royal Academy of Bards*, or the *Australian Xena Information Page's The Bard's Corner,* and find multiple new stories posted daily. Short stories, novellas, novel-length stories, and stories in a series were available. In the beginning, nearly all on-line lesbian-themed stories were about Xena and Gabrielle. Still, even so, in some of the stories, the plot, the level of thrill and adventure, the emotional complexity and depth of the characters, and the imagination and detail of the love scenes were better than what was available in published lesbian fiction.

For aspiring writers, the advent of on-line fan fiction was a paradigm shift. Anyone who wanted to write could. Many who had never considered writing before, inspired by *Xena* TV episodes or other fan fiction stories, sat down at their computers and began what, for some, evolved into a writing career. There was freedom in posting on-line, with no limits on plots, settings, or story lengths. While putting one's work out there was often a bit scary at first, readers of lesbian fiction were desperately hungry for new material. Nearly all stories were welcomed with open arms, and any bard who wished to could remain anonymous by using a pen name, and could choose whether or not to accept, read, or respond to reader feedback. In the world of fan fiction, if you could weave a good tale or write a steamy love scene, readers were willing to forgive a lot in terms of structural mechanics.

Soon after fan fiction was first posted on-line, editors known as beta readers emerged, offering editing skills for free to bards who wished to have their stories reviewed by a second pair of eyes, and cleaned up for content, grammar, spelling, and punctuation. Individual bard and beta reader partnerships developed, and eventually, on-line reader/writer/beta reader communities were established, most often in the form of e-mail based forums such as Yahoo groups.

One of the largest forums was The Bard's Village, which at its height, had around 2,000 members. Bards were encouraged to post drafts of their stories in progress and could receive instant reader feedback. The list also offered a group of beta readers willing to work with bards privately, and from time to time, the list hosted themed writing contests, encouraging bards to write for the first time or to stretch their writing skills to adhere to the theme of a given contest. It was a win-win situation. Readers looked forward to daily stories landing in their inboxes, and bards had a built-in cheering section and source of feedback to help them improve their writing.

As time went on, some bards developed large on-line followings, and several started their own mailing list forums where readers could read stories by and interact with their favorite bards and other readers on lists exclusive to the individual bard. Perhaps the largest of these groups was the Merwolf Pack, which is still active today for fans of writer Melissa Good, who has written thousands of pages of *Xena* fan fiction, and published a large body of lesbian fiction novels for her contemporary Dar and Kerry series and her Jess and Dev science fiction series. Good was also tapped to write four *Xena* scripts, two of which were filmed as sixth season TV episodes, and two of which were not filmed, but were later produced in other fan-based venues.

Fan fiction readers gradually began to expect more in terms of the quality of the stories they read, partly because the volume of available *Xena* fan fiction became so great that it became necessary to weed out the poorly written stories from the well-written ones. While readers relied heavily upon word of mouth, they also sought out sites such as Lunacy's Reviews for recommendations of *Xena* fan fiction stories to read. Other sites assisted readers in finding quality stories by reviewing and rewarding good stories, including the Amazon Ice Company awards, the Swollen Bud awards, the Royal Academy of Bards' Hall of Fame awards, and AUSXIP's XIPPY awards. Receiving positive on-line reviews and awards was also affirming for the bards, encouraging them to keep writing and improving their skills.

Writing *Xena* fan fiction was fun, and it was a safe and somewhat easy way to hone writing skills. The characters were already developed, and unless a bard chose an alternate universe, the setting was also at least partly pre-developed. Other elements were provided by the show, such as supporting characters and dialogue patterns, so that all a bard had to do was create an interesting plot to weave around all the pre-existing story elements. Because the stories were posted on-line for no monetary profit, there was no external pressure from publishers with deadlines and financial expectations.

Fan fiction writing could be challenging, but as time went by, some bards went in search of greater or different challenges. Many of today's published lesbian fiction writers started out writing Xena and Gabrielle fan fiction, and some also wrote fan fiction for other shows, including Willow/Tara fiction from *Buffy*, Janeway/Seven fiction from *Star Trek*, and Sam/Janet fiction from *Stargate.* Even hugely popular published author Radclyffe wrote on-line lesbian stories featuring Dana Scully from *The X-Files,* which amassed readership when they were discovered by the vast population of *Xena* fan fiction readers. On-line versions of some of Radclyffe's early published works, including *Love's Melody Lost* and *Safe Harbor*, are still available today at the Royal Academy of Bards.

As covered in another chapter, Uber is a genre of fan fiction that grew out of the *Xena* fan fiction world. Uber stories feature characters that generally bear personalities and physical traits similar to Xena and Gabrielle, but are given different names. These stories may be set in any period in history, with the majority taking place in modern times, and plots vary greatly, though nearly all contain the common theme of lesbian romance. The show itself delved into Uber storytelling, with the characters of Melinda Pappas and Janice Covington in the episode "The Xena Scrolls," Arminestra and Shakti in "Between the Lines," and Annie, Mattie, and Harry in "Déjà vu All Over Again" and "Soul Possession."

Not too long after "The Xena Scrolls" aired, *Xena* bards began writing their own versions of Uber Xena and Gabrielle characters, with bard Della Street leading the way with her western story titled "Toward the Sunset." The Uber fiction genre opened up a whole new world for *Xena* fan fiction writers. It was refreshing to write Uber stories. While the two main characters' personalities and physical traits might be patterned after Xena and Gabrielle, writers were presented with the often more interesting challenge of creating original character names, back stories, settings, and plots.

Over time, Uber fiction became more original, complex, and creative, and eventually someone decided some of the better novel-length stories should be published. The first publishing company to rise out of the *Xena* fandom was the now-defunct Justice House. The first story they sought out was the premier work in Melissa Good's on-line Dar and Kerry series, *Tropical Storm.* There was initial concern by Good, the publishers, and others within the fandom that Uber stories should not be published for fear that because they came out of the world of *Xena* fan fiction, they constituted copyright infringement. Although *Tropical Storm* contained no actual proprietary elements of the *Xena* television series, erring on the side of caution, Good sought Rob Tapert's opinion, and with his blessing, the first edition of *Tropical Storm* was published by Justice House in 1999. The next two Uber novels Justice House published were *Accidental Love* by B. L. Miller and *Lucifer Rising* by Sharon Bowers.

The pairing of tall dark characters with short fair characters is a literary device that pre-dated *Xena*, but the 'should they/shouldn't they' publish debate continued for a few years within the fandom. The flood gates were open, however, and a wave of on-line Uber *Xena* stories was published over the next decade. As a result, many *Xena* fan fiction writers were inspired to write their first Uber stories, often in the hope of joining the ranks of the published. Like Justice House, other publishing companies that formed out of the *Xena* fandom have come and gone, including Jane Doe Press, Fortitude Press, Cavalier Press, Dare to Dream, Bluefeather Books, and PD Publishing. Other Xenaverse based publishers are still in business today, among them, Regal Crest Enterprises (formerly Renaissance Alliance Publishing), Bedazzled Ink, Brisk Press, Affinity Rainbow Publications (formerly Affinity e-Book Press), Bossy Pants Books, Wednesday Afternoon Press, and AUSXIP Publishing.

While not directly formed out of the Xenaverse, Bold Strokes Books, founded by Radclyffe, is also worthy of inclusion. Several Bold Strokes writers came out of the Xena fandom, including Lambda Literary Award finalist Ali Vali, and Lambda Literary Award winners Gabrielle Goldsby and Georgia Beers. Even the other "giant" in the lesbian publishing world, Bella Books, which grew out of Naiad, has several Xenaverse writers under its umbrella, including Lambda Literary Award finalist D. Jordan Redhawk, and Lambda Literary Award winner and former Lambda Literary Board member, K.G. MacGregor. Even popular Bella writers and Lambda Literary Award winners, Geri Hill and Karin Kallmaker, both have stories posted at the Royal Academy of Bards.

There is not enough room in this chapter to list every published lesbian fiction writer who came out of the Xenaverse, but a perusal of the author list of nearly every lesbian fiction publisher will reveal at least one or two, while other Xenaverse bards have opted to self-publish their original lesbian fiction novels. Among the more prolific published lesbian fiction writers to come out of the Xenaverse that have not already been mentioned are Carrie Carr, J.M. Dragon, Blayne Cooper, Lori Lake, Lynn Ames, Mary D. Brooks (MaryD), Barbara Davies, Erin O'Reilly, Mavis Applewater, and Susan X. Meagher. It takes a village to publish a book, and that includes editors and book cover artists, many of whom also came out of the Xenaverse, including editors Cindy Cresap and Medora MacDougall, and cover artists

Lucia Nobrega, Linda Callaghan, MaryD, and Stephanie Solomon.

Xena fan fiction had a progressive impact on the quality of published lesbian fiction. In the early days of *Xena*-based publishing, many writers did not have to seek out and submit their manuscripts to publishers, but rather the publishers took advantage of the vast library of on-line Uber fiction, and contacted the writers of more popular stories to see if they would allow them to be published. Some publishing houses established rigorous multi-step editing processes for the books they produced, while others did little more than lift manuscripts from the web, run spellcheck, and clean up the formatting before publishing Uber stories. Publishers soon learned that readers who were willing to forgive a multitude of sins when reading free stories on-line, quickly became harsh critics once they forked over their hard-earned cash for the published versions of those same stories. This demand for quality forced some publishers to up their editing games.

Uber *Xena* fiction writers often overlapped their lesbian romance stories with other literary genres, including historical fiction, science fiction, fantasy, mystery, horror, and action/adventure. This was good for readers, who had a greater variety of books to choose from, and good for lesbian fiction writers, who were free to explore and write outside of the traditional lesbian fiction box of short, formulaic novels.

Some Uber fiction writers wrote long on-line stories that translated into 300-plus page printed novels. Longer novels presented cost challenges within the traditional publishing model of printing a run of books that had to be stored until sold, and some of which went unsold. Many *Xena*-based publishers moved to the innovative print-on-demand model, which meant books were only printed as they were ordered. Print-on- demand, and later the rise in popularity of e-books over printed paper books, eased production costs and provided an outlet for the longer novels some writers excelled at writing, and some readers enjoyed reading.

One very important lesbian fiction milestone that came out of the Xenaverse was the founding of the Golden Crown Literary Society, which was established in 2004 by a group of mostly *Xena*-based publishers and writers, to enhance and promote lesbian literature. The first annual GCLS conference was held in 2005 and included a format still adhered to today, of master writing and editing classes, panel discussions, social activities, book marketing, and the Goldie Awards ceremony. The awards ceremony is preceded by a formal and lengthy submission, review, and voting process. The conference and awards program has had a great impact on lesbian fiction by recognizing and promoting the careers of lesbian fiction writers and drawing in new readers and writers. Today, GCLS and its Goldie awards are well-respected within the LGBTQA+ publishing industry alongside other conferences and awards programs such as the Lambda Literary Awards and the Saints and Sinners Literary Festival.

In the past few years, what grew out of on-line *Xena* fan fiction has come full circle. Publishers report that e-books are outselling books printed on paper, and audiobooks are also rising in popularity. Many of today's queer fiction readers jump indiscriminately back and forth from reading on-line fan fiction to reading published e-books. Popular fan fiction site Archive of Our Own ("AO3") makes downloading stories for offline consumption as easy as pressing a button, and a glimpse at the libraries on many queer fiction readers' phones and tablets will reveal downloads of both fan fiction and purchased, published fiction.

The world of published lesbian fiction will be forced to continue to evolve. In addition to competing with fan fiction, it must fight for the attention of consumers with a growing volume of LGBTQA+ themed movies and television shows available through streaming platforms. The shift to self-publishing by many writers will provide additional challenges for publishing houses to continue to draw talent and remain relevant. Readers themselves have voiced a desire for more diversity of content, to include not just lesbians, but characters all along the gender identity and sexual orientation spectrums, as well as characters of diverse racial and cultural backgrounds.

Whatever the future of published lesbian and queer-themed fiction holds, it owes much of its current success to the *Xena* fan fiction community of the late 90s and early 2000s. What started with *Xena* is still going strong today. A key to its continued success may lie in its very roots, in listening to writers and readers of today's queer fan fiction to gain a better understanding of how to produce published works that those readers and future generations of readers will find relatable.

www.nextchapter.net

Chapter Twenty-Four

To Every Thing, There is a Season

by MaryD (Mary D. Brooks)

I HAVE KNOWN I wanted to be a writer since I was ten years old. In January 2001, I fulfilled a life long dream of having my first novel published by Renaissance Alliance Publishing. That novel had its roots back to when I was fourteen years old, but it would take twenty-three years before it was published. It was a long journey towards my goal.

I have been writing since I was eight years old; I cut my teeth on Six Million Dollar Man, The Bionic Woman and Charlie's Angels fanfic (even before I knew what fanfic was) and progressed from there. I'm a voracious reader of historical novels, police procedurals, and murder mysteries.

From the outset, I would like to out myself as being a history nerd (which will become apparent in this chapter). The drive to write happens when I'm passionate about the topic. It's not a switch I can turn on or off; if the subject matter ignites a fire, it stays lit. Boy, does it stay lit. I remember when Star Trek: The Next Generation ignited my writing muse. I wrote so many stories, but never shared them. I didn't think I was good enough to tell my stories of Captain Picard or Commander Data or Tasha Yar (every writer suffers from this malady). Then along came Star Trek: Deep Space Nine. Right out the gate, on the first episode, Major Kira Nerys was the fire that lit my writing muse. I sat down and wrote my first Star Trek fanfic called "The Price of Silence." I surprised myself by posting it online and then submitting it to a printed Star Trek fanzine called Outpost but didn't think it would be accepted. That story would be the first in eleven stories that would be published in various issues of the fanzine.

Then came Xena and I wanted to write Xena fanfic. My first Xena fan fiction was called *"The Price of Silence,"* and it was about Xena and her son, Solan, and Gabrielle. Throw in some Callisto, and it makes an interesting mix. I found that Xena and Gabrielle refused to talk to me, but I could hear Callisto loud and clear in my head (scary). Callisto, bubbled forth fully formed, and her voice was distinct, loud, and clear. I surrendered to the idea that it was going to be a Callisto story. The fanfic was posted on AUSXIP and shared with the rest of the Xenaverse.

I wrote a few other pieces, but not as extensively as Star Trek: DS9. If I couldn't write an Alt Xena Fic, maybe a Uber Xena fanfic would do the trick. Yes? No.

A Time To Love...A Time Of War, And A Time Of Peace

I would have to go back into my time as a youngster to explain why I wanted to write a Xena and Gabrielle Uber set in the 1940s. When I was ten years old, we moved into a new house in Sydney, and like all kids around that era (1970's), we had both parents working, but the school would be out by 3:00 pm. In between the time I left school and my parents coming home from work, I would spend time with the next-door neighbor. I fell in love with Oma (grandmother in German), and we adopted her. She was this larger-than-life character, with a smile on her face and never complained about anything even though she had problems with her health, especially her legs. She was positive and always saw the good in others.

I was a voracious bookworm, and she would recommend books for me to read, and we would discuss the book later. She didn't have children of her own, and I thought she loved the idea of having time with me to share the stuff she was reading as well (watered down for a ten-year-old). Oma introduced me to such classics as Charlotte's Web by E. B. White and The Lion, The Witch, and the Wardrobe by CS Lewis, and so many more. Those books remain my favorites. I think the characters of Charlotte (the spider) and Wilbur (the pig) in Charlotte's Web was a good representation of our friendship; two souls, vastly different, sharing a bond. She did have one vice that she shared with me. Oma got me addicted to licorice (black jelly beans etc.), and Smarties (a sweets addiction I still have today) and those massive hugs that only a grandmother can give.

I was also intrigued by the numbers tattooed on Oma's arm. At ten years of age, seeing a row of numbers on her arm got my little brain trying to figure out what it meant. I remember saying to my older sister that it might be her telephone number. Oma told me that she would let me know when I was older. As a child growing up in the 1970s, I didn't know much about the Holocaust. When I was just about to turn fourteen, she introduced me to a book called "I Am Rosemarie" by Marietta D. Moskin. "I Am Rosemarie" tells the fictional story of a young girl (sixteen years old) in a concentration camp during the Holocaust and their liberation. The book shook my world view and was outraged by the injustice. I have a visceral reaction when I'm confronted by injustice and unfairness. The rage I felt over that young girl's plight was what Oma would reveal that she knew she had done the right thing by giving me the book. I didn't honestly understand the real horror of the Holocaust at that time, but that little bit that I found out, was enough for me to be indignant as only a fourteen-year-old can be.

There was one passage in the book that made such a profound impression on me. The young girl, in the book, says that her symbol for peace is different to those of other people; many people would say that for them, the symbol for peace was a dove with an olive branch, but she saw the symbol for peace as seeing an army soldier coming through the gates of the concentration camp to liberate her. I read that and re-read it, and it saddened me so much I cried. It still has an impact today when I'm much older and know the real horrors of the Holocaust.

I asked Oma if she knew anyone who had gone through that terrible ordeal, and that was when she bared her arm and said, 'yes, I did, and that is why I have these numbers on my arm.' Of course, I was an inquisitive teenager, I wanted to know everything, but she was reluctant to talk about it other than to say she lost her entire family in the Holocaust.

She survived the notorious Auschwitz-Birkenau Concentration Camp. She was liberated in 1945 and ended up in a refugee camp (know as a "Displaced Person Camp," and it was run by the UN (United Nations Relief and Rehabilitation Administration) in Egypt. There were other camps in Aleppo (yes, the same Aleppo that was bombed out of existence) and other Middle Eastern countries. Oma met and fell in love with an Australian soldier, and they moved to Australia.

I was a clueless teenager until I got that book. It was also the start of my journey to educate myself about the Holocaust and World War II. I lost my Oma when I was sixteen years old, and I was heartbroken. She would never see how that little seed she had sown would ignite a raging fire within me.

The other person who helped shape my world view was my paternal grandfather. I was in Greece in 1978 on a visit with my family and was just about to celebrate my fourteenth birthday in the place I was born. That tickled me no end because Larissa is five thousand years old, and being a history nerd, it had me in raptures. This is where my grandfather would add to my knowledge about World War II, the Holocaust, and the Greek experience. Those two extraordinary people would shape my world in ways I never expected.

My Pappou (Grandfather in Greek) was a man of a few words and reserved. I had a lot in common with him because we shared a love for history, and we were the only introverts in a family of extroverts. His historical interest lay in Ancient Greece and in the war of 1821 to liberate Greece from the Ottoman Empire. It was two topics I was also interested in and peppered him with questions, and we would discuss the heroes of Ancient Greece. One of his heroes was King Leonidas of Sparta (King Leonidas of Thermopylae fame - see the movie 300 if you are not familiar with the heroics of the Spartans). My Pappou was born in Lakonia (where Ancient and Modern-day Sparta is located). He told me stories of the Ancient Spartans and the War of Liberation in 1821. Once started, it was difficult to get him to stop (not that I wanted him to stop!).

While we were discussing history, I wanted to know more about my birthplace. Since Larissa was an ancient city, I wanted to know all about it, and we would go up on the flat top roof with his homing pigeons in the afternoons. I also took the opportunity to ask him about WW2, but he didn't want to talk about it at first. I decided to try and get him talking about people that were involved in Resistance activities. Yes, of course, he saw through my ruse (being subtle is not one of my superpowers). One afternoon we were sitting on the flat-top roof with his pigeons, and he started talking about the war. It wasn't because he wanted to talk about it but because if he hadn't, I would never quit asking (never quitting *is* one of my superpowers). He began to tell me about his neighbors and the Resistance—manna from heaven for this nerd. I asked him if he was in the Resistance as well. He said, "Never ask a question you already know what the answer will be" and wagged his finger at me. Then he laughed. He knew I had already asked my grandmother because she told him! I told him about "I Am Rosemarie" and about Oma Evelyn and what I was learning about the Holocaust. I couldn't stop talking about what I found out.

He asked me if I understood what all of it meant and why I didn't know about the Holocaust in Greece. Did I know what the Greeks did during the war? I didn't know anything about the war in Greece. My Pappou said he was going to teach me how the Greeks won WW2 for the Allies. If you have seen the movie *"My Big Fat Greek Wedding,"* you would be familiar with the father's hyperbole about Greeks inventing everything. My Pappou's claim was not hyperbole. The Greek Resistance changed the course of the war and led to Hitler's disastrous foray into Russia.

When the Germans invaded, the Greeks started the fiercest resistance movement in all of Europe. The Greeks were so ferocious at it that Hitler's plans to invade Russia were delayed. That delay cost the Germans dearly because winter in Russia stopped the German juggernaut in its tracks. If it wasn't for the Greek Resistance, the Germans would have been in Russia during the summer. Those Greeks…just ten million of them, but they punched above their weight.

Now back to my story. After a lot of begging for him to tell me what he did during the war so I wouldn't have to bug my Yiayia (my Greek grandmother), he opened the floodgates. There was a sizeable Jewish community, especially in two of the largest cities in Northern Greece - Larissa and in Salonika (Thessalonica). He told me he was in the Resistance and helped Jews escape by hiding them in the fields before they could be moved. His home (the same one I was staying in) was used to protect Allied soldiers and also housed Jews before they were moved to another home or to the fields. He told me stories of his town and the Italian and then German occupation. All the stories he told me were archived in my mind for another day. I scribbled plans of the house, with its staircase that led down to the cellar—fodder for when I would write my novel.

Now back to Xena, and that's where the third element of this journey clicks into place. Xena is a lesbian icon. Being in the Xenaverse, I was fully aware of the horrendous discrimination and abuse of the gay community is subjected to. That's why I chose to write lesbian fiction; a straight chick was writing about lesbians. I hate injustice and unfairness with the fire of a thousand suns, and this was my way of changing hearts and minds. You have to start someplace.

A Time To Pluck Up That Which Is Planted
On June 15, 1999, we got word that beloved Pappou had passed away, and the story I wanted to tell about his exploits in the Resistance became stronger. I also wanted to bring Oma Evelyn's holocaust story into it as well. The more I thought about it, the more I also wanted to introduce the third element: discrimination and persecution of gay people.

I wanted to bring those elements into a Xena Uber story because of the episode "The Xena Scrolls" was set during 1940 and World War II. Xena and Gabrielle were Greek, and I could place the Uber in the Greek city of Larissa. The planets were aligned...or so I thought.

I needed to do more research and dived into it. I love research because it sends me down rabbit holes I never imagined existed. Through that research, I also learned about how gay men and lesbians were treated by the Nazis. To my horror, I discovered the atrocities of Dachau Concentration Camp, where gay men were tortured, and aversion treatments did not end with the Nazis but continue to this day (2020). Inhumane and shocking.

Armed with the research, the stories my Pappou told me, and the Holocaust that my Oma taught me about, I was going to write a Xena Uber set during WW2 with Uber Xena (who is German) helping Uber Gabrielle (who is Greek) to help Jews escape. I thought this time I will write a Xena story.

The Uber Xena story was the perfect vehicle to introduce two Uber characters. That's how Eva Muller (Xena) and Zoe Lambros (Gabrielle) were born.

I had everything lined up, but someone forgot to tell Eva and Zoe that they were Uber Xena characters because those girls had other ideas. After the first chapter, I realized once again that I could not hear Xena and Gabrielle in my head. The voices I was hearing were distinct and had no relation to the show. I had stumbled into creating my own characters, and they were not going to be pigeon-holed into what I wanted them to be. If you think writers have full control over their characters, I'm here to disabuse you of that idea. We don't have any control over them.

Thus the Intertwined Souls Series began. The title "In The Blood of the Greeks" came from the Greek National Anthem, the Hymn of Liberty (Freedom), which was penned by Dionysios Solomos in 1823 (with 158 stanzas), and translated into English by Rudyard Kipling in October 1918.

"And we saw thee sad-eyed,
The tears on thy cheeks
While thy raiment was dyed
In the blood of the Greeks.*"*

I chose "In The Blood of the Greeks" because it was a perfect title that represented the story I wanted to write. I read about the atrocities committed in Greece (more than what my grandfather had told me) and then the crimes against homosexuals (mainly gay men, but lesbians were also targeted, although not with the same ferocity as the men nor were they sent to concentration camps as a general rule).

I wanted to write about that; I wanted to expose the horror of those atrocities but also tell a story of hope, resilience, perseverance, and eventually of love. That was the core of what Xena was about, and if I couldn't write a Xena Uber, then I was going to bring those elements to my original story.

There's a saying in the Xenaverse – Feed The Bard.

So the process began, and the more I wrote, the more I was encouraged by the feedback I was getting from fellow Xenites. Feedback is manna from heaven for a writer, and I was blessed with having people comment on what I had written. They encouraged me to continue. Feeding the bard is not to heap praise on the writer to bolster their ego but to help, to praise when needed, to correct when needed, and to be there to bounce ideas. Beta readers shape the writer and, in my opinion, make the writers creatively stretch themselves.

Never in my wildest dreams did I think that my first novel would be published! Cathy C. Bryerose, the owner and publisher of Renaissance Alliance Publishing (now Regal Crest), took a chance with me, and on

January 01, 2001, "In the Blood of the Greeks" and the novella "You Must Remember This" was published under the title "Out of Darkness."

Cathy allowed many Xena fanfic writers to have their work published and thus set into motion these writers for even more significant opportunities.

"In The Blood of the Greeks" was a story that really started its life when I was fourteen years old. The building blocks were set, and the foundation laid. No other tale could my first novel because the people who lit the fire made sure of that. It's a book that holds a special place in my heart (other than it being my first published novel).

Since January 2001, it has been republished by various publishers over the years. When Oma Evelyn asked me what I wanted to be when I grew up, I said, "A writer," and she supported me, and later when I was older, she said, 'tell the stories of the Holocaust, so no one will forget.' It was a wish that came into being in 2001.

"In the Blood of the Greeks" was not a horror story of man's inhumanity to man, but of how two women survived the horror of the war. It is the story of a love two women found, of courage, and of faith. It's a story of the triumph of the human spirit. While I was doing research for my book, I read about many real women who had experienced what Eva and Zoe had gone through. They not only lived through that most horrific time in our history but also survived and found love and happiness. The novel doesn't dwell on the worst the Nazis could do/have done but on the hope of what was possible, on priests and villagers risking their lives to save fellow Greeks, regardless of whether they were Christians or Jews.

I received an email from Blaire Barnes, a fellow Xenite, and with her permission, I'm reprinting it here. It broke my heart to hear back from someone who underwent aversion torture (not just during WW2 but in our "enlightened" age that this barbaric torture is still being performed on young gay people).

Reading this series has been such an experience for me. I'm 29 now. I started reading this series when I was about 16. It began with Out of Darkness. As you have expanded the details through the release of later editions, you have been able to capture what it was to not only be in a war-torn country but to be a lesbian woman in that period. One of whom underwent torture to cure her "illness." You have been able to somehow step into those shoes. And let the readers experience a sliver of what so many on this earth have gone through. Be it straight, gay, Christian, Jewish. It doesn't matter. You have captured every character you have written with integrity. I have been able to relate to your characters.

Especially Eva. Your books have helped me heal in a way. The struggles she went through and continues to go through, and her ability to overcome them have helped me in overcoming my own obstacles. You have been able to capture those struggles as they would have occurred. Almost exactly. I essentially grew up with this series. And I am so excited to see what adventures await Stella and Tessa. And to see where life takes Eva and Zoe as they continue their journey. Thank you for continuing to write about these characters I have come to love.

Blaire

Blaire's email brought me to tears. To hear how the words and characters I had written have that profound effect is a real blessing. That's what every writer wants to see happen; their stories to have an impact.

Then came 2015...

In February 2015, I got the opportunity of a lifetime; my friends, Penny and Kat Cavanaugh gave me an incredible gift. The story of how I saw my characters come to life in the film is fantastic in itself. You can read about that in *Chapter 39: Watching My Characters Come To Life – The Intertwined Souls Series Promo.*

In March 2015, I decided that it was time to take control and dip my toes in the publishing world. I opened the doors to AUSXIP Publishing – a decision that I was told was long overdue and was destined to happen. The problem was that no one told me I was going to be doing that! It's been an incredible five years. In that time, I have published nine novels, three radio plays, and over twenty coloring books for adults. It felt serendipitous that the first book I published under the AUSXIP Publishing banner was "In The Blood of the Greeks."

You can read more about the birth of AUSXIP Publishing in *Chapter 40: Doing Something Scary - AUSXIP Publishing is Born.*

In September 2015, I had decided to create a companion book called *"In The Blood of the Greeks: The Illustrated Companion."* I wanted to shine a light on the Jewish Holocaust in Greece through real-life warriors and their stories. There was so much material about the Holocaust in other countries. The majority of the books that had been written were about Germany, Poland, France, et al. I reached out to The Jewish Museum of Greece (https://www.jewishmuseum.gr/en/).

The Museum has a massive archive of material – letters, photographs, and video. I emailed them to license the images from their archives for the Illustrated Companion. Of course, I was asked how I was going to be using them, and through email exchanges, I outlined the book and its purpose. They gave me blanket permission to use whatever I wanted from their archives without payment. They requested I send them a copy of the book once it was done for them to check on the work. Lucia Nobrega illustrated parts of the book, which included my characters, and there were a lot of historical details from the Museum. The Australian and New Zealand armies (ANZACS) were in Greece supporting the Greeks before the country was invaded by the Germans in April 1941. I approached the Australian War Memorial and the New Zealand War Memorial to use photographs from their collections and received permission to reprint images. Overall it took elements of the fictional story and merged it with the historical record.

Once finished, I sent the book to the Museum and hoped they would like it and not asking me to stop using their material. I included "In the Blood of the Greeks" to show how those two books complemented each other. Once sent, I didn't think much of it and thought if they had questions about the books, they would email me.

In 2016, I received the highest honor that I would ever get; it wasn't an award or anything like that, but, for me, it was the ultimate compliment. The Museum emailed me to say that they were going to add the fiction book and the companion book to their book collection in their Museum in Athens!

No awards, no best-seller rating can outshine the honor of having my books in the Jewish Museum of Greece. This is the highlight of my writing life. There are no words to truly articulate how much this meant to me. If you are in the area, pop over to Nikis 39, Athens 105 57, Greece, and see their collection of valuable documents, images, and videos about the Holocaust & Jewish Resistance in Greece

I think my grandparents would have been so proud of the fact that the fire they ignited within me made a difference and continues to do so. They were courage personified. I have been supremely blessed throughout my life (even during the darkest times). That why I used the quoted scripture of Ecclesiastes 3. 1-8 about there's a time for every purpose.

I don't know where this journey will take me, but it's going to be a fun and exciting ride!

GALVESTON 1900: SWEPT AWAY

LINDA CRIST

Affinity eBook Press NZ LTD

Chapter Twenty-Five

The Gift

by Linda Crist (Texbard)

"Gabrielle, I want you to understand something. We both have families we were born into. But sometimes families change, and we have to build our own. For me, our friendship binds us closer than blood ever could."

– Xena, Ties That Bind

I WAS SIXTEEN years old the first time I fell in love with a woman: deeply, madly, and in a way that only a sixteen-year-old heart can. Our love was mutual, but I had no definition for what I felt at that time. During the next dozen years, despite a lifetime of Southern Baptist guilt, I realized that I was gay. There was little time to process what I had come to accept, as three days before my twenty-ninth birthday, I lost my mother to cancer, and a little over a year later, my father died of a heart attack. In the year following, nearly all my time was consumed with settling their estate, but finally there was time to grieve, and to get on with figuring out what being gay meant for me.

Xena: Warrior Princess premiered when I was thirty-two years old, but I did not watch it from the beginning. I discovered *Xena* fan fiction before I discovered the television show, and I cannot tell the story of my writing without telling the story of the connections I made along the way, the Xenites who became my friends and eventually, my family. In the years between accepting that I was gay and finding *Xena*, there was no internet in my life. Although Dallas has a large LGBTQA+ population, finding my people as a young gay woman in a pre-Google world was not easy. I made a few lesbian friends but struggled to find a place where I felt like I fit in.

In the 90s, there was a bookstore in the Dallas gayborhood that has since closed, Crossroads Market, but it catered mostly to gay men, and the lesbian books occupied only a few shelves near the back of the store. Prior to discovering the store, I did not know lesbian fiction existed, and I was thrilled at their meager offerings. After reading several books, however, I found myself wanting something deeper than the short, formulaic novels I found on their shelves.

In 1995, the same year that *Xena* premiered, I accepted a paralegal job at a small law firm. One morning I logged onto my work computer and discovered we had acquired a connection to the "worldwide web," as it was called. Our manager told us that as long as we stuck to work during business hours, we were free to play after work. One evening while exploring, a thought came to me, *I wonder if there is anything good to read on the web?* Using the Alta Vista search engine, I entered a query, "lesbian fiction." A bunch of *Xena* sites came up. I thought I had made a mistake so I ran the search again, with the same results.

What in the world does Xena have to do with lesbians? Possibly the most ironic thought of my life. I knew who Xena was, but had only seen short clips of the show while channel surfing, and thought it looked a bit silly. Finally, I chose a site called The Scroll of Roses, thinking maybe it wasn't a *Xena* site. I was wrong. It was, and it had links to fan fiction stories by B.L. Miller, L.N. James, Melissa Good, and many other unbeknown to me at that time, well-known Xenaverse bards. I chose a story, "Heaven Down Here," by Rebecca Hall, and it changed everything for me. Everything. I devoured that story and several others. They were like nothing I had read in any lesbian novel before. These stories were full of depth, adventure, love, and an emotional, beautiful aching longing.

Finally I thought, *I have got to watch this show*! The first episode I watched was the second season's "Return of Callisto," in which Gabrielle marries a man, Perdicus. Not the most auspicious beginning, but there was that kiss on the lips between Xena and Gabrielle after the wedding, and Gabrielle talked at length about Xena on her wedding night. Then *the* scene came. Xena knelt down in that moonlit glade and prayed, "If anyone's listening, you know I'm not much for praying, but I don't know what else to do. I was ready to give up once and Gabrielle came into my life. Please, don't let that light that shines out of her face go out. I couldn't stand the darkness that would follow." My heart! My poor heart, that had been seeking something greater in life, was lost forever to this television show.

I never intended to write fan fiction. Once I discovered *Xena*, I was happy to watch the show and read the daily new fan fiction offerings. Then the fourth season cliffhanger, "The Ides of March," aired. From the moment Gabrielle picked up that spear and killed to try to save Xena, through the jail cell scene and their crucifixion, I sat literally on the edge of my seat, breathless. I had taped the episode and watched it several times more. Then I realized I couldn't wait until September to find out what happened next, so I sat down to write my own resolution.

It was supposed to be short, and I didn't intend to post it anywhere. It was for my own personal consumption. Eight chapters later, *March the Sixteenth* had become a novel-length story and with much trepidation, I

242   AUSXIP

sent it to Tom's Page to post. The positive feedback was overwhelming. I had interacted with a few Xenites on-line prior to that, in the form of feedback I sent to other bards, but posting that story was the first tiny crack in the doorway that led to what became my Xenite family. I continued to write additional fan fiction stories, and joined three on-line mailing lists, the Bard's Village, a community of bards and readers, the Merwolf Pack, Melissa Good's fan list, and Texas Pupmeet, a group of Texan and honorary Texan Melissa Good fans.

I attended one small fan gathering, the New York XenaFest, in 1999, where I briefly met Melissa Good, Susanne Beck (Sword N Quill), and TNovan, but my first big convention was DragonCon in 2000. Melissa was leading the *Xena* track and on her list said she needed panelists. I am an introvert, but something possessed me to e-mail her and volunteer. I flew to Atlanta, not really knowing anyone who was going. On Friday morning, I stood in the lobby of the Hyatt Regency, trying to figure out where to go. At a distance, I saw Melissa and some others walking past, and followed them to the panel room.

I filled out a name tag, adding both my real name and my on-line pen name, Texbard. As I walked into the room to find a seat, people began to notice my name tag and came up to introduce themselves, and tell me they'd read and enjoyed my stories. By then end of that weekend, I had met people who became lifelong friends and sisters.

Around that same time, some of the Dallas-Fort Worth area Xenites on the Texas Pupmeet list decided to meet in person at Sue Ellen's, our lesbian bar that is still open today. What started as a somewhat awkward gathering slowly became a rollicking great afternoon, and friendships that are still going strong today were born. Between DragonCon and that small gathering of Texas Pups, after years of searching, I had found my people. I had a place I belonged.

I kept reading and writing fan fiction, and one night at work, I received what became a life-changing e-mail from a reader named Lisa. I was looking for my evening's reading material, and she told me she was waiting for the next chapter of "Exposure," an uber fan fic story. I knew what uber stories were, but had not read any. She persuaded me to read "Exposure," which was written by Tonya Muir, TNovan, and XWPFanatic (Francine Love). I learned that they uploaded new chapters every Thursday evening, and if you could answer a trivia question, Fran would e-mail you the chapter early. Thus began my friendship with my first publisher.

The idea of writing my own uber developed gradually. The characters of Kennedy Nocona and Carson Garret slowly revealed themselves to me, and one day in 2000, I don't recall exactly when, I drafted character descriptions and the briefest of outlines for *The Bluest Eyes in Texas*. I began writing and posting chapters to the Bards Village mailing list, and then started my own Texbard list. By that time, Tom's Page had quit accepting fan fiction, so as I completed chapters of *Bluest Eyes,* I sent them to the Bard's Corner at the Australian Xena Information Page, and to the Royal Academy of Bards (RAOB). It was well-received beyond my wildest dreams, and in early 2001, Francine Love reached out, told me she was starting a publishing company, and asked if they could publish it.

In May 2001, thousands of Xenites descended upon Pasadena, California for the biggest *Xena* convention ever held. The show was ending later that year, but the fandom was far from over. In Pasadena, Fran held a reception for her publishing company and the authors they had signed, and in April 2002, Fortitude Press (now defunct) published *The Bluest Eyes in Texas*. The thrill of opening a box containing copies of a book you have written never grows old. The smell of the paper and ink, the smoothness of the cover, thumbing through the pages… It is exciting, every single time, but there is only one first book. As I held *Bluest Eyes* in my hands, I felt this sense of gratitude, that this crazy Xenaverse kept giving and giving, without end.

Sometime after the 2001 Xena convention, I received an e-mail message from Denise Byrd, whom I had befriended at DragonCon the prior year. She and some other Xenites, including Phil Schudde from RAOB, Carol Stephens, Liz Brock, Marsha Smith, and Trish Kocialski, were planning to hold a fan gathering at Walt Disney World in 2002, the Orlando BardCon. Denise asked if I'd like to join their staff and I enthusiastically agreed.

The con featured *Xena* music videos, pool parties, a charity raffle, scavenger hunts in the Disney parks, a bard brunch, book sales, author round tables, and games that focused on *Xena* fan fiction and the published authors that came out of the fandom. It was a lot of work and a lot of fun. We held four Orlando BardCons, culminating in 2005 when Renée O'Connor and her mother, Sandra Wilson, graciously attended the con and spent a lovely day with us. Sandra bought a copy of every book that was for sale that weekend, and Renée read from some of our books on stage, did some readings of her own, and also MC'd our talent show.

During those years, my friendships with Denise, Carol, Trish, and Melissa deepened, and someone in the fandom began referring to us as "the Posse." In 2004, the Posse went to New Zealand, where we spent three weeks driving in a van from Queenstown on the south island all the way to Bethells Beach and beyond on the north island, including a wonderful few days spent in Christchurch with fan fic cover artist and Xenite Kiwi Linda "Calli" Callaghan.

Before the New Zealand trip, earlier that year during the third Orlando BardCon, Denise and Carol asked me if I would like to join the staff of the

Xena Subtext Virtual Season (SVS) for its tenth season. The SVS is an on-line fan fiction series, not for profit, that began in 2002. It picks up where the Xena television show ended, and it went on for seasons seven through ten. Each episode is written in an expanded script format, taking the elements of a traditional television show script and adding descriptive narrative beyond what is usually contained in a script intended for TV. Original artwork and screen caps from the show are used to illustrate the story-scripts. The series was a collaborative effort among several Xenaverse bards, artists, and web masters, including Denise and Carol, as well as Melissa Good, TNovan, Susanne Beck, Trish Kocialski, MaryD, Lucia Nobrega, Linda Callaghan, Marsha Smith, and Judi Marr.

Writing collaboratively was a new experience for me. As we planned each episode, the person who was to write it would put forth their story idea for discussion, the group would provide input, and then the writer would take it away and write it, then bring their draft script back to the group. Feedback sessions went back and forth until the writer had a finished script. From there it went to the production staff and the artists, to edit and format it, and provide the beautiful artwork and screen caps that were included in each episode. When we started putting the tenth season episodes in order, quite randomly, I ended up writing the season premiere and what became the season and series finale. It was a privilege and a pleasure to work with that team, and is still one of the highlights of my writing career.

During all my adventures in collaborative writing, traveling, and working on BardCon, I continued to write my own stories. After I finished *Bluest Eyes,* I wrote its sequel, *Borderline,* which was also well-received, but my most popular work was yet to come. One day I was on one of the mailing lists, and a reader I had met in person at a Texas *Xena* fan gathering, Gova Rubio, said she wished someone would write an uber about the 1900 hurricane that destroyed Galveston Island. I remember thinking, *Hmmmm.* Growing up, my family and I went to Galveston almost every year. I knew the island well and had been to the hurricane museum and seen the film about the storm, but it had been years. As a result of Gova's comment, I began learning about the storm through adult eyes, and writing the story of fictional characters Rachel Travis and Mattie Crockett.

That book taught me the meaning of research. It also showed me in a new way what a joy a really good editing experience can be. I had worked with editor Cindy Cresap, whom I adore and met at DragonCon, on my other two books, but this was a much more seasoned process for both of us. As I read through her feedback notes, I realized that for every part of the book that I had known needed something while I was writing it, she had provided excellent guidance on what that something was. In 2005, the first edition of *Galveston 1900: Swept Away*, was published. A testament as much to Cindy's editing skills as my writing, the book was a 2006 Goldie Award finalist. In 2013, when the second edition was published by Affinity Rainbow Publications (another Xenite-formed publishing company), Cindy and I had worked so well together on the first edition, that there was little new editing required.

Galveston 1900 opened and continues to open doors for me in the world of lesbian fiction writing. It has been the primary reason I continue to be invited to participate in various writing conferences today. In some ways it is the reason I have continued to remain relevant as a published writer, but none of what *Galveston 1900* has given me would ever have been, if not for that Xenite friend Gova, who suggested the idea for the book in the first place. Since I began writing, I have been honored with several on-line writing awards. There have been Swollen Bud awards, XIPPY awards, and twice I won first place in the writing contests at the Bard's Village. In 2005, by reader vote, I was included as a top ten favorite bard in the inaugural season of the Royal Academy of Bards Hall of Fame. Some of my stories have also been voted into the Hall of Fame. In 2009, I was awarded the RAOB Lifetime Achievement Award. As exciting as that 2006 Goldie nod was, nothing compares to these on-line awards. They humble me, and they fill me with such great joy, because they come from the readers, my Xenite friends and family. If not for them, there would have been no writing and no published books.

It all goes back to those friendships and connections. I discovered the fan fic. I discovered the show. Through reading fan fic, I made friends on-line. I wrote, and because of friends made on-line, had the courage to post what I had written. Because of on-line connections, I went to DragonCon and that first gathering of local Xenites at Sue Ellen's, and made what became lifelong friendships. Those friendships in turn opened up more opportunities in more ways than I can possibly recall. Not just my writing, but almost every part of my life has been touched by being a part of this fandom.

Xena: Warrior Princess and its fan fiction saved me. It gave my life meaning, purpose, joy, adventures, and a place I belong. Most of all, it gave me a family. My writing is not just a gift to me, it is my small way of being able to give back to this crazy, generous, amazing Xenite family. The *Xena* fandom has been one of the greatest gifts of my life, a gift that keeps on giving. I am thankful every day, and cannot imagine what my life would be like today without it, and the amazing people I have met along the way.

Original Fiction: http://www.texbard.com/
Fan Fiction: http://www.texbard.com/online-fiction.html

Chapter Twenty-Six

Late to the Party

by Cheyne Curry

I WAS LATE to the party. As usual. I discovered fan fiction at the end of 2002. I don't remember how I happened upon it, but when I did, I knew I'd found a home for stories I never thought I'd ever get published (I just changed the names & descriptions to fit the TV characters). I started submitting *Law & Order: SVU* fan fiction to Passion and Perfection sometime around the summer of 2003. The focus of a majority of those stories was Olivia and Abbie. Then I submitted an *SVU/Cold Case* crossover and that little story changed my life.

I received a fan letter from another *Cold Case* femslash author named The Raven. We became fast friends and her fan fiction challenges inspired me to broaden my writing horizons. She introduced me to uber (I actually started to write an Olivia/Alex uber) and she is the person who got me interested in *Xena: Warrior Princess* in 2005. As I said, always late to the party. I had only ever watched one episode of *X:WP* when it was currently on the air and it was "Fallen Angel." Without context or history, my first thought was, "What the heck is this?" Later, when I really started watching the full series, I could not ignore the spark between Xena and Gabrielle. I was hooked. The chemistry of Lucy and Renée just jumped off the screen and right into my creative thought process, and from that point on, no other pairing would do. Even when I read stories I know aren't uber X & G, that's who the characters become in my mind. It's like a weird addiction I share with an entire Xenaverse.

So that uber Olivia/Alex story? I'd had trouble finding the motivation to continue it until I reimagined it with an uber Xena and Gabrielle. I finished it, submitting it to Passion and Perfection and Royal Academy of Bards a couple of chapters at a time. I called it Renegade. It went on to be my first published and most purchased book (PD Publishing, 2009, Bossy Pants Books, 2016).

Additionally, my connection to the Xenaverse also led me to making short films. In 2008, I submitted a story to a Royal Academy of Bards contest, "A Picture Is Worth A Thousand Words." The challenge was to select one of the twenty photographs displayed and write a story about in in a thousand words. I chose the picture of the cemetery and sent in "Requiem." It was about a mother taking the military to task at her daughter's funeral (during Don't Ask, Don't Tell). Her daughter, a soldier who had died in combat, had a wife and a daughter who were ignored by the military powers that be. They were not respected or given any of the compassion or benefits afforded to heterosexual soldier's widows and children. It won the challenge and I received so many letters telling me it should be made into a short film. So we did. "Requiem" became a twenty-minute short film we called "Survived by…". On that film, I was introduced to a cinematographer/writer/director named Chris who soon became my screenwriting partner and we went on to co-write, co-produce (and in one instance co-direct) over ten short films (three award winning) for local contests and one Doritos "Crash The Superbowl" commercial.

Doing short films also inspired me to want to create music, and through the magic of Logic and Garage Band, I now have a catalogue of approximately one hundred songs of all genres. I am considering making them available for book trailers and or/short film scores.

I met my wife, Brenda, through the Xenaverse. She wrote me a fan letter for The Tropic of Hunter, we met in 2007 and have been married since 2014.

I owe my published writing career to The Raven, and her introducing me to the inspired pairing of Lucy and Renée, whose portrayals of Xena and Gabrielle, so alive with sexual tension and all-encompassing love, reignited my passion for achieving a life-long dream. That led to realizing other lifetime creative desires as well. So… thank you and long live the Xenaverse!

Fan Fiction: www.ausxip.com/fanfiction/cheyne/index.html
Original Fiction: www.bellabooks.com/category/author-cheyne-curry

renegade
CHEYNE CURRY

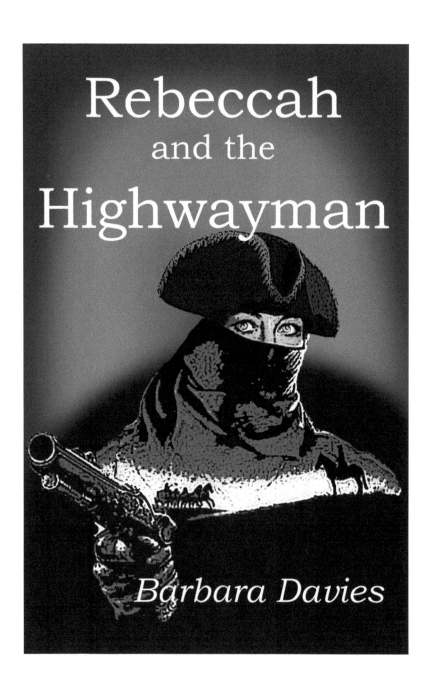

Rebeccah
and the
Highwayman

Barbara Davies

Chapter Twenty-Seven

I Wouldn't Have Missed It For The World

by Barbara Davies

MY FIRST BRUSH with *Xena* fan fiction left me unimpressed. At the time (1997/1998), I had no idea such a thing even existed, although, in hindsight, the two short stories I wrote in my teens featuring The Avengers and The Man from UNCLE surely qualify. I had no access to the internet, but my French penfriend Jay (whose classified advert in Starburst magazine asking for *Xena* fans I'd answered) did, and one day she printed off a couple of short *XWP* fanfic stories and posted them to me. One was a PWP (in which Gabrielle got her toe stuck in a bath tap, I seem to recall); the other was a romp involving Xena and Gabrielle trying to get rid of a clueless Joxer so they could have some alone time.

By then, I'd been writing crime, fantasy, and science fiction short stories for nearly ten years, trying to get published in the small press with limited success, and I thought, "I can do better than these!" So I wrote a short story, 'Like Pegasus,' told from Argo's point of view, popped it on a floppy disc, and sent it to Jay to do with whatever it was you were supposed to do when submitting fanfic. She sent it to Tom's Xena Page and he posted it on-line. Jay also printed off an appreciative comment from a reader –the first I'd ever received- and sent it to me. Like Gabrielle, I had dipped my toe in the water.

Fast forward six months or so, and I now had my own internet connection (primarily so I could email book reviews to Starburst). Those were the days of dial-up modems and eye-watering phone charges. I was always watching the clock, worried about the size of my next phone bill, so I developed a routine: send/receive emails a couple of times during the day and access the internet for ten minutes max in the evenings when it was cheaper. Of necessity, this meant using a targeted smash-and-grab approach to accessing websites rather than today's leisurely broadband browsing. Fortunately, I discovered Yahoo groups. Specifically, a UK-based group called the Xenanet. For the first time I could share my growing enthusiasm for all things *Xena* with other British fans via email. And it was on the Xenanet that I met fellow British bard Midgit.

Midgit knew all the *Xena* fanfic and index/review sites, and generously volunteered to be my guide to the best fan fiction out there. We restricted ourselves to completed stories, as those being posted in parts too often ran the risk of never being finished. Knowing I was clock-watching, she took it upon herself to download suitable stories, turn them into attachments, and email them to me. Now, whenever I downloaded my emails, dozens of stories thudded into my inbox, waiting to be read at my leisure. To say I quickly became addicted is an understatement. Our tastes didn't always mesh (Midgit soon learned not to send me PWPs) but mostly she was spot on. And she introduced me to that strange beast, unique to *Xena* fanfic, as far as I know: the uber. I was dubious as to whether I'd like ubers but willing to sample them, and they proved to be a revelation. I had to have a go at producing my own.

So began a period of intense creativity as I played in this wonderful new sandbox, aided by the directories of experts and beta readers provided by reviewer Lunacy on her website. It was my chance to try genres I'd not tried before, such as contemporary romance, historical fiction, and westerns, and experiment with different story lengths. I don't have the energy or patience to write novels, but an episodic approach makes them feasible. Ubers had few limits; if I wanted to make Xena a circus ringmaster, I could. So I did. And when 'Summer's Circus' received a coveted 'highly recommended' review from Lunacy herself, I was chuffed to bits.

I posted my stories on several of the websites dedicated to *Xena* fanfic that by then existed e.g. The Athenaeum, AUSXIP's Bard's Corner, The Academy of Bards, and also, in due course, on my own website. People read and liked them. I knew because they emailed me, something that rarely happens in the world of conventional publishing, and as well as thanks/feedback, some offered me cover art and in one instance a musical theme tune to accompany my story. So I set up my own Yahoo group, the better to keep in touch with my readers and vice-versa. Little did I know that among the group's members were two who were planning to start a publishing company.

By now, Midgit had introduced me to more *Xena* bards whose work I enjoyed and respected: Advocate, Redhawk, the late and much missed Nene Adams, and Tragedy88, among others, and we began reading each other's stories, offering constructive feedback and egging each other on. Some of us even got together to run our own *Xena* fanfic awards scheme for a while, until all the reading and judging became too time-consuming. Ideas for fanfic stories continued to come thick and fast: Xena as an outlaw, a pirate, a swordfishing boat captain, a famous violinist, a highwaywoman, a secret agent, a Regency viscountess, a Victorian romany, a Restoration actress, etc., and I gleefully set to work writing them.

As time passed, I couldn't help but notice that some *Xena* bards were publishing their fan fiction in book form and removing the original from the net. I had always approached fanfic as an amateur in the original sense of the word, so I had mixed feelings about this. Writing stories was my contribution to the Xenaverse—payment (if you like) for all the *Xena* fan feedback, fiction, reviews, artwork, videos, news, etc. I was receiving in my turn. The fact that some of the early books were poorly edited and full of typos didn't help. So I didn't go looking for a publisher. But in 2005, out of the blue, I received an offer from Bedazzled Ink (BInk) to publish my western uber 'Christie and the Hellcat.'

BInk were just starting out and had no books I could judge them by. I would be their first author; was I willing to take the chance? That I already knew Claudia and Casey (BInk's owner/publisher and senior editor) from my own Yahoo group was a huge plus. But I was cautious. After an exchange of frank emails discussing issues such as editing and quality control and a proviso that I could keep the 'warts and all' unedited originals on-line, I signed the contract. I'm glad I did. BInk have now published five of my *Xena* ubers and two specific short story collections. And receiving my author's copies of each book published is as sweet today as it was back then.

Which brings me up to date. I must confess that these days… whisper it!... I no longer feel the urge either to read or write fanfic. Just as well, as I believe many of the websites I used to haunt have vanished, been mothballed, or show little if any activity compared to the 'good old days.' A new generation of *Xena* fans may well be carrying on the fanfic tradition in a different way, of course, and if so, I hope they're having fun. The enthusiastic and supportive Xenaverse I experienced was a wonder to behold and brought me joy, a publisher, and lifelong friends. It was one of those exhilarating times when you had to be there, I think. And I was. I wouldn't have missed it for the world.

Fan Fiction: www.academyofbards.org/authors/barbara_davies.html
Original Fiction: binkbooks.bedazzledink.com/authors/barbara-davies/

INTERSECTION

Nancy Ann Healy

Chapter Twenty-Eight

Becoming the Bumbling Bard

by Nancy Ann Healy

"I'VE ALWAYS WANTED to become an author." I've been told that countless times. Two simple questions follow. "How do you become an author? How do you make your living as an author?" There is one solid piece of advice I can impart. Don't strive to become an *author;* be a storyteller.

I never imagined I would make my living writing books. I love books, movies, music, theater, and television. Exploring new worlds and meeting people from every walk of life, every period in history, and places I never dreamed could exist exhilarating. I can't tell you how many times I've placed myself in an imaginary world. I might cast spells, toil in a new land, fight in a World War, navigate the underbelly of organized crime, or the world of espionage. I've flown planes and visited distant worlds, all without leaving my couch. Stories live inside me. I believe they live in each of us.

My journey as an author is an unexpected plot twist in the story of my life. I didn't aspire to become a novelist. Years ago, I dabbled in stand-up and improvisational comedy. I wrote more monologues and plays than I care to count. Life has many crossroads. My choices led me away from my creative endeavors. Something was always missing in my life. I shoved it aside and pressed onward. It wasn't until I experienced a year of profound and tragic loss that I realized I had to change course.

I decided to return to college to pursue the ministry. I loved it. Assignments in ministry studies are both academic and artistic in nature. As I continued my education, the slight niggle at the back of my brain saying, "you're not listening," morphed into a loud bang demanding I pay attention. I needed to create. Writing, painting, music—these were not hobbies. Storytelling is what I was born to do. It is nothing less than the air in my lungs.

I felt compelled to write a play based on that year of upheaval in my life. I'd forgotten how to begin. My son suggested writing fan fiction. Coincidentally, my wife and I were watching *Xena*. The characters in *Xena* are rich. The stories are engaging, and the relationships resonate with me.

Like many, I left the end of the television series feeling deflated. I decided to give the characters I loved a new story, one called *Salvation.* It was the perfect place to start. I could draw from the spiritual aspects of the show and my theological studies. At the same time, I would write the love story I felt was screaming to be told. The title proved the perfect choice. In many ways, the story became *my* salvation.

I'd never *read* fan fiction when I started drafting *Salvation.* Endless discoveries awaited me. Thousands of stories were available. I immersed myself in the world. I couldn't stop. If I wasn't writing, I was reading. I found myself—*my* stories. In the world of fan fiction, Xena and Gabrielle were not represented as an implicit model of a romantic relationship. They got married! They had kids! Writers took them into new lifetimes. After all, they were soul mates who would travel together in every lifetime. I visited distant planets and foreign countries. I traveled with detectives, actresses, doctors, lawyers, warriors, and queens. I was hooked.

The more I read, the more I wanted to *write.* I was amazed at how many people were willing to read my story. I was invited to join groups on social media dedicated to fan fiction and the show. People encouraged me to write new characters. I mulled that idea over. What would I write? What did I love to read? Political thrillers. Bingo. My first novel, *Intersection,* took shape, and the characters of Alex Toles and Cassidy O'Brien were born. I couldn't wait to get to my computer to talk with them. Every day was like that. I loved every moment and every word I wrote. I didn't think about publishing a book. I took a journey, and it was the most amazing experience imaginable. It changed more than my career or my life. It changed me.

I would never suggest that writing fan fiction provides an easy path to writing novels that pay the bills. The *Xena* fan fiction community is unique. Xena and Gabrielle's relationship represented the first time many women saw their dreams of love and commitment reflected on television. A beautiful, implicit love story developed over six seasons of the iconic show. Implicit models possess an elegance that is hard to define. Fans, particularly lesbian fans, wanted something explicit. They wanted the relationship between the warrior and the bard to be *defined* as a romance. Lesbian viewers desperately craved a happy ending, something they could hold onto as hopeful in their lives. Fan fiction provided the remedy. Writers of fan fiction began to understand, as I did, that a hungry audience existed for lesbian models. That audience was undoubtedly broader than one fandom. Many lesbian fiction authors and publishers can trace their roots to *Xena* fan fiction. I'm not an exception.

Xena also offers a vast landscape from which to draw inspiration. Fantasy shows open realms that crime shows and medical dramas can't. Six seasons of adventures with a warrior princess and a bard explored everything from war to sex, Gods and immortality to mortality and loss, distant realms to historical events, and mythology to theology. The overarching story is one that speaks of heroism, forgiveness, redemption, and humanness. It was quirky, original, daring, romantic, adventurous, and even violent at times. Combining all these elements with two female lead characters makes the *Xena* fan fiction world a unique place to explore creative writing. *Salvation* was set ten years after Xena's death. I attempted to write the characters from the show as I imagined they would speak, feel, and appear ten years in the future. Writing a story in Xena's time and world forced me to expand my horizons. I wanted the journey to feel authentic. I also wanted to make Xena and Gabrielle's relationship clear. Those two goals required me to leave my comfort zone as a creator. I had to write romance and intimacy, and I also needed to depict violence and loss. I could've chosen to write for any number of fandoms. Few, if any, would've provided me the scope and the challenge that telling a story about Xena demanded. It served as excellent preparation for creating original characters and adventures.

Xena fans are dedicated, not only to the show but also to each other. It is a community that allows a writer to plant seeds and then helps water them. Devotion plays an enormous role in a fan fiction writer's ability to transition to a published author. The ability to form relationships with your audience is an asset when you reach the world of publishing. Your audience will follow. Your readers will be more than consumers. They will become your ambassadors. Word of mouth remains the most powerful marketing tool any author can hope to employ.

I can prove it. My first novel released the week of the annual *Xena* convention in Burbank in 2014. My fan fiction readers carried the book, took pictures of the book, tweeted about the book from the convention, wore T-shirts with Alex and Cassidy on them, talked to other convention goers, and served as unknowing press agents. I didn't ask for their help. I never needed to ask. The enthusiasm they created around the book sent it soaring to number one in Lesbian Fiction on Amazon, where it remained for nearly six weeks. *Intersection* also reached number five in general Political Thrillers. I am confident that the Xenite community is mostly responsible for the exposure the book received.

There are other tangible benefits to having experience in the fan fiction world. Not the least of these is interacting with public feedback. Exposure to public praise and criticism is beneficial for any person considering a venture into publishing. Praise feels wonderful, but it can surpass the casual, "I enjoyed this story." Putting yourself out into public in any way invites its share of challenges. People are vulnerable and emotional. There are times when a reader confuses the characters you create with the person behind the keyboard. Equally, some criticism moves beyond, "this wasn't for me." Occasionally, feedback gets nasty and personal. In my experience, this happens less in fan fiction. No one is paying to consume your content. It does occur. Learning when to engage, when to step back, what to take in, and what to let go helps when you step onto a larger stage. Experience, as they say, is a wonderful teacher.

Mechanics and style are elements of writing that develop over time. The more you read, and the more you write, the cleaner and more succinct your writing becomes. Practice will never make anyone perfect. It does improve imperfection. Fan fiction is a terrific place to practice. Often, the idea of writing tens of thousands of words is enough to scare people off the idea of writing altogether. They never start. Fan fiction provides an opportunity to pen short narratives and share work a chapter or two at a time. Writing for a fandom can help you find your footing, your confidence, develop skill, and cultivate an audience. All of these things are imperative for any person hoping to make a living as a novelist. But there is nothing more important than telling your story.

Something happens when you enter the world of publishing. When your writing becomes your livelihood, a new layer is added. You have bills to pay. You have to produce, and you have to perform. It can kill the joy of writing. You start to think about all the tangibles: your audience, the mechanics, the criticism, *and* the financial reality. That is the time to remember that you are a storyteller first and an author second. Losing sight of *why* you sit behind a keyboard for hours will negatively affect both your productivity and your product.

No one writes fan fiction for the monetary reward. It's written with joy. I've had many people tell me that they don't understand the concept of fan fiction. I take every opportunity to remind people that we strive for our goals, that we seek to explore our world based mainly on what has inspired us. It isn't a stretch to move from telling a story about characters you've enjoyed traveling with to creating unique worlds.

I worked as a retail manager for over twenty-five years. The latter part of my career was spent in bookstores. I met and worked with New York Times best-selling authors, hosted filmmakers and journalists for events, and sat with scientists and political figures during the doldrums that accompany book signings. One thing I have learned from every successful person I've met is that they were all inspired by someone or something. You might wonder how that pertains to making the leap from fan fiction to publishing.

It's not unlike making the leap from making movies on a super 8 camera or an iPhone to directing a studio blockbuster. You begin where we all start, inspired by the creation of others. I once hosted a physics professor and researcher who is considered an expert on theories relating to time travel. He told me he became a physicist because of H.G. Wells. Years later, after I'd started publishing, I was part of a panel at Comic Con. As luck would have it, I was invited to dinner with a successful movie producer and writer. He's had a hand in bringing numerous popular heroes to life. We sat surrounded by comic book artists. He told me he spent his childhood consumed by comics. He wanted to live with the superheroes he loves. Now, he brings them to life on the screen. Storytelling. We are all writing a story with every word we speak and every breath we take. Our stories become part of the fabric of the world. We aspire to create our lives based on what has moved us, and in doing so, we inspire others on their journey.

There is no unique checklist that guarantees success as an author. Often, when people ask my advice, I find myself scratching my head for a response. I didn't have a checklist. I didn't start with any expectations. I didn't even begin with a goal. I wanted to tell a story. As I began, I realized there were countless stories within me waiting to emerge. I could expound on the value of marketing strategies. I could impart my ideas on the subject of plot devices and character backstories. I could spend time sharing my experience in interacting with readers. I could write volumes about the reasons I believe *Xena* is responsible for growth in lesbian fiction. I could share countless observations I've made as I've transitioned from fan fiction to publishing, and to publishing full-time. It is imperative to always remember *why* and *how* the journey began.

Everything we create carries within it all that has inspired us. Why does a little boy want to become the president like Barack Obama? Why does a little girl aspire to win Wimbledon like Chris Evert or Billie Jean King? Why do you want to write a fan fiction about a warrior princess and a bard? Because you've been captivated by their story. Their adventures have inspired you in some way. We *aspire* because we have been *inspired*. If you have a story to tell, you must tell it. You should trust that someone will be captivated by it, and the circle of inspiration and aspiration will continue.

Writing *Salvation* started a new chapter in my life. Like all chapters, the time came to turn the page. Each line, each page, and each chapter is part of an ongoing story. How does a person turn a hobby of writing about television characters into a career of producing books about FBI agents, television stars, chefs, and senators? One word, one sentence, and one page at a time. Writing *Xena* fan fiction opened up new worlds for me. It was the catalyst for evolution with me and my life. Can anyone achieve the same thing? All that depends on the story *you* are writing.

Authors and publishers deal with dollar signs, marketing campaigns, event management, and a host of business realities. Storytellers embark on a journey. When I built my first website as a writer, I adopted a simple statement as my philosophy: "Life is a journey, not a destination. You create it." I may have known there was truth in the words before I wrote *Salvation*. I didn't understand what the statement meant. Whenever I revisit my path to publishing, I find myself humbled and grateful. I love *Xena*. I love the show because beneath its silliness and fantastical storylines, its heart is human. I fell in love with the characters—all of them. I laughed with them. I cried for them. I wished that somehow, that world might be real. *That* is what life is all about. Not warrior princesses and bards on the television screen: wonderment, curiosity, and connection. Our path isn't set by others. It is ours to navigate. As ancient travelers once did, we set our course by the stars, those distant lights that beckon us toward them. That is how I found myself typing furiously at my keyboard about ancient Greece. It's what led me to write the twists and turns in Alex and Cassidy's lives. No. Not everyone will write fan fiction and land a career as an author. Anyone *can* follow that path. It is your story to write. Don't be afraid to turn the page and start a new chapter. You never know; you might just find your *Salvation*.

Nancy Ann Healy's Xena Fan Fiction
https://www.thebumblingbard.com/fan-fiction

Original Fiction
https://www.thebumblingbard.com/

Chapter Twenty-Nine

Finding a Community and the Courage to Publish my Books

by Jae

I COME FROM a family of non-readers. I can't remember my mother, my stepfather, or any of my grandparents ever reading a book. They tolerated that I always had my nose in a book growing up but didn't understand or support it, so there weren't many books in our house. I read my way through the local library, and when I ran out of interesting books to read, I started writing my own at the age of ten or eleven. My family didn't know what to make of that either, but I didn't let that stop me.

I also grew up in a tiny little town of 800 people, with not one single out LGBT+ person. As a result, I felt pretty isolated as a book person and a lesbian.

It wasn't until I went to university that I met other people like me…and I met them through fan fiction.

I had no idea that stories about women loving women were out there until I stumbled across them on-line by coincidence. I remember I had googled "truth or dare," a party game that seemed to be rather popular in the US but wasn't played in Germany. Instead of an explanation of the game, a short story titled "Truth or Dare" by Meghan O'Brien, on a site called The Athenaeum came up. I started to read and… Well, needless to say, it was an eye-opening revelation because, as I know now, Meghan O'Brien is known for her steamy lesbian erotica!

Over the next couple of years, I read most of the stories that were posted on sites like The Athenaeum, The Academy of Bards, and Passion and Perfection. Most of what I read was *Xena: Warrior Princess* fan fiction. I had never even watched *Xena*—mostly because all English shows are dubbed on German TV, and the German version was horrible—but the fan fiction really resonated with me.

I must have devoured thousands of stories. I call it my free English language course. While I learned the basics of the English language in school, it certainly wasn't enough to write at the level of a native speaker or to read books with the same speed and enjoyment as I would a German book. But I hung in there, and soon, I didn't need a dictionary anymore. I absorbed new vocabulary just by reading, and believe me, I learned a lot of words and phrases that definitely aren't taught in school!

But what's more, I finally found what I never had growing up: a community of people who understood what reading means to me, especially reading stories featuring women who love women.

A community like that didn't exist in my native language, German. Back in 2006, there were no German websites where authors of lesbian fiction could post their stories, find beta readers, and interact with readers, so I became involved in the English-speaking fan fiction community instead.

After a few years, I decided I wanted to try my hand at writing my own stories with lesbian characters and posting them on-line for other people to enjoy, but I felt really insecure about it. I had never shared my stories with anyone but my twin sister. Was my writing ready for a bigger audience? What's more, I'm not a native speaker, so could my stories keep up with all the wonderful stories out there?

I decided to try. I found beta readers who volunteered their time to look over my stories before I posted them. I started to post my work on The Athenaeum, The Academy of Bards, and a couple of other fan fiction sites.

The feedback from readers was overwhelmingly positive! I got hundreds of emails from readers, telling me how much they loved the stories and begging me to post more. I still keep every single reader feedback email I got back then, and I sometimes re-read a couple when I'm having a bad day.

Backwards to Oregon was so well-received that it was the number one of The Athenaeum's top 25 list for two weeks in a row, and it even became The Athenaeum's Story of the Year in 2007!

Interestingly, *Backwards to Oregon* wasn't actually intended as a *Xena/Uber* Fan Fiction, but with a tall, dark-haired and a shorter character with reddish-blonde hair, many readers read it as an Uber, and the story certainly resonated with many Xenites. And who knows? Maybe I was influenced by all those fanfics I read.

The fan fiction community certainly influenced me. Not only did the feedback from beta readers improve my writing skills, but the success of the stories I posted on-line did a lot to boost my confidence as a writer. I don't think I would have had the courage to offer one of my manuscripts to a publisher if not for all the readers who sent me encouraging emails and some fellow authors who reached out to give me a virtual pat on the back.

In mid-2007, about a year after I had started writing in English, one of my beta readers encouraged me to submit one of my works to a publisher. She had heard of a new publisher specializing in lesbian fiction. L-Book was a pioneer when it comes to e-books, starting to publish them the year the

Kindle was first introduced.

At first, those old self-doubts crept up again. Was my work really good enough to be made into a "real" book? But with all the encouraging feedback I had received in mind, I finally hit the *send* button and submitted *Backwards to Oregon*.

Within less than a week, I had an acceptance letter in my inbox, and *Backwards to Oregon* was published in December 2007.

That was the beginning of an amazing publishing journey. I published five books with L-Book before switching publishers and joining Ylva Publishing, an international publishing house based in Germany, which allows me to translate my novels into my native language, publish them in English and German, and reach even more readers.

I actually first met my now-publisher, Astrid Ohletz, through *Backwards to Oregon* and The Athenaeum. Astrid is a fellow German who devoured all the stories posted on fan fiction archives too. She had loved *Backwards to Oregon*, sent me feedback, and eventually asked me to beta read her own stories. Later, she established her own publishing house to publish those stories.

So, in a way, fan fiction led to me joining Ylva Publishing.

I published my first contemporary romance, *Something in the Wine*, with them in 2012, and by now, I have published twenty lesbian romance novels, a novella, and thirty short stories. Most of them are available in German and as audiobooks too, one has been published in Italian, and there'll soon be a French version too.

But that's not all. My books were so successful that it soon started to look as if it might be possible for me to actually make a living from my writing. Being a full-time writer had been my dream since I had been a ten-year-old, scribbling my stories into old exercise books, but few people worldwide are able to make a living from their writing, so I thought it would forever stay a dream, especially since I wanted to write about women loving women.

After a lot of careful consideration, I took the leap at the end of 2013. I gave up my day job as a psychologist to become a full-time writer and part-time editor. It was a leap of faith, but one I had to take. I have never regretted that decision. I just celebrated my sixth anniversary as a full-time writer, and I'm still waking up happy every day that I get to live my dream, writing lesbian romances for a living.

But it's not about the money. It's still very much about the community for me. I'm still in touch with the beta reader who started it all by encouraging me to send my first book to a publisher. I met some of my best friends through writing fan fiction and lesbian fiction. Since I can work from anywhere, I get to travel the world and meet some of the wonderful readers who supported me over the years. I lead a very fulfilling, very busy life, yet I still try to make the time to give back to the community by mentoring new writers and giving them the help they need to get started on a similar journey.

So I have certainly come a long way, and it's all because of the amazing fan fiction and lesbian fiction community. I can only encourage you to reach out, build a network of support, and follow your dreams, whatever they might be.

***

Jae is the author of twenty award-winning lesbian romances. She lives in the sunniest city in Germany, near the French and Swiss borders. She used to work as a psychologist but gave up her day job in 2013 to become a full-time writer and a part-time editor. As far as she's concerned, it's the best job in the world. When she's not writing or editing, she is an avid reader of lesbian books, indulges her ice cream and office supply addictions, and watches way too many crime shows.

Website: http://jae-fiction.com
Facebook: https://www.facebook.com/JaeAuthor
Twitter: http://www.twitter.com/JaeFiction
Instagram: https://www.instagram.com/jaeauthor

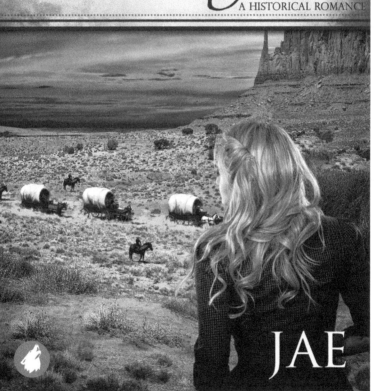

Backwards to Oregon

to Oregon

A HISTORICAL ROMANCE

JAE

Book One
The Shaken Series

KG
MacGregor

Without
Warning

Chapter Thirty

Look What You Made Me Do!

by KG MacGregor

WHAT'S THIS, ANOTHER 25-year leap? It sure went by in a *whoosh!*

I'm honored and proud to participate in this commemorative book celebrating *Xena: Warrior Princess*. I can unequivocally say that the show—and its passionate fandom—changed my life.

Now stop me if you've heard this: "*Xena* didn't change your life. *You* did!" That's the party line from the show's creators and stars, and I get how empowering it is. *I'm* the one who grabbed the opportunity, and who put the time and effort into my transformation. Still, I can't fathom any of it happening had I not walked a path through the Xenaverse.

I never aspired to be an author. My training was in social science—data and analytics—which I used in my career as a media research consultant. I'd convinced myself long ago that I possessed neither creativity nor artistic ability. No problem, since my work was numbers-oriented. So imagine my surprise to discover a latent interest in writing fiction. Not just any fiction—lesbian love stories. All it took was the right inspiration, which turned out to be a campy fantasy show featuring two heroines whose emotional and physical affection portended a romantic, sexual relationship. Oh girl, that was a mouthful. Let me put it this way: Ten minutes into my very first episode (FF&G), I said to my partner, "I don't know what this silly show is, but those two women are sleeping together."

Why did this quirky series resonate so deeply? Perhaps because Hollywood's meager rations for the lesbian audience consisted primarily of frivolous girl/girl kisses designed to goose the ratings during sweeps week, with predictable returns to character by episode's end. There was nothing on-air in the 1990s that depicted lesbians in love. I made do with shows that depicted intimate friendships between women who were especially devoted to one another—*Facts of Life*, *Designing Women*, *Cagney & Lacy*—even though all those characters were explicitly described as heterosexual. *X:WP* portrayed the deepest love I'd ever seen between two female characters, so intense that once I saw it as romantic, I couldn't see it any other way. Even when the show's plot lines explicitly departed from the lesbian subtext, there was no erasing the enthralling onscreen chemistry between Lucy Lawless and Renée O'Connor. Clearly, I had an unrealized need to see *my life* reflected back at me in the media I used, a need I didn't fully recognize until the series finished with Xena's death. About that…I thought it a ballsy conclusion to the hero arc, but it marked a devastating end to the love story—and to that sliver of lesbian representation that had become so precious to me.

Not long after the series ended, I started reading fan fiction to fill the void. I was especially drawn to uber stories that borrowed from the show's brilliant—and in light of the finale, comforting—the concept that Xena and Gabrielle were soulmates destined to meet again in all their future lives. Our modern-day heroes were doctors, ranchers, attorneys, detectives, and rock stars. I could easily picture Lucy and Renée in these contemporary roles. Many of the themes were authentic to my lived experience, with characters struggling against familiar obstacles: fear of rejection by family and friends, anxiety over losing a job, heartbreak from an unrequited crush on a straight friend. But they also celebrated strength, courage, selflessness and virtue, all traits that had drawn me to Xena and Gabrielle. Best of all, they ended happily with the couple together and in love.

Those happy endings were essential, and not just because we didn't get one with Xena and Gabrielle. We didn't get happy endings *anywhere*. Generations of lesbians grew up and came of age without ever seeing the girl get the girl. The only windows to affirmation were through obscure films like *Desert Hearts* and *Claire of the Moon*, and hard-to-find books by pioneering writers such as Jane Rule, Sarah Aldridge, and Katherine V. Forrest. Uber fan fiction, written for the show's subtext fans and posted on-line for free, was practically bottomless, with new stories posting every day.

Before long, I was spending all my work-related travel time reading stories I'd downloaded for the trip, including favorites that I read again and again. I suppose it was inevitable that I would eventually try to write the story I wanted to read. Wouldn't it be exciting, I thought if Xena and Gabrielle met…in modern-day Los Angeles…while climbing out from beneath the rubble of an earthquake…and then got separated…and found each other again months later…and fell in love? I'd call it *Shaken*. Clever, huh? I tapped a few creative neurons to come up with that premise, but the rest I figured I could manage using all those left-brain organizational skills that served me so well in my consulting work. All I had to do was picture Lucy and Renée as my leads and follow the tried-and-true template of the other Xenaverse bards, even appropriating their clichés and writing quirks. I then came up with a pseudonym to wall off my fan fiction from my consulting work: KG from my beloved cats Katie and Grace and MacGregor from my Scottish ancestors.

Over the next couple of years, I manically cranked out over a dozen uber works that included seven novel-length stories, all with lead characters who were facsimiles of Lucy and Renée. In that sense, the show and the actors were a primary inspiration. But by this time, there was something even stronger stoking my muse: the fan fiction community itself. There was a vibrant synergy of bards, beta readers, webmasters, reviewers, cover artists, publicists—all fueled by one essential group: the *readers*. They kept the ecosystem churning with notes of praise and gratitude, many talking in poignant terms about how our stories moved them. It's hard to overstate the effect their encouragement had on my motivation to keep writing.

Enter desktop publishing and print-on-demand. A number of cottage-industry presses rose up with the idea of turning our uber fan fiction into actual books we could offer for sale, as long as they didn't explicitly encroach on the *X:WP* creators' copyright. Suddenly the lesbian book market was flooded with hastily written, dubiously edited works (including mine) about tall, dark-haired women with short blond love interests. I'll spare you the horrors of my initial emergence as a published author. We were dilettantes working with amateurs, mostly well-intentioned but utterly blind to our deficiencies. What we *did* have was an incredibly loyal following of Xena fans supporting our efforts with their hard-earned dollars. It was on the strength of this built-in fan base (and four published books) that I was able to persuade Bella Books, the premier publisher of lesbian romance, to take a chance on me. I committed to learning my craft, engage with a broader audience, and put out the very best books I could. To follow this new bliss, I dropped all my consulting clients, closed my business, and began calling myself a writer.

One might say that signing with Bella in 2005 marked the end of my debt to *Xena* and the fandom. In order to publish my on-line novels, I had to rewrite the beloved uber archetypes as original characters, and I worked hard with experienced editors to clean up the endearing fan fiction tropes and platitudes. It paid off in 2008 when my fifth Bella novel, *Out of Love,* won the prestigious Lambda Literary Award for lesbian romance. That was a completely original—oh, wait. It was actually based on a short story I wrote for the Valentine's Special at the *Royal Academy of Bards*, so maybe I shouldn't count it as post-Xenaverse. Which means I ought not count five of my distinguished Golden Crown Awards either, since they too had their genesis in works I posted on-line as uber fan fiction.

Hmm…but all that was years ago, right? Surely, I've moved on from the Xenaverse since then. Except the book I just finished (*The Lucky Ones*) revisits characters from the uber tale, *The House on Sandstone*. And my next project is shaping up to be book five in The Shaken Series, that little earthquake story that launched me down this road. When it comes to inspiration, Xena's one of those catchy earworms that won't be suppressed. In fact, true story: I've heard from readers who followed me over from the Xenaverse that it doesn't matter how I describe my characters—they still picture Lucy and Renée because it enhances their enjoyment of the book. *I love that!* It's also a humbling reminder that once a book leaves my desk, it belongs to the audience, who will bring their own expectations and perspectives to whatever I meant to write.

By now, I hope you're completely convinced that *Xena* directly changed my life. In writing this chapter, I began to recognize tangential influences as well. "The greater good" is an enduring legacy of both the show and the fandom. Years of charity auctions and "Feel the Love" days have cultivated collective altruism that makes me proud to be a *Xena* fan. I especially appreciate that fans are encouraged not only to support the stars' chosen causes but to get involved in our own communities as well. In 2012, I was invited by my editor, the esteemed lesbian author Katherine V. Forrest, to join the board of Lambda Literary, a global organization whose mission is to ensure that LGBTQA+ stories are written, published, and read. I confess that my first thought was to write a nice check and decline, as a board commitment would seriously eat into my writing time. But Lucy Lawless, whose career I've continued to follow, had just made worldwide headlines for climbing atop a drillship to stop its Arctic exploration. *Mad respect!* If someone as busy as Lucy could risk so much for a cause she believed in, surely I could serve a two-year term on a nonprofit board. Well, I ended up serving *six* years, including two as board president, before bowing to term limits. And guess what? It was one of the most gratifying experiences of my life.

Storytelling also presents ways to advance the greater good, which circles back to where this essay started. Twenty-five years ago, lesbians living happily ever after was a radical idea for television. Hollywood still disproportionately kills off lesbian characters, a trope known as "burying your gays." We've finally gotten more lasting portrayals in shows like *Glee, Wynonna Earp,* and *The Good Fight.* One could even argue that *spoiler alert* *Orange Is the New Black* delivered the heroes' ending for Piper and Alex that we'd craved for Xena and Gabrielle.

As a romance writer, I'm wedded to conventions of the genre that flat-out *require* a happy or at least hopeful ending. Affirming stories of lesbians can be a lifeline for some, particularly those constrained by social, cultural, or religious influences. Seeing oneself portrayed positively in fiction validates their existence. For those who feel trapped or isolated, it can light a path toward fulfillment. I need not imagine that my work has impacted readers this way—I know it from their heartrending notes and from talking with them at book events. *Books save lives.*

As my readership grew, I began to recognize the potential—and my own responsibility—to amplify the greater good through my work. By rewarding heroes and serving justice to villains, I write the world I want to live in. In my world, women persevere against an evil system that lets star athletes get away with rape. Environmentalists expose the corporate and political malfeasance that allows oil companies to foul our waterways with impunity. And a small Southern town says no to the scourge of white supremacy.

Stories shape and reinforce our core values. We feel sympathy for people struggling with disability, addiction, or past trauma. We're inspired to aim high, to open our hearts, to forgive. And as lesbians, we celebrate our growing visibility in this vast, assorted game of life.

I can trace my small part in this historic progression back to that day I stumbled on *Xena: Warrior Princess*. A "goofy show for smart people," Lucy once called it. I'm forever grateful that it brought me to this wonderful place in life, where I'm KG MacGregor, author—and a very proud product of the Xenaverse.

***

KG MacGregor is the author of twenty-six books, including the romance saga, The Shaken Series. Her works feature strong, career-minded lesbians, and blend romance with intrigue and adventure. She has been honored with nine Golden Crown Awards, a Lambda Literary Award, the Alice B. Medal for career achievement, and the Lifetime Achievement Award from the Royal Academy of Bards. She served as president of Lambda Literary, the world's premier organization for LGBTQA+ literature. A native of the Blue Ridge Mountains, she now makes her home in Nashville TN with partner Jenny and warrior cat Rozzie.

Xena Fan Fiction: www.academyofbards.org/authors/kg_macgregor.html
Official Site: www.kgmacgregor.com

Awakenings

I Found My Heart In San Francisco
Book One

Susan X Meagher

Chapter Thirty-One

First Steps

by Susan X Meagher

A LITTLE MORE than twenty years ago, a friend suggested I watch this kind of crazy TV show that aired on my local Los Angeles network on Saturday afternoons.

I was an adult and hadn't watched an afternoon scripted show in at least twenty years, but I trusted her taste, so I watched *Xena: Warrior Princess* for the first time that weekend.

This was right before Thanksgiving, and they were airing a marathon, so my wife and I turned it on as we were preparing a meal for our guests. After about an hour, we were both sitting in front of the TV, giving each other puzzled looks. We weren't sure if it was supposed to be historical, deeply serious, slapstick funny, or a mash-up of every theme. But when we watched "One Against An Army," we were sure it was a subtext-dripping show that was blasting blatant lesbian signals into our humble home. (For those of you who weren't alive in 1998, let me assure you this was not common.)

So began my infatuation with all things *Xena*. At the time, I had just quit my job, where I'd worked, unhappily, for a large law firm. So I had some time on my hands, which I devoted to plunging into the *Xena* fanfic community, which was newish, and growing by leaps and bounds.

I don't recall the first story I read, but I'm confident I read dozens of them within a day or two. I was enraptured, and continued to read anything I could find until one fine day when I read Melissa Good's first story in the Dar and Kerry universe.

I had no interest in learning large amounts of detail about ancient Greece, nor trying to figure out whatever wacky timeline the TV series took place in, but I loved the dynamic between Xena and Gabrielle, and had the germ of an idea that I could tell my own story about the characters so long as I could put it in the present day as Missy had.

Over the next few months, I came up with, and quickly discarded many ideas. I finally settled on a story about a returning Iraq war veteran who enters Cal-Berkeley on the GI Bill, and meets a seemingly straight, very privileged woman who's younger and naive—but interested.

I wrestled with the idea for weeks, finally deciding I wasn't the right person to get into the head of a veteran. I did, however, have some insight into Irish-American families, so I made one character the only girl in a large extended family.

I swiftly wrote the first several hundred pages of "I Found My Heart In San Francisco," belatedly learning that long titles are not wise. I was at a stopping point—kind of—but had a lot more to say, so I wrote another few hundred pages.

During this time, I was avidly spending my evenings on-line with my hundreds of new friends—Xenites all. I posted infrequently, but I didn't have the nerve to share any of my work.

I regret that I've forgotten the name of the woman who wrote a story where you had to ask to read the last, very racy, chapter. My interest in racy chapters outweighed my shyness, and I wrote to her, telling her how much I'd enjoyed the story so far. I got a nice reply later that day, which made me feel like I'd interacted with someone *very* famous. I got such a buzz from that scant interaction that I began to truly wish I had the nerve to actually post my own work. But I didn't. Nowhere close.

By the time I'd written a couple of hundred thousand words, my wife took matters into her own hands, cut the story into manageable hunks, and sent the first hunk to MaryD, as well as the Royal Academy of Bards—without telling me. Days later, my wife showed me the responses, with both sites agreeing to post it.

I was more excited about having that story posted than I'd been to graduate from college or law school. That might sound funny, but this was the first time in my life I was able to express my *own* thoughts in written form, and that made me blissfully happy.

As soon as the story went up, I started getting reader feedback, which I printed off and have retained. It was what I imagine doing serious drugs feels like—where a substance fills a need you didn't know you had.

I worked twelve hours a day cranking out more, soon finding myself proclaiming I'd write twenty-six of these books. One for each letter of the alphabet. How hard could that be?

It turns out it's fairly hard to write twenty-six volumes of a series about two college students, but I'm getting close to finishing. To keep myself energized, I started to write stand-alone novels after a while, and I've really enjoyed going back and forth between the series and the stand-alones.

But all of my writing goes back to the Xenaverse. There was a zero percent chance of my trying to write fiction without the incredible support I enjoyed from the community. I was terribly lucky to stumble upon the fanfic community at the right time in my life. For someone like me, who can produce a lot once I start, the community gave me the confidence to actually begin.

Obviously, my wife was then, and is now, my biggest supporter. Early on, I agreed to a publishing deal for my first book. This was back in the day when publishers popped up like dandelions in the spring, and many of them died when the heat of summer hit. My wife decided it made sense for us to self-publish, since we knew we were serious about it and wouldn't overextend ourselves. Despite her full-time job, she's been my publisher for about eighteen years, and if there's anyone who loves her publisher more than I do, she's a very lucky woman.

My wish is that all of us who love reading about the lives and loves of women who love women take the time to encourage new writers like the Xenaverse encouraged me.

Writing is a scary proposition for anyone who isn't used to revealing all of her inner thoughts to perfect strangers. When someone makes her first stab at it, she deserves gentle treatment, along with enthusiastic support. If you can find a way to do that, whether through sending notes of congratulations to new writers, proof-reading for them, editing if you have the skills, or even mentoring them, I strongly encourage you to do so. Every fledgling writer you support will thank you.

Because of the Xenaverse, I've met people I consider sisters, and have a friendship network that extends into the hundreds. I've gained significant self-confidence, have overcome my terror of public speaking, and have never had to go back to work in an office. Much of that is from luck and circumstance, but, again, I can clearly trace all of it to my original support network. The Xenaverse has given me the life I hadn't known I craved, and I will never be able to repay them for helping me find my voice.

***

Xena Fan Fiction:
http://www.academyofbards.org/authors/sx_meagher.html
Official Site:
https://www.susanxmeagher.com/

LOVE
BEARETH
ALL THINGS

REDMOND CIVIL WAR ERA ROMANCE SERIES ~ BOOK 5

T. NOVAN
TAYLOR RICKARD

Chapter Thirty-Two

Confessions of an Ancient Bard

by T. Novan (Morgan Sams)

I WAS DELIGHTED and greatly honored when Mary asked me to be a part of this project, and I readily agreed.

Then a day or two later, my brain went, oh shit!

Personal perspective pieces are tough for me, especially when the subject is so important and special. I have been working on this project for six months. I have started and rejected three different attempts. I have spent dozens of hours with fingers poised over the keyboard, feeling like nothing I could put down on paper would ever make people understand what this quirky little show could mean to me and so many others all over the world.

There is no way for me to adequately explain the depths of emotion associated with something we hold so dear and important.

I know people wonder how a TV show, and one described as campy at that, can become so important in the lives of its fans.

Every good fandom gives its audience something it can connect with. In the case of *Xena*, two strong female characters, flawed and trying to find their paths and answers for their lives. Set in a realm of fantasy, anything was possible, or most anything.

There is something about it that speaks to our spirit and catches our imagination.

I have been a *Xena* fan from the original airing of the second episode (catching the first episode in the second airing that evening). We are lovingly referred to as Elders in some circles and I am proud to be a part of that group.

I was going through a tough spot when *Xena* premiered. A long term relationship had just ended. I had moved from my home to the attic space that a friend offered me until I could get my bearings. I was changing jobs. It was just a difficult time, and *Xena* offered an hour of respite from the frantic unknown.

For sixty minutes, I got to watch someone whose life was worse off than mine. I might not have a girlfriend, or a house anymore, but at least I didn't have grungy warlords chasing me.

And it didn't take long to fall in love with the characters, all for very different reasons. *Xena* was one of those shows blessed to have a cast that meshed perfectly. While Lucy Lawless and Renée O'Connor were the stars of the show, they shared the screen beautifully with their ever-changing and rotating list of co and guest stars. The casting was so seamless that when Lucy Lawless was injured during a publicity junket, the show was able to write and produce "Ten Little Warlords," with Hudson Leick stepping into the role of Callisto inhabited by Xena, and it worked beautifully and is considered a fan favorite.

That kind of chemistry among the entire cast is a rare and precious thing. They brought the characters to life in a very tangible way. They made you care about them, and the moment you start caring about someone, they become a part of you. They have an impact on your life.

Xena became so beloved that the fans became a force to be reckoned with. If there was a need, the fandom came together. Twenty-five years down the road, fans are still giving, and have raised millions of dollars for many, many causes.

It gave us hope, it gave us confidence. It helped so many of us find those families that finally accepted us for who and what we were. So many of us were young and struggling with our own identities and directions in our own lives.

The fans formed chosen families. There have been dozens of commitment ceremonies and weddings between people who met as a result of the show. People have moved to other states and countries to be with someone they fell in love with all because of this silly little program.

Over the last two and a half decades, we have shared the news of, births of children and grandchildren, the loss of loved ones, marriages, divorces, and illness. Everything typical family experiences and shares, we have done on a global scale.

I had always been a very quiet and private person, but with the people I met in this fandom, I had no choice but to expand my world, and I was made so much richer for it.

I felt compelled to write about these characters, and I was encouraged in a way I had never experienced before. People I had never personally met, from far-flung corners of the world, reached out to offer me support when I began my fledgling attempts at writing fan fiction. People who had never laid eyes on me, took the time to contact me to tell me what I was doing was good and that they enjoyed it.

Suddenly, I was an artist within my new family and community. It is a role I enjoy a great deal. I am in my comfort zone telling stories, weaving a tapestry of words that form a rich fabric in which someone can wrap themselves for a few hours. I feel complete when I am writing. I have grown as a person from my writing; it has helped me work through more than one difficult issue. I would never have found any of that if it were not for *Xena*.

I am fortunate some of those people wrote to me and shared stories about how my writing, my efforts had helped them. The one that will always stick with me is the young woman who wrote to say that she had finally come to recognize her relationship was abusive because of something I had written about domestic violence and its impact. She related to me that she had found the courage to leave, the strength to end the relationship, and that she had given birth to a healthy baby boy a few weeks after establishing her own home. She named him Kai, after a character in the story I had written.

I am forever grateful to the powers that be for letting us play in their sandbox. They allowed several of us to launch careers. They allowed this family to come together and remain together. They allowed us to flourish and help each other in every way possible, some of which we could never have imagined.

As we gather in Los Angeles in April 2021 for the twenty-fifth anniversary, if there were a category for "most changed," I'd probably be in the lead for that one. I have honestly changed inside and out. Big changes that allowed me to be honest with myself and those around me. Changes that would have been far more difficult without the support of my Xenite family.

I am a transgendered person. Over the last fifteen years, I have been able to live my life as I want, as I need to, as a man. When you begin the process of transition, it is a profoundly frightening experience because you must tell those you love and care about.

Many people like me lose family and friends over our choices. We become outcasts in many cases, having to rebuild a circle of friends in a world that does not even want us to be real.

In my case, I did lose some family members, none of them worth being concerned about. Like the friends I knew growing up, they abandoned me as well. But not my *Xena* family. I did not lose one person from this group. In some cases, it strengthened our bond, as these people were glad that I would share this with them.

That kind of strength and courage does not come along very often, especially in a large diverse group of people. It does take a great deal of both to open your heart and home to someone that society has branded deviant and unworthy of consideration, let alone love and respect.

It has been said that trans people are brave, courageous for living our truth. In reality, it is those around us who don't turn their backs who are truly worthy of those accolades. People like me have to live our truth, our lives in order to be happy. It is our friends and family who remain with us and help shield us from a cruel world that are the heroes in the story.

If there is one thing that *Xena* created, it was a world of heroes.

Even if most people don't realize they walk among us, we are all so much better off for it.

Don't discount where the next heroes we need might rise from.

It might be because of a silly little TV show.

***

Publishers Note: T. Novan is published by AUSXIP Publishing and his latest novel is called "Love Beareth All Things". It's written with his wife and writing partner, Taylor Rickard.

You can find out more about T. Novan's work here:

T. Novan's Xena Fan Fiction:
http://ausxip.com/tnovan/

AUSXIP Publishing Author Page:
http://ausxippublishing.com/authors/tnovan/

Facebook T. Novan Fan Page:
https://www.facebook.com/Wordsheard1

Chapter Thirty-Three

Beyond Thousands of Words!

by Sherri Rabinowitz

I STARTED WRITING *STAR TREK* FAN FICTION many years ago. I loved it. Back then, we sent them out in magazine form—what we used to call fanzines. They were made for and by fans. Long before the internet, we used to buy and sell them at *Star Trek* cons and from the back of Starlog Magazine. I used to sit in my university library, writing fan fiction instead of studying. Bad me. It relaxed me and comforted me during stressful times; it was as much for my comfort and fun as it was for the enjoyment of those who bought the zines. It was also a creative outlet when I badly needed one.

Though I never stopped writing stories and poems, I did stop writing and reading fan fiction until *Xena* came along. I was very busy with the hurried and crazy world of gainful employment. Then one day I got my first computer, and I had just started to watch *Xena*, so I wondered if there was anything on-line. I discovered fan fiction. I used a lot of paper downloading stories so I could read them in bed (no laptops or android cells then).

At first, I just wrote poems, then what were called fixer-up stories, which were very, very short. Did you ever watch an episode of a favorite series and not like the ending or thought there was no ending? That is what fixer-uppers are. I know that they leave the ending of episodes to the viewers' imagination. Well, my imagination just didn't want to stay inside my head; I had to get it down on paper. Then they became longer and longer stories. And then, boom! I was writing fan fiction. I was hooked again. From *Xena* fan fiction, I was introduced to Uber stories, which are original creations from the author based on the characters from the TV show. I really became hooked on that even more because it was more fun. You had more leeway and, to be honest, my characters got really far, far, far away from the shows. I was just enjoying myself too much. I wrote pretty much original stories and people would read them. It was a fantastic school, really. I got feedback from readers on what was good and what was not. It was the beginning of everything for me.

I played with several of my stories to see, which would translate into a book. I worked with several editors and it was hard to find a fit. I am rather sensitive, so really abrupt people hurt my feelings. Still, I didn't want namby-pamby people who agreed with me. The best editor I ever had was my dad, and he really was a godsend on my first book. Finally, I decided on Murder Inc. as the fan fiction I would turn into my first book. I worked hard. I tore it apart and put it back together, I added characters and took characters out. I cut favorite scenes and added a cat. I restructured the book to focus on my characters and it became a real book. It was a very hard job and when I was done, my editor (I finally found the right person) nodded and let me know that it was ready.

I sent it out. It was accepted on my third try. My dad was so excited! He always wanted to be an author himself and he was just so proud that I was about to be a real published author. He took the cover my talented artist friend Anja Gruber had created and made a lot of copies to pass them out as a flyer to everyone he knew. Then a tragedy struck (not intense or personal, but pretty damn painful): my publisher went bankrupt. They sold to a company which said they would publish all the books, but then they dropped several of them, including mine. Even small independent publishing was a difficult world. I was going to give up, but my fan fiction fans and my family encouraged me to try again. So I did. After about another year, I found a new publisher and my very first novel, Murder Inc., came out into the world. My first book, my first child, was born.

My dad was a one-man publicity man, and he told everyone about my book; even our relatives were not immune. At dinner with one of my uncles and his guest, my dad regaled them about my storyline, according to my mom, pretty much telling them the whole story. She said she kept kicking him under the table, but he ignored it and blithely went on. He was so proud of me; my whole family was proud of me.

After Dad passed away I stopped writing, except for very depressing poetry (my poetry tends to be depressing and even more so when I was suffering such a huge loss as that of my beloved dad). After encouragement from my mom and brother, I started to fiddle with a new idea for a novel. It all started during Christmas time at the mall when I started to jot notes about what was to become my second novel, Fantasy Time Inc. No relation to the first, but they both have the 'Inc.' for different reasons.

[Sherri's story continues as she navigates her way to a hit podcast show and radio playhouse in the section: Xena Is Responsible For...)

Xena Fan Fiction:
http://www.academyofbards.org/authors/ri.html
Original Fiction site:
http://authorpage.com/rithebard

Murder Inc.

RI

PART 6

THE SOCIAL XENAVERSE

Chapter Thirty-Four

Xenaverse Social Presence

by MaryD

AH, THE SOCIAL Xenaverse! How much it has changed in twenty-five years, and it will continue to change as the years go by! It goes without saying; nothing ever stays the same. That's progress!

I'm going to take you through the time tunnel back to the dawn of a new age (I feel there should be some Enya music as I write this). An astonishing thing happened in the late 1980s and early 1990s. The internet was readily available to the masses, and anyone who had a modem could have the world at their fingertips.

The speeds ranged from 1200, 2400, 4800, and 9600 bps, and then in 1991, it reached 14.4 kb, and in 1994 it reached 33.6 k, and then it hit the motherlode in 1996 at 56k. Trust me, the leap from 14.4 to 56k made a HUGE difference.

Back in the day, you had to know how to use Unix. For the Mac lovers reading this, if you go into terminal, you will find the raw power of Unix. For the Windows users, select the Windows + Q and you will get the search bar, then type 'cmd,' and you have the command line (Windows DOS terminal, also built on Unix). Both operating systems were built from the Unix system.

Hey, you, the one whose eyes just closed…wakey wakey! That trip down memory lane didn't last a long time. Now back to our topic. It was a period that would introduce us to the world of Usenet. Usenet was (and still is) a worldwide distributed discussion system. It had what we now call forums, but they were called Groups on every conceivable topic.

Usenet was the original Facebook, Twitter, Tumblr, and a host of other social sites. From Usenet came Fidonet – specialized groups (think Google Groups), and then we branched out to Bulletin Boards (BBS) – the ORIGINAL message forums. 60,000 BBSes were serving 17 MILLION users in the United States in 1994. Back in the day, I set up a couple, and they were fun!

All this happened right on time for a new show to be born and a new fandom to emerge (see, I was getting to this point). *Xena* came at the birth of the internet on September 04, 1995. In 1996, the modem speeds went up and allowed everyone with a decent connection and a basic knowledge of Unix -or that perennial favorite America On-line (AOL)- to connect. The new breed of social interaction was ready to take on the new frontier (I am writing this with Captain Picard's voice in my head and Enya's music in the background. Heady combination).

The social Xenaverse was born in 1996 with on-line message boards, mailing lists, and the USA Net Forum. This allowed Xenites to gather, to discuss, to ship (we didn't call it shipping back then...wonder what we would have called Xena and Gabrielle... XeGab? GabXe? XGab?). The fans found their mini tribe within a tribe.

Xena Mailing Lists

This is just a small sample of the *Xena* Mailing Lists that were active (and some still are).

- Chakram
- Down Under Xenites - The Australian Xena Fan Club List
- Flawless
- Friends Forever Mailing List
- Gabchat
- Gabsclan
- Herc-Xena
- MacConnor
- Merwolf Pack
- Pacific Northwest Xenite Mailing List
- Sisterhood of Subtext
- Subtext in Xena
- The Tavern
- The Twisted Tavern
- Xena Club
- Xena_Gals
- Xenaverse
- XMR

A LONG list of Mailing Lists is on Tom's Xena Page
http://www.xenafan.com/links2/Mailing_Lists/

Xena Chats
- Aussie Xena Chat
- Pan & Yah's Xenaverse
- QWorld Xena Chat

- The Babble On (virtual ship sailing to NewXenaland)
- Xena: Warrior Palace

A LONG list of Xena Chats is on Tom's Xena Page
http://www.xenafan.com/links2/Chat/

On-line Forums / Message Boards
- USA Xena Warrior Princess NetForum (Closed)
- AUSXIP Talking Xena (Active)
- Whoosh! On-line Forum (Inactive)
- XOC (Xena On-line Community) (Active)
- The Xena Library (Active)

A LONG list of On-line Forums is on Tom's Xena Page

Those lists are just a sample of the plethora of links that were active. Now, of course, we have Facebook, Twitter, Tumblr, Instagram, et al.

For a huge list (but not complete because you couldn't list everything), go over to Tom's Xena Page and have a look! Most of them, unfortunately, are no longer active, but it's still an impressive list.
http://www.xenafan.com/links2/

AUSXIP

TALKING XENA
FORUM

Chapter Thirty-Five

Creating a Safe Haven for Xenites –
AUSXIP Talking Xena Forum

by MaryD

IT WAS THE last season of *Xena*, and we were months away from the show's series finale; rumors were running rampant and people's emotions were running high. Universal Studio's Official NetForum was ablaze and tempers frayed. It wasn't generally a place of respect and acceptance. There had to be another way for Xenites to express their feelings without their words wounding others (compared to today's Facebook and Twitter hangouts, it was tame). I felt it was time for something better and one where AUSXIP's rules of respect could be enforced.

It was time for AUSXIP to have it's own message board where our moderators could enforce those rules rather than a free-for-all. AUSXIP Talking Xena was founded back in January of 2001 by Redhead and me, with Redhead being the admin. It was a place for people to have a friendly discussion about the show Xena, its companion show Hercules: The Legendary Journeys, and the stars of the two shows, Lucy Lawless, Renée O'Connor, Kevin Sorbo, Michael Hurst, and all the rest.

Since then, it has grown to over 3,200 members with well over one million total posts and is still going strong. Over the years, it has also changed ownership several times—first when, after a year of co-ownership, I stepped aside to leave it in Redhead's hands.

In February 2009, I stepped back in and brought Talking Xena once again under the AUSXIP umbrella. The mods and former owner EZ Ryder had made it a great meeting place for people to chat about Xena, Lucy Lawless, Renée O'Connor and the rest of the Xena family. It was with that in mind that I agreed to bring TX back into the fold and have it become AUSXIP's official message board. Tobias now runs the board with the help of other moderators. I go in for the occasional, "Hi, I'm still alive, just checking the place out and back out I go."

As time went on, the number and type of forums, along with the look, have changed from the original to the present with many incarnations in between. The one steady thing has been our members, who may come and go, but are always part of the family and the heart of the board.

We had the pleasure of having Rob Tapert, Creator, Writer and Executive Producer of *Xena: Warrior Princess,* doing a Q&A with our members; he answered 121 questions! You can read Rob's Q&A here:

https://www.tapatalk.com/groups/talkingxena/20-answers-from-rob-tapert-t754.html#.TwAodkrQ-jF

or

http://ausxip.com/one/robtapert.html

Our forums are:

- Main Board
- General Xena Chat
- Subtext Central
- Shipper Heaven
- Fencesitters Forum
- Xena Polls
- ROC Chat
- Lucy Chat
- Herc Chat
- TV, Music, Movies, Games
- Reader's Review
- Sci-Fi Central
- Sports Center
- Off Topic
- Current Events

You can now find AUSXIP Talking Xena here:

https://www.tapatalk.com/groups/talkingxena/

Chapter Thirty-Six

A Xenite in the Closet –
Xena & Ubers Podcast (XNU)

by Cas

WHAT STARTED OUT as a little quirk to pass the time actually wound up being a massive endeavor that I did not realize would attract so much attention.

My name is Cas, and I am the creator/host for Xena & Ubers Podcast, also known as XNU. It all started out on Monday, February 18, 2008, as a fluke crazy idea. I had been surfing the net looking for some fandom that would strike my fancy and came across a few sites that listed some stories, which of course, lead to other sites and then video clips.

As one of many, I was late to the table to discover the *Xena* fandom universe. Oh, don't get me wrong. I was well aware of *Xena*, having watched the show when I was not working or doing family activities. It's just that I had no knowledge of MaryD's site nor of any others except what I found in my surfing adventures.

After many, many months of reading and YouTubing, I craved more. Reading required you to actually pick up a book or Kindle, spend time on-line at the sites reading or downloading to read later, which would, of course, interfere with other tasks such as work or eating, sleeping, etc. Then there was the watching countless videos, which also was frowned upon at work, as I was getting paid to actually do work (darn the inconvenience) and not use precious streaming resources for my fantasy escapades.

One day at work I had the epiphany that maybe I could listen to books being read, thus allowing me to continue to work, commute, etc. I began searching in earnest to find something that I would enjoy. Although audiobooks had been around for some time, the advent of podcasting didn't start until around 2005, so it was still in its infancy when I was looking around.

With a limited number of audiobooks to fit the genre, I was looking for, I listened to those that I could find and any podcasts that were of interest. There really are only so many Harlequin Romances a girl can take before she gets migraines from rolling her eyes at "…he wanted her to want him, to feel his need rising."

Finally, I stumbled upon "The Athenaeum" http://xenafiction.net and AUSXIP http://www.ausxip.com/ and a handful more that gave great reading ideas, downloads, and suggestions to listen to. One of them along the way mentioned the *XWP* Podcast, so I googled that and started to listen, happy that finally there was something I could sink my teeth into.

I noted that there still was not a *Xena* fanfic podcast out there that I could find. I surfed on to XenaCast by Amy Boatman and listened to her show for some time. Hers was about the show and episodes, plots, characters, etc.

But something was missing.

I did a search, trust me. I looked for all those that I could find and listened to their shows, hoping to find one that would be reading fanfic based on the Xenaverse and all parts thereof. A podcast that would be more of an audiobook giving us great stories yet showy stuff that we all come to expect when listening to a podcast.

Alas, I could not find one to suit my desires.

So, when faced with the ongoing dreary thought that I was not going to find something that tickled my fancy, I decided it was time I put my money where my mouth was; in this case, more like microphone where my mouth is.

It would be a bit narcissistic of me to say I wanted to hear my own voice read to me, so fear not, I didn't and don't! The only time I listened was when I was editing the shows for upload, and even then, I cringed.

It took me many moons to figure out what I had to do to even start.

First, I had to get the concept down. What was I going to do? Where was I going to get the stories to read? How could I do that? Then the layout of how I was going to present the story. What about a blog to host the site? What about the art design? How do I do the audio? Is there music involved?

The list went on and on!

I had to make a full list of possible questions to ensure I covered all the bases. To just sit down and talk into a microphone actually doesn't work... Well, it does, but not for the purpose we had in mind.

So, back to basics, I went.

What to call my show? *Xena*? Nope, can't do that. What about *Xena* Podcast? Nope, can't do that either. The list of show names became, I think, one of the most challenging things until finally, I was just doodling words from all over the net that I had come across. Since Uber was being bandied around and its definition is "over, beyond," I just happened to have the words 'Xena' and 'Ubers' in the same scrap piece of paper that I doodled on. The light bulb moment hit, and XNU was born!

So, the first hurdle was cleared. We had our name. Then the next was where to put it? (No snide remarks, please!)

I found that you could get your own blogsite for free and that's where it went. Then it was to design a logo of sorts and add on all the little nuances that make it a presentable site. Of course, it was ever-evolving and changing as one does, but the initial rollout had to have the right clicks.

Next, I had to figure out what I was going to even record, otherwise nothing but dead air. I scoured the internet and found some really great stories to read, but you just can't read someone's writings on air without their permission, otherwise, the legal side of things gets really harrowing. Then what?

Where do you find the authors' contacts? Email? Phone? Smoke signal?

After deciding on a few stories to start off with, I attempted to contact the author only to find out that the initial story's author L.J. Maas had sadly, passed away. I did some research and found her partner, who had authority and granted me permission to use her story. A very grateful thank you goes out to Carolyn Boone for assistance.

Okay, name – tick. Blogspot – tick. Storyline – tick. Permission – tick. Now to get down and dirty with the recording.

Well, what the hell am I supposed to do to record? I just can't sit in front of my computer and start talking! There has to be some format, audio equipment, a program that I need.

Alright, I can do this. eBay and Amazon, here I come! After purchasing the equipment (microphone, stand, filter), I had to find the right program to run and learn how to use it. That's where I discovered a nifty little program called Audacity.

Audacity started out in 2000 but soon developed into the go-to program for bloggers and recorders. It is an amazing resource that is super user friendly and enables podcasters (or like me, a wannabe) to record from multiple sources and edit afterward.

Now I had to figure out the format for my show.

I had to have an introduction explaining who, what, where, why, etc. Then, if I wanted to have some music (which I later added), I needed a brief descriptor and maybe add in things like movies or books. Then maybe a location to send emails to or from, which begged the question, I needed to create an email just for this particular endeavor.

Hmm, okay, my show is Xena & Ubers, so I might as well make up an email that is the same. Well, I can't use the ampersand symbol (&), so I guess we go without the symbol.

I introduce to you Xena.Uber@gmail.com.

After numerous scraps piles of paper being wadded up and thrown at every conceivable surface and animal venturing into my office, I finally settled on the rough draft of my introduction. Lame as it might have been, it was a work in progress and at least something to start the show with.

Show? So, you mean this is really starting to come together? Yup!

Okay, so I've got to do the introduction. Should I talk about myself? Nah.

How about what the show is about? Yes! And also do a little recap maybe; throw in the music and then do a little research about a topic we all would like to know, such as movies that might be coming out or some that are just old gems. Then there are the countless thousands upon thousands of books that cover almost every conceivable storyline that one can imagine (joy!).

Also, announce where to send any emails if one were so inclined.

Finally, I sat down in front of my computer, turned on the microphone and started talking just to get the hang of it.

"Ahem, Ahem. Hi, everyone. I'm a dork recording my nonsensical whimsy of fantasy."

Well, that's not what I actually said, but that's what I felt like, let me tell you.

I had to learn where to talk, how to talk (you'd be surprised everything that you do when speaking normally and how it comes across), when to talk, how to structure my sentences, how to change my voice (if so required – note: this is a very cringe-worthy moment in afterthought) and how to express emotion. I even had to learn how to take breaths in between!

After sitting down for the first few hours, I realized that there were many components to putting this show together (I hadn't really put them all down by the way) and that there was some organization required in what goes where and when.

Of course, first is the introduction (duh) but should I talk or just explain the things that are just happening? Such as: The music you hear in the background, the book review this week, the movie review this week.

Well, you get the idea.

Then I had to announce the story for the week, who the author is and where one could purchase the book if so desired. To that end I always gave credit to the authors, their websites and where you could purchase their books, as I always told each author that I would do when I contacted them for permission for the use of their story.

That permission always required me to send multiple emails out to many authors at a time, as due to time constraints, some didn't get back to me for the next cycle of the show. I wanted to have a few up my sleeve whilst one was in production.

Then there was the searching for movies. I could and would search through Google or just go to many known sites that were specifically geared towards the many listeners I thought I might potentially have. Wolfe video,

YouTube, etc. were great resources.

Books, wow. Where do you not go to find a book in this day and age? What genre hasn't been explored exponentially? I would read reviews on-line and then suggest to them if it struck a chord with me or if it was recommended by someone else (after some time they started coming in.)

Now down to the nitty-gritty!

I started reading the story that was for the show that week. Generally, I liked to read a bit of the story before I started recording so that I knew what frame of mind/voice I would need to be in. But this little tidbit of vital information I didn't realize until after a few stories had been read.

If you listen in to the first few episodes and then to the later few, you will notice a considerable difference in style, layout, format, and also hear the relaxed manner vs. my initial almost robotic style.

While reading, initially, I would try to correct any errors I made in voice, grammar or just reading. This led to only being able to record minutes at a time and having to go back to correct. Bear in mind that this is the initial recordings. I soon determined that it would be futile to continue on that style of work.

And as I began learning the program, I discovered that I could record as long as I deemed necessary or was able to, and I could continue the next day or multiple days later.

Another great aspect was that I could read multiple individual tracks and mix them in when required, such as when one person was interrupting another or talking at the same time. This would then sound as if there were in fact two people doing the show. I could also inlay sound effects (another cringe worthy moment, but not the least fun!).

And I did have fun! There were times when I had to stop recording as I laughed at myself, making the sounds of amorous moments (omg, so embarrassing!).

I generally finished reading the story in one to two days and then began the task of editing. That was the most tedious task of the entire process.

I had to listen to myself (ugh!!) and correct all the errors made. Sometimes there were whole lines that had to be deleted. But the good thing was that I had continued to record the correct sentence (in whatever format necessary) so it was just a matter of taking out the bad section and shifting the track for continuity.

That's when I laid in the sound effects tracks. Some were the ole' "Kablam, kapow" effects that you either heard or read in the TV shows of the '70s. Yes, I am dating myself here – I'm feeling as old as dirt.

The tracks often had to be shifted up or down, back or forth, to get the storyline to flow and the characters to talk in the right sequence.

And characters… There's another head-banging moment! I had this idea of what some of the characters should sound like.

Whilst overall, it was okay, I did get some negative feedback that I made one of the characters sound like she was a little nine-year-old girl and another like she was a man. (Really? I sound like a guy?)

I did attempt to change that a bit as well, but for the most part, I just tried to talk and use the program to change pitch and tone for the characters.

After I felt like it was all done to the best of my novice ability, it was time to learn how to upload.

But to where?

How do I get my hard work out there?

Back to learning again. I found out that to upload a show, you have to store it to some server. Then to get it to be on a podcasting platform, you have to register the show, but first, you have to register to the podcast platform. (Have I lost you yet?)

I registered with iTunes/Apple then over to Podcast Pickle and several others. Then I found a storage server willing not to charge me an arm and leg. Then I had to upload my show, which generally took about one to two hours. In the interim, I would get on my blog and type up the latest show notes and then go have dinner whilst the voodoo was brewing.

Once I received confirmation that the show had been uploaded to the server, I could then go to the platforms and link the show as well as to the blog.

Then there was the RSS Feed and all the little things that went with ensuring the show was ready and on air. Finally, I would click on the stream and listen to make sure it actually was done.

From the moment I sat down until the moment, it would go to air, it would take approximately five to six working days. That was a lot of work, considering I still had a day job as well as a family to attend to.

I don't regret a moment of it, all cringe-worthy parts included.

Out of this endeavor, I've made some immensely dear friends. One couple of individual listeners became friends, and I actually played matchmaker for them, and they got married!

They became fierce friends and even traveled across the country to attend my 2nd wedding (in the US with my family.)

Another friend is someone who I've characterized now as my little adopted sister, and I've traveled to see her when visiting my family back home.

Overall, it has been an enlightening experience on so, so many levels.

It's taught me some self-confidence to put myself out there for strangers to critique (good or bad), it's shown me how to appreciate what some people do on a daily, weekly basis for a continued length of time. It's also opened the door for me to meet some amazing people who have changed my life in one aspect or another.

The opportunities have been boundless and still continue, like now, when the venerable MaryD of AUSXIP was kind enough to extend this honor for me to talk a bit about my show.

I guess to end, what lesson I drew out of the amazing experience is that there is nothing you can't do or learn to do, not if you have the desire to see it for the pleasure of others without any reward for yourself.

Thank you for peeking in the closet to find out what it was all about.

All the best!

Official Site: http://xena-ubers.blogspot.com/
Podcast site: https://www.stitcher.com/podcast/xena-ubers
You can find a spreadsheet (Excel) of all the podcasts here:
http://xena-ubers.blogspot.com/p/listing-of-all-episodes-and-information.html
Facebook: https://www.facebook.com/Xena-Ubers-174585116020195/

Chapter Thirty-Seven

The Babbling Bards –
A Xena Warrior Princess Podcast

by Trista L. Holmes And Liliana C. Costa

WHEN ONE TRIES to escape the mundane activity of day-to-day life, there is no limit to the things they'll try. That is precisely how *The Babbling Bards: A Xena Warrior Princess Podcast* was formed. As we like to say, it's a podcast made by Xenites, for Xenites. What started out as a *Xena: Warrior Princess* fan fiction challenge to one of the hosts, spanned into so much more. Let's go back to the beginning, shall we?

I (Trista), absolutely **hated** *Xena* the first time I watched it, which was about four years ago now. However, Liliana, the other half of the podcast, was insistent on me watching it. After much protesting, I gave it a second chance. Unlike a chunk of the Xenite community, I didn't catch on to this little thing between Xena and Gabrielle called subtext. That is, until "A Friend in Need Part 2," so, needless to say, my partner in crime was pretty insistent that I watch it again, after I swore the show-off, because, well, we all know how it ended. Little by little, I started catching onto the subtext, the second time through, and then I was met with a challenge: to enter a fan fiction contest with a Xena/Gabrielle pairing. In order to publish the fanfic before I submitted it, because I don't want anyone snatching my blood, sweat, and tears, I built a website. Before I was finished building, Liliana chimed in with, "We should do a podcast!" The rest, as they say, is history.

We try to keep *The Babbling Bards* pretty simple. Mostly, it's just us, well, babbling at our listeners. We divide and conquer. It is awesome to have Liliana recording alongside of me, since she's been following the show since it originally aired, and I'm still new. She does a phenomenal job of keeping the flow of the episode straight, especially when I start getting excited. Sometimes, I still manage to teach her a thing or two, with my random, little known facts about the episode. She loves taking on the "Oopsies," as we call them—the little mistakes that weren't caught until after the episode had already aired. The area that gets us every time, however, is something that a couple of our dedicated listeners have told us they enjoy: Subtext Time with Trista. Because it took me *so long* to catch onto it, finding and dissecting subtext from every single episode was so generously given to me by Liliana... usually while she giggles. Typically, just for the subtext portion, I research anywhere from twenty to sixty forums, both archived and active, to make sure I hit every little piece I can find. Some of them, especially some of the ones written by psychologists, have really made me stop and think. I even wrote a rap, which can be found in one of the podcast episodes.

Usually, when putting the entire thing together, it takes us about six takes to get it where we want it, and then, the fun part—the editing, which is a feat that Liliana has taken on. Otherwise, our listeners would have less podcasting and more dead airing. One amusing fact that we've learned since starting this podcast is that the two of us can talk *Xena* at length, without a pause or a breath. However, when that microphone comes on, it seems like all the words just fade away.

You can find the Babbling Bards at: www.thebabblingbards.com/podcast
Facebook: www.facebook.com/BabblingBardsPodcast/
YouTube: www.youtube.com/channel/UCAl_JildEgGaPgm7ihHCybA
Pinterest: www.pinterest.com.au/thebabblingbards/?autologin=true

PART 7

BECAUSE OF XENA...

Chapter Thirty-Eight

From Xenaverse Bard to Xena Show Writer

by Melissa Good

SO. WHAT WAS it like?

There is a hoary old story that has been a part of fandoms forever—the one where a fan gets to be invited into their favorite show and be a part of it.

On *Xena*, that happened. Between the fifth and sixth seasons of the show, after a fandom uproar over the stories in the fifth season, the production staff decided they wanted to see about getting a fan involved in a script.

That is how I happened to be sitting in my house, writing a fanfic story, minding my own business, as it were when I got a ding from AOL Messenger. (Those of you saying 'what?' just google it.)

It was Steve Sears, a well-known and beloved by fans writer from *Xena*, whom I had met at several successive Dragoncon conventions where he had been one of our *Xena* track guests.

Steve is a fantastically engaged, kind, ferocious writer who had written some of the stories we all loved, and he was special to the fans in that he was always there, always right out in the fandom, always approachable and available.

So, of course, I was glad to hear from him and anticipated some sort of conversation about charity items, or upcoming conventions, or something like that. Steve was always the go-to for that—he was the conduit in a way between the fandom and what I think the rest of us called TPTB: The Powers That Be.

At conventions, he could always be found in the public spaces talking to fans, taking stupendous photographs, glad to talk about the show, the stories, the characters, his views…

Anyway, when I answered, I thought it would be that. What I did not expect him to say was, "Hey, how would you like to write a *Xena* script?"

Nothing really prepares you for that, by the way. It's like buying a lotto ticket on a whim and then watching your numbers come up on the screen.

I do think I probably said in response, "Wait…what? What do you mean?" There are memes on the internet now that encapsulate the feeling—

that staring-at-the-screen moment when your mind tries to accommodate a shift in your own personal reality and sort of fails.

What did that mean, actually? It meant, he explained that they had been having a talk in the office about getting a fan involved in a script and he thought I might be interested. So, was I?

Was I interested? Yes, of course, I was interested. There are moments in life when you have an opportunity to have a unique experience and this was one of those moments, so I didn't hesitate to say, "Absolutely."

I ended the conversation with a phone number in California and a time to call it, and I remember going downstairs to tell my mother that this somewhat obscure fandom hobby of mine had just taken a sharp left turn.

It was, and still is when I look back now a very surreal experience. Even after making that phone call the next day and talking to both the writing team and Rob Tapert, it was very difficult to really digest that this was actually happening.

How did it feel? Was I scared, or nervous, or deliriously happy? The answer is none of the above, really. Intrigued and very interested to see what this experience would be like is probably the most accurate answer.

I think most of all I felt a very strong sense of responsibility in taking this on. It was a risk for Rob to want to do it, and there was resistance to the idea because television shows are expensive things to assemble. Their time is money, and taking that valuable time dealing with a fan's involvement was in question. I also felt a responsibility to step up to the fact that Steve had recommended me. I did not want that to reflect poorly on him.

Of course, I didn't know if I could produce anything useful for them. I write long form prose. I had never dealt with the formatting of a screenplay or the constructs of television writing. I am by trade an IT professional—I manage network and server infrastructure and engineering on a day-to-day basis, so this was very literally out of my wheelhouse.

But they wanted to give it a try, so I told them that first day to let me know what they wanted me to do and I would do the best I could for them.

They asked me, in that first meeting, what kind of story I had in mind to write for them, and on that phone call I could all but hear them kind of steeling themselves for what I was going to answer, because not only was I some random potential nutcase from the internet, I was also an alt-bard.

Well, half alt, anyway.

However, I didn't really feel it was or should be about me, and so what I said to them was, "It's your show and your budget; what story do you need?"

Because that was always the core of *Xena*, wasn't it? The greater good and all that? I was honored and happy to be even the smallest part of the magic around that show and I didn't want it to be a horrible experience for them or a total waste of their time. I wanted to do the best I could to give them something useful.

That broke the ice a bit. They relaxed. I figured I had said more or less the right thing and they started talking about an episode they were doing called "Who's Ghurkan" that was set in the desert. Could I think of a story, also in the desert, they could leverage being on location for?

I said I thought I could. They sent me out a big packet of what television writing looks like—what a beat sheet is and how to write one, and I went off to come up with a story and send it back to them.

At the time, my thought was that I would construct this storyline and give it to them, and then -if they liked it- they would take it off and make something that had some of those ideas in it. To me, that would have been a great result, so after I came up with the storyline for "Desert 2," I sent it off to them and waited to see what happened.

I had no idea what that would be.

We had a network outage that next day and I was standing behind our operations desk doing triage when my phone rang. It was Rob.

It was a nice distraction. I figured he was going to politely thank me for my ideas. What he thanked me for, on the other hand, was for not making him look like a jerk.

I had apparently done all right, and as a reward for that, I was now going to be asked to write the script's first draft.

At that moment, it all became real.

Real as in we were going to actually do this.

Real as in they sent me a contract to sign outlining the story and the obligation to work on it with them until they were done with my participation with it, making me a freelance employee of Universal. I had to report this to my then-current employer, who had a secondary employment policy mostly designed to keep technical staff from moonlighting as IT consultants, and now had to be educated on why one of their technical supervisors was going to work writing television scripts.

With the contract also came the realization that I was going to get paid for the effort, which to me was a surprise. I was not, of course, a member of the Writer's Guild, but the contract was for the minimum of what a Writer's Guild writer would get.

Participating is important because you get paid in milestones, but going the distance is the point, so that was a view into the business side of content production that was unexpected and very interesting to see.

TV is also a team sport. You are a small part of a very big machine full of large numbers of talented people working in all directions. It's a business—a high pressure, intense business with a hard bottom line where what we see on the screen is just the tiny visible tip of the iceberg.

There are a lot of moving parts, and when you come in like I did from the outside, there is a huge amount of things going on you know nothing about that affect what the team wants to put on the screen, which might have to work with what you are doing.

In *Xena*'s case, they were also coordinating writing team calls now across three time zones—Auckland, Los Angeles, and Miami, which actually worked out for me because it meant most of the time they were in the early evening and I took them before I went home for the day.

I did have one or two calls from home, though, and there were a few times when yelling at my dog, a cream-colored Labrador named Gabrielle, caused some confusion.

The writing team was very gracious. I tried not to ask too many dumb questions. I tried not to make the same mistakes more than once.

I figured out how to use scriptwriting software (Final Draft) and what settings to use to make my pages match their pages (very important!) as I worked my way through completing this four-act and prologue first-draft script.

I remember printing it out and then measuring it against the pages of samples they had sent me to make sure I had the font size right and the spacing adjusted for the fact it was from New Zealand and had been printed on New Zealand size paper.

I finished it and sent it off, and waited to see what would happen.

My assumption always was that the next step would be taken over by someone who professionally did this, so every time I got a step further it was kind of a delightful little surprise.

Even when I got to the point of them calling the draft a final one, I don't know that I really expected it to be what ended up on the screen, or if any of it would at all.

People have asked me, and I know it sounds like I am lying when I say this, but the thought that it would be changed for whatever reason, either because the story didn't work or there was something in the production that would require it to change, didn't bother me at all.

If they had decided not to do the story in the end, I would have understood because it was a business, and I knew I had done the best I could do with it, and if that wasn't good enough, well, it wasn't.

I write because I enjoy it. I like storytelling and I enjoy the process of creating stories and images inside my head and then putting them on paper. I like inventing characters and dialog, and hearing their thoughts, and describing their emotions and what they see and feel.

So, I completely enjoyed the process of working with the *Xena* writing team and with Rob, and getting to go through this very technical workflow and produce this script, no matter what would happen with it in the end.

It was difficult and uncomfortable at times. There were expectations and perceptions and I don't know what else that were in play in the overall maelstrom of the internet and fandom, but I honestly would not have opted out of a moment of it.

Having said all that, I submitted this final draft, dusted my hands off, and thought, "well, that's that, anyway."

I did, however, apply for a passport at this point. I thought if they were going to end up filming any of this, it would be an amazing end to this story if I could go out there and see a day or so of it while it was being done.

Thus, a couple weeks after I turned in the last draft of the script, I asked if it would be okay if I could fly out there for a few days, see a bit of filming, and maybe get a handful of black sand and see a kiwi.

Getting to Auckland from Miami is not a trivial trip, but I had done some checking on the internet and thought I could get the flights arranged. I had never been out of the US, so I figured, why not start with the longest trip I could think of?

That was just before the DragonCon weekend that year, and I was heading up to Atlanta to attend and coordinate the *Xena* track for that convention. On the way to the airport, my phone rang, and it was Rob.

He told me that yes, of course, I could come out to Auckland, but since he wanted to give me another script to work on, he'd instead I do that and come out to New Zealand after.

Wait. What?

They already had some other episodes lined up to start season six, but it seems the season launch would coincide with the Super Bowl, and they didn't want to have "Heart of Darkness" compete with that, so they needed another, smaller script to go in that position.

Was I up for that?

Sure. Why not?

I didn't get a chance to see my first script filmed. Still, I did go out for a few days to see the second one in progress. While I was there, I had the most surreal moment of what had been months of surreal moments, when I got to see the almost final cut of the first episode there, in a small office at Pacific Renaissance, right down the hall from where they were setting up an office for Renée to work out of for her directing debut.

It was a very bizarre thing to happen, because there is a discontinuity there, at least for me. I don't have a lot of short term memory. I have been hit by lightning twice.

Although I had written the script and been a part of the whole process, by the time I saw it, I didn't really remember the details, and so it was an hour of watching Lucy and Renée do and say things I'd never seen before that all of a sudden became familiar because I'd written them.

It was awesome. It was the moment I realized that the words and the mental images I had typed into my keyboard were real, and on the screen, and they had actually done it.

My mother liked the second story better than the first one. It had Ares in it, and that was her favorite character, and while I was there in Auckland, Kevin was kind enough to sign a picture for her.

I was so glad I got to write him as Ares. He was happy to get to ride a horse in the script, and while I was there, I got to see a bit of a scene where Lucy kicked his sword out of his hand, just messing around. It was so heartbreaking for us to lose him the way we did.

It was awesome to see how they made the show, and amazing to be able to witness for a few days the process they have to use to assemble all the parts and bits and non-sequential activities into a coherent end product.

Putting this kind of thing together is a complex process and requires a large, diverse team. There are things that are hard, and sometimes tiring. Sometimes you have to go through things and deal with how it works in ways that are often uncomfortable and don't turn out how you want them to.

It's technical and full of logistical problems—a very mechanical process that is used to put something up on our television screen that can reach out and engage our hearts with a kind of lightning strike magic.

In the end, for me, the amazing part of the journey was the fact I was able, for a little while, to be a part of that process and of the team that made it happen. Even the parts that sometimes weren't fun were full of emotion, and I'm glad I got to be a part of it.

I sometimes get asked why *Xena* was so special, not only to me but to many other people.

I think the answer is not because they gave us everything we wanted. They never did. Rob and his team walked to the line and never crossed over it while the show was airing.

They never said yes, but what I think made *Xena* so important to all of us was that they never said no either.

I was a weird little kid. Nobody really got why I read out the sci-fi section of three libraries. I was a nerd. I liked robots and spaceships and taking apart telephones and I knew I was weird.

Then I saw an advertisement for a little *Star Trek* convention in the Howard Johnson's in North Miami Beach, where I lived.

So I went, and I walked into that small conference room full of posters of spaceships and people walking around in Starfleet uniforms and it was a shock, you know? To understand that you are not alone. That you have a tribe, a community of people who think like you do and care about what you care about.

That's what *Xena* gave us.

Because they never said no, because *Xena* came into being when the internet was born and it amplified the fandom's reach, it gave us community and visibility, and we loved these characters who were gorgeous and funny and unique and maybe...maybe like us?

Well, maybe they were. Walking into a *Xena* convention and seeing thousands of people who share a common love and a common view of love changes you.

It's an honor to have been there in that time, in that place, and see that happen and be a part of this fandom and get to do what I got to do.

AUSXIP
PUBLISHING

Intertwined Souls

SERIES PROMO

Forbidden love, heart racing suspense, an epic tale set in war-ravaged Greece.

Starring

Kat Cavanaugh, Penny Cavanaugh & Special Appearance by Adrienne Wilkinson

www.nextchapter.net

Chapter Thirty-Nine

Watching My Characters Come to Life –
Filming the Intertwined Souls Series Promo

by MaryD

"WE HAVE A GREAT idea!" Hm. That sounded familiar. I was on a Skype chat with my editor Rosa Alonso and my good friend Penny Cavanaugh. Getting those two together is a recipe for mayhem! I need to go back in time a little to allow you to see how we actually got to this point in time.

Let me tell you about a girl called Penelope Glasswell. Penny is a force of nature, no doubt about it. Anyone who can convince me to come to an after-party (eek! A party? I don't do parties!) and cut a cake in front of a crowd is practicing some serious juju. Introverts don't go to parties or cut cakes or talk that much for that matter. Yet, here I was at a Xena convention, and it was the first after-party that Penny had organized. My introverted self said "no," but "yes" came out of my mouth (I was possessed or had just drunk a Crown and coke because that's the only explanation I can come up with). I have a lot of time for Penny, her bubbly personality won me over the first time we met. I have a gut reaction to people, and my gut is always right (not listening to the gut is a bad thing). If the request was made by anyone else, I would have said 'no.' It was Penny, so I heard myself saying, "yes." I shocked myself and my mate Christa. We were still a bit shell-shocked all the way back to our room. The cake cutting was a success (putting that on my CV in case I'm called again to perform that duty), and the night was a blast!

Fast forward a few years, and Penny tells me she's got her eyes on a girl. That girl had better be good enough for our Penny (I am very protective of Penny, she activated the mothering gene in me. I am old enough to be her mother). The girl who won Penny's heart was Kathleen Cavanaugh. I didn't know her, and when I saw a photo that Penny sent I thought she looked familiar, but I couldn't place her. They got married (aww!) on January 13, 2013, at the Official Xena Convention. Unfortunately, I couldn't attend that year. Penny talks about her marriage to Kat in *Chapter 41: Love Blossoms In the Xenaverse.*

In late 2013, I was in New Zealand to watch Lucy Lawless perform in Chicago, and I met up with Penny and Kat for an early dinner. There was something about Kat that bugged me (not in a bad way but in an 'I know who you are, but I don't remember where and when kind of way). I have the memory of a flea UNLESS I write stuff down. She didn't give any indication we had met before, so either we were both suffering from amnesia or I may have been wrong. I was pretty sure we had met before, and she made an impression because she managed to get stuck up there in my swiss-cheese noggin. I didn't say anything about my memory problems on that occasion. Nor did I say anything when we met up again for dinner in 2013.

A few months later, at the 2014 Xena convention, I was sitting at the long table in the lobby of the convention hotel. One of my books, *Book 3: Hidden Truths,* was in my hands (I need something to hold while I'm thinking…I'm sure there is some reason this helps the thinking process but who cares, it works), and I was talking to Angela, a fellow Xenite who was working on short video promos for my series. I was just twirling the book around while we talked.

Kat saw me and came over to ask me something. I looked up, and then it hit me. I remembered where I had seen her before! I'm going to leave this part of the story here for a moment.

I am always forgetting all types of stuff UNLESS I write it down or see an image. Then it sticks in my head forever. When I started to write my first novel, "In The Blood of the Greeks," in 1999, I wanted to write a Xena Uber story. You know the drill by now: dark hair and blue eyes for Uber Xena, and blonde hair and green eyes for Uber Gabrielle. I had it all planned out. This was going to be an epic story of Nazis, Greeks, and lesbian romance. Hey presto, I would write an Uber fanfic!

Not so fast. As I outlined in my chapter about turning into a published author, I forgot one little thing. YOU, the writer, don't get to choose your characters (no, I'm not joking). The characters choose you (much like our pets).

I should have been seeing Lucy Lawless as I was writing Eva, but instead of Lucy's gorgeous face, I saw another image. It was a mixture of Ava Gardner and Angie Harmon. Why? I don't know, but that's where my head wanted to go. Rather than fight it, I gave in. I left Eva with dark hair and blue eyes because that is just a beautiful combination. For Zoe, I wasn't seeing the gorgeous Renée O'Connor, but someone else. I couldn't quite pin down who she resembled. I know it's weird, but I gave up a long time ago trying to figure it out. I knew one thing about Zoe—she was a redhead, she was a loudmouth and a hothead. I loved the combination of the two: Eva, an introvert, a damaged soul, meeting the opinionated, take-no-prisoners green-eyed redhead. Phew!

LJ Maas was the first one to try and conjure up Eva and Zoe in her art, and she did a pretty good job of it. Then along came Lucia Nobrega. Let's just say that NO ONE comes close to what Lucia has achieved in drawing my characters. I have so much art that Lucia has made for the last twenty years, and she doesn't tire of it (I think she's in love with Eva). Thus Lucia's art of Eva and Zoe would grace the covers of my books.

Back to Kat. I looked up, and from the angle where I was sitting, it finally dawned where I had seen Kat before. She was looking up at me from the covers of my books. No joke. Lucia's artwork of Eva Muller was almost a dead ringer for Kat.

I may have jumped up like someone had put a firecracker up my posterior, and I may have yelled in triumph that I finally connected the dots (it takes a while some days). I know Kat must have thought I was a raving lunatic, as did everyone else around us.

When I finally calmed down, I let Kat in on the secret. She agreed that Eva did look like her. One thing led to another, and my mate KT Jorgensen, who is an excellent photographer, volunteered to do an impromptu photoshoot that someone suggested (I don't recall who; it may have been me or KT but you know…fuzzy memory) with Kat as Eva and Penny as Zoe. That was one hell of a fun photo shoot. I do remember one moment that almost made me cry. We were out near the pool, and everything was going well. Rosa (who loves Eva and Zoe even more than I do, if that's possible) mentioned something from a scene from the first book.

It was a pivotal moment where Eva meets Zoe for the first time. Eva had just been struck by a defiant Zoe with a pebble out in the streets of the Greek town. KT was going to photograph that exact moment so I could use it in my promos. Kat asked me about the scene, and I described it and discussed Eva's vulnerability at that moment. Then I saw the transformation. It blew me away and almost made me stop breathing. It was PERFECTION. It turned out really well, and we all agreed it would be even better at the following year's convention because they would be ready and better prepared.

Let's go back to the start of this chapter. Rosa and Penny had an idea. Instead of a photoshoot, they came up with the idea of filming scenes from the five books in the series (so far).

I'm sorry, but what? I was on the receiving end of one of my own 'I have an idea' moments. It was very strange. I think I may have uttered the words "you want to do what?" a little louder than I should have. Did I want to see scenes from my books, which I wrote and had already seen in my head, come to life before me? Yep, sure did! Sign me up!

There was a lot of preparation and little time, but we had a lot of spirit and ingenuity at hand. Penny got things moving; our director was Karyn Ben Singer, and everything else clicked. I found a sound studio and props. One of the scenes called for Zoe to aim a gun at Eva, so I needed a pistol. A replica 1940s pistol. I couldn't actually believe that I was looking through Amazon for a gun! I bought a Denix P-08 German Luger Parabellum World War-II Non-Firing replica pistol and notified Christa that she had an incoming box from Amazon!

For Eva, I purchased a Victorian-style wood walking stick/cane with a brass handle. Those were two of the many props that would be used for the filming. I then called a dear friend who is actually quite good at this acting business—Adrienne Wilkinson. I'm quite sure she must have thought I had gone totally nuts. I asked her if she would like to play the role of Zoe's mother (spoiler alert…she dies). Adrienne, without hesitation, agreed.

Penny wrote the script, and let me tell how odd that was for me. Someone else was going to write my characters…weird.

It was a revelation, and it blew my mind to watch the characters I had created and to hear the lines I had written come to life. Every author needs this gift. Penny and Kat were out of their comfort zone and were outstanding. Just simply outstanding. It was tough work, but they did it with style and grace. Karyn Ben Singer was terrific; she conjured up set designs where there had been none before, other than a bare concrete floor. Her direction was a marvel. Her assistant was Anthony M. Sannazzaro, and the two of them worked so well together. The crew was something else. They are a resourceful and fantastic group of women who made it all possible: Arielle Strauss (clapperboard), Sam Silva (set designer), Deborah Rizzo (set designer), Rosa Alonso (Producer/do-everything-be-everywhere goddess), KT Jorgensen (Photography), Pat Vowels (Assistant) and me. All of us were brought together by the idea that we could bring to life two characters I had created. It was the ultimate gift, and it lifted me to the stratosphere.

Karyn created something that, up to that point, had lived only in my head and on paper. Several scenes stand out in regards to Karyn's direction that I marveled at her ingenuity. One of the scenes called for an abandoned hospital corridor; you know the type that hasn't seen a soul in decades—the stuff of nightmares. I looked at the area in question when we got to the studio, and it was a plain corridor. It got transformed in ways I hadn't thought of. There was another scene that I honestly couldn't figure out how Karyn was going to do it. It called for something extraordinary, and Karyn created it. Add in Kat, and it was the most powerful scene of the entire shoot.

It was a scene that was one of the most pivotal moments in Eva's young life—she was subjected to aversion therapy (read that as torture) because she was a lesbian. Aversion therapy is the way to retrain your brain to associate pain with a feeling or an action. It doesn't "cure" you, but you feel pain when you are doing the activity that your brain has been trained to trigger a negative response against. A simple example is if you bite your nails. You put a bitter polish on your nails, and when you attempt to bite them, you are repulsed by the taste, and you stop. Simple. Aversion therapy for sexual orientation is far more sinister and far more of a torture than bitter nail polish. It was not invented by the Nazis, but they used it, especially on gay men in Dachau and elsewhere. Karyn was going to recreate the scene where Eva's mind and body are shattered. Heavy stuff. It's the only scene I could not watch as it was being filmed. I had seen this in my head, and I didn't want to see it live. I stood behind a corner and listened. I got to see the results of Karyn and Kat's work in the quiet of my hotel room. I was floored and very emotional.

Another scene that stands out for me is the one featuring Adrienne and Penny. I was standing behind the director, in the dark, in front of a green screen. Adrienne had come all the way from the other end of LA for this one scene. It was the pivotal moment in Zoe's life and one that would shape her worldview. I have read that a talented actor can lift the other actors around them; it's a gift they impart to their fellow actors. I'll be honest and say I found it hard to believe. That was until I saw it happening before my eyes.

As I mentioned, I stood behind Karyn, watching Adrienne and Penny. I was transfixed on Adrienne because she was staying in character in between takes. Then something happened when Karyn called 'action.' Penny is a decent actress, but playing off Adrienne, I could see her posture change—her bearing was Zoe-like, her stance was perfect, her acting was superb. Adrienne knocked it out of the park (naturally), and the death scene was perfection. I was in awe watching it. Adrienne, is a tremendous voice actress and she also did the voice over for the promo!

KT was taking some incredible photography, but it's a photo that I shot stands out, for me, as an Eva and Zoe moment. Outside, the studio was a wall that was colored blue and looked very much like it could belong someplace in Greece. We got lucky because we didn't know about this wall when we rented the studio. We filmed a scene outside with the blue wall as a backdrop, and again it was a pivotal scene where a spunky and angry Zoe throws a pebble and hits Eva in the head. I was standing across the road, watching the scene being set up and then I spotted a perfect moment in time. What I captured with my camera was a quiet moment between takes when Penny was rehearsing with Kat, and it was pure Zoe that the camera captured. You couldn't see Kat's face, but the black cloak she was wearing was blowing in the wind, and it gave me goosebumps at the perfection of it.

There was this scene we had to film back at the hotel because otherwise, we had no bedroom scene (no, it's not what you are thinking!). The scene was from *Book 2: "Where Shadows Linger"* Eva is hesitant about making love to Zoe because of what the aversion torture did to her. Eva was scared. For those that haven't read the book, look away I'm about to spoil it: Eva decides she's had enough of waiting and is going to push through. Here is where Kat truly shined. Everything I wanted Eva to be at that moment, came through. Just brilliant. Penny had the easy job of laying in bed, acting up a storm as Zoe pretending to be asleep.

After that scene was filmed, that was a wrap! We finished filming after five days, and the results were fantastic! Check out the photo below of my wonderful cast and crew. I'm behind the camera taking the photo!

That was one of many special moments in the filming of the Intertwined Souls Series Promo. I wouldn't mind it becoming a series because it is a great story to tell. Maybe one day. I was blessed with getting a taste of what might be and now I understand the addiction of bringing your dreams to film.

What about the props? The gun was thrown on the floor so many times by an irate Zoe that I felt sorry for it. By the way, if you're going to give a gun to a sixteen-year-old, don't choose a Denix P-08 German Luger Parabellum pistol. It's heavy and hard to reload (says the non-gun owning Aussie...although that isn't true now, is it?). I donated the pistol to the studio–it's not a good idea to get on a plane to Australia with a WW2 handgun in your luggage.

I was left with a lot of happy memories, a whole lot of film to process, and the desire to see my characters as a series. One day it might happen, and that would be thanks to Kat and Penny Cavanaugh and their willingness to give me this opportunity, to Adrienne Wilkinson, who just blew me away with her generosity and love and to the rest of the crew for working on this unique project. Last but not least is my editor Rosa. She makes my work shine!

You can see the video promo here:
https://www.youtube.com/watch?v=pGQg3SzSKLo
You can find out more about Eva and Zoe on my fiction site:
http://www.nextchapter.net

Chapter Forty

Doing Something Scary –
AUSXIP Publishing Is Born

by MaryD

NINETEEN SUMMERS AGO (sounds like the start of another *Xena* flashback episode), my first novel, "*In the Blood of the Greeks*," was released along with a short story called "*You Must Remember This*" in one volume called "*Out Of Darkness*" by Renaissance Alliance Publishing (RAP). A wish fulfilled. Like all writers before me, I wanted more; I wanted to tell more stories, especially of my newly minted characters (who didn't want to be Uber Xena characters no matter how hard I tried). Over the years, I've had novels published by various publishers, and the idea of self-publishing my own fiction never entered my head. That was until 2014...

In 2014, I found myself standing at a crossroads – the self-publishing world had matured to the point that authors could take the reins of their careers (if they had the willingness) and publish their own work. The question that occupied my mind was, should I continue to be let my work be published by others, or should I take the reins? In 2014, the idea was planted in my noggin. I tried to ignore it while I worked on two novels for an early 2015 release date.

Lucy Lawless likes to say, "*Do something scary, the payoff is awesome*'. The question I asked myself was, 'am I prepared to be scared out of my mind to get the payoff?'. I've been doing a lot of scary stuff by challenging myself and pushing my limits, but this was different.

Towards the end of January 2015, I decided that I've had enough of thinking about it (was anyone surprised?), and I needed to act. I was ready to take that next step and see where I landed. I knew that failure was part of the process; every time you do something new, you will fail at it, at first. When you fail, you reassess the methods you used, but you don't give up. You get back up and try again. Yes, a lot of hard work was in my future. I needed to get my hands dirty if I wanted control over how my work was presented.

In a move not for the faint of heart, I decided to take that step and open my own publishing company. Not just be a self-published author. Half-assed measures are not my thing. Opening my own publishing business was the way to go, but I didn't have a clue about where to start or how it was done.

When I confided to a few close friends (aka mates) about what I wanted to do, they didn't seem all that surprised; they thought it was bound to happen. They were astonished it hadn't happened sooner. These mates never steer me the wrong way; they bluntly tell me if I'm going be doing something stupid or they encourage and support when they think it's a great idea.

My dear mate, Rosa Alonso, and also my supremo editor, was already aware of the idea and jumped on board wholeheartedly and without reservation. Cindy Tingley is another mate that jumped on board the speeding train. I was sitting in her kitchen, giving voice to my ideas and bouncing them off her. Cindy was right behind me, providing valuable advice and encouraging me all the way. You have to surround yourself with people like that, not because they say what you want to hear, but they will give you their honest opinion.

WHAT DO I NAME THIS NEW BABY

The easiest part of the whole process was naming this new company. I bounced names around as if it was a newborn baby. I shouldn't have bothered trying to come up with a name because the answer was right in front of me.

AUSXIP Publishing.

The business motto of the new company was: *Inspire, Strengthen, Enrich The Soul* because that's what I wanted the books from this company to do, and that was also the ethos of the main AUSXIP site.

I registered my new business name and got the right tax permits, dealt with the Australian Tax Department, and the United States IRS (since I was going to be publishing my work using US-based companies), etc. I registered the domain name – ausxippublishing.com and having learned my lesson from AUSXIP, I also nabbed the domain auspixpublishing.com because I found that people misspell AUSXIP into AUSPIX.

TIME TO SCARE MYSELF…

I researched the heck out of the various aspects of publishing while I was going to test the waters with my first project. As a graphic designer, I knew some incredibly talented cover designers, including the supremely gifted Jazzy Trafikowska. I chose Jazzy to create my covers and to typeset my first novel until I got my sea legs. For my own books, I needed another pair of eyes because authors can't divorce themselves from their work. The role of Chief Editor was the domain of my editing goddess, Rosa Alonso. I also gathered a group of proofreaders (having learned that aspect from Xena fanfiction days). AUSXIP Publishing was now fully staffed and ready to go.

While doing all of that, I wanted to publish my first novel early on to get AUSXIP Publishing off and running. The first book published was… *In The Blood of the Greeks* – the cover created by Jazzy and it featured Penny and Kat Cavanaugh from the filming of the Intertwined Souls Series (the filming is described in detail in Chapter Thirty-Nine: "Watching My Characters Come To Life – Filming The Intertwined Souls Series Promo." My first novel was going to be the first (of many) books under my newly minted publishing company. There wasn't any doubt about what to publish first; it had to be In the Blood of the Greeks. The book was published on March 26, 2015.

Was it scary? Heck yes. It scared the living daylights out of me, but seeing my novel under my own publishing company name was just so thrilling. What's even more special that book has been so successful – even though it was fifteen years old since it was first published.

In Chapter Twenty-Four: For Every Thing There, Is A Season, I outlined how the inclusion of the novel and a companion book, "*In the Blood of the Greeks: The Illustrated Companion,*" was selected to be part of the Jewish Museum of Greece's book collection. Both books are part of their library about the Holocaust in Greece, and the museum is located in Athens, Greece. https://www.jewishmuseum.gr/en/

MAJOR CHANGES IN 2019

At the start of 2019, I made the decision to start publishing the work of other authors. Back in 2014, I was given some advice that I listened to. I should make all the mistakes (and there would be a lot of them) with my books, refine the process, learn all aspects of the business and then when I'm ready, publish others. It was time for the next step in AUSXIP Publishing's future.

On the fourth anniversary of AUSXIP Publishing's birth, March 01, 2019, I made the announcement that the first author to join AUSXIP Publishing would be Susanne M. Beck. I had known Sue for over twenty years, and I loved her work. I was thrilled she came on board with her Ice and Angel Series. Unfortunately, we lost Sue when she passed away on April 21, 2019. On September 19, 2019 – on Sue's 56th birthday, I published her first novel Redemption, quickly followed by her other books.

Since then, the author ranks have swelled, and we publish Historical Romance, LGBTQA+ fiction (in particular lesbian romance and transgender romance), Children's Books, Science Fiction, Coloring Books For Adults, and Non-Fiction.

In addition to all of that, we offer author services such as book covers, editing, book trailers, web site design and hosting, and social media image creation and a book and merchandise store.

From 2015 to 2020, it's been a whirlwind of change. Looking back on the last five years, AUSXIP Publishing had exceeded my expectations. It has published award-winning bestsellers, signed up authors who are gifted storytellers and artists to showcase their extraordinary talent. I'm proud of what AUSXIP Publishing has become and excited by the possibilities of what it will achieve in the years that follow.

What is absolutely fascinating is that if I hadn't listened to my friend Xero who wanted me to watch Xena: Warrior Princess, there would be no AUSXIP and no AUSXIP Publishing. Lots of crossroads that if the decision was different, none of this would have happened.

All of this is BECAUSE of *Xena*. You're reading this book BECAUSE I listened to Xero. BECAUSE I created AUSXIP to show my love for the show. BECAUSE I had first my novel published by Renaissance Alliance Publishing, who gave me a chance. BECAUSE I wanted to branch out and take control of my publishing future and, in turn, publish others, AUSXIP Publishing was born, and the end result is this book.

It boggles the mind to think of the massive impact that little show had on so many lives. Serendipity.

Scary part? Check. What about the payoff?

You're holding it in your hands.

***

AUSXIP Publishing Site: https://ausxippublishing.com
AUSXIP Publishing Store: https://store.ausxippublishing.com
AUSXIP Publishing Newsletter: http://newsletter.ausxippublishing.com

Kat & Penny Cavanaugh & photobomber Lucy Lautex

Arielle Strauss-Brueland and Erin Brueland

Chapter Forty-One

Love Blossoms in the Xenaverse

by MaryD

WE KNOW THAT *Xena: Warrior Princess* brought about positive change in people's lives, but one unexpected change that happened was the blooming of love (everyone, say aww!).

There have been so many stories of relationships formed (and weddings) in the Xenaverse that listing them all would require its own book! Here are some of the relationships that blossomed because of *Xena*. The Xenaverse is a diverse group of people from all over the world and many found friendship and love.

In 1996, it was unheard of for the LGBTQA+ community to freely marry—it was fraught with so much heartache, subterfuge, and sorrow. However, things never stay the same, and sometimes unexpected events surprise us all, which is what happened when same-sex marriage was legalized in the United States, Australia, UK, New Zealand, and all over Europe.

In 2003, when I attended my first official Xena convention, I was meeting people who I had only communicated with via email or message forums. One Xenite approached me and told me a story that left me utterly gobsmacked. She thanked me for AUSXIP, and then she said that she had met her life partner because of the site. As you can imagine, I felt inconsequential because all I did was create a website, but here was a person was telling me she had a life-changing event because of the site. What do you say to that? 'Thank you' seems inadequate, right? The cast and crew of *Xena* have heard that same stories of love that blossomed because of *Xena* for the last twenty-five years. The actors say they were just doing a job (which is true), but the bottom line is this: this show brought people together in a lasting and meaningful way.

I decided that instead of writing what I knew about the couples that got together, I would ask them to write about their experiences! It wasn't difficult finding Xenites who got married because of this show. I put the call out to the Xenaverse that I needed some stories about their experiences of finding love and getting married because of *Xena*. No sooner had I sent that request out, my inbox filled with stories. Enjoy their tales of love and marriage!

Marilyn and Tiger

I have known these two extraordinary women for over twenty years, and it's been a great friendship. They recently tied the knot, but those two lovebirds have been together forever.

In 1999, I joined a Yahoo group called Merwolf Pack (for fans of Melissa Good) because I'd been watching a show called Xena. In April of that year, I was having a cornea transplant and reached out to the Pack. One of the first to answer was a woman named Tiger. She knew someone who'd had eye surgery.

We started emailing and I found out that she lived in Los Angeles. We set up a day to meet and had lunch at Ruby's at the end of the Huntington Beach pier. I found out that she's gay. Being raised Southern Baptist, I thought of her as a friend and nothing more. We were both annual pass holders at Disneyland and went on the weekends that summer and into the rest of the year. Slowly, my feelings moved from friendship to something more. I startled her one day at Disneyland when I slipped my hand in hers. I must admit that I was surprised too, but it felt right.

We've now been together for nineteen years. We've traveled across the country and made many friends around the world, all because of a TV show called Xena. Love comes in many shapes, and I'm glad that it did come to me.

Arielle and Erin

In April 2019, I was walking up the path to my cabin at the Xenite Retreat in Lake Hughes, California and I came upon on a dear friend of mine, Arielle Strauss, who looked ecstatically happy. In my usual bumbling way, I had crashed into her life-changing moment; Arielle's marriage proposal to her beloved Erin (not the actual popping of the question, but the happy aftermath of it), and they were deliriously happy. I'll let Arielle tell you the story.

Seven years ago, at Xena Con 2013, my sister Talia and I were waiting in line for autographs. Talia turned to me and said, "We have to find you a girlfriend." I was not about that. I'd recently broken up with a long-term boyfriend and was still grieving and needed to move on. But mere seconds after saying, "no, thanks," the most beautiful woman I'd ever seen walked by. It was a true Romeo and Juliet moment—the moment in the crowded festival when Romeo is with his best friend Mercutio, mourning his lost love of Rosaline when all of a sudden he sees the woman he's meant to be with for the rest of his life. Only he doesn't know it yet. I never believed moments like this existed, but they do, and I've experienced one.

I didn't see this mysterious woman again until the 2014 convention when Talia and I proudly donned our Xena and Gabrielle costumes. She approached us and asked to take our picture. Later on that same day, she snapped our picture again. I didn't know what to make of her. I figured she probably wasn't as nice as she seemed, we most likely had nothing in common, and she had to be straight. I couldn't have been more wrong.

While waiting in line for Brittney Powell's autograph, my crush snuck in behind us so we could chat. She was curious and engaging, and I could see by the way she treated Talia and me that she was kind-hearted. Her name tag read 'Erin.' "It's nice to meet you, Erin," I told her.

"It's nice to meet you, Arielle," she replied, reading my name tag.

The Xena convention held in February 2015 was to be the final one. My dad and sister were only going to be there for one day, which at first, I was upset about. Con was supposed to be our thing, and I had to go it alone for most of the last one, but I knew Erin would be there, and this would give me the opportunity to get to know her better.

Erin and I spent the whole convention together, even after Dad and Talia arrived. When the two of us parted after con, we missed each other terribly. A week later, she sent me a heartfelt email about how much it meant to her that we had shared the last convention together. And the very next day, she admitted her feelings for me and bravely came out as bisexual. Since then, we kept a long-distance relationship on opposite coasts with frequent visits. She's the joy and love of my life.

We've since moved in together and have every year attended Xenite Retreat as a couple. Growing up with XWP as my guide, I knew the warrior and the bard and those adventures. They became part of the inner landscape of myself. The episodes felt like my own memories. Then, beginning my journey with Erin was like living the story all over again. I was the storyteller that left home to do life with a strong supportive woman, who happens to have a dark past who tries to do right by everyone. She carried the weight of the world on her shoulders, but she doesn't have to carry it alone; not anymore. At last year's Xenite Retreat, I got down on one knee and asked Erin to be my wife. And she said yes. With the help of my maid of honor, Talia, of course, I have chosen a beautiful white dress to wear at our wedding.

Penny and Kat

These two are dear friends and I simply adore them. This is the story of their friendship, love and marriage in the Xenaverse. Dearest Willow (their baby daughter), if you are reading this in a few years from now, this is how your mothers met, fell in love and married. You're in for a treat! I love a good love story. This is an excerpt from Penny's chapter about how she met her wife Kat. You can read Penny's chapter in Part 7: Because of Xena, Chapter 47: From Life At 10 To A 10/10 Life.

I remember inviting this really cute girl to an after-party one year. I didn't know her name, but she knew mine, and when she said it, I just about lost my legs from under me. It would take me another two years to finally get enough courage to speak to her again (she never showed to the party the year I invited her!!).

Here is where I owe MaryD a pretty massive thank you. Mary asked if I was going to get a photo with Lucy. I told her that I wasn't. She asked if I had ever met Lucy. I said no. So, Mary gave me her photo op ticket. She also asked me not to tell anyone, because that is the kind of wonderful giving person Mary is. She doesn't do it for the props. But sorry, Mary, the cat's out of the bag, because that gesture led to the Kat being IN the bag... Let me explain.

I remember Lucy saying, "Do something scary; the payoff is awesome."

Moments after meeting Lucy, when I was still in what they call the "purple haze," I saw Kat. The cute girl. At that point, Creation had told us this was the last con (spoiler: it wasn't) and I figured I was going back to Australia never to see her again, so what would it hurt to tell her that I thought she was cute? I marched up to her, and in a way not dissimilar to the way that Joxer confesses his love for Gabrielle (I'm pretty sure I even borrowed Aphrodite's advice of not expecting anything), I let my mouth babble.

What I said I couldn't tell you, but by the end of it we had exchanged contact information. This is where I'm going to make a long story short and say that in true U-Haul fashion, we got married at the following convention. Katherine Fugate stood up in our wedding and gifted us a special lesson in love that we remember to this day, and I walked down the aisle while Lara De Wit played the Xena theme song on the piano. It was a damn fairytale.

Barbara Bassett (aka bjStranger) and Linda Brault

In 1996, I met a fellow Canadian woman —screen name Nova— on those XWP mailing lists, and before long, a romance blossomed between us. She wooed me with her poetry, and I fell hard. Nova lived in Halifax, Nova Scotia, and was an out lesbian there, though not entirely out in her small hometown. Her family knew and were accepting, but in 1996 they still didn't really talk about it. I was a closeted lesbian, married to a guy, and not out to anyone in the city where I worked or in my own hometown, especially not to my parents.

I am an only child and an introvert. The internet was my coming out mechanism because it put me in touch with lesbians and queer-friendly people. Xena and Gabrielle lit a fire in me. I was captivated by the show, so when the internet finally arrived at my workplace, I dove in looking for everything Xena. It's funny now to remember that my experience with the internet was solely text-based that first year. The Saddlehorn mailing list introduced me to Xena/Gabrielle fan fiction. After reading some of those lovely romance stories with sex scenes, I realized I needed to get the heck out of the closet. I had been too shy, afraid, and unlucky to meet women like me in real life, but now I was talking to them daily and falling in love with one of them on the internet.

Nova had three siblings and is less of an introvert than me. She'd been dating women (in RL) for a few years before we met. Nova had a home computer and was one of the first people I know of to have Windows. She'd experienced interacting with people on-line already, but after discovering and loving Xena on TV, she immediately sought out and enjoyed the joys of XWP on-line fandom. She became obsessed with Xena just like me, and our paths crossed on-line.

Long story short... I met Nova three times in person before we began to set in motion the cascade of events that led us to being together for good. For our first RL visit together, Nova flew to Ontario and we drove to the New York City Xena Fest with two other women from the Toronto area (Liv and Merope). That was a transformative trip. In New York City, I slept with Nova, and it was everything. Nova and I clicked in real life so it was on. In our second visit together, I flew to Nova Scotia and we spent a few days sightseeing and getting to know one another better one-on-one. She took me to her hometown and introduced me to her mom and one sister. (That went really well.) In our third visit together, Nova flew to Ontario and we drove to the Xena convention in Valley Forge, Pennsylvania. During that visit, we discussed practicalities like who should move where and who should change jobs, etc.

Around that time, we were in touch with other women who had fallen in love on-line through Xena fandom and who were experiencing the same ups and downs of long-distance relationships. Dialogue with them was very helpful. Like me, a couple of other women were married. We faced the daunting task of ending our marriages. Lucky for me, there were no children involved, but it was still difficult. I found it so hard that I had to employ the guidance of a social worker psychologist through the family assistance program offered by my employer. She helped me set up a plan on how to approach coming out to my parents, how to initiate the end of my marriage, etc. Initially, my parents were not pleased to learn I was gay and gave me quite a hard time, but eventually, they came around and accepted Nova into the family.

At her end, Nova told her mom and three siblings she was moving to Ontario to live with me. Once a move date was established, she put in her notice at work that she was resigning. It was a time of upheaval and change but Nova coped quite well. In years past, when she was a soldier in the Canadian Armed Forces, she had already lived in the province of Ontario when she was based in our nation's capital and worked at a military hospital there.

Step-by-step, we finally achieved our goal of living together. By the spring of 1998, I was legally separated from my former spouse. In the summer of 1998, Nova moved to Ontario and changed jobs. She had worked in hospital sterile processing in Nova Scotia but was ready for a change. During our first three years of living together, she was a student with a part-time job at FedEx Ground. In October 2001, she graduated with a Bachelor of Science degree in Computer Information Systems and *immediately found a good job in IT with a major Canadian bank. And after the waiting period required by law in Ontario between separation and divorce, I was finally legally divorced around the same time. Living together was everything we'd hoped for.*

On June 10, 2003, same-sex marriage was legalized in the province of Ontario, and on July 24, 2005 same-sex marriage became legal throughout Canada. But Nova and I have not married. We're content being common-law spouses. We have all the same privileges as a married couple. We bought a house together in 2004 when we were both still working in the city. In 2017, after we had both finally retired, we sold it and moved to my hometown, Collingwood, Ontario. I am finally out in my hometown—at least as out as one can be when they introduce their wife to friends at their high school reunions and at social events at the Legion.

Over the years we've had many adventures together. We love camping and road trips, riding our motorcycles and doting on our two cats. Among other activities, I work on genealogy and history projects, and Nova writes fan fiction when the muses strike. Her pen names over the years have been Nova and AliceBB. Besides XWP fan fiction, she's written fan fiction for Star Trek Voyager, Criminal Minds, The 100 (Clexa), and Fear of The Walking Dead. The most recent story that she wrote is called Summer Girl— https://archiveofourown.org/works/21889816.

On August 1, 2019, we celebrated our 21st anniversary. We have a wonderful life together, and we owe it all to Xena: Warrior Princess and the wonderful fandom it created.

Barbara is sixty-four and Linda is fifty-four

1998

Demeter and Wishes met on-line through a Xena fan list in 1998. Wishes retired and moved to Canada in 2001. We were married on May 14, 2016. A cardboard Xena standee was in attendance, to the delight of our wedding guests and the hotel guests, who all wanted their pictures taken with Xena and us.

1999

Carrie Carr and Jan Carr have been together since August 1999 and married since September 2003.

2006

My name is Agnes Hagadus. I met my better half about six years ago. We met in Jay Tuma's Xena group. I was writing fanfics for Xena and Jason was a reader. At the time, I was with someone else. Ja was luckily patient and happy with a friendship. Once things ended, Ja was there for me and things went from there. We started dating in 2015 and were married in 2016. Jason even immigrated to the US for me from England. He'll be sworn in as a US citizen during the new year!

2007

Martine De Grauw and Karin Oosterveen got married on February 24, 2007. You can read more about Martine and Karin in the second chapter about Webmasters called "How Xena Changed Our Lives – The Xena Film Locations, by Martine De Grauw And Karin Oosterveen."

2008

Jennifer Cantley and Diana Leah Cantley got together in 1999 and were married in 2008. They met on the USA Xena NetForum. Unfortunately, Diana passed away on September 08, 2018.

Diana and I were together for twenty years. We did a joining first and then got married in 08. I adopted her last name. I lost her last year due to strokes. If it weren't for Xena, my life would have never changed, at least not the way it did. I'd probably still be in the closet and not know it.

2009

My beautiful wife, Alison Wilcoxson, and I, Bobbie Halchishak, met in an on-line Xena chatroom. We were married on Sept 28th, 2009, in Iowa, the closest state to us at the time (we live in Michigan). We tell everyone the show was the reason we met!!!

2011

My name is Tash Karoly. My partner (we are legally married) and I met because of Xena. We were both on Talking Xena first and then moved to the Xena On-line Community (XOC). We met in 2011 and got together the same year. It was long distance for quite a while since I lived in Mississippi and he was in California. We now reside in California and were married on June 12, 2015. We also have a five-year-old son together.

2016

We are Caroline Beattie and Heike Stewart. We both are from the Edmonton, Alberta, Canada area (45 minutes apart) and met at the first Xenite Retreat in California in April 2016. We went on our first date on May 4th and have been together since then essentially, but our official anniversary is May 18th, 2016.

There are so many stories such as the ones above... Indeed, love blossomed in the Xenaverse.

Chapter Forty-Two

From the Xenaverse to
Winning Daytime Emmys

by Christa Morris, KT Jorgensen, and Maria Webster

IN 2002, I WAS working in Los Angeles, helping to build a new television station. The work was long, hard, and tedious. I spent weeks at a time in hotel rooms or build sites in a city I didn't know and was a bit afraid of.

Surfing the internet one night, I discovered Renée O'Connor was scheduled to perform in a production of *Love Letters* in Pasadena that weekend as part of a convention. To see the play, I had to purchase a pass to the convention itself.

I wasn't overly interested in the convention part but was amazed at the people. The place was packed—merchandise everywhere, people in costume. After making a couple of rounds through the expo floor, I decided to head to the hotel bar and wait for the play…and this is where it all truly began.

The bar was quiet. I was sitting at the end of the bar, minding my own business, when the woman next to me tried to strike up a conversation. I was nice, but not interested in talking. I was pretty shy back then, and to be honest, still a little unsure of who I was as a person, so I wasn't interested in talking. This woman was having none of it. She kept pushing and I kept retreating.

Out of nowhere, another woman stepped between us. She had long braided hair and was dressed in a black shirt and leather pants, and the first woman backed right off. My knight in shining armor was Maria Webster and we have been friends ever since.

Our friendship turned into a yearly pilgrimage to the annual *Xena* convention, which led to the building of a tribe of friendships, including MaryD, Desiree Lauro, Pat Vowles, Ruth Roddis, Kathleen Mayer, and KT Jorgensen, the other person who would become vital to my journey.

Like Maria, KT came out of nowhere. During one *Xena* con, MaryD insisted I go to some bard thing in a large room with a bunch of tables. As we sat at one chatting with a few other people, MaryD suddenly started speaking another language to one person who then responded in the same language. Confused, I jokingly said, "Whoa, who changed the channel?"

Everyone at the table fell over laughing, including the photographer for

AfterEllen…KT Jorgensen. Drinks in the bar that night led to me telling her that she was welcome to come to hang in L.A. anytime, which she did, a lot.

All the friendships I built during this strange but magical annual four-day pilgrimage helped me become more and more comfortable with who I am as a person and in my career.

***

I first became aware of *Xena: Warrior Princess* at work. Following in my grandfather's footsteps, I went to school for Television and Radio just a few weeks out of high school. By the time I was in my mid-20s, I was a manager at a TV station in Dallas, Texas.

One night while I worked late, a master control operator asked if I had a few minutes to look at a feed we had just received for one of our weekend shows. That show was *Xena,* and "checking it for air quality" became just sitting and watching the show. I was hooked. I'd never seen anything like it. I learned later that I was watching the end of the series and not the beginning.

Obviously, I went back to watch the show from the beginning.

Within a few years and after a lot of bumps, bruises, blood, sweat, and tears, my career led me to NBC Los Angeles. Eventually, I settled into a management job at KNBC in Burbank. I wasn't sure about L.A., but I loved my job and boss, so I figured the rest would come with time. And I was still making my annual treks to the *Xena* con.

On October 27, 2008, my boss, Michael McCarthy, climbed up the back stairs to our office. He hadn't been feeling well and had spent time in and out of doctor's offices. NBC was pushing budgets hard, and Mike felt like he just couldn't take time off. He kept saying, "Maybe after the holidays."

Mike was winded and took a moment to sit in one of the assistant chairs. After a moment, he fell to the floor. There was panic and a call to 911. One of the account executives performed CPR, but Mike never got back up. This kind and generous man whom we all loved so much died right in front of our eyes. In hindsight, I think he was dead before he even hit the floor.

As I stood in the ER listening to the doctor and then the crying of Mrs. McCarthy, I was lost. What the hell was I doing in this town, alone, working endlessly? Over the holidays, I sat on the beach alone trying to figure out what I wanted. Should I go back home to Dallas or stay in L.A.? This was the place I had always dreamed of, the industry I always wanted to be in.

My grandfather hadn't lived long enough to see me in his world, working in the industry just as he had. I had just become a member of the Academy of Television Arts and Sciences thanks to Paula Madison, but was it all for nothing?

I looked out at the ocean, wishing my grandfather was there, wondering what he would say.

That night, I read an article about Ashton Kutcher and how he had taken his canceled television series and put the remaining episodes on YouTube. It had developed a cult-like following. The article also mentioned an actress, Crystal Chappell, who was working on a web series. The name seemed so familiar. Google informed me that Crystal Chappell played Dr. Carly Manning on the long-running soap opera *Days of Our Lives*, a show and character I had loved during high school.

One of the perks of working at KNBC in Burbank was that *Days of Our Lives* was filmed on our lot. Live feeds of the daily filming were displayed on in-house monitors. One day, I saw Crystal Chappell filming. A few days later, she walked into the NBC commissary, where I was eating lunch.

Intrigued, I researched the web series to see what Crystal was trying to accomplish. After a lot of over-thinking and back and forth with friends, I decided to write an inner-office memo to Ms. Chappell explaining who I was and what I did. If she was interested, I would love to meet with her to learn more and see if there was anything within my experience that might help her.

I had been in TV for a long time, and I could see that things were changing. My grandfather had talked about the transition from radio to TV. Now, broadcast media was on the verge of another massive change and my bosses didn't want to acknowledge it. But I wanted to stay relevant.

A couple of weeks later, I got an email. Crystal wanted to meet. Holy crap! So, we set up a lunch and if you believe in signs, well…get this. Crystal walked in, and as we were doing introductions, I felt a hand on my shoulder. I turned to see Lucy Lawless standing behind me, smiling. I'd had the honor of being around Lucy a few times, but in all the years I'd lived in L.A., I had never run into her out and about.

After a quick hello and hug, I introduced Lucy to Crystal, and then we both went to our separate meetings. Even more hilarious was the fact that most of my *Xena* buddies were camped at my apartment because we would all soon be heading to *Xena* con!

That lunch turned into more meetings and talks, as well as an interview for AUSXIP. Then one day, Crystal asked if I would help her production manage the second season of *Venice The Series*.

After I recovered from the shock, I called my *Xena* tribe.

Desiree Lauro came on board to help with crew hiring, equipment, and more. KT Jorgensen aided with production and behind-the-scenes photographs. Ruth and Kathy helped get actors where they needed to be, and when the *Venice* site crashed, I was asked if I knew anyone who might be able to help fix it. Maria!

Before we all knew it, a bunch of women who had met because of *Xena*:

Warrior Princess were now helping Crystal build a web series. Crystal had given me the chance of a lifetime and I was very, very lucky to have friends behind me who were willing to come on the journey. They believed in me, I believed in them and we figured it out as we went, together.

***

By the time Season Two of *Venice The Series* was released, the Daytime Emmys had added a new category – "Outstanding Special Class Short Format."

The night of the Daytime Creative Arts ceremony, I don't think I have ever been so wound up. When Crystal texted, "you're getting a gold statue!" I just started to cry.

I was a kid from nowhere, born into a life that wasn't exactly picturesque. Dysfunctional family, bad student, horrible grades, moved every couple of years, not expected to be much or do much in life. Yet somehow, my friends and I helped create something that had won an Emmy Award!

I remember the day my actual statue arrived. Crystal had fought to make sure I got it due to some paperwork issues, and it came to the office delivered by the same mail person who had delivered my original memo to Crystal.

I opened it and as I pulled the Emmy out of the box, I thought, "Look, Grandpa, look what we did." Not only had Crystal and Open Book Productions won, but we had also made history by winning the first Emmy ever given for our format of digital media.

***

In production, the triumphs, although life-changing, are short-lived. You have to keep moving forward through the ups and downs—scripts to write, crew to hire, websites to fix, stories to tell.

I was lucky enough to co-executive produce two more seasons of *Venice The Series*, as well as *The Grove The Series, Beacon Hill,* and the feature film *A Million Happy Nows.* But on the personal side things were getting harder and harder at the day job, NBC. My boss, who in some ways had grown up with me in the industry, and I were not seeing eye to eye. As the world now knows, the media industry was a man's world, a very hard world for women for many reasons. The man running my division should have never been put in the seat he held. I believe he knew it and he was willing to do anything to keep it. My time at NBC was coming to an end and I knew it.

One day I got an email from MaryD telling me that Lucy was going to be at the studio to do *The Tonight Show.* We were in the middle of moving offices. NBC had built a brand-new station for us over at the Universal lot and my team was going with the news department early to move in. I found out when Lucy would arrive and ran down to wait for her.

The security guards can be a little grumpy about staff hanging out waiting to catch a glimpse of celebrity guests, so I did a lot of nothing to look like I was doing something until the limo pulled up.

Lucy got out and promptly looked up the ramp to me and said, "Well, hello, Christa!" I laughed and said, "Hey, Lucy."

The grumpy security guards made a path.

As we walked to her dressing room, she congratulated me on my success and the Emmys. I looked at her and said, "Thank you. If it hadn't been for you and *Xena: Warrior Princess,* I would have never gotten them."

She laughed and said, "It was all you. I had nothing to do with it."

She couldn't be more wrong. Without *Xena* and the tribe I found because of it, I wouldn't be the person I am today. I would never have had the courage to do the things I've done since the night I went to watch Renée O'Connor perform *Love Letters.*

They say that life is a journey, and truer words will never be spoken. I have always known I wanted to work in TV. Always. But it was the friendships I gained through *Xena* that gave me the courage to become me, not just the version I thought people wanted me to be. I'm not saying it was all roses and wine (still isn't), but all the good and all the bad are lessons learned.

If you had ever told me when I was in my twenties that I would have two Emmys, I would develop shows for major networks, I'd be building a business with my partners Maria and KT creating original content for TV, film, and digital, I would have not only called you crazy, I would have given you all the reasons why it was crazy to look at me of all people and say that.

But here we are…life just keeps Moving On.

Chapter Forty-Three

Xena Made Me Do It!
Standup Comedy & Podcasting to the World

by Cat Crimins

LUCY LAWLESS IS CRAZY

Lucy Lawless crank-called me. It was December of 2006 and she got my number from a mutual friend, dialed it and at some point decided, "I should fuck with her." (This would prove to be a recurring theme). And she did. She disguised her voice by using some strange high-pitched American accent (she's really good at accents, go figure) and asked if I knew anyone with a Xena costume, she could rent. There was a long, confused pause from my end of the call before Lucy chimed in again with her normal voice.

"Hey Cat; it's Lucy."

She quickly got to the point of the real reason for her call without missing a beat. She wanted me to be the MC of her Roxy show.

At this point, she had known me for about two months. In those two months, we had said goodbye to a mutual friend, had both been there as that friend passed away, mourned together at her funeral, and celebrated her life with laughter at her memorial service. At that same memorial service, Lucy saw me tell some jokes. Let me explain.

Our friend Aleida had led an extraordinary life, and her partner of twenty-five years, Grace, wanted her memorial to be a joyful celebration of her life with lots of laughter. Grace had asked that I be the de facto officiant of the memorial service. They were not a religious couple, and Grace wanted someone who knew Aleida to lead the service. I was honored to take on this role. It is the most important thing I've ever been asked to do and I really didn't want to screw it up. And I didn't. Apparently, Lucy agreed. I guess if you can get laughs at a funeral, you can handle a crowd of five hundred Xenites. It makes perfect sense.

Back to the crank call. She got right to the point.

"I need an MC for the Roxy. You'll be good. And you can tell some jokes".

It was more of a statement than a question. When Lucy freaking Lawless tells you to do something, you do it. I was still trying to wrap my head around what she was asking me to do when I said yes. I hung up the phone an instantly regretted saying yes. I had never done standup and I had never performed anything like an MC gig in front of a group of people before, unless you count Aleida's memorial, which Lucy apparently did.

Let me take a moment to discuss Lucy Lawless. She's crazy. Completely nuts. What was she thinking? I could have been terrible. What was I thinking? I could have completely bombed! I should have said no. Any rational, self-respecting person would have. But I said yes. Because I am also crazy.

I've been a huge fan of standup comedy since I was a kid. In my hometown, Thousand Oaks, California, we had a local AM radio station that only played comedy—standup bits during the day and classic radio shows at night. I was obsessed with this station. When I left for school in the morning, I'd leave a cassette recording the station in case I missed a new comedy bit from one of my favorite comedians. And at night I would go to sleep listening to classics like Jack Benny and Burns and Allen. I memorized my favorite comedy sets: George Carlin, Elayne Boosler, and (the now very problematic) Bill Cosby. I mimicked their timing and delivery. I was pretty good for a ten-year-old. If I had a presentation to give in class, I would warm up my "audience" with a few jokes. Comedy was on my radar. Maybe this was a career option? But then someone told me something that ended my aspirations of being a standup comedian. Apparently, you had to write your own material. I couldn't just go up there and perform other people's jokes. And that was the end of that. How could I possibly ever write jokes as funny as the comics that I loved? I was not the kind of kid that put a lot of stock into 'hard work will get you what you want.' If something looked impossible, it probably was, so why bother trying (not good advice, kids; do not write that down)? So the idea of me ever doing standup was filed away, deep in the back of my brain. Until the crank call.

Getting a phone call from your idol is an amazing thing. If, during that call she asks you to join her on stage because she thinks you'd be great, that starts to creep into surreal territory. This is the sort of thing that happens to other people. If someone told me this story, I would just assume they were lying. This kind of thing doesn't just happen on a regular Tuesday afternoon. But it did. Part of me was expecting her to call me back the next day and call it off, having thought better of it. I would have been totally OK with that. She did call me back a few days later, but it wasn't to fire me; it was to discuss details.

I would be opening both nights of the show with a five-minute set, then introduce the opening act, Tig Notaro, an actual comedian and old friend of Lucy's, then the lights would go down and Lucy would do her thing. Then she would call me up halfway through her set and I would ask her questions from the audience. Great, simple, easy. Oh, and one last thing; Lucy felt it would add to the show if I wore some sort of sexy costume.

Allow me to take another moment to discuss Lucy Lawless. I mentioned before that she liked messing with me. Telling me that she wanted me to wear some sort of sexy nurse or sexy cop costume is just another example. Giving me the nickname 'Kit Kat' and subsequently only referring to me in writing as Kat was another way. The thing you need to know about Lucy is that when she does something, she commits to it fully, and messing with me was no different. When my name appeared on the Roxy marquee, it was spelled with a K. In the weeks leading up to that first show, she took me to at least half a dozen lingerie and sex shops searching for the perfect costume for me to wear. What I didn't know at the time was that she was never going to make me wear a sexy outfit. She just liked to see me squirm. Commitment to a joke. I respect it. Eventually, in 2009, the last year of her Roxy shows, she did get me in a costume, but not a sexy one. If you look hard enough on the internet, you will find a photograph or two of me in a nun's costume. Commitment.

Don't Screw This Up

I had about a month to prepare for the shows and it didn't take long for me to figure out what my jokes were going to be about. I knew the crowd very well. So well in fact, I would have been in the crowd myself if Lucy hadn't asked me to be her MC. I knew what Xenites wanted—jokes about Xena and Lucy. And I knew the same crowd would be at both shows, so I had to come up with a completely different set for each night. Let's recap. Ten minutes of untested comedy (no one had heard any of my material before the performances) delivered by someone who had never performed standup before (if you don't count a funeral). What could possibly go wrong?

For the record, Lucy never asked to see or hear my material before the show. Her confidence in me is what kept me focused on doing a good job. I couldn't let her down.

The night of the first show arrived and I was freaking terrified. I was running through my set obsessively in the hallway outside of Lucy's dressing room on the second floor of the Roxy because it was all I could do to not have a panic attack. Lucy could tell I was a little tense, so she invited me to hang out in her dressing room for a bit to try and distract me. That's where I met Tig Notaro, the actual standup comic. I knew who she was from her appearances on Comedy Central and The Sarah Silverman Program, and she was the real deal. When Lucy introduced me as the night's MC, Tig asked me how long I had been doing standup. I smiled and said, "Tonight's my first night."

I'll never forget the look on her face, a mix of skepticism and sympathy.

"Well, good luck," she said with her famous dead man delivery. I thanked her and excused myself so I could go back to rehearsing my set, the only thing that seemed to be calming me down.

Five minutes until showtime. Lucy wished me luck and sent me downstairs. Standing behind the curtain, I could hear the chatter of the expectant Xenite crowd. I had friends out there, but that didn't help to calm my nerves. What if I forgot how to speak? What if I forgot my set? What if I bombed and got booed off stage by a room full of angry lesbians who are intimately aware of how to crucify someone? It was too late to back out. The house lights went down and someone shoved a microphone in my hand and told me to start the show. I stepped through the curtain and walked onto the lonely, bright stage and took a deep breath.

I didn't forget how to speak, I didn't forget my set, and I didn't bomb. The crowd was generous and wonderful and so supportive. As soon as my first joke landed, all the anxiety and nerves I had been feeling for the last month disappeared from my body and I had the time of my life. I didn't want it to end but those five minutes went by very quickly. I wrapped up my set and introduced Tig. As I passed her the microphone, she shook my hand, and with a smile said, "Nice set." And that, ladies and gentlemen, might be the coolest thing that anyone has ever said to me.

Lucy, of course, had a fantastic show and brought the house down. The next night was just as much fun and before I knew it, the weekend was over. I didn't embarrass Lucy or myself, and I got a taste of my standup dream coming true.

The Payoff For Doing Something Scary Is Awesome

Two months later, I was preparing for my first open mic night. I had to give this standup thing a shot. The Roxy shows gave me a lot of confidence, not only to give standup a try but to do something that scared the crap out of me. I wrote and worked on a new, Xena-free five-minute set and found a bar in West Hollywood with an open mic night. I reached out to my friends with the date and time in the hopes that I could stack the crowd with friendly faces. My friends answered the call and showed up. The one person I was not expecting to show up was Lucy freaking Lawless, but she did. Insert head exploding emoji here. This was going to be great. Best first open mic performance ever. I'm probably going to be on the news.

I made my way over to the bartender and asked where I could find the sign-up sheet, the list where you put your name down to be called up on stage.

"What sign-up sheet?"

"The sign-up sheet for the open mic tonight."

Funny story, they had discontinued their open mic night weeks before and had not yet updated their website. The good news was there was a comedy show that night, but the bad news was it was with booked talent. This was not good. This was actually terrible. I had at least ten people there waiting to see me perform, including Lucy freaking Lawless, and I was not about to tell them I would not be going on stage. I had to do something, but what? Well, I did what any self-respecting Xenite would. I asked myself, what would Xena do? Now, to be fair, I could have actually asked Xena what she would do, but I didn't need to. I knew what she would do and that's what I did. Without all the punching.

I marched over to the comedy night's MC, explained that I had a bunch of people waiting for me to perform because I thought it was an open mic night so he had to let me go on stage. Please.

"Are you any good?"

"I mean, I'm not bad."

He must have seen the desperation in my eyes because he let me perform, thank the gods! And once again, I didn't completely embarrass myself. I sent Lucy a thank you email the next day. Her reply included one of my favorite lines, "The payoff for doing something scary is awesome, right?"

Awesome indeed.

For the next year I performed standup all over Los Angeles. Mostly in bars and restaurants. I scored a few regular gigs and I only bombed a few times, but I started to notice something happening over that year. My anxiety before each show slowly increased. I went from having stage fright right before going on stage, which is totally normal, to having nerves a week before the show. My anxiety was slowly turning my standup dream into my own nightmare. I wasn't eating or sleeping, leading up to a gig. Once I got on stage, I would be able to perform, but as soon as I was done, the anxiety from whatever upcoming show was next crept back into my mind and body.

Hiatus Is Another Way Of Saying I Don't Want To Do This Anymore

Lucy asked me back for her 2008 Roxy show, which I gratefully accepted, but after that weekend, I pumped the brakes on my standup performances. I would perform once or twice a month that next year, but only when invited by a friend. In 2009, Lucy performed for the last time at the Roxy. She invited me back one more time (nun costume, remember?) and as much fun as it was, on the ride home from the theater I told myself I was going on hiatus from comedy. My body and brain needed a break from the constant dark nagging of my performance-induced anxiety.

That last Roxy show in 2009 would be the last time I would perform standup in front of an audience for eight years. Until I got a message from one of my favorite humans, Penny Cavanaugh, director of the Xenite Retreat. She was putting together a comedy night for the 2017 Xenite

Retreat and wanted to know if I'd like to be a part of it. During my eight-year, self-induced hiatus, I had gone through a lot. My partner Leah and I were celebrating ten years of being together and I had changed careers twice. But a few things did not change. I was still a Xenite and I was still a sucker for someone with an accent who thought I was funny. I, of course, said yes. Because A) when Penny Cavanaugh tells you to do something, you do it, and B) I'm a Xenite for life and will never say no to celebrating this incredible fandom. The night was a lot of fun and I had a blast performing at the Xenite Retreat. There were lots of familiar faces from the old Xena con days and some brand new ones. I performed all-new Xena material, including a 'Joxer polishing his sword' fanfic joke I am very proud of.

So You Want To Be A Podcaster

I am constantly listening to podcasts. On my way to work, in the shower, at home doing chores. They are a constant in my life. I have been dabbling in producing podcasts since 2013 but I wasn't serious about it until 2019. My goal that year was to produce and co-host two new podcasts. I knew it would feed that creative need I had since quitting standup. I like to think of it as standup without nausea.

By early 2019, one of the two podcasts I wanted to produce was already in development. It would become the "My Mistake Podcast," where my friend John Fitzgerald and I tell funny stories about mistakes we've made. For the second podcast, I knew I wanted it to be a look at pop culture through the lens of queer women and I knew who my perfect co-hosts would be. Wendy Woody and Tara Chadwick had made a name for themselves in the Xenaverse for their fan films. We had a lot of mutual friends and had crossed paths numerous times. Wendy had just moved to Los Angeles from Dallas and so I asked them both out for drinks. I was actually very nervous to ask them to be my podcasting partners. It was like we were on a co-host first date, except they didn't know it yet. We spent most of the evening catching up on what we all had been up to. I waited until the very end of the night to ask them about podcasting with me and thankfully they said yes. And so the "She Nerds Out Podcast" was born.

https://podcasts.apple.com/us/podcast/she-nerds-out/id1459003657

There are many things I love about podcasting, including the way it allows me to express myself in a creative and funny way (without nausea). It's a great excuse to hang out with friends and talk about our passions, including the one passion that brought us together in the first place, Xena.

Chapter Forty-Four

From Published Author to Radio Host to Playwright and Producer

by Sherri Rabinowitz

IT ALL STARTS WITH a spark of an idea… I had just published Fantasy Time Inc and well on the way to promoting the book. I was invited to be interviewed on a radio show.

It took me by surprise that the interviewer didn't ask any follow-up questions and seemed unprepared. It was disappointing, and I was somewhat perplexed by the presentation. All subsequent interviews, from various podcast shows, were lacking the same attention to detail. I was talking to my Mom one day, explaining how frustrating it was, and she suggested I do a show. "After all, you're an actress, and you studied journalism." I blinked and thought she was right. The answer was right there in front of me.

My guests trusted a new broadcaster with their interviews, and they keep coming back to the show, which means so very much to me. I love them all. If it weren't for them, I am not sure I would have had the courage to keep going. And now, I have just entered my seventh season, and I am still writing my novels and other books. Here are some of the radio interviews and plays that have featured on my show

XENA: WARRIOR PRINCESS

Steven L Sears was the first guest I had on either of my shows, Chatting With Sherri and Sherri's Playhouse. He has always been very supportive of me, and when I asked if I should do either of the shows, he said I should go for it. Steven had no idea if I could do it. Neither did I, but he believes in encouragement, and he has given me a great deal of strength through the years. Steven is also the best storyteller ever, I get so caught up in his stories I sometimes forget to watch the time, he has such extensive knowledge, he can talk about anything and be funny, charming and very informative. Thank you, Steve. http://tobtr.com/11366725

Adrienne Wilkinson was on that first year too, she has been super supportive too. She is so funny and tells a lot of great stories about working on shows like Xena, Star Trek, and Star Wars! Adrienne also has a huge heart and gives time to a lot of charities. Adrienne holds a big auction every year to raise money for a family in need. She is utterly charming and fun, I adore having her on my show. http://tobtr.com/11703099

Hudson Leick also came early on, she is so much fun! We talk about everything under the sun. She is very deeply into Yoga and Meditation, her yoga class is not to missed, it is fantastic. http://tobtr.com/10911375

TJ Scott is utterly charming and funny, he is like Steve Sears, he is a great storyteller and I get lost in his stories too. He is just so much fun, he can talk about anything, and they are always entertaining. TJ has directed a lot of iconic television and he always has a cool backstage story to tell us about. http://tobtr.com/11666727

MaryD from AUSXIP (Mary D Brooks) devotes a lot of time to writing, her websites and communicating with her fans. She loves *Xena* and she is always warm and funny, with her sweet Aussie accent and her 'hello Mate', she always makes me smile. Mary published this book via her publishing company AUSXIP Publishing which was a huge effort and she is an amazing talent and even more amazing friend. My first writing award came from Mary, for a story I wrote for my Mom called "Happiness", because Mom said all my stories are so sad. Thank you Mary, you are the best! http://tobtr.com/11366725

Melissa Good - I met Missy at one of my first *Xena* Cons, I had written some fan fiction but since it was not under my name I was deeply undercover. But we had chatted via email so she knew who I was, she cheerfully introduced me to a group of her fans, who to my shock had read my stories. She also came on my show early, she is always cheerful, funny and really supportive of my show. Thank you Missy. http://tobtr.com/11670694

MISS FISHER'S MURDER MYSTERIES;

Nathan Page was the first person I interviewed for another of my favorite shows; Miss Fisher, he plays Detective Inspector Jack Robinson. I very soon discovered, how very down to earth he is and very, very funny and easy-going. We have talked about his chickens, his garden, new dog (at the time Lola is a big girl now,) and his family. We always laugh and chuckle during the interview but not as much as we do before and after. Nathan is a lot of fun to chat to and very generous with his time. http://tobtr.com/11433805

Anthony Sharpe and his wife Julie Sharp are just such a great couple; you never know what you are going to talk about, burlesque, singing, redoing homes or film projects. It's always a blast to chat with them. We had a lot of fun last time talking about his newest YouTube project, and I even subscribed! http://tobtr.com/11726030

Brice Bexter: is new to the Miss Fisher world. He was surprised by the fandom and how people were interested in him since he does not have a big part. He is a delightful young man with some great new projects ahead of him. What was really interesting is that he is not only funny but really insightful, and he was educated at the very prestige's Actors Studio in New York. Wow! http://tobtr.com/11645505

I LOVE LUCY (TV SHOW)

Gregg Oppenheimer: it was so much fun to talk 'I Love Lucy' with Gregg, his dad was the producer of the show and his stories about how specific storylines came about blew my mind. The part where Ethel cuts Lucy's spaghetti was from his Mom always carried nail scissors in her purse or the Ricky going bald was curtsy of his dad who bald young. Just a charming and delightful guest. http://tobtr.com/11484465

SHERRI'S PLAYHOUSE

I had another idea to expand my platform, and that was to produce radio plays. I called it "Sherri's Playhouse". It came from hearing a reading of one of my plays by professional actors. I thought it would be great to give others a chance to do that and to give actors some credits for live radio performances. It has worked out so well, I am on my third season!

Here are some of the highlights (with links to download the mp3 files!)

A Heavenly Hand was my first radio play, I was so nervous, I wrote and produced and directed it. I had done a little of each before but never for a big audience. But I had a lot of joy from it because everyone loved it. http://tobtr.com/6454691

Murder At Home; I produced and acted in, I played a part of femme fatale, if I auditioned for a play on the stage I would have never have gotten the part. But you can do anything with just your voice, not only did I do it, the audience loved it, I received some of my best reviews. http://tobtr.com/6886383

A Widgie Knight by MaryD (Mary D Brooks) was so much fun, it was Mary's first play with us, and it was a smash. I got to play an Auntie Mame kind of character. It was a blast! It's part of the Eva and Zoe series.

http://tobtr.com/9213229

Sherlock Holmes and The Terror By Night Train was our first attempt to do a classic, it worked really well, it was a lot of fun too. This time I produced and acted, I played a British Aristocrat, that was a blast! Of course, we were all suspects, love a good mystery. http://tobtr.com/9768533

Cat's Pajamas, this was another play I wrote, produced, directed, and this time I acted in too. It was fun but hard because I had taken up so much responsibility. I played another over the top character, a lot of fun. It takes place in one of my favorite periods, the 1920's which was the beginning of a forward movement for women and talked about the good, the bad, and the ugly in it. I am very proud of it. http://tobtr.com/11726808

Mabel of the Anzacs was another play by MaryD (Mary D. Brooks), it was very close to Mary's heart, and I was playing the second lead in it, I was so nervous because all I wanted to do was to make Mary proud of me, we all worked very hard, it is part of the Eva and Zoe series, and I think it is one our best efforts. http://tobtr.com/11103379

Mishpucha was a short play written about my family for a contest, I adapted into a radio play, and I was thrilled that people seemed to love it. The cast really got into it. (I was smart that I didn't cast myself in any part other than the narrator.) http://tobtr.com/10987227

Joe Kronus was a romp I created at the request of one of our regular actors, it's all about time travel and saving the world, and responsibility. It was one of our most successful shows, I wrote, directed, and produced it. http://tobtr.com/10710077

I spoke to Steven Sears again at a *Xena* con about all that I was doing, and he said it sounded like fun and suggested he come on my blogtalk show and interview *me* about it. He did, and we had a blast! It helped launch another series of shows that are very dear to me on my platform.
The Xenaverse changed my life. Thank you, *Xena*!

Visit Sherri's BlogTalk Radio Show – Chatting With Sherri and Sherri's Playhouse https://www.blogtalkradio.com/rithebard

Chapter Forty-Five

From Xena to Producing Films and Going Mainstream

by Wendy Woody

"WELL, THAT'S DUMB." That was my first thought upon hearing that a *Hercules* spinoff about a woman named Xena was in the works. I mean, *Hercules* was a cute show, but did the world need another one like it? Boy, did we. Lives were changed by *Xena: Warrior Princess*. The show and its story of Xena and Gabrielle helped many people either discover or finally become comfortable with who they truly were. It motivated people to come out of their shells (and closets!) and travel across the country, or often from other countries, to celebrate the show and meet other like-minded fans. It helped forge lifelong friendships not only between fans of *Xena*, but also between some fans and the creators, writers, and actors who helped bring the show to life. It also cultivated amazing creativity in the form of homemade costumes, fanfic, art, and in my case, filmmaking.

The first time I decided to dabble in the world of *Xena* videos, it was to make a video for Creation Entertainment's music video contest in the early 2000s. I had some editing experience so I figured this was something I could definitely handle. I made a finely crafted video celebrating some of the battles from the show set to "Charging Fort Wagner" by James Horner from the score to the film Glory. It was an epic video with creative transitions that slowly built to a thrilling ending. I was sure it would be picked to play at the convention, so of course... it was rejected. At least my mom liked it. My later music video contributions would include the *Xena* intro in the style of other shows' opening credits and some sort of "follow the bouncing ball" sing-along video. I guess I redeemed myself! Little did I know my video-making exploits would get much bigger in the future. But first, my eyes needed to be opened to what was possible.

My friend Deborah made a short film for a local video contest way back in 2001. She shot it in a hotel room in Dallas using myself and some of our friends as actors. It was definitely a low to no budget production made with a simple home video camera, a couple of lights on sticks, and small microphones strategically clipped to various pieces of furniture. It wasn't the greatest thing we ever made but we sure had fun doing it, and it even made it into the contest! For me, the most important thing to come out of that experience was to see that anyone could make a movie. You didn't need any experience, fancy equipment, or even professional actors. All you needed was an idea.

The first video I remember directing, if you can call it that, consisted of me being attacked by small toys, including stormtroopers and Lala from Teletubbies. You've got to start somewhere. I eventually ventured into the world of directing actual actors with my first film for the Star Wars Fan Film Contest, 8 Minutes. It told the story of Star Wars fans attempting to get tickets to the upcoming Star Wars movie, told in "real-time" following the style of the TV show 24. It actually did pretty well!

It made it into the contest, won the Spirit of Fandom award, and got me a very cool trophy consisting of a golden R2-D2 and C3P0, not to mention tickets to San Diego Comic-Con for the awards presentation. My other Star Wars films, Tiny Toys and Star Bars didn't fare as well, but they were fun to make, and both consisted of actors interacting with action figures come to life. With every video, no matter how they turned out, I was getting experience and getting better.

My relationship with Creation Entertainment started after a memorable trip to New Zealand in 2002, during which Deborah and I visited many *Xena* filming locations. We even got the opportunity to ride (while dressed in Xena and Gabrielle costumes no less!) up and down the beach in chariots from the show. After returning home, I decided to put together a travelogue video of sorts featuring our photos and videos of the *Xena* locations along with scenes from the actual show. We thought it might be something Creation would be interested in playing during a *Xena* convention, so we sent them a copy. Much to our surprise and delight, they ended up playing our little New Zealand video during a couple of their conventions, so Deborah and I decided we would see what else we might convince them to play.

We went on to make several films for Creation's conventions, including True Love Never Dies, Spirit of Xena, and DeliverX. All were fun and very challenging to make. While filming True Love Never Dies, our *Xena* fanfic story, I'll never forget the long walks (while carrying heavy equipment) into the wilderness of Austin, Texas to reach the perfect shooting location. It's not easy to replicate that beautiful New Zealand scenery in Texas! We also had the good fortune to be able to use the Texas Renaissance Festival near Houston to capture that *Xena* village feel.

I'm not sure we really got permission, but that's what makes low-budget filmmaking exciting! Fun fact: the actress who played young Gabrielle in that movie even went on to star with Lucy Lawless herself in the TV movie Vampire Bats! Most of the films Deborah and I made together consisted of putting the camera on a tripod, standing in front of it, and doing the scene. One of us might be able to hold the camera if only one of us needed to be on camera or occasionally, we had a friend help out. Over time, however, I started realizing that the films might be best served by my staying behind the camera and concentrating on directing.

At the 2005 *Xena* convention, I met Tara Chadwick, a fellow filmmaking enthusiast. Our similar tastes in videos and a shared sense of offbeat humor led us to work on several movie projects together over the years. From *Xena* convention videos such as Foes, Femmes & Djinns, and Inappropriate Stranger to pet video contest winners like World Cat, to even starting our own production company, 55 Mile Entertainment, we covered a variety of topics and styles. As much fun as those videos were to make, nothing would compare to our experience in making Wicked: A *Xena* Musical in 2009.

I had always loved the idea of making some sort of musical, and Tara and I had tossed around several ideas for one focusing on *Xena*. One evening it seemed like a light bulb literally lit up over Tara's head when she got the idea to adapt Wicked. I had not seen the musical at this point, but was familiar enough with it to realize the music and the story were a perfect fit for Xena.

We decided it would be a somewhat loose look at the story of Xena over the course of the show, and we immediately set to adapting the music and lyrics. The next step was casting. This was our first venture into using actual actors who weren't our friends. It was exciting but also a bit scary! We had great luck in casting all of the *Xena* roles like Ares, Joxer, the various Amazons, and especially Gabrielle. We used a variety of locations around the Dallas area, including Scarborough Faire for the village scenes (we had permission this time!), a local nature park (despite getting kicked out once for building a large set), a castle in Oklahoma, and even my house and backyard. We rented a real recording studio to record all the songs, hired a local seamstress to make the Xena costume, and even managed to borrow a real horse to play Argo. This was definitely our most ambitious endeavor yet! That year, Tara was moving to Los Angeles, so our plan was to drive in her moving truck from Texas to California in time for the convention. Our trip was delayed by an ice storm, but we used that time to continue to improve the editing and effects. We fine-tuned the movie right up until we finally had to head out on our non-stop drive to the convention.

The fact that we never got sick of watching the film while editing or checking for mistakes over and over led us to believe that we had done an okay job. Of course, you never know until an audience sees it. The convention room was packed for the viewing, which only heightened our nerves (thank goodness for the hotel bar!). While Tara and I hid in the back of the room, the rousing cheers we heard from the packed audience after the first Amazon dance number gave us hope.

The audience really understood what we were going for, and getting a standing ovation at the end was a moment we'll never forget. Immediately afterward, we were shocked when Rob Tapert called us backstage to tell us how much he had liked the film. He even said we had come up with a better ending for the show than he did! Making the film was an incredibly memorable experience and will always be one of the highlights of my filmmaking life. We had such excitement and passion for that project and I think it came through. When I look at the film now, I see things I wish we had done differently or what we would be able to do better now. Still, I will always be so proud of what we accomplished and the work we put into making *Xena*: A Wicked Musical.

Tara and I had often talked about doing a film with an original story and characters, something that wasn't a parody or fan film based on another copyrighted property. That project ended up being God Complex. Soon after starting the creative process, we discovered that coming up with something original is not as easy as adapting from preexisting material. Nothing is off limits! Only your limited imagination can stop you! The sky is the limit! It all sounds great, but being creative when you don't have any restrictions is hard. We did many, many rewrites, reshoots, rethinking of ideas, etc. The core story remained the same: a modern-day girl finds herself in possession of the powers of the ancient Greek god Artemis and finds love with the modern day Athena, currently living in an apartment complex in Los Angeles with other modern-day Greek gods. Hence the name God Complex! We wanted to tell an action-adventure story where the girl, not the guy, gets the girl at the end. Though I was still living in Texas, we decided to shoot the film in Tara's current residence, Los Angeles, for the simple reason that I had more vacation time. There are definitely some perks to shooting a movie in Los Angeles. There are a large number of actors ready to audition for your film, so we had quite a few options when it came to casting and ended up with a fantastic cast. There are also very talented lighting and audio professionals, and we were lucky enough to find some wonderful crew members to help us along the way. We were especially thankful for the invaluable contributions of fellow Xenite Beth Parks, who was the best production assistant anyone could ever ask for.

It was a large production with a big cast, and sometimes we were at the mercy of their availability. It took so long to complete filming that one of our actors had to start wearing a hat in scenes to hide the fact that he was losing his hair! We learned a good many lessons in bringing God Complex to life. We were working with real crew members and actual L.A. actors (several of whom had worked on major film and TV projects) for the first time. We were also fortunate to find enough people willing to share their land and property for us to have several fantastic locations at our disposal. We might have shot in a few places without permission but, like I said, that's the fun of low-budget filmmaking! We could not have brought this project to life without the incredibly generous donations from Xenites, who believed in us based on our past *Xena* films. We will always be grateful to them for their support.

Without my exposure to *Xena*, the people I met through the fandom, and the inspiration from the show itself, I'm not sure I would have found myself venturing into the world of filmmaking. I had always had an interest in it, but never saw it as something I could actually do myself until I watched my friend make that first little movie in a hotel room. The films have gotten bigger, and the challenges steeper, but it has always been fun to direct movies and videos and be involved in filmmaking on any level. I now find myself living in Los Angeles, and thanks to my job as a director for KNBC, I am a member of the Directors Guild of America. I'm not sure what my next project will be, or when it happens, but the way I see it, I can't really call myself a Los Angeles director if I don't make a film while I'm living in the film capital of the world... so stay tuned!

Chapter Forty-Six

From Xena to Novels to Films
Creator of Kaia Saga

by Lara Vezzani

FIRST OF ALL, how wouldn't *Xena* change my life? From the very first convention or the first time I met Lucy …what a ride it has been!

I recall when I first got hooked on the show; it was the episode "The Titans." I have been and always will be an equine enthusiast, and when I was channel surfing, I saw the gorgeous Palomino running through the woods and a beautiful woman on its back! I realized quickly that this was that show I had heard about that spun off from *Hercules*—*Xena*! And that gorgeous Palomino will forever be known as Argo.

For years I watched the show and discovered the previous episodes before "The Titans." Honestly, "The Reckoning" with Ares hooked me. I was very sad about the loss of Kevin Smith, a man taken far too early in his life.

The Amazon episodes really got me. "Hooves and Harlots." I loved that one! And I loved the character of Ephiny. The entire Amazon nation enthralled me—so much pride and so much culture! I loved how Renée O'Connor embraced the role of the Amazon queen, and the episode had so much humor! I can thank Steven Sears for that as he WROTE that episode! As years went by and I continued to love the series, I found I loved the Amazons the most.

About seven years went by, and I moved from California to Arizona to buy a house, of all things. Arizona was so boring I took up writing again. You know how they say, "Be careful what you wish for"? Needless to say, Kaia, an ancient Greek Amazon has taken into outer space, was born.

If it hadn't been for *Xena*, I would never have come up with Kaia. I based her on the Amazon nation in Ancient Greece from *Xena*. Kaia was a Celtic (Northern Amazon) captain of the army of her tribe.

The twist was the Amazon is abducted and taken out into space!

Years went by, and nine books were written about the Amazon's journey—the Kaia Saga was born! I went through rejection and abuse–the entertainment industry is a hard nut to crack.

I recall going to the many *Xena* conventions and the stars mentioning the rejection that comes with the trade. I also learned a lot about perseverance.

If it hadn't been for some great things happening along the way -Lucy herself was interested in the project and told me to "Make it happen!" when I pitched it to her, along with a few other industry types who told me I really had something-, I don't think I would have pursued it the many years I did.

A chance encounter with the late Leonard Nimoy also steeled my resolve. I saw him at a Phoenix Comic-Con. He passed on his wisdom to those in the audience about his life story and early struggles in the industry. He at one time, was an NYC cab driver, and very early on in his career, he was getting nowhere and almost quit. A very important person entered his cab and he struck up a conversation with him. That man told him if he wanted it bad enough he would get there—he just had to work hard for it. That fare was none other than John F. Kennedy Jr., a senator at the time. So Leonard was MY inspiration as John was his.

I had this wonderful concept that even Lucy and others liked. Once I connected with a producer that liked the concept as well, I was able to meet with studio execs. If ANYONE tells you differently, you heard it here: it is all about who you know to get somewhere in the entertainment industry. This producer, who believed in my creation, connected me with a big hat. This very well-known person told me to make a trailer promoting the first book. Now, my first thought was… HOW am I going to come up with the money to make it? Soon I found out first-hand what it was to be an executive producer of my own project. You get INVESTORS, and I did just that. We are in post-production for the trailer to come out as of this writing, and by the time you all read this, it will be out and the movie may possibly be in production. I must credit my good friend Cheryl for this latest production of a promotional trailer. Thank you, Cheryl!

Kaia (2019); that's how it reads on IMDB. We have a short, and I am the creator, writer, and exec producer, and it would NEVER have happened without *Xena*. The location where it was filmed is Belfast, Ireland, and the cast includes Stephen Presley, Margarita Murphy, and Angus MacFadyen. The latter is most notably known as Robert the Bruce from Braveheart. Okay… how did we get a big A list star like him? Do you recall I said the only way to get through is with referrals? It is really true. Angus heard through a friend about Kaia and wanted in!

So the book became a trailer just like that, and it was a book that was embraced by the Xenites because it was forged by Xena herself.

This Xenite known as Kimba in fandom went on to write a sprawling nine-book saga about an Amazon in space who causes a civil war in the universe and becomes a female Spartacus… Watch for it on the movie previews… Because it's coming soon!

I thank Lucy Lawless first and foremost for making this happen, and I thank Stephen Presley for believing in the dream and taking on the risk of the Amazing Amazon Kaia. Though this is a *Xena* book, I have to say the industry didn't turn around until Wonder Woman hit the big screen by storm, so I would be remiss if I didn't thank the success of the Wonder Woman movie to bring Kaia forward as well.

This was a long and sometimes very trying ride… 8.5 years before it was finally adapted and produced. I must quote both William Gregory Lee and Adrienne Wilkinson when they once commented on stage together about being actors or getting into the industry at all. William said, when asked by a fan about how to get into the industry, that, unless it was something you wanted REALLY, REALLY bad, you shouldn't do it. He said, "The only way I recommend it is if it is the first thing you think of when you wake in the morning and is the last thing you think about when going to bed." I realized it WAS! So without his words and Adrienne's agreement on those words, along with Lucy liking the concept and urging me to make it, NONE of this would ever have happened. Yes, *Xena* changed my life in a very major way.

Kaia made it through, all thanks to a television show called *Xena: Warrior Princess*.

As of this writing, an independent movie is in the works and a promotional trailer about that movie—*Kaia Saga: Kill or Be Killed Part 1* is in post-production, and by the time you read this, it will be circulating. Again, thank you to Lucy Lawless, Stephen Presley, and Cheryl for making my dream come true.

You can watch the trailer of the movie on YouTube:
https://youtu.be/Ixzepfp7a7c

Chapter Forty-Seven

From Life at 10 to a 10/10 Life

by Penny Cavanaugh

"I WONDER WHAT Gabrielle's real name is," I mused.

"It's Renée," my dad responded from behind me, watching the TV too.

"How do you know?" I asked, in awe that Daddy knew everything. I was ten years old and I didn't pay attention to small details like names in opening credits.

I was a total tomboy as a child. One of my favorite toys was a short section of a wooden curtain rod that I referred to as my "Bommy Knocker," and I would swing it around in the back garden, pretending to be Gabrielle. Of course, I had about as much skill as Season 1 Gabrielle, and as much excitable energy too.

I think I related to Gabrielle because she was wordy. She talked, and dreamed, and knew she was meant to do so much more. For Gabrielle, it was so much more than the typical village life. For young Penny, the verdict was still out, but I knew that I too was meant to do so much more. Than what, I didn't know. I just felt a yearning for... more.

I had posters of Xena in my locker in 7th grade—that puts me at about twelve years old. I used to share my (innocent) fanfic stories with my teachers, and I even left my best friend's birthday party one year because I didn't want to miss an episode. Sorry, Cazz. (She'll never let me live that down!)

My little sister, Dad, and I started karate together, and I begged my dad to allow me to begin gymnastics too. I wanted to combine the two, so I could "be like Xena."

I once told a random kid on a swing set beside me that I was Renée O'Connor's daughter. She believed me. Always telling stories...

I learned the Greek alphabet and would write stories in code, with English words and Greek letters. My password for ICQ was 'Callisto.' My wallpaper was that faded background from Tom's Xena Page. Posters of Xena and Gabrielle peppered my room. We even made a collage of shells and sand from Bethells Beach.

I was obsessed.

I strongly recall talking about an episode in a cooking class (home economics, we called it). A girl in my class told me, "That's a lesbian show, isn't it? Aren't Xena and Gabrielle lesbians?"

I don't think I fully understood what lesbians were, but the way she said it, her tone, sounded like it was a bad thing.

"No, they're not," I said defensively, not even sure what I was denying.

Teen life took over and Channel 10 moved Xena to a later and later timeslot. I recall being mortified and broken-hearted that Gabrielle had her hair cut—long blonde hair was something she and I had in common, and when that changed, I was sad. That and my obsession with the Spice Girls took a firm grasp of my entire being. Xena slowly fizzled from my life.

When I graduated at seventeen, DVD stores had started to pop up everywhere. I was determined to have a massive DVD library and would visit a local store frequently. One day, I saw it: the entire series collection of *Xena: Warrior Princess*, just in and sitting on the shelf behind the counter.

How does it go? The heavens opened up and a light shone down on the box set. The angels sang, "Aaaahhhhhh!" You know the sound clip. I had to have it. Ten-year-old Penny would want me to.

I don't think I realized there were three seasons of the show that I had never seen.

The re-watch was amazing, and memories came flooding back. I didn't remember every single episode, but more importantly, the ones I did remember took on a whole new meaning now that I was an adult. I was instantly re-hooked, and I jumped on a meetup website to see if there were any other Xena fans in my area.

I watched the entire series, falling deeper and deeper in love. Season 4 came along and I remember telling my mother, "I'm probably going to want to cut my hair, because Gabrielle just did. Don't let me do it."

Of course, I ended up cutting my hair. "Honey, I can't make you look like her!" the flamboyant hairdresser exclaimed when I pulled out a photo of Season 5 Gabrielle holding her sais and staring into the distance. You know the one. But he did nail the haircut and I was super proud of it.

I found friends and we formed the Canberra Xena Gang. This is where my path started to become clear. We made plans to go to the 2007 convention, and while we waited, we watched fan club kits, old Con DVDs, and anything else we could get our hands on. We also produced a special DVD and CD Rom set that we called FOF ("Faces of the Fans"—even back then it was always about the fans!) and all profits went to breast cancer research. I think we raised over a thousand dollars. We asked MaryD if she would let us advertise FOF on AUSXIP. The day we got an email back from her saying yes, there was a LOT of squealing involved. MARYD! THE MARYD! A brush with fame!

Around the time I saw the final episode, I was also figuring out that maybe Xena and Gabrielle were lesbians, but perhaps that wasn't such a bad thing. It wasn't the 90s anymore, but I still felt weird about the word 'lesbian.' I was more comfortable with the word 'gay.' But Xena and Gabrielle weren't gay. There were just super besties that liked to cuddle at night and belonged together for the rest of their lives... right? Right, until the moment in FIN when Gabrielle needed to give Xena water from the fountain. "KISS HER!" I remember screaming at my TV. And she did. That was no damn water transfer. That was a freakin' kiss, and it was a good one. That's when it hit me. I wanted that kiss to happen, and when it did, it did something to me. I was shaken, I was tingling, I felt RIGHT, like the missing piece of the puzzle was finally in place. Holy s**t, I liked girls! It would take me a little longer before I could really, truly admit it to anyone else.

I was twenty-one when I went to my first Creation Xena con in 2007. I remember watching Pat and Mary Sue slow dancing at the dessert party, and in that moment, I realized that I could still have the love I dreamed of. The love I watched my parents share. That two women could promise to be together forever, and then do it. That it wouldn't be living my one life the "wrong way." (I like rules. Hi. Capricorn.)

I made some strong friendships in the Sais and Chakram Tavern over at the Xena On-line Community (XOC) in 2008, and by the 2009 con, we had planned to hold a friendly softball game on Friday morning before the convention kicked off. Amphipolis Warriors vs Poteidaia Battling Bards. It was some of the most fun I have ever had, and the first time I ever played softball.

We also decided there needed to be a real "end" to the conventions, since there was no scheduled event dedicated to saying goodbye to everyone once it all ended on Sunday. If you didn't see people in the lobby, you didn't get a chance to say goodbye. So, we started to host an after-party. We booked the room and asked for donations at the door to cover the cost. Anything left over after we paid the hotel was donated to a charity. Usually Starship Foundation.

The after parties were a lot of fun, and we eventually added a table with merch items and other cool things that people could buy tickets to, thus raising more money for charity. A chakram was donated; we got it signed by Lucy and Renée and we took donations for people to have a chance to win it. The first person who won it took it home with her for one year and then gave it back to us the following year so we could do it all over again. This happened year after year—that chakram has probably raised in the vicinity of $8,000.

I remember inviting this really cute girl to an after party one year. I didn't know her name, but she knew mine, and when she said it, I just about lost my legs from under me. It would take me another two years to finally get enough courage to speak to her again (she never showed to the party the year I invited her!!).

Here is where I owe MaryD a pretty massive thank you. Mary asked if I was going to get a photo with Lucy. I told her that I wasn't. She asked if I had ever met Lucy. I said no. So Mary gave me her photo op ticket. She also asked me not to tell anyone, because that is the kind of wonderful giving person Mary is. She doesn't do it for the props. But sorry, Mary, the cat's out of the bag, because that gesture led to the Kat being IN the bag... Let me explain.

I remember Lucy saying, "Do something scary; the payoff is awesome." Moments after meeting Lucy, when I was still in what they call the "purple haze," I saw Kat. The cute girl. At that point, Creation had told us this was the last con (spoiler: it wasn't) and I figured I was going back to Australia never to see her again, so what would it hurt to tell her that I thought she was cute? I marched up to her, and in a way not dissimilar to the way that Joxer confesses his love for Gabrielle (I'm pretty sure I even borrowed Aphrodite's advice of not expecting anything), I let my mouth babble. What I said I couldn't tell you, but by the end of it we had exchanged contact information. This is where I'm going to make a long story short and say that in true u-haul fashion, we got married at the following convention. Katherine Fugate stood up in our wedding and gifted us a special lesson in love that we remember to this day, and I walked down the aisle while Lara De Wit played the Xena theme song on the piano. It was a damn fairytale.

The following year, once Creation announced its final Xena convention, I realized that this magic couldn't end. Xenites loved each other too much. We were a family and I wasn't ready for it to end yet. I wouldn't accept it. (Again, hello, Capricorn). So I added some friends to a Facebook group that I had created, called "Xenite Retreat Planning Group," and I told them what I wanted to do. We started brainstorming in 2014, and by 2015 we had the bones of the Xenite Retreat.

The idea was to create a safe space where people could get together, share their love for the show, but also do fun summer camp things, like archery, high ropes, hiking, swimming, and of course, softball!

We started teasing people (pissed off some people, oops!) and launched the website ahead of the final con in 2015. We launched ticket sales the night of our last after-party. We sold out the early bird tickets in record time. I was shocked—people actually wanted to come to this. It started to get real.

Over the course of the next five years, we learned as we went. I listened to camp podcasts, I read about running events, and after a lot of trial and error, and learning from each year that passed, in 2019 we sold out ahead of the 2020 Retreat for the first time ever!

To explain Retreat would be way too difficult to restrict to a few paragraphs—I think I'd need a whole book to do it justice. What I can say, though, is that we have really carved out our own special place in the Xenaverse that is unique and safe, welcoming, and life-changing. Those are the campers' words—I have had countless emails and private messages from people telling me that their lives have changed because of the Xenite Retreat. That is so special to hear, because I feel like, in my own little way, I am continuing the legacy that Rob Tapert started when he decided to make *Xena: Warrior Princess*.

If Rob hadn't decided to create Xena, I would not be where I am today.

I am now thirty-three years old. I live in Illinois with my wife Kat, my daughter Wilhelmina (Willow), my step kids, my grandson (yep, I'm a grandma at thirty-three!), and my dogs. I have a beautiful home that is filled with LOVE and laughter. I work hard every year to create a Xenite Retreat that is different and special, so that no two Retreats are ever the same. I am so proud of the person I have become and the life I lead; it is truly a 10/10 life. Of course, there will always be moments of stress or sadness, but that is life. The important thing though, is that I am happy, I am fulfilled, and I truly believe that I am doing "so much more" than I ever expected I would or could.

Just as Gabrielle grew from village girl to Battling Bard, I have grown too. I will never stop reaching for more; never stop thinking of ways I can create special moments for Xenites to come together from all around the word to share and experience.

Thank you, Rob Tapert. Thank you, Lucy and Renée. Thank you, Steven, Adrienne, Brittney, Jacqueline, and Musetta. Thank you, MaryD. Thank you, Team Awesome. Thank you, Amazons. Thank you, Bards. Thank you, Cut-Throats. Thank you, Immortals. Thank you, Valkyries. Thank you, Warriors.

Thank you, Xenites. We are so damn lucky, and I'm in love with you all.

***

You can find out more about the Xenite Retreat at:
https://xeniteretreat.com

Chapter Forty-Eight

Shh... Don't Tell Anyone...

by CH

I WAS FIFTEEN and starting high school when Xena premiered. I stumbled upon it one afternoon while channel surfing and was quickly drawn into what I thought was a show tailor-made for my interests: mythology, martial arts, and strong female characters kicking ass. To this day, it feels as if the show was fated to last through my most formative years of high school and college, the time when I struggled to find an identity that I could meld all the different personalities I conveyed according to what audience I had. I was an honors student and varsity athlete, but still painfully shy in public.

I never fit in with either the scholars or the athletes. I preferred hanging out with my teachers during lunch period, daydreaming of a day when I'd be comfortable with myself. When the virtual chat world of Xena Palace came into the picture during my senior year of high school, I was enveloped by such a comforting and accepting group of folks from around the US and the world who practically adopted a tiny blue ball named CH.

I "attended" a virtual wedding, Amazon dance parties, birthdays, singalongs, and for those that remember the dial-up modem days of the internet, suffered from being caught in lag hell and chakramed out of the Palace. I would stay up until the twilight hours of the morning on school nights forming friendships and bonds as we chatted about not only our love for Xena and Gabrielle, but our colorful backgrounds and daily lives. We were all different ages, my teen self being one of the younger members, but it never really mattered to anyone. They comforted me when I stressed over school, celebrated when I overcame a challenge, and scolded me after finding me still on-line after they had gone to bed the evening prior! My imagination ran wild with comedy and action fics

I wrote for my fellow hardcore nutballs chronicling our off the wall adventures. When I finished high school, my graduation cap had pictures of a chakram and tiny smiley face balls in honor of the default avatars of the Xena Palace. I am fortunate to still have some of these friends more than twenty years later.

By the time I started college, Xena was still battling on. I loved following Gabrielle's journey and transformation alongside Xena. The theme of fighting for the greater good and protecting those you love drew me in strongly and stayed with me to this day. Around that time, I started forming different pieces of my life that eventually crafted the person I am now. I began training in different forms of martial arts and became an instructor.

I competed as an amateur kickboxer, wrote for martial arts magazines, lived and worked at a fighter's camp in Las Vegas, all while studying for my degree in criminal justice. I exuded the warrior spirit on the outside but still had the shy heart of a writer and a musician. It was an interesting combo to reconcile, but I couldn't help but find inspiration in both characters as I paralleled my journey with the laughs and heartache I watched our favorite duo endure as they came to terms with the pasts that helped craft the individuals they had become. That motivation and acceptance of my duality helped me wrap myself into a nice little package of fighter and finesse that made me become a special agent with the U.S. Secret Service.

Admittedly, my job as a Secret Service agent caused me to focus mainly on my career and everything that got caught up in it. I was supposed to protect everyone. Failure wasn't an option. So my fervent following for the show and actors dimmed over the years in my career, overshadowed by, well, life! But the enduring lessons of Xena and Gabrielle stayed just under the surface. Their strength, love, and the important lesson that it's ok to be flawed, recently came roaring full force back into my life.

Within the span of a year, I suffered through deaths of friends, family, and the sudden collapse of my marriage. Shocked and broken, I was also thrust into single motherhood and had to redefine what I pictured a family was supposed to be.

I couldn't fathom how I had fallen so fast. Trying to make sense and maintain order took its toll. Frankly, it was my return to my love for the show and to the inspirations of its actresses that helped me focus and rebuild. Xena wasn't just a show but a philosophy I took to heart, of never giving up and fighting to find love for yourself, of knowing you have a purpose in life.

There is a beauty in imperfection, and a world that blurs the lines between black and white is okay. It's still a work in progress, but I'm sure fellow Xenites understand that making the journey is part of the beauty.

To them I say, "Battle On!"

PART 8

THE GREATER GOOD

Chapter Forty-Nine

Changing our World for the Greater Good

by Denise Byrd

ON SEPTEMBER 04, 1995, a campy, little spin-off of *Hercules: The Legendary Journeys* made its television debut and exploded into a cult classic legend that is still popular and loved by millions of fans twenty-five years later. That show was *Xena: Warrior Princess*, and its tag line –*Her courage will change the world*– became its own prophecy… because Xena did change the world for so many that watched her. She gave marginalized people a voice and a safe place to be who they truly were, she broadened horizons and helped banish prejudice, and she created new friends and families.

But Xena was more than just her influence on the world as it was. One of the most important things Xena did was create a fandom that wanted to follow her example and make a difference in the world—a difference that would create its own legacy. And she, and the fandom that followed, have done so with aplomb and generosity for twenty-five years—to the tune of MILLIONS of dollars.

At the end of Season 1, there was an episode called "The Greater Good," in which Gabrielle is forced to leave a dying Xena behind to protect Salmoneus and a group of villagers being threatened by a marauding warlord. Written by fan-favorite Steven L. Sears, it was the first mention of the Greater Good in the Xenaverse, but it wouldn't be the last. Xenites took the gauntlet that had been thrown down in front of them and ran with it. In some ways, Xenites were the perfect candidates to accept the challenge they'd been given. Many were people that were old enough to have settled into their chosen careers; they had disposable income they could put into charities and causes they believed in. Many of the charities they supported were chosen because of their importance to different stars of the show itself, but they were also causing that fans found worth supporting.

One of the causes Xenites took up was very near and dear to the heart of Lucy Lawless—the Starship Foundation… one of the first and the largest children's hospital in New Zealand. She was informally involved with the Foundation for several years before she became a trustee on the board of directors in 2001. Lucy brought her appeals to Xenites around the world, and they responded overwhelmingly. That support continues even today (September 21-28 is 'Lucy Lawless Feel the Love Week') when the fandom comes together as a whole to continue to make their mark for the Greater Good in appreciation of not only her work on Xena, but also her acceptance of the fandom and all its varied glories. To date, thousands have been raised for the Starship Foundation, as well as for a number of other charities, which include Greenpeace and the Richmond/Ermet AIDS Foundation.

In 1997, Debbie Cassetta (Mist) was the first to promote a fan-run charity event which raised more than $3,000; the proceeds went to support a drug treatment program in New York City. She and Tom (of the site Tom's Xena Page at http://xenafan.com) went on to hold the New York Xenafest in 1999. It was actually one of the first fan-run cons in the Xenaverse and it brought to light just how anxious Xenites were to be part of spreading the Greater Good. The Sword and Staff auctions started then, raising a total of $5,400. It was just the beginning of what would become decades of charitable contributions. Debbie began something more important than she realized at the time. She set a precedent for giving and those that came after followed her example and continued to raise the bar a little higher every time. In doing so, Sword and Staff have raised more than half a million dollars for charity thus far. But they were not alone in their efforts, and we're not done yet.

In 2006, MaryD brought the power and reach of AUSXIP into the mix and began holding an annual charity auction where 100% of the proceeds would go to the Starship Foundation. Many people who took part in *Xena* both on and off camera have donated one-of-a-kind pieces to this endeavor. Still, it's been everyday fans that have made this venture the success it has become. Xenites are the ones that continue to contribute items for use in the auctions, and they're the ones who continue to bid on auction pieces year after year. As a result, $221,245.00 has been raised by AUSXIP thus far.

Renée O'Connor has become quite involved in charity work as well. There are several charities with which she is associated and one that she organized. Along with contributing items to the Ausxip auction for the Starship Foundation, she has also been a huge supporter of the Alisa Ann Ruch Burn Foundation since 2007, participating in car washes as well as the Southern California Firefighters Burn Relay. She also set up the Renée O'Connor Outreach Fund to help raise money for families in need, especially those hampered by serious medical bills due to a dire, unexpected illness. Her Season 5 leather patchwork coat was auctioned off to raise money to help a family that contracted some overwhelming medical bills. The coat sold for $7,800 and the money raised went directly to the family in need. Her outreach efforts also extend into the world of theatre. The summer of 2002, she participated in Shakespeare by the Sea in San Pedro, CA. The following year, the production company lost their audio equipment to theft, and the fandom stepped up and raised $3,200 at Renée's request to replace it. These days, she has her own theatre company; one of their goals is to introduce young people to the joy of all aspects of live performance.

Another *Xena* star that embodies the idea of the Greater Good is Hudson Leick. Though much of her current work is focused on yoga and self-healing, she first came to the attention of Xenites when she became involved with the James W. Ellis Jr. Scholarship. She co-hosted a charity breakfast with Anita Ellis, giving fans direct access to her (something that was relatively unheard of at the time) as well as auctioning off from the stage items of clothing that she was wearing during her Q&A sessions at Creation conventions. In total, she has been able to raise thousands of dollars simply by being generous with her time and her clothing.

Speaking of losing clothing, Brittney Powell has become quite infamous for losing her bra to the highest bidder, or the winning side of the room, at almost every *Xena* convention she has attended after the 2001 "Big Con." Through her work on *General Hospital*, she became involved with the Desi Geestman Foundation, which helps provide support for families with children battling pediatric cancer. She brought that cause to Xenites, who joyfully embraced her charity and have contributed over the years. To date, she's lost a considerable amount of matching underwear, but those bras have gone out into the world to support yet another example of the Greater Good that Xenites are proud to be a part of.

Adrienne Wilkinson accepted the mantle of humanitarian that Xenites offered and ran with the idea of being part of the Greater Good. Instead of choosing one, two, or even three charities to support, she set up her own foundation and chooses from a variety of recipients from causes that have touched her in some way. They run the gauntlet from literacy and animal welfare to scholarships for cancer kids. Her annual fundraiser, started in 2003, was done in collaboration with the fandom and has brought a number of other stars into the Greater Good fold.

In addition to these stars, there are a number of other *Xena* alums that have also embraced the idea of being a viable part of the Greater Good. Ted Raimi returned to DragonCon at his own expense one year to participate in an auction that was happening in the *Xena* track room because he'd promised to participate… even though he'd flown home from Atlanta to Detroit the evening before to attend his parents' fiftieth wedding celebration. Tim Omundson supports the #SuckItStroke Campaign, as well as Alzheimer's research. Jennifer Ward-Lealand is a board member of the Actors Benevolent Fund. Danielle Cormack is a ChildFund ambassador. Alexandra Tydings has become an outspoken advocate for LGTBQA people as well as women's rights. And those were just the ones that could be found simply by glancing at the front pages on their websites; it doesn't include anything not posted or discussed by them, or things they prefer to keep private. Xenites may never know the true reach of the Greater Good movement.

Aside from all that, even if we removed the stars and the monies raised on their behalves for the charities they support, there is still a lot of Greater Good to talk about, because this fandom has stepped up and raised thousands upon tens of thousands of dollars to support other causes we care about.

I personally can speak of a few examples of the Greater Good that the fandom has provided, because I was there when they happened. In some cases, I was a facilitator—I just happened to be lucky enough to be in the right place at the right time.

**

The Merwolf Pack was started as a mailing list for readers that were fans of Melissa Good's writing. It was a place to hang out and talk about her writing particularly, and the show in general, while we waited for the next update in her Journey of Soulmates series. It wasn't meant to be anything special, just a mailing list. Then we realized we could do amazing things and be amazing together, and we turned our attention towards giving back for the show that had brought us together and given us so much. We became part of the Greater Good.

Between the years 2001 and 2003, the Pack raised $71,900. Most of it was donated to Kids Cancer Camps, but part of that was the $3,200 that went to Shakespeare by the Sea for their audio equipment.

In two years of DragonCon, 2001-2002, Xenites put forward $8,700 for charity. Part of the monies were collected during a live performance of Missy Good's Sappho script "Last Chance," which went unaired in Season 6 for a number of reasons. Those funds went to the American Cancer Society. The following year saw the untimely death of *Xena* favorite Kevin Smith, and the money raised that year was specifically marked for the Kevin Smith Foundation.

From 2002 to 2005, there was a fan-run con that took place in Orlando known as Orlando BardCon. Its purpose was to bring together readers and writers to talk together, to buy and sell books, and to have a place to get together that wasn't a Creation con. Because the focus was on reading and writing, most of the $15,350 of charity money that was raised went to literacy programs like StoryPlus and FirstBook, though some went to the Kevin Smith Foundation in that first year. There was also some that went to help Noah's Wish and Hurricane Katrina victims through Habitat for Humanity in the final year. And that doesn't even begin to count the money that folks spent on books for children's hospitals. Xenites' generosity allowed nearly 900 books to be collected and sent out to thirty-five non-profit children's hospitals across the United States.

DC Bardfest was another fan-run enterprise that promoted writers and their books. They secured between $5,000 and $7,000 in their two years of operation that were subsequently donated to the Ohio State University Children's Cancer Hospital. Their charity was chosen for reasons that were personal to one of their organizers, but once again, Xenites showed up and offered their financial support for the Greater Good.

All of these things, except the Merwolf Pack, are defunct now, lost to real life and adult responsibilities. Even the Pack is much subdued from what it once was, mostly because we've gotten older and have slowed down, and several of our number have passed. But there is a new generation of Xenites that have accepted the mantel of responsibility for the Greater Good, and we are proud and happy to pass the torch of the challenge to them.

Some of the most proficient purveyors of the Greater Good in this younger generation are the organizers of the Xenite Retreat. They have managed to take the best of the fan-run cons: giving folks a place to come together, adding in a few guest stars, and including the Xenites' penchant for charity, and they have come up with a winning formula that thus far has raised over $50,000 for close to ten charities in the four years they have been active.

This second generation of Xenites that have stepped up to continue to make a difference for themselves and the world around them (people who were just kids when *Xena* originally aired) offers hope that the Greater Good will extend past our lifetimes and theirs, and will allow *Xena* to leave a lasting legacy on the world.

***

Before I go, I have a story I would like to share. This is the kind of story that you hear about, but you never really expect to be a part of, the kind where you actually get to KNOW the difference you made in someone's life because of a choice you made to be part of the Greater Good in some way.

At what is now known as 'The Big Con' (2001 Pasadena), the on-line community known as the Merwolf Pack got together for a huge charity dinner and raffle.

The raffle was two-part: part of it was held on-line and part of it took place at the convention dinner. The on-line part included a consortium of 128 people who came together to bid on a copy of Melissa Good's *Last Chance* script. On its own, that one project killed one printer, a ream of paper, and half a dozen ink cartridges… and it also raised nearly $20,000.

The charity raffle that took place in Pasadena was made up of a plethora of boxes that contained merchandise and autographed pictures and a myriad of other *Xena*-related items. People were excited to participate, both in donating items and in purchasing tickets. We structured the ticket pricing to allow for as many people as possible to take part: one for $5; five for $20; twenty for $50; fifty for $100. And we sold a LOT of tickets. Those boxes raised about $40,000 in the raffle.

Those events alone raised close to $60,000, which were divided up and sent to five different cancer camps for children. You cannot imagine what it felt like to be carrying around close to $60,000 cash; I prayed the entire flight home, and turned them into cashier's checks the minute I was able to.

When we got ready to send out the checks to the camps, I discovered I needed a contact name and a physical address to which to send them. There was no way I was sending that much money to a PO Box with no signature. I picked up the phone and called the four different directors and explained the situation to them. All of them were quick to comply, of course, and were grateful for the added funds, but they were also pretty perfunctory about the situation as well. The money we were sending meant they could add more campers because they already had their complete operating budget for the summer. Not that giving more kids the opportunity to just be "regular kids" for a while wasn't a good thing—I'm sure it mean everything in the world to those kids who were able to go to camp that year because of the money we donated. Still, it wasn't life changing.

The fifth call, however… When I told the woman who I was and why I was calling, I heard her gasp and her voice started to shake. She asked me how much we were looking to send. I had the check in my hand, and I read off the number to her. I don't remember the exact amount; I just know it was shy of $12,000. She gasped again, and this time I heard her begin to cry.

"Ma'am… are you all right?"

It took a minute or two for her to catch her breath, but finally, she responded. "You don't… you can't understand what a blessing this is," she said, and the smile was clear in her voice. "We just had a sponsor pull their support from our camp this week. We were going to be $10,000 short of meeting our goal. You're an answer to prayer."

I don't know that I've ever been the answer to anyone's prayers so directly before, but I do know that that conversation still gives me goosebumps whenever I think about it. Because that wasn't ME—that was US. That was Xenites who wanted to make a difference, and that day, we made the difference for a whole lot of kids who might otherwise not have been able to go camping that year.

So never let it be said that Xena didn't change the world. It certainly did… and still is. Xenites wouldn't accept anything else.

Chapter Fifty

Sword and Staff – A Legacy of Giving

by Debbie Cassetta (a.k.a Mistopholees)

XENA: WARRIOR PRINCESS. The internet. Sword and Staff. Each of these entities came into being at about the same time and when combined, they brought to life an idea that was new to television viewers as access to social media allowed them to communicate with each other and exchange ideas and opinions about the show and its writers, producers, and actors. Nutballs (as Lucy Lawless labeled them) saw the internet and Xena evolve as a means to construct an interactive online fan community. Writing from behind screen names that hid their identity, fans got to know each other by exchanging ideas anonymously. Through their interactions, they were able to establish themselves in a community of like-minded individuals. It didn't take long for these fans to begin to establish friendships with people from around the country, and it wasn't long after that that the online aspect of the Xena community became live interactions as fans gathered for the annual Xena Conventions in Burbank, and the many regional XenaFests drew fans from all corners of the globe.

The Xena online community grew rapidly as more and more television viewers were able to access the internet and thus meet other fans of the television show. The internet opened up a new avenue of communication, and it was through chat rooms like "The Pub," which was hosted on the official *Xena: Warrior Princess* website, that Xena fans from around the world came to know each other (if even only by their screen handles). At the Pub, fans had a virtual drink (mead was a favorite) and were able to share their penchant for this show. Debates about plot lines and nuances of the week's episode were discussed in great depth and detail. Minute details of the weekly episodes were dissected, and the exploits of Xena and Gabrielle were discussed by a legion of the fans who seemed completely invested in the trajectory of their relationship. Through this campy television show, Xena fans found a niche that allowed them the freedom to discuss the show and how it affected them on personal levels.

Xena fans were, and are, a diverse group in terms of backgrounds, nationalities, and ages, but each of them is drawn to the show and messages it conveys. Fans found that there was something magnetic about the show, and that intangible something fostered camaraderie among them and forged for many what have become lifelong friendships and relationships. As fans continued to seek out the company of other fans, and they were never shy about an impromptu party or episode viewing, the Xena conventions and XenaFests became staples of Xena fandom.

Sword and Staff was born from the first New York City XenaFest, a fan-sponsored event that garnered a great deal of interest and support from Xena fans from across the United States. Not only would fans spend the day with other fans, they would also have the opportunity to explore all the wonders and attractions that New York City has to offer. The organizers of this event were brought together by their interest in *Xena: Warrior Princess* and the fact that they all lived in or near New York City. Together, the NYC Xenafest Committee set out to put on a mini-convention for a growing number of fans whose interest in Xena was quite unlike anything that any of the XenaFest organizers had done before. Excited by the prospect of hosting so many fans from around the country, plans were set for a fest in a mid-town Manhattan hotel and after an endless number of meetings in restaurants, coffee shops, apartments, and after haunting many a restaurant, bar, and coffee shop in Greenwich Village to exchange ideas and plan for the day's festivities, the First Annual NYC XenaFest fest took shape.

When the day of the Fest arrived, we were pleased that turnout was far better than we had expected, and fans had a great day attending seminars, discussions, and demonstrations. One feature of the Fest was a charity auction of Xena memorabilia. The auction items were all donated by fans, and they included autographed photographs of Lucy Lawless and Renée O'Connor (rare commodities in those early days of Xena), and other show-related articles that were of interest to fans who could not get enough of the Xena merchandise we had for auction. In addition, we had other merchandise for sale, with profits from those sales going to charity. XenaFest t-shirts, photographs of the show's stars and co-stars, and any other Xena-related items resulted in a donation total of $5,400 that went to a local charity that cared for infants and children afflicted with AIDS.

What happened next proved to be the catalyst for the creation of Sword and Staff. Upon contacting the charity to arrange for the donation, we were told that they would not accept the donation because they didn't "want to be associated with a bunch of Amazons." Needless to say, we were stunned by the rejection of a donation that was meant to help children who truly needed support. We eventually made the donation to a different charity that did similar work with AIDS afflicted children, but I was particularly stung by the reaction of the first organization. In part, that rejection rested on the fact that Xena had a large lesbian following, and the people who headed up this charity obviously let their own issues come before the welfare of the children entrusted to them. Sadly, at that time, those sentiments were not uncommon.

Determined to change how Xena fans were often perceived, the idea of Sword and Staff was born. Sword and Staff was designed to be a means for fans to organize their efforts to donate Xena-related memorabilia to raise money donations for charitable organizations. Charity auctions were held on the Sword and Staff website with all proceeds from the events going to the named charity. Added to these efforts, the charitable donations raised at the many national and international XenaFests fell under the Sword and Staff umbrellas as fans from around the world began to participate in Sword and Staff activities designed to raise donations for charities in their respective countries. Fans from many nations, including the United States, Canada, Brazil, Argentina, New Zealand, Israel, the United Kingdom, the Netherlands, France, Spain, and Germany, participated in Sword and Staff activities.

It wasn't long before Sword and Staff became a source of pride among the fans who donated items for auction and fundraising, or who bought the items that were auctioned on the Sword and Staff website. In addition to raising over a half-million American dollars in direct donations to charitable organizations, we were able to donate money that was used to set aside approximately four-hundred fifty acres of Amazon rainforest in South America, an area estimated to be approximately three-quarters the size of New York City's Central Park. Quite a legacy for a group that literally couldn't give money away only a few years earlier.

Xena fans made every effort to support a wide variety of causes, and to give a hand up whenever it was needed. For instance, after the 9/11 attack on New York City in 2001, when most of us were reeling from the loss of the World Trade Center, Sword and Staff began to encourage fans to make blood donations at their local blood banks in memory of those lost in the attack. That ongoing blood drive resulted in several hundred pints of whole blood and plasma that were donated by fans to sustain the critically important supply of blood in their own communities.

Another non-monetary activity that members of Sword and Staff participated in was the annual International Coastal Cleanup. The Cleanup is a worldwide event aimed at cleaning up our waterways. Xenite volunteers cleared shorelines in New York, California, Florida, and Connecticut, removing seemingly endless amounts of trash and debris from our waterways. We individually and collectively removed and counted thousands of cigarette butts, straws, Styrofoam cups and dishes, plastic utensils, tires, nets, fishing line and hooks, and various other trash items that had been carelessly tossed on the shorelines or into the bays, rivers, and oceans. Preserving our oceans and wildlife is everyone's responsibility, and here again Xena fans stepped up to the plate when it mattered.

Another great fundraiser that Sword and Staff helped to facilitate was the sales of a special edition Monopoly game to benefit the Starship Children's Hospital in New Zealand. We had conducted several auctions to benefit the hospital, and I was contacted when they were putting together the new game board for the game. Sword and Staff was able to sponsor two properties on that board. Fans contributed to make that happen, and once the games were printed and packed, Starship gave American fans the opportunity to get one of the games. Five hundred Starship Monopoly games were shipped from New Zealand to Sword and Staff on Long Island in New York. As a nod to Xena fans, every one of these game boards was autographed by Lucy Lawless, who is a great supporter of Starship and its mission.

Perhaps one of the most memorable episodes related to acquiring Xena merchandise for a Sword and Staff auction was when Kevin Smith, Ares himself, donated one of the Ares prop swords to Sword and Staff for auction. I was invited to meet Kevin at a brunch for his fan club in Orlando, Florida, where he presented me with the sword and signed autographs for fans as we chatted. He was amazingly kind and it was a pleasure having the opportunity to speak with him. Not wanting to ship the sword and risk it being lost or damaged on its way to New York, the sword was packed into a carryon bag and, I'm loathe to admit, cushioned with about ten towels swiped from a cart at the hotel. On arrival at the airport I presented the bag, not thinking twice about how the airline might feel about my bringing a sword on board the plane. Needless to say, the sword never made it into the cabin of the plane and I was lucky not to be picked up by the police, where I was concerned about explaining about the towels.

Sword and Staff facilitated direct donations to charitable organizations in the amount of $527,000 over a period of approximately eight years, and as a group, we shared some exceptionally good times and made lasting memories. Through my affiliation with Sword and Staff, I had the opportunity to meet some amazingly generous people whose efforts to provide for the greater good always filled me with wonder. In a world where we tend to get wrapped up in our own lives, I am grateful for this great community, for the generous fans who participated in the auctions and bought the items that raised money for charities on three continents, and for the thousands of fans who always supported our efforts and provided the physical and financial support that it takes to put on fan fests and auctions.

If there is a single legacy of Sword and Staff, it is that it set the stage for other fan bases to do what we did. Auctions and donations continue on today in Xena fandom, and fans of other shows including some Star Trek fans in Canada, have taken a page out of our book and set up their own network of giving similar to what we've done with Sword and Staff.

Chapter Fifty-One

AUSXIP Greater Good –
Together We Can Make A Difference

by MaryD

AUSXIP GREATER GOOD was created to celebrate all that is good about the Xenaverse; to give back and support others. It was born because we wanted to celebrate a milestone, and once it was over, we enjoyed it so much, we continued to hold the AUSXIP Charity Auctions! Since 2006 we have raised $221,245.00 for various charities. How did this all start?

It was a quiet September 2006 evening, and I had been thinking about how I was going to celebrate AUSXIP's 10th Anniversary which was due on December 15, 2006. I could raffle something off, and that would be it, but I thought that sounded a little lame. Ten years is a big deal in internet years. The more I thought about it, a tiny germ of an idea started to form and as usual, this idea turned into another sequoia.

This was a project that would require a great deal of help and support from the Xenaverse. I could not bring about this project that I had in mind on my own; it would be impossible. I sent an email to my dear friend Roger (not their real name because they have an aversion to publicity, but Roger has to be one of the most generous souls alive), and I voiced my idea and how much work will be involved. The response was, "Yes, let's do it."

Firstly, we needed Xena goodies to auction off. We needed a way to auction them off without incurring fees. We also needed a means for us not to handle the money. We wanted 100% of the funds raised to go directly to the charities. Not an insurmountable obstacle but a challenge. I love a good challenge.

Roger and I raided our *Xena* collections of photos and memorabilia and put them aside. We bought stuff off eBay to add to the collection. I searched the net for a way to hold an auction and found a site that would allow me to do it without fees being involved. Two problems solved.

We decided that The Starship Foundation from New Zealand was one of the charities we would like to direct some of the money to. The goal was to get us out of the money side, but that would require Starship's help. I decided to take the most direct route; I emailed Starship and outlined that I wanted to run a charity auction and I didn't want to be responsible for the money, but for it to go directly to Starship. How could we make this happen?

Emails were exchanged, and then I called Starship HQ and spoke to Mrs. Bobbie Brown, who was the Fundraising Director. Thus, the AUSXIP and Starship relationship began in September 2006. We devised a plan where we hold the auction, the successful bidder pays Starship directly via their on-line donation form, Starship collates the information of the donor (name, address and amount that had been given), and then send me the spreadsheet to match our spreadsheet. Then Roger and I take over and ship the items. It was a relationship that was born out of a desire to do good. Starship was overjoyed by the idea, and I was energized because another issue had been sorted. Bobbie Brown and the whole team from the CEO on down were and still are extraordinary and that relationship has blossomed over the years.

Roger and I also wanted to donate to one of Renée O'Connor's chosen charities, and we chose The Alisa Ann Ruch Burn Foundation. Unfortunately, the arrangement that was put in place for Starship didn't quite work out for The Alisa Ann Ruch Burn Foundation.

A roadblock is only a temporary block if you have the will to find a way around it. We were determined this wasn't going to deter us, so we decided to do the next best thing—the winning bidders would pay us by check made out to the Alisa Ann Ruch Burn Foundation (once again taking us out of the money loop) and all we had to do was send them the checks. Problem solved.

What we also wanted to do was get our newly released cache of goodies out to Los Angeles to get them autographed by Lucy and Renée. With the help of Melissa Good, who volunteered to take everything we wanted to be signed to Lucy and Renée plus to offer some goodies of her own, we got that squared away.

It was now November 2006. Everything was falling into place. We were getting donations of items from the other cast and crew, and I began to sign COAs that everything we were going to auction off was 100% legitimate and the autographs were real. I uploaded all the images and information about the items to the charity auction site, and we started to promote the auction to the Xenaverse.

I love this fandom. I love their reaction to the auction. Fans began to rally to the idea and the excitement built. We made one crucial mistake that we would never make again. All the auction items were sent back to Australia instead of the US (where we currently house our auction items). There was a significant issue with Renée's autographed items. Renée's items had decided to take the scenic route and, apparently, the box of goodies were shipped to AUSTRIA instead of AUSTRALIA. Luckily, they got rerouted they arrived the day before the auction was to start. No pressure!

The auction was held on December 10-15, 2006 , and it raised a total of

$15,158.56. The Starship Foundation received $11,917.74, and $3,240.82 went to Renée O'Connor's Outreach Fund for The Alisa Ann Ruch Burn Foundation.

It was a great deal of work. We loved the experience and decided we wanted to continue doing the auctions. The AUSXIP Charity Auctions would continue and they have. We have raised just over $221,000 for Starship and other charities since 2006.

We needed some changes since we wanted the auctions to be a long-term project. We couldn't rely on external sites because they could easily disappear or change their priority. We needed something stable; something we could have complete control over. With AUSXIP being housed on a dedicated server, we had the resources to host an auction site that was dedicated to raising money for charity with no fees being involved and the certainty it would not disappear.

Lucy, Renée, Adrienne, and all the other actors and production crew that donated items for the auction. They willingly give their time and energies to sign everything placed before them. They also sent along messages of thanks to the fans. The CEO of Starship (Andrew Young at the time and later Brad Clark) and the entire Starship Foundation team have also sent along their thanks for the Xenites for their support. The Alisa Ann Ruch Burn Foundation also sent their thanks and subsequent ROC Outreach beneficiaries. The Starship Foundation has been an enormous help in our efforts to streamline the process. I couldn't have asked for a better partner. With support like that, it makes our job so much easier. I had the pleasure of going into Starship HQ in Auckland, New Zealand, to see all the staff and spend time with them. They floored me with their generosity and appreciation of AUSXIP and the Xenaverse.

We could not have achieved all of the above on our own. This was an 'it takes an Amazon village' kind of response. It took the effort of a lot of people to go from a tiny seed of an idea to a charity Sequoia and a lot of money raised. The fans rallied and loved the experience; watching them in bidding wars is a sight to behold. Roger was (and still is) EXTRAORDINARY. Roger and I were bowled over by the response. Over the years, we were joined by Christa Morris and Lori Boyles in helping us out.

The Starship Foundation, ROC Outreach Fund (The Alisa Ann Ruch Burn Foundation, the Tumbo Foundation in Peru and later House of Bards) have publicly thanked AUSXIP and in turn, the Xenaverse, every year for the donations. Starship has included AUSXIP in its official supporters list in their yearly report. The House of Bards included AUSXIP in their official program for their production of Macbeth (2019). You can find out more about why we chose The House of Bards in the next chapter.

Lucy Lawless and The Starship Foundation have sent along messages of thanks to AUSXIP and the fans for all the money that has been raised:

To Mary and the fans:

I have been very remiss...In not expressing my humblest thanks for all your kindness to the Starship Foundation over the past weeks (and years). You raising over $20,000 for Starship this past week shocked me. Mary, you, your posse and the greater Xenaverse have challenged my own view on my career and it's place in the world. I honestly just took the role of Xena because the chips fell my way. Ren and I acted the words that someone else put in our mouths and wore the costumes given us. We were paid pretty well for that time and we were grateful. But, and I think Ren would agree, we NEVER foresaw the kind of community spirit that has long survived the show itself. How could we? I do not believe there has ever been a precedent for this kind of fandom. The Xena fans are beyond generous, beyond loving and ever faithful. Because of your Kindness to the Starship Foundation, the sickest children of NZ have been the recipient of so much love from afar. Please rest assured that every penny is appreciated and thoughtfully spent. Brad and his team are worthy members of our team. I love you all! I wish you peace and laughter all the days of your life,
Yours truly,
Lucy Lawless

**

On behalf of Starship kids and families from all over New Zealand who will benefit from your support - a huge Starship Foundation thanks to all the winners and bidders in the recent Lucy/Xena memorabilia auction!
- Brad Clark,
CEO Starship Foundation

To Mary, and the phenomenal members of AUSXIP,
THANK YOU!
On behalf of the Starship Foundation and the children and their families who use Starship's world class, lifesaving services, we would like to thank you for raising an amazing $18,062.58 for Starship in 2016! Thanks to your amazing community's incredible generosity, Starship's children are continuing to have access to the best possible medical care at the time they need it most urgently. It is only with generosity like yours that we can access the latest technology and minimize the distress and disruption for a child during treatment and improve their chances of survival in their brave battle against illness and injury. Your generosity will continue to have a great impact on children - thanks to you, the foundation provides funding for state-of-the art technology, world class facilities and highly trained staff. We feel exceptionally privileged to have the kind-

hearted, on-going support of AUSXIP. Once again, our most heartfelt thanks for your kindness.
Yours sincerely,
Krissy Garnham
Community Fundraising Executive, Starship Foundation

Hello Mary!
I want to acknowledge the organization and implementation you provided for the entire charity auction, and especially for the Outreach Fund. It is an honor to be a part of it! I hope each person who made a contribution can see how their generosity is as far-reaching as Peru! Please read the letter attached from Arthur, who plans to provide all of us with updates on the school's progress. I have an inspiring friend, Chris Howard, who has the goal of eradicating poverty on the global level. I will continue to get involved with his projects around the world, as it is my desire is to see these models of communities enable themselves in an enriched sustainable way. Again, thank you so much for contributing to the love and gratitude in my heart as well!
my best,
Renée

Read the letter from Chris Howard here:
http://www.reneeoconnor.info/renee-outreach-fund/letter.php

Renée also reached out and thanked the fans for their support for the House of Bards for Renée's 2019 production of Macbeth. The program guide for the show had the names of those who supported HOB via the AUSXIP Charity Auction. You can read more about that in Chapter 53: *Renée O'Connor Feels The Love - Supporting Our Bard.*

A job well done but we are not finished. We strive for more and that's why the royalties from *Xena: Their Courage Changed Our World* will be donated to The Starship Foundation and House of Bards.
Together we can make a difference.

Chapter Fifty-Two

Lucy Lawless Feels The Love – Supporting Our Warrior

by MaryD

THEY SAY WHEN an actor is superlative in the role, and no one can envisage any other person in that role but that actor, they were born to play the part. Such is the case for Lucy Lawless. She was born to play the lead in *Xena: Warrior Princess* as Xena.

When given the opportunity of a lifetime (Lucy was the only one available after five actors turned down a three-episode arc on Hercules: The Legendary Journeys), Lucy made the role her own, and *Xena: Warrior Princess* became a legendary show. Now armed with the newfound fame, Lucy would be excused for seeing this as just a job, but her name had power. Many actors find that if given half a chance, they could use their fame to be an instrument for good.

Lucy is revered around the world and even more so in her native New Zealand. Lucy chose to use her fame to promote environmental causes and the health of the children of New Zealand. The fans were right behind her and have followed her example by reaching out to help in their own communities. This isn't a complete list but an example of the efforts that were made.

2000: A Time For Action

Lucy gets involved in the Safe and Sound Appeal (known as CARES). It was August 2000, and Lucy Lawless sat at her table at home and wept for yet another child beaten to death by their parent in New Zealand. Lucy had to act, so she picked up the phone to the Commissioner of Children's Office and offered to do whatever she could to help stop the abuse. Lucy took action, and with her friend Liz Gunn they founded "The Safe and Sound Action Group." The Appeal raised funds for specialist centers for child and adolescent recovery, a place of empowerment. For safety centers – they brought together, under one roof, all the different community agencies to treat and prevent child abuse. The Xenaverse got involved and raised $12,000 to help with the ongoing fundraising effort!

2006: Lucy Lawless Feel The Love Day (Week)

It's not every day an actor gets a week named in their honor, and it becomes an annual event, but that's what happened to Lucy in 2006. A member of the Official Lucy Lawless Fan Club, Rebekah, came up with a great idea called the "Lucy Lawless Feel The Love Day (Week)" that would run from September 21-28. It would involve a week of doing good for the community around the world. The initiative was approved by the Fan Club President, Sharon Delaney, and passed on to Lucy, who was overjoyed by the idea. It was also enthusiastically embraced by Xenites around the world. The long list of works included: helping children with sports and the Scouts, helping out in hospitals, working in food pantries, helping the elderly with groceries and other chores, helping neighbors and relatives, donating to the Starship Foundation, donating to Red Cross and shelters, breast cancer research, Alzheimer's and Cystic Fibrosis walks, cleaning up neighborhoods and so much more! Lucy was very proud of the annual event. She took every opportunity to praise the fans online and to mention the "Feel The Love Week" in media interviews.

Messages from Lucy to the fans for their efforts can be found on the fan club page: http://www.lucylawlessfanclub.com

News about the event from 2006 to 2015 can be found on AUSXIP Lucy Lawless: http://www.lucylawless.net/events/Feel_The_Love_Day/

2009: Lucy Supports AUSXIP Charity Auctions

Lucy always went out of her way to support the AUSXIP Charity Auction and signed whatever we asked of her. She never said 'no' to anything, including panties that were 'thrown' at her during her 2012 Auckland concert. One of my favorite stories is about a pendant she donated. Lucy donated a shark tooth pendant (costume jewelry) she wore at her first Roxy Concert in 2007. The pendant ended up having some wicked frequent flyer miles. Sylvie, the Xenite who won it, donated it back to the auction the following year. She gave it to Lucy to wear during her Photo Ops and also on stage, then Lucy would hand it back to Sylvie. It was then handed back to us, Sylvie would repurchase it and repeat the process for many years. It became known as the Boomerang Pendant. That pendant raised just over $5650!

2010: Lucy & Starship Foundation

Lucy donates her Xena Costumes for the Starship Spring Clean and raises $17,925.00 plus an additional $6,922.21 for other Lucy items! In 2011, Lucy donated her Lucretia Spartacus Costumes For Starship. Lucy auctions off her Spartacus costumes for Starship Spring Clean, and the fans rally to buy them with the total amount raised $14,838.

Now here is my favorite story involving Lucy, a horse, and AUSXIP.

A Horse Is A Horse Of Course Of Course...The Story Of Argo, Starship Warrior Princess, And The AUSXIP Horse Committee!

It was December 7, 2010, and Ellerslie Racecourse announced that it had set out to create a unique charity event called the Resene's Fastest Art Exhibition. One of the celebrities who were given a fiberglass horse to paint was Lucy. They had a couple of months to create their artwork. The horses were put on display in Auckland during Auckland Cup Week. After that event ended, the painted horses were to be auctioned off with the proceeds from each horse going to charity. Lucy chose the Starship Foundation and Xenites were ready and determined to win this horse race!

Lucy named her horse, Argo Starship Warrior Princess. Argo was the name of Xena's beautiful Palomino-colored horse played by the gorgeous Tilly. In 2011 Lucy began her Argo painting project and sent along with photos and reports to AUSXIP to keep the fans up to date with Argo's progress! Lucy was inspired by the ancient Egyptian faience sculptures of the water-horse or hippo, most fearsome of all African animals.
https://www.metmuseum.org/art/collection/search/544227

"I was intrigued by the idea of a 'water-horse,'" Lucy said. "It is a very serene piece and would look good in a garden setting or close to water. It made me feel good to have it around, and I wrote words up the legs which seem to me, the components of joy."

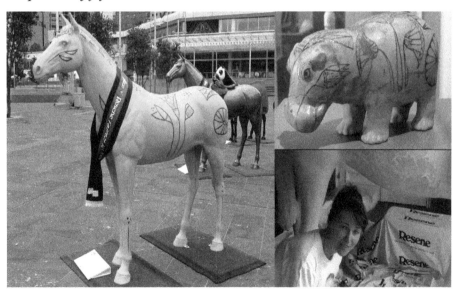

The words written upon Argo's legs were *"Love," "Peace," "Gratitude," "Argo Starship Warrior Princess." "Generosity, "Wisdom, "Courage," "Kindness," "Spirit,"* and *"Inspiration."*

On February 16, 2011, Argo made her debut and a decision was made that AUSXIP was going to win and donate the horse to Starship. I sent out 'I have an idea' email to a group of friends and we formed the AUSXIP Horse Committee. Committee member and New Zealand based, Jo, was our scout and would report on Argo's movements. Jo was also in charge of photographing Argo Starship Warrior Princess while she was being shown off at Aotea Square, Auckland, on February 18, 2011. You can see the photos and video from that event here:

http://www.lucylawless.net/events/2011/resenehorse/argo-on-display/

When the day finally arrived for the auction, Jo and I were the only members of the committee who were in the Southern Hemisphere. The bidding was going to close in the early evening, and we were on tenterhooks. We wanted to win this auction! Despite some connection problems (from my end), we managed to win! We bought Argo for $2500.00!

That wasn't going to be the end of Argo raising money. There was also a Facebook Like Campaign, and that mobilized the fans. The Xenites won (of course) and Ellerslie donated an additional $5000 to Starship. $7500.00 was raised from those two auction events, but that was still not the end of Argo's money-raising efforts. Since the AUSXIP Horse Committee now owned Argo (never imagined I would ever own a horse... real or fiberglass), we wanted to donate her to Starship to display at the Starship Hospital. Unfortunately we ran into an Occupational Health and Safety issue; having a giant horse and children playing around her could be a recipe for disaster. We changed our plans. We decided to auction her off in our upcoming AUSXIP Starship Auction! But wait, there was another problem Shipping her overseas was going to be an expensive exercise, more than Argo cost to buy. Argo was not a small horse, She was 229 cm (9.98') long, 50 cm (1.64') wide and 208 cm (6.82') in height and weighed 52 kg (114.6 lb).

While we were trying to find her a New Zealand buyer, we needed to give Argo a place to stay. The AUSXIP Stables (aka Jo's home) became Argo's temporary home. I didn't realize how much of a presence Argo was until I visited and was surprised when I rounded a corner and found myself staring up at a giant blue horse! Pictures of her didn't do this horse justice. We laughed so much over that horse.

We eventually found Argo her Forever Home in June 2013 and she left AUSXIP Stables soon after. She was sold to a horse loving family in Auckland, NZ. Argo Starship Warrior Princess raised a total of $11,970 for Starship. A stellar job by Lucy Lawless, Argo's Caretaker Jo and Xenites everywhere. A lot of money raised for the children of Starship Hospital. Win/Win!

Chapter Fifty-Three

Renée O'Connor Feels The Love – Supporting Our Bard

by MaryD

RENEE O'CONNOR IS an incredibly gifted, amazing woman; love her spirit, sense of humor, and her acting/writing/producing is phenomenal. I'm a massive fan of her work, and I discuss one of her movies that touched my soul in *Chapter Four: When The Xena Horde Gathers – Xena Conventions.* The first time I met Renée was in 2005; they say not to meet your idols because you will be disappointed, but the reverse happened with Renée.

I could write several chapters about Renée's work, but this chapter is about her generosity of spirit and as an advocate for social justice. Renée has been extremely generous to us for the AUSXIP Greater Good Charity Auction. One of my favorite stories is from 2017 when Renée saw a poster with Xena and Gabrielle holding a banner proclaiming "Support Equality/Love is Love" at a convention she was attending. Renée went to the vendor, bought it, autographed it, and donated the poster and autographed photos for the AUSXIP Charity Auctions. I was gobsmacked when I received an email from AUSXIP's Lori Boyles, who was with Renée, to tell me about her generosity. That poster generated $640 for The Starship Foundation! It's the little things that matter.

Renée is also an advocate for social justice by supporting marriage equality, environmental issues, and racial equality. Here are some of the charitable events that Renée attended and was supported by Xenites.

Xenites love to support the Xena cast, so out they came to put their words into action for the Greater Good when Renée took part in the Southern California Firefighters Burn Relay on May 31, 2003. Renée was surprised to find that when the relay arrived at their destination, there were Xenites out in force to support her in her endeavors.

Renée was raising money for The Alisa Ann Ruch Burn Foundation. They are an organization that raises money to enhance the quality of life for burn survivors and promotes burn prevention education. Renée started her association with the Foundation via the Firefighters Burn Relay event. The Foundation was created in 1971 and named after an eight-year-old girl who was fatally burned in a barbecue accident in Southern California.

In July 30, 2005: Southern California Firefighters Car Wash - Renée participated in the Southern California Firefighters Car Wash as a fundraiser for the Alisa Ann Ruch Burn Foundation. Fans pitched in and also washed cars with her. The car wash raised $2000 (with 400 cars washed). An additional $1000 was donated by the fans. Whenever Renée attended the Southern California Firefighters Burn Relay event (2005 to 2010), the fans were there to support her and the Foundation in their work.

October 2014: Renée was part of a photoshoot for TJ Scott's In the Tub photo book where the proceeds were donated to Breast Cancer Research. The fans got involved by buying the book, and AUSXIP Charity Auction auctioned off the coffee table book to raise funds for the ROC Outreach Foundation and Breast Cancer Research.

April 28, 2019: Uncle Vanya / Little Fish Theatre Company Fundraiser, where Renée was appearing in Uncle Vanya. The fans helped by coming to the performances and also donated to the theatre company. It was a fantastic performance, and I was stoked to get to see Renée performed. Win/Win.

We had been looking into how we could come to an arrangement with charities that Renée supported that would mirror what we were doing with Starship. We managed to find a way to help them even though the method we wanted to implement wasn't available. That all changed in 2019 when Renée's House of Bards Theatre Company became a reality!

In June 2019, Renée opened the doors to the House of Bards Theatre Company www.houseofbards.org. In consultation with Renée, HOB became one of AUSXIP's Official charities. We chose HOB because of what Renée and her team wanted to do. AUSXIP and AUSXIP Publishing share the same goals. We need storytellers, and we need people to help others fulfill their dreams. We live in a world that is increasingly difficult and distressing. Storytellers have taken us out of our world and transported us as far as our imaginations, and their storytelling could take us. Renée has worked behind the scenes with young actors to reach their potential, and that needs to continue. During HOB's first production, Macbeth, we included HOB in the 2019 AUSXIP Charity Auction. Renée donated items, and we raised $4500. Renée also included the AUSXIP Greater Good logo and the names of the fans who contributed to the auction in the official program!

Since 2006, the AUSXIP Charity Auctions has raised just over $25,000 for the ROC Outreach Fund. The charities supported included The Alissa Ann Ruch Burn Foundation, Haiti/Chile Earthquake Relief, and The Tambo Foundation in Peru to construct a high school for the Huilloq community and others. We plan on supporting Renée in her charitable endeavors and helping her make a difference for many years to come.

Chapter Fifty-Four

Adrienne Wilkinson Feels The Love – Supporting Our Jr. Warrior Princess

by MaryD

ADRIENNE WILKINSON IS one of those people whose personality, when you first meet her, instantly impresses you; there is an authenticity about her and a sense of playfulness. She's fun, warm, and open. Adrienne was Xena's daughter in the dual roles of Livia and Eve in Seasons 5 and 6 of *Xena: Warrior Princess*. It's not surprising that the Xenaverse has fallen in love with her.

Adrienne is the powerhouse behind the Adrienne Wilkinson Charity. She raises money for families in need and has done so for many years. She comes up with new ways to make the fan experience exciting and different at every event.

Adrienne started this charity drive back in 2003 when she began to host an annual event to raise funds for a family in need to meet their medical expenses. From memorabilia auctions and cast-dinners to celebrity meet and greets, she has established a long history working with Xenites and celebrities to raise money for the Greater Good.

I've been to several charity dinners and they are such fun with various celebrity guests and fans who have a great time. It is a beautifully organized event that has left many fans delighted.

In addition to her own charity, Adrienne has worked with more than two dozen charities, including literacy programs, animal welfare organizations, and scholarship funds for students whose lives have been affected by cancer. I asked Adrienne about her charitable endeavors and how the Xenaverse has played a part in helping her in her various fundraisers:

It has been an absolute privilege and an honor to be part of the Xenite community and to watch, witness, and participate in so many charitable projects and events over the years, and to see first-hand so much support for the Greater Good in action, to see such valuable difference being made in so many lives. I've lost count of the number of charity-focused events I've had the joy to be part of and the generous souls I've connected with through this community.

It has been exciting to watch as the Xenites constantly challenge each other to give bigger, to support more and greater causes, and to take a stand on issues that need a voice, need attention, and need support. The effect this has had, the outreach that has happened, the positive change, and the continued positive results can't be underestimated. The epic ways in which this community has created waves of change, combined with the intimate way this has strengthened the bonds within the Xenite community, are glorious to witness and even more magical to be part of.

I am always inspired and so grateful to be part of this community. To have had the opportunity to champion people and causes that inspire me to learn and grow and reach further, and by their nature, they also enable so many to challenge others to do the same. To be surrounded by such an extravagant tapestry of phenomenal humans working together to make the world a better place is absolutely beautiful... and breathtaking and humbling and inspiring and just damn delightful. I'm so proud of this community and honored and thrilled that I am part of it.

Thank you to the Xenite community, and here's to a lifetime of this tsunami of good continuing across the globe.

A tsunami of good is a pretty good way of describing it!

I have a wonderful story about Adrienne during the filming of my Intertwined Souls Promo; I was in awe watching her work. You can read about it in *Part 7: Chapter 39 - Watching My Characters Come To Life - Filming The Intertwined Souls Series Promo.*

You can find out more about Adrienne here:
https://www.imdb.com/name/nm0929330/?ref_=fn_al_nm_1

Adrienne's official site:
http://adriennewilkinson.com

Adrienne's Official Fan Site (run by AUSXIP):
http://adriennewilkinson.net

Chapter Fifty-Five

Brittney Powell Feels The Love – Sacrificing a Few Bras for the Greater Good

by MaryD

I WAS AT THE 2008 Official Xena Convention in January 2008, sitting down to listen to one of the funniest, absolutely adorable women I had ever met because of *Xena*—Brittney Powell. Brittney played Brunhilda in the spectacular Ring Trilogy—Season 6 Episode 7: "The Rheingold," Episode 8: "The Ring," and Episode 9: "Return of the Valkyries."

There is NO subtext in these episodes whatsoever! (I'm joking. Subtext became maintext in Season 6). Good ol' Brunhilda fell in love with Gabrielle (get in line lady, the entire Xenaverse was in love with Gabrielle!).

Brunhilda was a Valkyrie of great integrity, valued by Odin for her paradoxical combination of loyalty and independence. She had been given orders to betray Xena and Gabrielle, but she fell in love with Gabrielle. The Valkyrie sought to capture Gabrielle to exchange her for the ring, so she rode in on a horse and took Gabrielle. She turned herself into an eternal flame that kept a sleeping Gabrielle and the ring safe from getting into the wrong hands until Xena returned with Beowulf. Only Xena, her soulmate, could pass through the flame. - Courtesy of: https://hercules-xena.fandom.com/wiki/Brunhilda

Brittney's enthusiasm for everything is infectious, and her drive to raise money for the *Desi Geestman Foundation* inspired the Xenaverse to give her a hand. She is a fan favorite because she does what Xenites love—be themselves with a whole lot of spunk, honesty, and the ability to laugh and play with the fans. We like our cast (our cast? Aren't we the possessive kind) to be themselves, and that honesty forms a bond with the fans. A bond that will follow that actor through everything they do; Xenites will support them because they have fallen in love with THEM and not just the character they played. Brittney is also responsible for one of the best traditions in the Xenaverse...

Let's talk about Brittney's Bra...

How could Brittney's Bra not feature in this discussion about charitable events? Brittney's Bras have a special place in the Xenaverse. I wouldn't be surprised if they have their own fan club!

How did this all come about? Creation Entertainment was in charge of holding the Official Xena Conventions from 1997 to 2015. January was usually Xena Convention Month, and so it was in January 2007. That convention was Brittney's first Xena Convention, and boy was she in for a surprise! I wasn't present at this convention because I was back home in Australia, and I'm sorry I missed the entire con because a lot of things happened that year!

A couple of months ago, I was being interviewed along with Steven Sears on Sherri Rabinowitz's podcast "Chatting With Sherri," and we were discussing *Xena: Their Courage Changed Our World.* We came round to talking about the Greater Good and Brittney's Bras. As Steven recounted this story, I was laughing so much, the back of my head hurt. I had to mute my phone because of all the guffawing I was doing.

The story is legendary and pure Xenaverse shenanigans (of the good kind). Before we get into Brittney's bra (so to speak), many thanks to Steven L. Sears for his recollections about the convention that started the tradition.

Brittney took to the stage for the first time in a room packed with Xenites, and she was nervous. We usually have some sympathy for first-time guests because they don't know how to deal with us; the Xenaverse is different to any other fandom. Once the guest figures out that Xenites love to play, then they relax and play off the fans. That's how things progressed with Brittney. The fans could see her nervousness. Added to that nervousness, Brittney noticed that her bra strap was showing. Brittney tucked it back in and said, "Oh, my goodness, I can't show you that" to a room full of Xenites.

Let that marinate for a little bit. She said it to a room full of Xenites who don't need a lot of encouragement to have fun. Well, that's an opening that no self-respecting Xenite would let pass. Steven recollects that someone from the back yelled out, "$100!"

Welcome to the Xenaverse, Brittney! The Xenaverse ice breaker and we were off and running! It's a Xenaverse in-joke that given half the chance, Xenites would have an auction and bid on two flies walking up a wall to raise money for the greater good. We once had an auction where a COKE bottle LABEL with Lucy's signature went for $500. No, seriously. It wasn't the label or the autograph; it was the act of giving. Now back to Brittney and her bra...

We don't care what it is; we just want to be generous, and if it's a bra that someone is wearing, then that's what the auction item will be. It sounds unbelievable but that's our way; give us the opportunity, and we will grab it and raise money for a worthy cause. No one told Brittney that Xenites were these gloriously generous souls. Brittney was quick on her feet and not shy. She realized she had found her tribe, and we found yet another guest to bring into circle of crazy fun.

That "$100!" started an auction frenzy where half the room was bidding against the other half of the room! While I wasn't at that convention, I've been to several conventions where the exact thing happened (it became a Xenaverse tradition for Brittney to lose her bras and raise money for the Desi Geestman Foundation). It's a joy to behold as both sides, in a friendly way, go at it—bidding wars galore until one side wins.

Brittney realized that we were no ordinary fans; she played up to the fans, and that endeared her to us even more. She was no longer that awkward convention shy guest; she had become family.

What about the auction? Here's the absolute kicker: the two sides COMBINED the amounts raised and gave it all to Brittney for the Foundation. The auction raised $1100. The winning side then took possession of the bra (not with Brittney in it, of course), and it went on tour. You think I'm joking, don't you? I'm not! There are Brittney Bras tours! Those bras have some serious frequent flyer miles.

The generosity of spirit mixed in with the quirky (and insanely generous Xenites) is the stuff of legend and The Xenaverse Way. Thank you to Brittney for being such a good sport and being so adorable while doing it. Genuine kindness shows through.

Watch the Bra Auction in action on YouTube – you're in for a lot of laughs.
https://www.youtube.com/watch?v=dVVmvvgyYOw

You can find out more about the Desi Geestman Foundation here:
http://www.desigeestmanfoundation.org/

You can find out more about Brittney Powell here:
https://www.imdb.com/name/nm0694044/

PART 9

FRIENDS IN NEED – THE XENAVERSE CODE

Chapter Fifty-Six

We Help Our Friends In Need

by Jackie Larson

IN 2002, I ATTENDED my very first *Xena* convention. I was dumbfounded by the generosity of the *Xena* fans I encountered there. Thousands and thousands of dollars were bid on banners by several hundred people. I would listen to the bids increase and increase until finally, there was a happy winner. I always wondered what the person who won would do with those huge banners. Still, then I discovered that people were as much about giving to a charity as they were about winning the banners.

Next up would be Hudson Leick and the auctioning of her dress. I always thought that the people bidding were doing so to have an opportunity to own a dress that "Callisto" wore, but once again, I was wrong. Well, sort of... People loved owning the dress, but the idea of helping out a charity, the James W. Ellis Jr. Scholarship, was the real reason why they would bid a thousand dollars on a "used" dress!

Brittney Powell got into the act one year when she followed Jay Laga'aia and didn't know how she was going to top his singing and guitar playing, so she auctioned off her bra. The crowd went wild, and Brittney's bra auction grew each year until both sides of the auditorium were throwing money on the stage. One side benefit was that the winner was able to unhook the bra. But again, the charity was the main reason for such generosity.

Money was raised for Kevin Smith's family, and for Lucy's favorite charity, Starship, and the list goes on and on.

Each year, I went home feeling good about the Xenaverse and the positive and very tangible assistance that these kind people gave to charity.

I never dreamed in a million years, though, that the kindness and generosity of people scattered all over the globe would have such a huge impact on my life and the life of countless others. We can talk about living for the Greater Good and believing the message of *Xena*, but it is another thing entirely to see the love that people have for one another in action, to see the impact of the hand that is reached out to help another person and how that hand can benefit not only the receiver but the giver.

In 2016, after the first Xenite Retreat, a good friend and founding member of the Retreat was diagnosed with ovarian cancer. Ann's job did not include sick time or any payments for being out of work while she received treatment. I was asked to create a GoFundMe account so that we could get a bit of money for her until she could get back to work. I was hoping for a few hundred, just enough to tide her over. I was shocked to find that in just a couple of days, we reached and exceeded our requested amount. I would never have dreamed that we would raise so much money in such a short time. The story doesn't have a good ending. When Ann died a few weeks later, I reached out and asked for assistance with the funeral expenses, and within a short time, the money was raised.

Money is only one aspect of the support that we gain from our Xenite family. When Ann was sick, many Xenites rallied around. They sent in video messages of support to give her strength and energy.

The first year of the Xenite Retreat, over $14,000.00 was raised for charity in three short days. Several charities were given a cash infusion and were able to continue to help people in need. Xenite Retreat has been going strong for four years, and each year a sizable donation has been given to many, many different nonprofit organizations. Xenite Retreat has also provided twenty-one scholarships to people around the world so that they can experience the friendship, acceptance, and belonging that is the Xenaverse.

Our community is based on working for the Greater Good and choosing the Way of Friendship. How we live up to these labels is shown in a million different ways and through a different million people. I have "Xenite" on my license plate, and a friend told me that as I am driving, I am also representing my Xenite values and will have to not go into road rage and give someone a bad idea of what a Xenite is.

As we celebrate the 25th anniversary of *Xena*, the message of the Greater Good and our code of love, acceptance, and friendship is maintained and strengthened by each random act of kindness and each gift of love that we do for each other and our communities, both Xenite, local and worldwide. Here's to another twenty-five years celebrating all things *Xena*!!!!

Chapter Fifty-Seven

I Will Always Be With You

by Heather Parker

XENA BECAME AN important part of my life at the beginning of 2016 when in six months, I lost four members of my extended family and friends. I felt disconnected from support for some reason, and my family members were struggling too, so I didn't want to pull from them. The only thing I felt I could connect to and pull from was my best friend, Wendy, who had died in 2003. The show helped me do that. Wendy was my Xena, but she was absolutely a Gabrielle, like me, and I garnered so much strength from watching the show. When I laughed, I could almost hear her laughing with me. When I saw Xena's exasperated looks, they were all too familiar and made me smile. And when the ending came around, I knew that I would have fought like Gabrielle did to save my friend, but I didn't have that chance. Then, when I saw Xena on the boat, I cried for hours because I knew Wendy was still with me, and it was not crazy to feel like she was helping me through everything.

After digging a bit, I found Xenite Retreat and decided that it would be my reward for surviving what I had just gone through. I signed up to go and started connecting with others that were going. I connected with Jackie Larson and Penny Cavanaugh a bit, but then right around the anniversary of Wendy's death, they lost their dear friend Ann. I looked at Penny and saw the devastation that I had felt when I lost Wendy. My heart broke for her, and so I reached out to her, and then something amazing happened that had not happened many times in my life—she reached out in her pain and gave something back to me. She shared an extraordinary moment with me from Ann's service that floored me.

A woman who barely knew me gave me something special from herself to help me with my own grief and loss. It was a defining moment for me and went a long way towards helping me feel like I had possibly found a group of people that I could relate to. By the time I got to Retreat in April, I had bonded with several people. I had also gone through a divorce from my best friend of twenty-six years, and it did not go the way I thought it would. So I was desperate for connection by the time I got to Retreat, and not only was I not disappointed, I was floored at the genuine kindness, love, concern, empathy, and support I was getting from total strangers.

See, I used to be really bad at attention-seeking, I used to use the hard things in my life to get love from other people, and I had finally determined that I was never going to abuse people's kindness that way again, but I was still trying to find a balance in that process. So even though a few people knew what was going on, I did my best to smile and not show the anguish I was feeling. On Friday afternoon, I got a phone call that upset me greatly. I could not hold back the tears, I could not function, so I walked to a bench a good ways away from everyone to call the woman that had been my dear friend for about seven months, and who I had just started dating, Shawna.

She talked with me, and she made me feel a bit better, but I still could not stop crying. As I sat there, two of my fellow Warriors, Sarah Erickson and Lupe Pacheco, saw me and started walking towards me. I almost panicked. I didn't want these women who barely knew me to see me so upset, but it was too late. I started to shut down so that my unhealthy patterns from the past would not come up, and I would not pull from them, but I didn't have to, because they gave... freely, no questions asked. They wrapped their arms around me, they walked me back to the cabin, and then they listened to what was happening with so much love and concern on their faces that you would have thought we had been friends forever.

It was magic, it was love, it was another experience that let me see that there were other people out there, like me, who just wanted to love and help others, and that I could trust what I had found. Later in the Retreat was my moment with Brittney Powell that showed me that even the stars of the show are amazing. Cindy Classen, who is an amazing friend and the person that convinced me that Xenite Retreat was going to change my life, was determined to get a bra from Brittney to take back to South Africa to help raise money. And so I, being who I am, wanted to make that happen, but also being who I am, I had to make an ass of myself in the process.

I saw Brittney sitting alone and went and sat by her, introduced myself and basically asked if there was a way that I could get a bra from her if the one they were talking about went to someone else. I had no idea it was a charity auction, I had no idea how everything worked, and I had just put her in a horrible position. She was gracious and kind but basically said something to the effect that it would depend on the auction. When I found out what the process was and what I had done, I was mortified. I felt horrible, so I saw Penny talking to Brittney and went up to apologize and asked Penny to please vouch for me that I was not a complete jerk.

Penny did and then asked me to tell Brittney what had happened to me in the last year. Brittney put her hand on my shoulder and looked me in the eyes and so sincerely said she was sorry for everything that I was going through. It was genuine and beautiful. When the time came for the bra to be given away, someone else won it, but Penny called Cindy and me back to the green room. Brittney, being the wonderful woman that she is, had autographed another bra and gave it to Cindy, telling her how lucky she was to have a friend like me. Not only did she do something amazing, but she also gave me credit for it.

That night, I cried like a baby. I had found my people, and there was no way I was letting go of them. Over the next year and a half, I became friends with many more Xenites, Shawna moved in with us, my children and me, and my life felt like it was finally getting back to normal. In August, we were able to fulfill one of Shawna's lifelong dreams, and she met Lucy in Salt Lake City at FanX. Then about a month later, totally unexpectedly and suddenly, the light that had carried me so far in the last two years was gone.

Around 11pm on Sunday, September 23, Shawna passed out and went to the ER, and by 4am on the 24th, she was gone. I was in shock and utterly devastated. Later that morning, I started reaching out to my closest Xenites. Jackie was already planning on meeting us in St. Louis, where we had Shawna's services. My sister Heidi drove to Denver to pick me up and then drove me to St. Louis the next day. I asked Penny if she would let our tribe know what was going on. I wanted it out there and not going by word of mouth so that my friends would have no questions about what was happening with me.

On that twelve-hour drive, my phone never stopped. Now, to some people, that sounds horrible and taxing, but to me, it was terrific. It was a constant stream of Xenites checking on me, just letting me know they were there. Every beep was like a piece of cloth stitched together to form a blanket that covered me. I couldn't eat or sleep for a couple of days, but I didn't need to because, for almost an entire week, I never went for more than an hour without someone reaching out to help hold me up. Even people I had not met were reaching out to help me.

Jackie and Heidi became my personal guards, but the Xenites were my army of love and support. Jackie suggested starting a GoFundMe page to help cover my expense of flying Shawna from Denver to St. Louis. I thought I would be thrilled and grateful to get $500, and I should have known better because we got enough to cover the expense almost to the dollar—a little over $2,000.

As grateful as I was to see the dollar amounts, it was the notes that were there that made the experience so amazing. Then, to top that off, when we got to the service there were the most beautiful flowers and an amazing note from my tribe to me and my girl, but that was not all that they did, because while I was asking upfront for help through GoFundMe, my tribe had already started voluntarily, without anyone asking, sending money to Penny to help me.

They bought these amazing flowers, which Shawna would have loved, and there was so much given that by the time I got home, they had given me another $1,000 to help with travel expenses and whatever I needed. I have never experienced such heartbreak and gratefulness at the same time. Jackie drove us home from St. Louis, and we settled in to try to figure out what our lives were going to look like without Shawna.

We were home for a week, and I got a call from Heidi that our baby sister Holly was in the ER, and the prognosis was not good. By the next day, Maddie (my oldest daughter), Heidi, and I decided we'd better get to Norman to see her. I started a separate Facebook group where I could keep my Retreat Xenites informed of what was going on because I was lost without Shawna and desperately needed them. I had Heidi, Holly's twin; my other sister Lisa; Rob, Holly's husband, and their amazing group of friends, but my people were gone.

My ex-husband was gone, Shawna was gone, my grandparents that raised me were sick and I knew they were not long for this world. So, of course, I reached out to them and to my cousin Jeff a bit, but it was my Xenites that I leaned on the hardest. Every night when I could not sleep Cindy Classen was in South Africa helping me.

When I thought I was going to lose my mind, Sharon Glasswell became the mom I needed and held me all the way from Australia to Oklahoma.

In my moments of panic and desperation, it was my Xenites that I railed against the gods with and that I asked to help me beg for my sister's life. But it did not work. It took three weeks of us keeping constant vigil with her, but eventually, Holly left us. And through those three weeks, I was never alone.

The messages and support continued. Jackie insisted that there would be more financial support if I needed it, but I could not take one more cent from my friends. All I needed was their love, and I had that in abundance. There was never a moment that I could not find people to talk to, and there was never a day that my phone went silent, and I didn't have people reaching out to me.

Again, I got home, I thanked my friends for their love and support, and tried to figure out what my life was going to look like. The one thing that I knew was that we would be okay and that I had my tribe no matter what.

Two weeks later, on November 6, 2018, my grandmother passed away. Even though it was expected, it was devastating.

My grandparents took me when my parents did not want me. My grandparents were all that was left of my foundation, and the first one was gone, and I knew it would not be long before my grandfather followed. By this time, I started shutting down. My tribe would check on me daily, and they gave me incredible amounts of support and love, but I could barely feel or connect with anything. When I got home, I just kinda gave up and did what I had to in order to keep my kids up and going, but I was broken and done. I started shutting my friends out because I could not put this level of pain on them.

There were only two or three Xenite friends that I would let in, but they were there. They absolutely carried me. And as I began walking through trying to find any sense of steadiness, it was my friend and fellow Xenite, Janine Morales, that became my steadfast rock. She would check on me and do her best to make me laugh. I would tell her I was going to hide for a day or so, and she would give me space until the next day and then come looking for me.

Life started again; it was the holidays and time to pull myself together for my kids. I did the best that I could, but I was broken, absolutely broken. A few weeks before Christmas, I put a post on my Facebook page asking people if they wouldn't mind sending a few trinkets to the kids from where they were. A pencil, or a postcard from the town that they lived in, to help distract the kids from the losses they were feeling. I was thinking that we would get a few small things for Brynn, who was eight at the time, and Garrison, who was five. Stuff that they would get to enjoy getting from the mail. Within a week, things started arriving, and none of them were the trinkets that I had asked for. They were boxes of comfort for all of us. I, Maddie, my daughter that is twenty-one, Brynn and Garrison, were included in everything. From the end of November to after Christmas, there was a steady stream of love that came into our home and all but one of the packages were from Xenites.

Three to four times a week there was something that had toys for the kids, a journal or a book for Maddie, and something of comfort and a note of love for me. It became another visual portrayal of what it is to ask a Xenite for help. Packages came from all over the states and even one from my bard family in England. I feel like there are no words that can convey the appreciation that I have that our holiday was about love instead of death, that my kids' memory of this time will always include the kindness of helpers and not just the ache of the missing.

The new year started and I knew that my grandfather was probably going to pass soon. I continued to keep myself isolated and my Xenites continued their constant support but respected my need to be in my cave. On February 25, 2019, my grandfather passed away. That was it; that was the end of my foundation. My parents, my grandparents, my husband of over twenty years, they were all gone from my life.

I felt lost and untethered. As broken as I imagined I could ever be. Then three days later, the unthinkable happened. I was home in Waxahachie waiting for my cousin Jeff and his family to leave Austin to meet me that afternoon to finish preparations for my grandfather's funeral and I got a phone call that Jeff had suffered a heart attack. My mind went numb. You see, Jeff was not only my cousin; he was my brother, my confidant, my protector, and my buffer.

Like many Xenites, I grew up in a very religious family and when I walked away from the church, it was always Jeff that I could vent to when my grandparents laid into me. It was always Jeff that understood me and supported me with that side of my family. And now he was in the same place that my baby sister had been just five months earlier. That was it for me; I was done. I could not believe that there was any way that this string of deaths would continue. I closed almost every door to me but three or four. The only person I talked to daily was Janine.

After about three weeks of isolation, she came up to get me out of the house. My ex-husband had moved to Texas in October and so I was doing the single mom thing alone and had not had any time to myself, other than to attend funerals in five months. She had planned, as best as she could get me to commit to, a weekend that would get me out of the house a bit and even throwing axes. I asked if we could stay in after dinner on Friday and we just chilled and laughed. Then on Saturday morning, I got the call that they were going to take Jeff off life support. It felt like any little pieces of my heart that had remained intact shattered all at once.

Not him, not Jeff; it was too much. I could not deal. So Janine, a Xenite that I barely knew seven months earlier in Salt Lake, but had decided I wanted to be better friends with, in true Xenite fashion, took over. She didn't know Jeff or anyone else in my life that had passed except for Shawna. It was the first time she had even been to my house, but she let me put my head on her shoulder and held me tight while I cried, for I don't know how long, until I fell asleep.

I could not tell my tribe; she did it for me without me even asking. She stayed with me while I coped as best as I could and showed me nothing but love and concern while I went through one of the hardest weekends of my life. It absolutely felt like it was the day that hope died in this eternal optimist, and if she had not been there, I know I would have ended up in the hospital too. Again, for days, while I drove from Denver to Austin and went through yet another funeral, my phone rarely stopped.

My tribe was there, with love and support the entire time, but it all felt like it had become too much. I was beginning to hear that old, familiar, and ugly voice telling me that I was too much. That my tribe, no matter how they were acting, was done with the drama and tired of my life. I almost decided to skip Retreat at the end of April because I could not face any more rejection or loss.

About two weeks before Retreat, my five-year-old, Garrison, had an episode in the car. He grabbed his heart and started gasping for air. Now, this is after Shawna, Holly, and Jeff all died from events that involved heart attacks. And both my grandparents and my dad suffered from some sort of heart failure. I looked up to the sky and said, "no f****** way, this is not happening!!!"

The drive that should have taken about twenty minutes to the hospital took ten. I was running red lights. Brynn, my now nine-year-old daughter, was in the back with Garrison trying to help me keep him conscious and holding a cup as he threw up and turned the palest I have ever seen anyone. I honestly thought my baby was going to die before we would make it to the ER.

When we got there, and the dust settled, it was my Xenite family that I reached out to first. It was Janine and my closest Bards that I told first. It was them that I wanted in my corner immediately. When it came time for what I was afraid was going to be the battle of my life, my first line of defense was going to be them because they had earned that level of respect in my life. It turned out that Garrison is okay; he has a manageable heart condition and a whole team of Xenites that will always be there for him too.

When it came time for Retreat, I knew that I needed it. I knew that I had to go, even if I was a little shaken about Garrison, even if I was afraid of all the drama that surrounded me being seen as a negative, I needed to see my tribe. From the moment I arrived at the Marriott in Burbank, it was like the day after Shawna died.

You see, we have a tradition of sitting in the lobby or the outside patio so we can hug everyone as they are coming in, and it is absolutely one of my favorite things. This year, even more so, I could not wait to hug the necks of my chosen family and give them back just a bit of the love that they had supported me with for the last six months. As my tribe came in over the next two days, I was filled with excitement and joy to see each new face.

Xena: Their Courage Changed Our World

The Marriott and then Canyon Creek felt like home as much as my grandparents' house in Waxahachie. If you are lucky enough to belong to a tight-knit family that is spread out and does not get to see each other often, then you know what comes next. I had four solid days of love and support, so much love and support that it became overwhelming to this person who used to lie and manipulate just to get a little attention.

This family encircled me, validated me, supported me, and sent me home with gifts of love and memories that I know will be with me for the rest of my life. And all of this comes from the random happenstance of surfing Netflix, clicking on Xena, and seeing my Wendy thirteen years after she died. So I sit here after two years, not twenty like a lot of you, or even five, but just two years, and type all of this out to acknowledge who we are and what we do.

There are quips about Xenites changing light bulbs in Vegas, there are instances of financial support, and incredible acts of loving-kindness, but I feel special because I feel like my situation is a true representation of the best of our tribe. I'm no one special, I'm not a celebrity, I have no real connections. I'm just a woman who has been through a lot of stuff for the last three years and who was lucky enough to stumble into Xenite Retreat. As a result of that luck, I get to be the one to write this chapter on how Xenites rally around each other, and it is my absolute privilege to help the world know what an amazing group of people we really are.

After just two years of friendship, there are people that I know would do absolutely anything for me, and I don't know that through faith in them—I know it because they have walked through Tartarus with me, some have even carried me through the flames, and they still love me and are here for me any time I reach out. This chapter is my love letter to all of them.

This chapter is a thank you for saving my family and me in our darkest hours. I would not have made it through this without all of you. And to those of you whose names I did not mention, please know that your name is written on my heart. If I could write my own book of thank yous, I would mention every name because you have all impacted me in so many ways. #ToAStrongAmazonNation

Chapter Fifty-Eight

Keeping Track of Our Xenite Family In Times of Distress

by MaryD

DISASTERS, CALAMITIES, AND EPIDEMICS are part of life, and at times we are overwhelmed by it all. We feel alone and in need of comfort. Xenites have a system in place (as the previous chapters indicated) to support each other. In addition to helping one another, we also reach out and help others in the tradition of the Greater Good. The following chapter will showcase some of those times.

2001: The Horror of 9/11 and Acts of Kindness

In 2001, I decided that I was going to go on my first solo adventure to the United States, my first trip to visit friends I had only spoken to via email—my Xenite tribe. I planned on blogging about the adventure and Mesh was at the helm of AUSXIP to steer the site while I was away for six weeks. I landed in Los Angeles on August 25, 2001. I fell in love with the country, the warmth and hospitality, the wonderfully quirky nature of the people and my fellow fans. I was feeling so upbeat and positive.

On September 10, 2001, I flew out of Washington DC. I headed to Syracuse to meet up with the woman who had introduced me to *Xena*. Susan "Xero" Podd. She was waiting for me, and we were going on an adventure of a lifetime.

September 11 was the day I was going to finally see a site I had been dreaming about—Niagara Falls. It was a three-hour drive so we needed to start early. We couldn't take Xero's beloved dog with us so we drove to her mother's home for her to dogsit while we were away. That was the last thing that would be normal for the rest of my trip.

I stood in the lounge room half listening to a conversation between mother and daughter and watching the television. You know those moments when you remember everything you were thinking and doing? This was one of those moments. I thought to myself, "Why are they playing a disaster flick so early in the morning?" I failed to notice the CNN logo on the bottom of the screen; I was transfixed by the plane that was flying into the building. It was then that I noticed that this wasn't a disaster movie, but live news from New York. The terrorist attacks on America were underway.

The country was under attack and all I could do was watch with my mouth agape at the carnage being replayed, the towers going down, and the utter helplessness we all felt.

Over the coming hours we were glued to the television or ringing friends in New York or DC to find out if they were okay. Added to the stress, I was worried about my mum turning on the news, on the other side of the world, and finding out her youngest was in a country under attack.

Then something extraordinary happened (I shouldn't have been surprised). Mesh started to get emails asking about my whereabouts. The planes had been grounded as soon as they could land; no matter the location and travelers were stuck on the ground regardless of where they were going. Those who were following my blog knew I had just been to Washington DC, but other than that, there was no word on where I was that moment. Mesh got offers for me to stay at Xenite homes if I were in their area. I was deeply moved by their love and generosity.

It was an extraordinary time in history. The Xenites stepped up and were a force for good once again by helping their fellow fans in dealing with the grief and the loss, by raising money and offering support.

Friends in Need: the Xenaverse Code.

2002: Xenites Support Kevin Smith's Family Trust Fund

We lost our beloved God of War, Kevin Smith, in a tragic accident in China in 2002. He passed away on February 15, 2002. A Trust Fund was set up for his family and the fans donated to it to help his grieving widow and children. It was shocking news that left the Xenaverse heartbroken.

More about *Kevin in Chapter 64: Our Fallen God of War - In Memory of Kevin Tod Smith.*

2005: Hurricane Katrina and the Race To Save Lucy Lawless

On 28 August 2005, New Orleans residents were told to evacuate the city because Hurricane Katrina was barreling for them with winds measured at 175 mph. It was going to be deadly. Lucy Lawless was in town to film the movie "Vampire Bats." Despite the warnings that Hurricane Katrina was going to be catastrophic, Lucy chose to stay until the very last moment. It was a gamble she would never win against the might of Katrina. The roads were clogged, Katrina was wreaking havoc in the city, and people were trying to flee. The Xenaverse went into meltdown with concern over the city, their fellow fans, and Lucy. The idea of sending a plane to rescue her was put into action but Lucy couldn't get to where the plane had landed. It was an all hands on deck type of emergency. Lucy managed to get to Baton Rouge, but it was a close call and one she would never forget.

The New Orleans newspaper "The National Ledger" on August 31, 2005, had this report and quotes from Lucy:

"I was staying in a lovely little house in the French Quarter, and at first, I was planning to ride out the storm. Then we heard it was going to be a Category 5 storm, and I rang the producer and said, 'Let's get out of here. This is crazy," she recounts. Initially, Lucy planned to get to Los Angeles. Realizing that had become impossible, *"We lowered our sights and thought we'd get to Houston. Then we found that was impossible and thought, 'Hell, let's try to get to Baton Rouge.' Our choices were eroding by the hour. The local crew left days ago. We took the film stock with us and the payroll."*

On the road Sunday evening, "It took us nine hours to travel a distance that usually takes 15 minutes. We knew they were going to sandbag off the road, and our big fear was that we'd be turned back and get caught in the storm."

Lucy and the executive producer of Vampire Bats, Jill Tanner, ending up staying with a Baton Rouge family they met through a special effects artist. *"I've never depended on the kindness of strangers before, but here, with the generosity of these people in the South, it seems appropriate,"*

Lucy made it out safely and she set to help New Orleans after Katrina wreaked havoc. Xenites mobilized to offer assistance.

2005: AUSXIP Xenite Watch Launches to Keep Track our Xenite Family during Hurricane Katrina

The devastation of New Orleans was unbelievable; the loss of life was horrendous and then the generosity of spirit that is the Xenaverse kicked it up several notches.

On August 31, 2005, AUSXIP set up Xenite Watch to track down and make sure that our fellow fans were safe. It was at times deeply distressing but it concentrated our minds on tracking down our friends.

- A network of Xenites were formed to get in touch with other Xenites that could be affected and see if they needed help.
- Xenite Watch Mailing List was created to keep everyone updated
- A Xenite Safe List drawn up so we knew who was safe.
- Xenite Waiting Info List to monitor those we were still waiting to hear from and the efforts that were made to locate them.

2005: The Xenaverse Mobilizes For Katrina Relief

- On September 02, 2005, Renée O'Connor was at a Red Cross Donation center, helping out and spreading the message for assistance.
- The Golden Crown Literary Society (GCLS - Lesbian Fiction Writers) went into action; many on the board were *Xena* fans and then issued a press release to say they had set up a fund.
- On September 04, 2005, auctions were held and the money raised went to Katrina relief through the Red Cross.
- Cindy Tingley (from Forevaxena web site) and Xenaverse writer Robin Alexander called in for Xenite help for those affected in Baton Rouge. They asked for baby items: food, clothing, and bottles, summer clothes, shoes, personal hygiene items, deodorant, toothbrushes, toothpaste, soap, tissue, toilet paper, first aid supplies, non-perishable foods, bottled water, bedding supplies, and toys for the kids. The Xenaverse responded.
- Lucy, Renée, and Lucy's husband Rob Tapert (executive producer of *Xena*) autographed artwork for an auction for the American Red Cross.
- On September 24, Renée put up for auction two of her original watercolors to raise money for Katrina relief.
- Lucy created an artwork that was auctioned off by the Starship Foundation in July (before Katrina) and a fan won it.

That same fan (Drummerliz) that won Lucy's artwork, donated it back and money raised from that went Katrina victims. Sandy Verner from Atlanta, Georgia, sent me a note offering to help Xenites in need:

In a community that has given me so much over the years, I am offering my services to anyone who will eventually need them. I have owned and operated a Disaster Restoration company for the past eighteen years. We restore contents and structures after fires, floods, tornados, hurricanes, etc. I realize many have lost everything, but on the off chance they have not, I will be more than glad and willing to help in any capacity I can. If it's advice or hands on work, I will be available to those who want it. I know many do not have access to internet use and may not for some time. I will leave my cell phone # to anyone who wants it through MaryD

2005: First AUSXIP Charity Auction For Katrina Relief

On September 15, 2005, I turned on AUSXIP Charity Auctions for the first time as a buy/sell way to raise money for Katrina relief with a call for people to donate their goodies. The only proviso was that 100% of the money was to go to the relief. It was a huge success. That auction site was located at (the now deleted) cgispy.com site and would serve as the location for more AUSXIP auctions.

2006: A Friend In Need Books, Cards & Toys Campaign Helping Hurricane Katrina Survivors One Step At A Time

In January 2006, The *"A Friend In Need Books, Cards & Toys Campaign Helping Hurricane Katrina Survivors One Step At A Time"* began. The campaign was initiated by fans from the Official Lucy Lawless Fan Club after a news article on an angel called Lily Duke.

As MSNBC reported: *Within days after Hurricane Katrina hit, Duke managed to do what other relief agencies couldn't—get food and water to her neighbors. Since then, she's expanded her network, distributing medicine, packaged lunches, and bags of ice to as many as 20,000 people a day."*

Xenites mobilized and started to send care packages from ALL OVER THE WORLD, and some even drove there to hand their boxes to Lily.

Those were some of the examples of our how the Xenaverse mobilized into action when our friends were in need.

Chapter Fifty-Nine

Xenite Refreshes Campaign
Supporting our Xena Writers
During WGA Writers Strike

by MaryD

XENA ENDED IN June 2001 with the final two episodes called 'A Friend in Need'. Throughout the show's six-season run we got to know the cast and crew. Steven L. Sears was one who would mingle with the fans and later he was joined by other *Xena* writers such as Katherine Fugate. We knew them, we loved them and supported them post-*Xena*.

November 05, 2007 was a momentous day in the television industry. All 12,000 film and television screenwriters of the American labor unions —Writers Guild of America East (WGAE), and Writers Guild of America West (WGAW)— went on strike.

How did that involve the Xenaverse? Our *Xena* writers were involved. That was all we needed to know. Our show had ended in 2001 so it wasn't going to affect the show we loved, but it was going to affect the writers we love. We are a family and when family is in need, Xenites rally!

A brilliant idea was emailed to me by a Xenite. Was there a way we could help our *Xena* writer during the WGA strike. Our show had been off the air since June 2001 but as I mentioned in the opening chapter, Xenites support our *Xena* cast and crew throughout their careers. I thought about how we could implement this idea. Our striking writers were: Steven L. Sears, Katherine Fugate, and others. After thinking about different ways we could do it, I sent an email to the one person who would have the answers. My mate, Christa Morris. Being in the industry, Christa was aware of why the writers were on strike and what it meant for them. Was there a way we could help? Of course! The Xenaverse Refreshes Campaign began on November 30, 2007.

The Xenaverse Refreshes Campaign was organized to raise money so we could purchase water, Gatorade, tea, vitamins, and other goodies. That call to arms was answered in droves! Christa Morris volunteered to make cookies (trust me, they are really great cookies!) and to drop off the water and other items. It took a lot of effort by Christa in baking the cookies and other goodies plus the shopping. We had raised $2005 to get supplies and it was appreciated by the striking writers and those around them! We had such a huge impact on morale that Katherine Fugate sent the following note:

Hey all and sundry —

Yet ANOTHER generous drop came to the Disney gate today from the Xenaverse. Have to tell you - it's so humbling and inspiring. The mostly male WGA writers always walk up to me with shock on their faces when I arrive, saying, "they did it AGAIN!" and I smile, realizing, then say, "you don't know the power of the Xenaverse…" …Katherine

We continued the drop-offs of refreshments and cookies until the writers' strike ended on February 12, 2008. None of what we did would be possible if not for the support of the Xenaverse or Christa Morris who baked, shopped and dropped off supplies. She was the Xenaverse Drop-Off Elf!

The photo below is of Christa's car, packed and ready for another delivery for our striking writers.

We didn't just stop there. Read the next chapter about how we marched in support of our writers outside NBC. It was a fantastic day filled with laughter, friendship, a *Xena* battle cry or two, rain, hail, sunshine and wholehearted Xenaverse support!

Get to know more about Christa in *Part 7: Because of Xena and Chapter 42: From The Xenaverse To Winning Daytime Emmys, by Christa Morris, KT Jorgensen, And Maria Webster.*

Chapter Sixty

Xenites March in Support of our Xena Writers During WGA Writers Strike

by MaryD

FROM EARLY NOVEMBER 2007 to February 12, 2008, all 12,000 film and television screenwriters went on strike for increased funding. Television shows shut down production, and writers were marching in the streets outside studios. Our Xena writers were also on strike, and as you've read in the preceding chapter about our Xenite Refreshes Campaign, the Xenaverse were supporting them. On January 12, 2008, it was announced that the Xenaverse was going to march in front of NBC to show our solidarity for our writers. OUR writers? *Xena: Warrior Princess* had been off the air for SEVEN years (at that point). We had no skin in the game (our show was not impacted).

Why were we going to march for our writers? If you have to ask that question, you don't know the Xenaverse.

It doesn't matter that our beloved show was off the air for seven years. The writers on strike were OUR writers, and we supported OUR actors. Yes, we *are* a possessive lot.

No, seriously, it's not that we are possessive (too much), it's just that we have come to know our writers over the years and we consider them friends. Steven L. Sears can be frequently found in the middle of a horde of Xenites at conventions. No one bats an eye unless they are con virgins, and in which case, they hyperventilate until they get used to seeing Steve. Then it's "Oh, it's Steve! Hi Steve!" It's the same for our other writers. We all have our favorite episodes and know who the writer is (on the other hand, I can't name any writer from my favorite tv shows and wouldn't be able to recognize them in a lineup). So what is so special about the *Xena* writers that we were willing to stand out in the cold and march in support? It's what we do. It's our superpower!

We support our writers, our actors, and even the stunties (slang for stuntmen/stuntwomen) who we also know by name (Hi, Zoe Bell!). The Xenaverse is a close-knit community, and it's what we do. Now that we know WHY we are marching let's get to the actual day. We were going to join the actors, writers, and producers for a march on January 24, 2018.

In attendance from our show were Renée O'Connor, Claire Stansfield,

Rob Trebor, Adrienne Wilkinson, Rob Tapert, RJ Stewart, Chris Manheim, Katherine Fugate, Liz Friedman, Victoria Pratt, TJ Scott, and Steven L. Sears. Lucy Lawless couldn't make it because she had a series of concerts and had to protect her voice.

It was such a great day, and the Xenaverse believes it sent a loud message that our writers were valued, even after Xena was off the air for years. I went into the AUSXIP Archives to dig up my report of the event. It was such a great day, and we had so much fun, even if it was cold and wet.

***

Before I flew down to Burbank to join the Xena March, Steven Sears sent me an email about the latest update about the march and to alert everyone about the weather conditions. I remember writing back to him saying... "through rain, hail or shine, we will be there" – I didn't think it would literally come true, but that's what happened! What a fantastic day – over 200 Xenites walked up and down the footpath outside NBC studios.

To see all those fans support the writers – WOW! I know our show of solidarity buoyed the striking writers. It meant a great deal to Steven, Katherine, and the rest of the Xena writers and Rob Tapert. I had such a great time, and that day created some exceptional memories:

Have I mentioned how cold it was? The rain pelted down; it would stop for a bit, then the sun would briefly make an appearance to lull us into a false sense of security, then it would rain. I've never been happier to stand in the rain! This was Xenaverse support at it's best.

The writers (from various shows who march with our writers) asked me to pass on a message to all the Xenites. The appreciated the goodies that the Xena fans have provided. They couldn't stress enough how much it meant to them. Having 200+ Xenites marching with them gave them an even more considerable appreciation of this fandom.

You can watch highlights of the Xena March, including interviews. AUSXIP's Lori Boyles was behind the camera!
https://www.youtube.com/watch?v=PYI6qMSG3l4

Thank you to my dear friend, Lida Verner, who took the amazing photographs from the event. There were so many images but I ran out of space to show them all!

That was such a fun day!

PART 10

HOW XENA CHANGED OUR WORLD
XENITE STORIES

Chapter Sixty-One

How Xena Changed Our World
Xenite Stories 1995 – 2018

by MaryD

WE ASKED XENITES from all over the world to submit their stories on how *Xena: Warrior Princess* changed their lives and these are the responses!

1995

- Lani Hilton
- Tank
- Melissa J. Aldrich
- Amanda
- Lara
- Gloria (Flabbi)
- Jamie Byrne (Jimmy Graham)
- Roxanne Thibault
- Richard B. Kloosterboer
- Tash Karoly
- Krislene Hancock
- Meg Arrow
- Hayriye Makas Uygun
- Aixa R.
- Patricia O'Leary
- Leanne Fisher
- Ladykimp
- JS Stephens
- Jacki Wyman
- Amanda E
- Gayle McDonald
- Paully Adams
- Julie Hupp
- Maria Aquino
- Jen Tucker
- Luciana Rodrigues da Silva Sampaio

- John Terrell Jacobs
- Carolyn Kroll

Lani Hilton
Country: United States

This is how *Xena: Warrior Princess* changed my life. I began watching the show when my now ex-husband told me I needed to check out this show he had come across. He said I would love it because I am a badass like Xena. The very first episode I watched was "Is There a Doctor in The House?" I was hooked from the beginning. I was struggling in my life at the time. I was in an abusive marriage which was repeating patterns from a violent and horrible childhood living in an alcoholic home. The character of Xena was so relatable to me. I was full of anger and rage. I had my light and my dark side, and it was a constant battle over which one would emerge. I knew I had a capacity for great love and compassion, but my anger and temper would take over. I watched as Xena and Gabrielle went through so many struggles and yet, no matter what, they loved each other.

That never went away. They always found their way back to each other through forgiveness. Love was the one thing that mattered most. It was because of their relationship that I could see how unhealthy my marriage was. There was one more important factor…I realized I wanted a Gabrielle in my life. In the span of the *Xena* TV show, I had two children. I just knew I needed to get them away from my marriage and give them a better life. A lot has happened in my life since the show ended in 2001. I've had relationships with a couple of Altis. I have always kept in mind one line in *Xena* that still sticks with me: "I don't accept defeat." I got into therapy and found my warrior spirit again. Today I am forty-six years old and I am in college. I am going to be a therapist.

The greater good is the only way! We have to fight for people who cannot fight for themselves. I want to help people overcome bad pasts and live happy lives. I want to help other people who are disabled like me to still be happy despite having a broken body. I want to help people that were victims of child abuse heal their souls and find peace in their lives. Xena and Gabrielle are fictional characters, but the writers gave us a strong message of love and peace that I will always carry with me. No matter what life throws at us, remember to BATTLE ON!

Tank
Country: United States

I had just turned fifteen when *Xena* began airing and I was already realizing that I was not like the rest of the teens around me. As I watched the show, Xena's courage gave me the courage to stand up and fight for the various injustices I saw around me. I became friends with those that were being bullied and we all stood together. The courage of Xena stayed with me and made me be a better person. To this day. Thank you, Xena, for being a beacon of light in the darkness for so many of us!

Melissa J. Aldrich
Country: United States

Xena changed my life by helping me become a strong independent woman and learn to stand up for myself. I made a lot of wonderful friends over the last few years and attended the last *Xena* convention in Burbank, California. I've become a strong woman and learned to do things on my own. *Xena* helped me get through my divorce and helped me realize that I don't need a man to take care of me. I want to say thank you to Lucy and Renée for giving me the courage to do that. Xena and Gabrielle are very two independent and strong women and could basically do what any man could do. They will always be my heroes.

Amanda
Country: United States

My mom was a huge fan of *Hercules*, and so when *Xena* premiered she was so excited that she kept me home from school to watch it. I adored the badass female character and had a massive crush on Lucy Lawless (still do). We would watch it every day as it came out because it aired right after I got out of school. I adored the show as I got older, so it was always on in my house just because it made me happy (still does). Once I moved out of the house and into my own place, I went through a horrible depression because there was so much happening in my life that was bad. I didn't feel like living anymore, and I just kept thinking, "It's ok; no one will miss me." *Xena* was on in the background, of course, and it was the Academy of Performing Bards episode. Xena said, "Even if I had an army around me, I'd still notice you were missing." I know it wasn't directed at me, but it stopped me in my tracks and I've never been that bad since.

Lara Vezzani
Country: United States

I was told back in 1995 that there was a villain in *Hercules* that was spun into her own show. I was intrigued about *Xena*. It was actually her horse that made me watch it—I am an avid equestrian. The beautiful palomino Argo caught my eye (along with the warrior) and I was hooked. Xena inspired me to write the nine-book galactic series Kaia Saga based off the Amazon Nation. Without *Xena*, there would not have been a Kaia—in development in 2018. Yes, *Xena* changed my life and I am forever grateful. *(MaryD: You can read Lara's story in Part 7: Chapter 46 - Because of Xena - From Xena To Novels To Films! By Lara Vezzani)*

Gloria (Flabbi)
Country: Italia

I do not remember what was the year that *Xena* came out in Italy. I would have been twelve years old or so. As soon as I started watching I was hooked; I did not want to miss a single episode. I liked it a lot because it had everything I believed in and hoped for, everything I had always missed in my life: true values, love, affection, protection, friendship... I did not feel loved by my parents. I do not know the reason or what I was doing wrong. I was very shy, but if I was attacked I defended myself and I refused to be stepped on. I knew how it felt to get kicked or hurt with words, but not what it was like to receive affection, or a simple hug. I have always missed having a sister or a friend with whom to share things.

What my family taught me was that I should dismiss others, despise my relatives, think only of my own interests, and not listen to anyone. I did not like this; I was not like them. I spent a lot of my time looking for movies where I saw on the screen what I was missing in real life. I watched several television series, but in *Xena* I found what I was looking for.

I felt a bit like Gabrielle when she met Xena: I wanted to go with her, travel and learn new things from a strong person. I needed this too. And I felt like Xena as well: she tries to change and redeem herself for the things she did in the past, and fights to help the weak and the people she loves. I had always felt I did not deserve to love or be loved, as if I had been a bad person in a past life, and that's why I had to pay the consequences by not having friends or anyone who cared about me.

I seemed to have been cursed and I didn't know how to break out of it. I had to redeem myself like Xena, and I became a person devoted to helping others in any way I can. I'm always afraid of making mistakes but I put my heart and soul in everything I do even if nobody cares or if people hurt me.

Xena didn't give up when she was challenged, and I like challenges too. I would fight for the people I love, I would go across the world to reach them if they needed me, and I do not leave anyone behind.

This show has given me courage to not be trampled by others, to defend myself, and to follow my heart.

Everyone tells me I'm strong, because being and looking strong is what I have to do to survive. Those times that I was hurting, I never asked for help. I find it hard to trust others, but having someone close to you, like Xena and Gabrielle do, gives you strength to face life.

They no longer broadcast the series in Italy, but this year, which has been hard for me, I have wanted to watch it again. I searched the internet, and I have watched many episodes on YouTube. I found videos about the conventions and the coffee talks. I did not know all this was out there!

I wanted to find out what Lucy and Renée have done in addition to *Xena*, what other films or shows they've been in, and understand what kind of people they are in real life, outside their characters in the series.

I have found that they are two beautiful people who care about family, friendship, charity, the environment… They are very inspirational.

I did not know about all these Xenite fans and groups existing in many parts of the world, and it's beautiful to see how many people still love the series.

I have always wanted to travel, and this year, I faced my fear of traveling on my own, without understanding or speaking English well, just to meet Renée. And I was fine—it was the best trip ever!

I do not know what my life will be like in the future, but I know I will never stop trying to do good, to follow my heart, and to fight for the greater good.

Jamie Byrne (Jimmy Graham)
Country: Australia

Xena came into my life at the age of seventeen. I was suffering from anxiety and depression, coming to terms with my sexuality, and feeling very alone in the world. I remember when Xena aired for the first time and feeling instantly connected to this amazing character. I connected to her need to change who she was and to become a better person no matter the cost; she had a dark past, she had her flaws, but she wanted to turn that all around and that resonated very deeply with me. She gave me something to believe in and has continued to this day to be my hero and to inspire me to always strive for the greater good. The love and strength of Xena and Gabrielle gave me hope and I never missed and episode.

Seeing Gabrielle evolve season after season was amazing. Xena gave me strength to accept who I was, to come out to the world and embrace who I was as a gay man. The Xena community (Xenites, as we are lovingly known) became and continue to be a family, and I have truly made lifelong friendships from this community. I have also been a collector of memorabilia from the show and continue to collect to this very day. I have been incredibly lucky to have had the opportunity to meet Lucy on three occasions. To be in the presence of someone who means so much to you is a truly beautiful gift.

Lucy and Renée gave us something incredibly special and I will always be truly thankful to both of them and all the amazing cast and crew who gave us this amazing show. It has changed my life forever.

Roxanne Thibault
Country: Canada

The show impacted my life oddly enough in a subtle way. I was sixteen years old and my life was a ball of chaos when I first saw a Xena episode. I was angry at the world as to why I wasn't like other girls and not accepted. Watching Xena and Gabrielle's friendship slowly evolve into an amazing relationship made me slowly begin to accept myself, and it gave me peace of mind, body, and soul. It showed me that with patience and endurance, anything can be overcome and that we are all searching for truth, acceptance, and forgiveness.

Richard B. Kloosterboer
Country: New Zealand

My mother was a raven-haired beauty and one belt higher than me in Shaolin Kempo. She had a dagger stare that would slice through fools like a hot knife through butter. She was also kind, and animals and children always felt safe with her. Mum passed away in 2016 and I miss her greatly. I have always been attracted to strong women—warrior women who could take on anything despite the odds.

The first episode, "Sins Of The Past," where Xena buries her weapons and armor only to dig them up again while rescuing some villagers, got me hooked. Xena helped me face my fears and my doubts and accept who I am no matter what anybody else says. It also made me a better New Zealander, as I am now prouder to be a kiwi than ever before.

In 1997, Xena stopped being aired on free TV and went to Sky. I did not know that so I missed out on Season 4. During that little break, I wrote my first fan fiction, Xena In Timewarp, which sends a descendant of Xena back in time. Around 1998, I joined the internet and a whole new world opened up to me. I entered the Xenaverse and found that there was an overwhelming Xena following. I checked out Star Trek, Star Wars, and later on Stargate SG1, the X-Files, and all these fandoms were intricately connected to this phenomenon.

I discovered MaryD's AUSXIP by pure chance and found myself to be the on-location go-to guy with local publications. Everything was still sourced the old-fashioned way—the discussions and differing points of view, the bickering, and the overwhelming feminism which I do support, by the way. fan fiction was brought up to a whole new level with virtual scripts and seasons. There were two main groups, and I was with the one that stayed true to the format of the show, whilst the other explored subtext. They had the advantage of a fanfic author, Missy Good, who wrote the episode "Legacy." It was such a privilege to have been close to fans who got the dream job.

I also created MuseVid music videos which allowed me to learn to edit and tell the Xena story in a different way using scenes from the show. But then the copyright cops came and stopped it all. My last MuseVid took almost a decade to be published on-line, but it's there now to be enjoyed.

After the series wrapped in 2001, I had just started working in the security industry. I kept running into people who worked on Xena and Hercules and was told of all the locations, and during this time, I acquired some unique props from the show. Around 2012, I sold a large proportion of my prop collection to a private collector in America. We have an understanding that any other props he finds on-line in New Zealand, we will buy.

My interest fizzled out a bit due to other commitments in life, but during my work as a security guard I have had a few confrontations, and then I would think, "What would Xena do?" And this gave me courage to stand firm against aggressors. On-line, I tackle cyberbullies head-on too. As soon as these thoughtless provocateurs speak their vitriol, I ask them, "Why the hate?" Bullies do not like being confronted.

As both my parents have passed, I have moved to the Waikato region, and I have reconnected with Xenites from the past and we still all watch our favorite episodes. Mine is "Been there, done that," which is one of many phrases from the show that I use in conversation.

Xena is your ultimate imaginary friend who has always got your back. People come and go, but Xena is forever.

Tash Karoly
Country: United States

I originally watched the show as a kid but revisited it in my early 20s. Rewatching began to direct my path in new and wonderful ways. For much of my childhood, I was abused, and the first people I told were Xenites who I had met on the Xena On-line Community. They believed me and accepted me, even when my own family didn't. My soulmate was among that group of friends and we've now been together over seven years and have a four-year-old together. *Xena* has always been there for me, even when my trauma had me at my lowest. *Xena* has impacted my life in so many ways I don't know where or who I'd be without this show. Some people might say it's just a show, but to people like me, it was literally the difference between life and death. Xena was my hero and she changed my world for the better.

Krislene Hancock
Country: United States

Wow, what an opportunity. I was raised by a single mother; we were a total of eight children. Two of my brothers died in a swimming pool accident and my parents blamed each other. They divorced back in the 60s, when women didn't raise children on their own. This left my mother very angry and she hurt us more than she should have. I stood up to her at thirteen years old; I got beat but she never hit me again. I came out of the closet in 1986. I held a lot of anger inside for a lot of years. When *Xena* came on I loved the relationship between Xena and Gabrielle. My little sister and I were very tight and I protected her from our mother. I finally started to forgive my mother. It was slow, but she finally saw me as her daughter. She died nine years ago and I miss her. Thank you, *Xena*.

Meg Arrow
Country: United States

I started watching *XWP* during the first season. I was amazed. I come from a very abusive family and childhood. Who knew women could be so empowered? Strong? Beautiful?

I grew up in such a broken home that food was not readily available. Beatings were regular. I had no peace. But Xena … She filled a void in my dark life. She was something I could look up to. I knew I was hooked. I knew I could one day become like her. The years dragged on. Eventually, *XWP* left TV. I cried, but I didn't forget. Her theme song still fills my mind. Through the years, it has given me strength. If I'm depressed, the show lifts me up. When I go to sleep, I still play that song in my mind. If I'm in a scary situation, I play that theme song in my mind and ask, WWXD?

Xena saved my life. It gave me courage. It changed my life.

I'm here today because *XWP* gave me enough strength to escape a bad situation in my life. More than once. Battle on forever!

Hayriye Makas Uygun
Country: Turkey

Dreams Do Come True

As I watched my mother's funeral in tears, I could feel a part of my heart being buried with her in the ground. Her unexpected death had broken my heart into a thousand pieces. She was a vulnerable woman, and I always tried to comfort her, but now I was completely out of power. And I felt lonely. All I wanted to do was cry and scream, but my employees and my kids were looking at me. My 80-year-old aunt, who had lost her sister, was leaning against me. Well, who was I to lean on?

Suddenly I felt a warm voice inside me that I hadn't heard in a long time. Then a strong hand on my shoulder. She said, "I am here for you." I hadn't heard Xena's voice in a long time because I was now a strong, grown woman and not a helpless little girl anymore.

That was the hardest year of my life. I became ill, and it was Xena episodes that kept me company in my hospital room. When my friends told Lucy Lawless that a single word from her would make a difference, she sent a message: "Kia Kaha! You will come through this and live a wonderful, long, and joyful life. Wishing you the best!" That night I let the warrior princess comfort me again, just like I had done in my teenage years.

My father was over-conservative. He was financially wealthy and a firm believer in old traditions. Women in our house had no rights. For my dad, girls couldn't go to school, talk to boys, or have a job. No guests ever came home. My father never thought that girls could be as smart and successful as men.

I spent my days at home, usually in a dream world of my own. One day, I saw Xena on TV. She could fight against men, she wasn't afraid, and she saved girls like me and changed their lives. I admired her and wished I had someone like her in my life, so I created her as an imaginary friend.

I often heard her voice in my mind saying that I, like her, had many skills. I realized she was right. I liked drawing, and I could sing, and dance, and act. I could even write stories.

I told my father that I wanted to go to school and study art, but he thought art is immoral and would never let me pursue that dream. I once applied for a college admission exam and he used his power to have my application cancelled.

For years, Xena inspired me and helped me fight against my father's tyranny. Eventually, I married my husband, who was the first man to make me feel really special, and I had two children.

I was no longer afraid of the world. I studied preschool teaching and child development at university. I later studied public administration. I opened a kindergarten school and taught my students to be warriors, to fight for what they believed in, to be kind to the elderly and to take care of animals and trees. All lessons I had learned from Xena.

I decided to start acting, which is my biggest passion, after I got my life on track. I applied for a position with a theater company. My skills were appreciated and I got the lead role in my first play. I was then elected to the board of directors of the theatre company. I started writing plays about solidarity among women. I collaborated with women's associations and wanted to publish my plays in my own language and donate half of the profits to women who are victims of violence. In memory of my mother. I've had small roles in some movies and series. Xena has been my inspiration in this area as well.

When I was a child, my birthday wish was to meet Lucy Lawless one day. Her activism for children, for minorities, for a better world had greatly increased my respect for her. She was a warrior princess in the real world and I was ready to do what I could to support her.

I spoke to MaryD about wanting to meet Lucy. She is the owner of AUSXIP, where I had been following Xena news since I was young. She was absolutely kind-hearted and never let me lose hope. "You never know what's going to happen," she said. Then I found out in April 2016 that there was a comic con where Lucy Lawless would appear. If I attended, I could have my picture taken with her, get her autograph, and even have the opportunity to have lunch with her after her panel. I took my daughter with me. She knew how precious Lucy was to me and I wanted to show her the importance of pursuing your dreams.

I screamed Lucy's name when I saw her, and she looked at me and smiled. "Oh, my God, I can't believe you're here!" she said. That was the nicest thing ever! I felt like I had come home. We had dinner together. I also had the opportunity to meet Hudson Leick, who is a wonderfully humble and elegant lady. Lucy talked about her memories of Turkey. One of the women at the table said that the reason Xena became popular in Turkey was the Amazons, because legend has it that the Amazons lived in our country. I disagreed. When Turkish women feel powerless, they take Xena as a feminist role model. Xena is an inspiration for us. Lucy found that interesting. At the end of the night, as she was saying goodbye to everyone, she stood up and kissed my daughter on her head. Then she stopped and came back to me and kissed me on my head as well. She said, "Thank you for coming all this way to see me. I'm proud of you. Take very good care of yourself and your daughter. I wish you a safe travel back to Turkey, darling."

My heart completely melted. I had dreamed of it, but I never thought it'd happen. Then I turned my story into a book. I translated it into English and went to New Zealand and gave it to Lucy Lawless and Rob Tapert when I went there to see Lucy on Pleasuredome. It was nice to see them both. Sometimes I wonder if they knew about it when they were planning or writing Xena, if they knew a story can affect the lives of people in many parts of the world.

I'm very lucky because my guide in life was extraordinary. Xena was the power inside me. 'I still haven't found a show that can replace *Xena*, but there are still so many people who need to discover the power inside them. Especially girls. Thanks, *Xena* team. You are unique.

Aixa R.
Country: United States

When I first saw the show I remember thinking how amazing Xena was. I grew up as an only child in a single-parent home and felt a strong connection with the Xena character. Every time there was a new episode I was ready for the next adventure of Xena and Gabrielle. I didn't understand how large a following there was until I was in high school wishing I could go to the conventions in California. Then, once I moved to California as an adult, I was able to go to my first official *Xena* convention, where I met amazing people who loved the same show I loved. That is probably one of the coolest feelings in the world. Through this show, I've met such kind people from all walks of life who have become my friends and I will always be grateful for that. After all these years, I still find the lessons and the stories told on *Xena: Warrior Princess* to be far ahead of their time and still relevant to this day. She taught me that it's ok to be different, that the family you end up with doesn't have to be blood-related, and that pushing yourself to be a better person every day is okay. This show means the world to me, along with the beautiful people I've become friends with because of it. Thank you!

Patricia O'Leary
Country: United States

I remember watching *Xena* with my family every Saturday. Through my eyes as a teenager, I noticed a pattern. The characters fell, but always got up again. At the time, I was taking horseback riding lessons. Unlike Xena, I wasn't a good rider. My instructor took away my stirrups, saddle, and reins on a regular basis to improve my skills. During my lessons, I'd ride an old horse named Mikey. He was a brown chestnut with a white blaze on his face, and he had the patience of a saint. His gait was as slow as my wit in the saddle and we were perfectly matched. When I wasn't riding, I was navigating the land mines of young adulthood. Each weekend I took respite watching *Xena* with my family, always knowing that, no matter the challenges she and Gabrielle faced, they would get through it together. Heading towards her next adventure, Xena would run alongside Argo while he ran at a canter and with three hops Xena was back in the saddle. In contrast, I'd go off to try to stumble through another week of middle school. What I didn't know at the time was that Xena and Gabrielle were teaching me a valuable lesson. They were teaching me how to fall.

During one of my horseback riding lessons, I walked Mikey into the ring towards the mounting block and pulled myself up into the saddle. First, I placed my boots in the stirrups and then I gathered the reins in my hands. After a few laps around the ring, my instructor told us to trot and I urged Mikey forward squeezing my legs. My legs were so weak he probably barely felt it, but Mikey obliged anyway and off we went. Next, I guided him towards the center of the ring and we jumped a low cavalletti. My instructor then had me bring Mikey to a canter. After a few strides, I felt myself slipping from the saddle and my left boot locked into the stirrup as I fell. I knew that I was about to end up under Mikey's hooves and that I was going be dragged. As I was falling, I made a choice. With my left boot locked in the stirrup, I landed on my right foot and grabbed the horse's mane with my free hand. As Mikey continued to canter, I hopped on my right foot once, twice, and on the third time I pulled myself back into the saddle. "How did you learn to do that?!," my instructor yelled across the ring. "I learned it watching *Xena*," I yelled back over my shoulder as I slowed Mikey from a canter down to a walk. In life, you can't always stop yourself from falling off the proverbial horse. However, you can choose how to fall and how to get up again. *Xena* taught me that.

Ladykimp
Country: United States

My first time watching *Xena: Warrior Princess* was when I had just moved into my parents' dark, cold downstairs apartment. I was forty-two years old, single, and had a brand new baby. I had been forced out of my large, comfortable home by my baby's father, who had become my stalker. I tried to remove myself from him hoping that 'out-of-sight meant out-of-mind'... but no such luck! He had, up to that point, not shown any interest in our son but had only been interested in cruelly punishing me for leaving him.

I watched the first few episodes of this action-adventure TV show to take my mind off of the trauma I was experiencing. This type of action genre television program had never appealed to me before, but I needed something to escape into and watching the first few episodes captured me in a way no other TV show had ever done before!

Becoming involved in the fantasy world of Xena and Gabrielle helped me relax and broke the pattern of fearful thoughts that had dominated my previous year.

Gradually, the storyline evolved and I fell in love with these two fictional women. The fierce protective emotions of Xena toward Gabrielle gave me hope... could I foster those deep emotions toward myself? Could I be brave like Xena and face down the man who was constantly harassing me? And could I eventually find a way to keep myself and my son safe?

When my adversary finally tracked me down to my parents' home, I remember standing up for myself for the very first time ever. The look on his face was priceless when he realized I was changing into my own version of a warrior princess! I was calm like Xena in the face of a callous person whose sole purpose was to hurt me, and I stood my ground and let the spirit of a strong warrior woman speak up for me. I refused to listen to his verbal arrows attacking me and got off a volley of measured verbal punches of my own instead. When he quickly left, I knew then what the series *Xena: Warrior Princess* really meant to me...I wanted to cry with relief! Xena was my sacred role model and her mental/emotional strength was to be trusted.

The years passed by after that impactful showdown, and soon my son was watching Xena and Gabrielle on television with me. We strained at her and Gabrielle's tight jams, we laughed at Joxer's antics, we booed at Ares, and I could see that my son thought Autolycus was a cool character. We never missed an episode. Today he is twenty-five years old and we still watch the boxed DVD sets together and it brings back nothing but good memories for us both.

I later bought the Broken Chakram prop from It's A Wrap, the company that sold the show's memorabilia after *Xena: Warrior Princess* went off the air, just so I could have a tangible piece of the show to hold in my hands. I knew the series had to eventually end but I was very reluctant to let it go.

This physical reminder of Xena's courage in the face of danger, pain, and adversity, as well as the protective love for her partner Gabrielle, will be passed down to my son when I am no longer here. I hope he will look at it, handle the polished metal chakram pieces and remember the close bond we formed while watching that magnificent television series for so many years.

I give my deepest and profound thanks to Lucy Lawless and Renée O'Connor for their inspired playing of two beautiful and strong women characters on the best television action series of all time. I will never forget them.

Leeanne Fisher
Country: Australia

I was thirteen when Xena came onto Australian screens. I saw her in Hercules first and then she got her own show. Xena and Gabrielle changed my teenage life. I came out as gay at eighteen. The bond and love Xena and Gabrielle had was incredible. Now, at thirty-six, I bought it to watch it again and my connection with Xena is stronger than ever. I understand their love better now and how hard things were between them at times. I have been through a lot myself over the last ten years, so I feel heaps more connected with Xena and Gabrielle. I love these characters and also buying lots of Xena stuff to decorate my room.

JS Stephens
Country: United States

I started watching *Xena* when some friends recommended it, and it was love at first sight. Finally, a show that not only had two badass women in the lead, but had major hints that the women were more than friends!

Then came that awful second season episode, "Ulysses." I was stunned at Xena falling for a lackluster man (the actor playing Ulysses was not convincing at all) after she and Gabrielle had kissed in "The Quest."

I was so stunned and angry by the episode that I decided to write a story to explain why Xena fell for such a wimp. I decided that it was Poseidon's Revenge, which became the name of the first fan fiction I ever wrote. I decided to post it somewhere to share my story/theory with other fans. Only one tiny issue—I didn't know HTML.

No problem. At that time, AOL offered free space to members for web pages, so I bought a book on HTML 2, taught myself enough to post the story, and started receiving feedback.

I was hooked.

I kept writing stories and learning more HTML, which led me to a fork in my career. My company had started an internal website and my manager decided that I would start a page with links to useful websites as our department's contribution. This skill, combined with my willingness to learn more about HTML, databases, and other related areas, led to a job offer when my company merged with another company.

I kept writing stories, gradually moving them away from the AOL space to GeoCities, then allowing other *Xena* sites to host my stories. By this time, I had taught myself enough HTML, CSS, and ASP to create search forms for an internal records database, and was also tapped to maintain the website for my local library association.

Life changed again in 2002. My company decided to move my department across state, and my partner at the time and I decided to stay put. My skills with websites and willingness to learn new skills was noticed by another library director, who offered me the job I have to this day.

Writing *Xena*, Uber, and later original fiction helped me get through some difficult times in my life. Writing fiction helped me with mergers (late 1998), the death of my grandmother (1999), my mother's death from ALS (2008), and the end of a nearly twenty-year relationship (2011). The love of *Xena* was also a bond with the woman who walked back into my life in 2011, whom I married in 2016.

Xena and Gabrielle showed me that two very different women could forge a bond of deep love, and gave me the courage to make radical changes in my life. Their willingness to battle the status quo and call out those who do harm has given me the courage to face challenges head-on.

Battle On!

Jacki Wyman
Country: United States

It is difficult to put into words what a show truly means when it has become a part of your very being. It seems silly to some people, but completely understood by others without saying a word. *Xena* was a refuge away from the denigration and submission of life. A place to remind me of my strength and courage when the world wanted less from me. A place that expressed my passion, pain, anger, frustration, fight, and love. A place that was mine, where no one else could belittle my desire. A home for all of us that expected more from life than the feminine expectations that were handed down. *Xena* was more than a show; it was our potential and expectations others dismissed.

Amanda E
Country: US

Girls can't be heroes. They're weaker than boys and the only purpose they serve is as damsels in distress to be rescued from situations they cannot escape on their own. This is what I had always been led to believe when I was young—that is, until I discovered *Xena* at eight years old. My young mind was quickly enthralled by the idea of women who were not only as capable as men, but who could handily defeat them (and look good while doing it). I became addicted and lived vicariously through the adventures I saw play out on my television screen, but I did not realize at the time how much these were shaping my impressionable mind.

Ten years later, when I decided that I wanted to become a United States Naval Officer, I was not prepared for the sexist comments I would receive. That the military was not a place for women. That maybe I'd be happier doing something that wasn't so "butch." It sounds funny, but the lessons I learned so early on from watching *Xena* helped me to rise above it. I am now a Lieutenant Commander in the Navy and I love my job and I love leading sailors.

I'm also happily married to a beautiful woman who is way too good for me and we have a beautiful son together. You see, I didn't know it at the time, but one of the things that initially drew me to Xena was her relationship with Gabrielle. I didn't understand it then, but seeing these two women together who were so clearly in love was the first time that I understood that the type of relationship that they had was even a possibility. Just being exposed to that at such a young age opened doors for me to learn to accept myself for who I am later on in life, and I will be forever grateful.

I will never be able to adequately express how much the story of Xena unexpectedly shaped so many aspects of my life, but I can say that I would not be the person that I am without her.

Gayle McDonald
Country: Australia

As a young woman, I was always muscular and strong and it made me feel like an outcast because other girls were so thin and barbie like. When Xena came along, her hair matching mine, her body muscular, I truly was able to embrace my strength. Years later, I adopted the attitude of an Amazon and it got me through four broken relationships and six kids, and it gave me the strength to beat a brain hemorrhage while pregnant.

Through Xenites I made the best friends and even had the opportunity to meet Lucy Lawless and Karl Urban, something I didn't even believe possible. I took the six-hour flight alone, I went to the comic con alone, and within seconds of being in line I made a new friend who was also a Xenite and then met up with another friend I had met on Twitter through our mutual love for *Xena*. I no longer felt alone in my fan world.

I felt like I could do anything if I just told myself to channel my inner Xena. I even have a pair of Nike ID shoes that say INNER XENA. It is fair to say that *Xena* changed my life, my attitude, and my strength, and I will forever be thankful to the cast and creators for making such an amazing show.

Having such a love for the show also created some future geeks as my daughter, who is one of six of my kids, loves all things geek too so she understands my passion and embraces it with me. My collection of the series has also kept me company on so many levels. While I was awake at nights feeding my twins, it was watching *Xena* that kept me sane and kept me awake to cope with those long and torturous nights. It was *Xena* that kept me company when my ex walked out and broke my heart. It was *Xena* that kept me in a good mood while I was sewing for days on end too.

There are so many times and ways that I owe my sanity to *Xena*. That show is a religion to me. The sheer joy it brings me is better than any drug and I will be forever grateful.

Paully Adams
Country: United States

This show has and still means the world to me. I grew up in NYC in a very Christian, conservative and black household. Being LGBTQA+ was not an option. I was not out to myself, much less others.

I could not deny the love between Xena and Gabrielle, nor could I deny the way I felt when a certain bard appeared on the screen. I finally came out to myself and accepted who I was because of this show. I came out to others because of this show. I learned what true love, soulmates and friendship was about, and I strived to be a true friend to others.

I learned that I have gifts and stories to tell. My first published poem, 'Her Eyes,' was inspired by a photo of Xena and Gabrielle smiling at each other. I have written stories, and because of the show, I have made tons of friends who also like to read and write fan fiction. Now I write for three different fandoms.

Most of all, I learned to be myself. I like to think I am a Xena (who is still looking for her Gabrielle), but honestly, I am more like Joxer. And that is okay too, for he played a special role as well.

This show has given me so much. Yes, there have been times I have become angry at the show and even stopped watching, but the love eventually won and suck me back in.

So thank you, LL, ROC, TR and TPTB for a show that inspired some many of us to be more... More honest, more loving, more creative and braver than we thought we could be!

Julie Hupp
Country: USA

The Courage To Ask

At last... what a performance! Lucy had come to the Midwest and I finally had the opportunity to hear her sing. Joe Lo Duca's band had been smokin' hot, and Lucy had just given us a performance to remember.

I stood waiting for the crowd to dissipate. I'd decided to eat in Greektown instead of catching the bus back. I had also hoped, of course, to have the chance to speak with Lucy. But if I was tired... I knew she had to be exhausted.

Time passed and still no Lucy. If she needed to call it a day, perhaps the best gift I could give her was not to ask for anything. I gathered my bag in anticipation of leaving, but before I turned away I sensed a quiet presence at the edge of the room.

She entered silently, dressed in jeans and chaps, head down in humility and perhaps a bit of that tiredness.

Then she looked up.

I can only describe the look in her eyes as magical... so full of love... like the look when Xena gave Gabrielle the scroll on the cliff in "Many Happy Returns."

Earlier, Lucy had shared with us her own moving spiritual experience, one that had set her firmly on the path of helping others. I'd had a similar epiphany from watching *Xena*, and I decided to tell her. To tell not as a "laundry list" about me, but as a wish to convey to her the depth of my thanks for the show and this community. It's a thanks I believe that is shared by many of us for similar reasons.

The few remaining fans began to drift over to her, asking for autographs and pictures, speaking a word or two.

No, I did not want an autograph. What I wanted was the courage to talk to Lucy face-to-face without most of those barriers between "celebrity" and "fan." I simply wanted her to hear the words of my heart, and in that sacred moment an autograph would've felt... profane.

As other fans began to drift back, Lucy turned in my direction. Though I thought I would be nervous meeting her, I found, to my surprise, a deep stillness inside of me.

It was strange.

It was like talking to my sister, or an old friend I hadn't seen in a while. I held out my arms and she came forward, and suddenly all else in the room seemed to stop...

"Hi, Lucy, I need to speak with you," I said.

Lucy hugged me. "Sure, sweetie, tell me your story..."

I paused for a moment to gather myself. "I just wanted you to know... that when I was a child I was sexually molested for sixteen years, from the time I was an infant... and I kept that inside and didn't even tell my therapist for twenty years until I saw *Xena*..." Lucy's face, only a foot from mine, scrunched up in pain as she shook her head. There were tears in her eyes, but her deep gaze never left mine for an instant.

"It wasn't until I saw a scene in *Xena* that..." I started to say when Lucy interrupted in a soft voice... "What scene, tell me, I really want to know...?"

"Um, it was 'Callisto...' the campfire scene..."

"Yeah, yeah, I know that one... go on..." Lucy nodded, her face still close.

"Well, I don't usually cry... like most survivors; it just gets pressed down inside of me... so I don't usually cry, but I started crying..." I said. "I remember saying to myself that this is silly, crying over a TV show... I mean..." I pointed to my MSU Spartan t-shirt, which is Rob's alma mater and my home town.

"I mean, I started watching *Xena* because of Rob... I tried to watch everything he did... so I was crying over a silly TV show, and then a voice inside of me said: 'No, that is YOU, and you've got to own that!' So I told my therapist for the first time in twenty years, and that's when my healing finally began. I just wanted to thank you for the part you played in that... and I try to pay it forward every chance I get..."

Lucy started to speak. "It's good that you talked about it; you've got to keep talking about it. Thank you... thank YOU for that, but..."

"And thank YOU for everything that you do... and thank God for all the wonderful and supportive women in this community..." I interrupted, gesturing to where some fans were sitting to our right.

Lucy smiled. "Yeah, aren't they GREAT? Really, just remarkable!"

"And I hope someday to be able to work as a Court Appointed Victims Advocate..." I continued.

Then Lucy's face suddenly inclined close to mine, her voice a high, angry whisper... "Unfortunately, there's such a need for that... Oh, God, it's everywhere... It's BLOODY EVERYWHERE!!" Her eyes brimmed with tears as she struggled to compose herself.

"Yes... it is..." I replied softly.

"Oh, I've just got to hug you, baby..." She whispered as she pulled me close in a tight hug.

"Thank you..." I whispered back.

Then Lucy stepped back, her tears suddenly replaced with a look of determination... "The most important thing you can do is you've got to stand up in your life... Stand up in YOUR life!" She said, pointing at me. "I know it's hard but you CAN do it! You can DO it! You've got to stand up in YOUR life, because standing up in YOUR life IS... of greatest benefit... to others."

We looked at each other as a moment of silent understanding passed between us... and then... we quietly embraced.

Lucy would return often to give me hugs between the photos and autographs she gave so generously. I watched for a while. As we all drifted our separate ways, I was left with a deep sense of peace that is difficult to convey.

How can I sum up this experience when its meaning and depth are so beyond the ability of words to express? I would like to think that she gained as much meaning for what she does as I have gained from her doing it.

One thing I AM sure of beyond doubt is that I have been immeasurably blessed. Blessed not once but twice... and I will carry the great goodness and healing of her words forward into my life.

A continuation of the healing which started thirteen years ago.

Sometimes you really do get what your heart has the courage to ask for. Thank you, Lucy. Thank you, Xena. Wishing blessings on your house, forever, and with love.

Maria Aquino
Country: United States

Xena has helped me identify and define myself. The impact the show has made in my life was unmatched! I was eight years old when *Xena: Warrior Princess* was introduced in my life, so I pretty much grew up with Xena and Gabrielle as role models. They showed me that it's okay to be tough and kind at the same time, which I can honestly say helped shape the person I am today. I never found any other show more enjoyable to watch! The characters were full of light and soul regardless of all the battles they endured. It is definitely something I will never forget and can call home—as the saying goes, "Home is where the heart is." Thank you, *Xena*, for changing my life!!

Jen Tucker
Country: USA

Twenty-five years ago, little did I know that a warrior princess and her bard would change my world. I had turned into *Xena* since day one. I was in college and had recently escaped a very homophobic and oppressive household. Watching *Xena*, I felt like I too was on a journey of self-discovery. What I was seeing between Xena and Gabrielle was something I had never seen on television. I wasn't even sure I was seeing it. I joined the Xena Net forum and quickly discovered I wasn't the only one seeing something.

It became a ritual to run to the school library after an episode aired and to hop onto the Net forum to discuss and dissect the episode. There were artists and writers sharing art and fanfic and it felt like family, all of us sharing our love for this show. I was struggling to accept my sexuality and depression was really pulling me down, but *Xena* was that bright spot that kept me going. An acquaintance had introduced me to IRC (Internet Relay Chat) to try and help with my depression. He asked me if I was a fan of anything. I replied with *Xena*. I met someone named Tigger. This was way before social media existed and everyone on-line was pretty much anonymous. You had no way of knowing their gender or age. It could be dangerous but it was also freeing. No preconceptions. Tigger begged me to come back the next night to meet his friend, so I did.

On Sept. 3, 1996, I logged into channel Xena and met Turayis. The name didn't click, plus it was spelled differently. I thought Turayis was a boy. We hit it off immediately. I went home that night completely enamored. Turayis and I shared everything we loved via chat. We discussed the episodes and both agreed there was something going on between the bard and the warrior princess. This went on for two weeks and then Tigger jumped in and teasingly warned, "Watch out, sis. She's a lesbian." I froze, staring at that little type-box blinking on the screen. There it was. That thing I was afraid to admit. I decided I was tired of not being who I really was. What would Xena do? I wanted to be brave, like the warrior princess, so I replied, "So what?" She said, "Really?" It was the first step.

We continued to meet up in channel Xena every second we could. Over the next three months, we got to know each other on an incredibly deep level. I was convinced I had met my soulmate. Turns out I was right. Less than a year later, she flew 3,000 miles to come live with me. Twenty-three years later, we're still together. She went on to get a bachelor's degree in anthropology with a minor in history inspired by the "Xena Scrolls," and then a master's in professional writing inspired by the bard herself.

Xena gave me the courage to be myself and understand that you sometimes have to make your own family. There's a chakram atop our Solstice tree every year. We spent our 15th Anniversary at our first ever *Xena* con and came back every year after. We still have friends from that con we keep in touch with regularly. *Xena* is the reason we found each other. I can't imagine my life without Xena and her Battling Bard. Happy 25th, Xenites.

Luciana Rodrigues da Silva Sampaio
Country: Brazil

I'm a big fan of the *Xena* series. I remember watching in my childhood, after getting home from school. I played and wanted to be Xena, while my sister was Gabrielle. Years passed and I watched the series again as an adult. I still loved it, so much so that I ordered a sword and chakram, bought the doll, and my pet cat is named Xena. I made several friends through the show and we have a fan club called Xena Brazil. I am an administrator, together with my sister Caly, who is still a fan, and a friend of ours named Kesita, who was very important in the setup of the group. I am a Xenite today, tomorrow, and forever.

John Terrell Jacobs
Country: United States

Xena was impressive from the first time I ever saw her on *Hercules*. The way she had her own army and was such a formidable villain for Hercules was so (for lack of a better word) cool! Then it was super exciting to find out this character had her own show on the way. While I thought Xena was the epitome of cool, I never would've thought the character would resonate with me and inspire me throughout my life. My first dog was even named Xena. By the end of the first season and ever since, Xena has been my hero.

It is the philosophy of the warrior princess that got me through good and bad times. From being bullied when I moved to a new school to my first job, to losing my mother, Xena has always been there to cheer me up and keep me optimistic... Things will get better either on their own or through my hard work. Xena does not back down in the face of adversity and neither will I. As one of her allies told her in my favorite line any of them ever said to her (in maybe her only time of doubting herself), "You have always succeeded where others have failed. Why should this day be any different?" In all honesty, I do say this to myself in times of doubt, "You succeed where others fail. Don't be nervous; keep going." Xena succeeds where others fail. She calculates everything she does and I have emulated that since I first started watching the warrior princess when I was nine.

One of my most important memories of *Xena: Warrior Princess* comes from my first *XWP* convention in New York City. I couldn't wait to meet Hudson Leick, and last minute my family member taking me canceled. Knowing how much *Xena* meant to me, my mother took me to NYC herself so that I would not miss Hudson, who plays Callisto, my favorite character next to Xena. This is special because my mother, who has since passed, was afflicted with multiple sclerosis and her mobility at the time was extremely limited. Barely being able to stand on her own as well as other problems, my mother made it through train transfers, city blocks, and made her way through the hotel limping most of the way followed by sitting in one spot most of the day as she would have difficulty walking.

I did not beg her to do this; it's just how important *Xena* was not only to me but to our family. She made it through the day and it was something I will always remember. My mother was a strong woman who reminded me of Xena in her own way. This is one of my fondest memories of her, and I have *Xena* to thank for it. Like Xena, she was courageous when facing adversity, and through her and Xena I was taught to do the same.

In the twenty-five years since *Xena* began, I have lost my mother to MS, my best friend passed away, and the family separated to different areas. We all once shared *Xena* as something to do together as a family. I feel it's the influence of *Xena* that instilled hope that I can always work to get to where I need to be, I can craft my own future, and support the greater good whenever the need arises. I will finish with another *Xena* quote: "We make our own fate." If we have regrets from our past we cannot change them. We can only work to make the future better. I'm grateful *Xena: Warrior Princess* became part of my life. I appreciate the philosophy and values of the show. It changed me for the better. BATTLE ON, XENA!

Carolyn Kroll
Country: United States

Xena started out for me as a television show that hooked me in by episode three. It gave me an hourly escape when life took a rough turn. Ultimately, *Xena* turned into one of the most profound influences on my life and it means so much to me to this day. The show was about friendship and family, and that's part of what I got from it. I have made friends from all over, many of whom I consider family, two of whom I still speak to almost daily. I went to fan conventions without knowing anyone, leaping outside of my comfort zone and gaining an appreciation for adventure and experiences. Lucy and Renée are (and played) such strong women and some of that bled into who I am as well.

Above all, I witnessed the difference that a group of people can make when they come together in a positive way, spreading love and kindness. The good that the *Xena* fandom has done in the name of the show and of the cast members is truly amazing. I am so fortunate to be a part of the *Xena* fandom, which is still running strong after twenty-five years! I never would have thought it possible for a show, a crew, and a cast to mean so much to me and to impact my life the way *Xena* has. Thank you!

1996

- Brenda Bridgers
- Leyla Eide
- Lis Venedin
- Sylvie Schmidlova
- Dave Mifsud
- Gabe
- Carmela Scalzo
- Lynne Krause
- Macgrrl
- Luci Dreamer
- Claudia Haase

Brenda Bridgers
Country: United States

This show and its characters helped me come into my own. As a woman, there were really very few strong female characters on television at that time. Even Wonder Woman, who up until Xena was my favorite, was made to wear support hose! That kind of took away from her overall toughness in my book. Xena followed her own moral compass and didn't bow down to the rules as laid down by men. She didn't let them run her down. I've been working for the railroad (REALLY) for eighteen years now, and I am the only woman that works out of my terminal. The men want me to do things their way, but I think to myself, WWXD? and follow that philosophy. They seem to have learned over the years that I will not be run over and that things run smoother if they listen to me. Thank you, Xena!

Leyla Eide
Country: Norway

In Norway, Xena didn't start airing until 1996. I was fifteen and we didn't have a TV at home, so I would watch at my best friend's place. I am pretty sure the first episode I saw was "Callisto," and straight away I was drawn like a magnet to the character of Xena and the woman who played her. I had realized the previous year that I was gay, and it didn't take me many episodes to pick up on the subtext. This was the first lesbian couple I had ever seen on TV, and I was hooked. I grew up in the countryside, and having been a victim of relentless bullying since 3rd grade, coming out whilst living there was never on the cards for me (why add fuel to the fire?) So Xena became my refuge, the promise of a world where women loving women was accepted. It helped me cement within myself that 'yes, being gay is not just ok; it's wonderful.'

Despite the bullying, I have always walked to the beat of my own drum, not letting what others think or say about me influence who I am. Being true to yourself when you don't fit the mold is not easy, and particularly not when you're a teen. Thus, I would draw on Xena's strength to be who she wanted to be, despite others' preconceived conceptions of her. The show also fostered in me the courage to stand up for the underdog—I became a very vocal support to the other bullying victims at my school. Whilst it certainly didn't make life easier for me, it resulted in them being targeted less. *Xena: Warrior Princess* fueled my innate passion for social justice and equity, and continues to do so to this day.

Lis Venedin
Country: Russia

In 1996, I was six years old. I wasn't allowed to watch TV after 8 o'clock and had to go to bed, but once, when nobody was at home, I switched on the TV and saw HER. I can't say that I understood much, but it was love at first sight. At the beginning, we played on the playground: I was Xena and could save everybody. I made a Xena costume from my pants. Two or three years later, I began watching all the episodes from the start. I got posters, photos, and everything that was possible to collect at that time in Russia during Perestroika. When I was a teenager, my passion continued and *Xena* helped me to cope with all my troubles. The strongest effect she had on me was two years ago, after my disease. I couldn't walk and went through awful pain. I knew Xena managed with all the difficulties (her legs were broken and she limped, afterwards she could recover and defeat all her enemies). My thoughts gave me power, so I trained hard through the pain, and I knew I could do it, because she could. I haven't recovered fully yet, but I believe in my power; she inspired me. Now, twenty-three years have passed and I live with my true friend, my Gabrielle, my love and my passion. As you can see, *Xena* helped me to find my destiny and accept my choices.

Sylvie Schmidlova
Country: Germany

When *Xena* was released in Germany I was seventeen. When I was about fourteen, I had started to doubt myself because of my feelings and thoughts about girls. I felt lost and alone in the world; at that time, not many people talked about being gay and, if they did, they just quoted the usual stereotypes: short haircut, butch, hates men, etc. I'll never forget the Sunday when I first saw *Xena* on TV. I was obsessed right from the beginning and the show every Sunday was my highlight of the whole week.

I was mocked (nowadays it'd be a case of bullying) at school for as long as I can remember. I was different—I was taller than the others, I hadn't been born in Germany, I never liked dresses, I was a tomboy... All those things where reasons to be bullied. My mom did her best, and she always told me that differences are good and make the world colorful. I believed her but I always thought she had to say those things because I am her daughter.

When I was in my teens, I started having different feelings: I started looking at girls/women differently, and the world around me had no clue. My sister was the daughter every mother could wish for—beautiful, with long blond hair, always wearing girly clothes, and she had a boyfriend whom she brought home. Well, I never did those things. My mom and my sister grew closer together and I drifted away till I was isolated and felt alone and unloved. I really thought I wasn't lovable, and I tried to convince myself my feelings were wrong. Back then, many people thought that being gay was a sickness and it could be cured. I tried to be normal; I kissed boys and bought girlie stuff, but it never felt right inside and it wasn't me deep down; it never was.

Then that Sunday came and I saw *Xena* on TV. I thought, "Wow, this woman is badass; she does things no woman does, and Gabrielle wants to be her friend because Xena is so full of strength and courage, plus Xena does what she wants and what she thinks is right." I saw myself kinda like Gabrielle. I kept watching episodes and got lost in my own world, which wasn't an empty hole anymore, but a world where two women could be who they really were and love who they loved. With every season, it became more obvious to me that this was more than friendship. Yes, it was subtle, but I could see it so clearly, especially after season 3. I got often asked, "Why are you watching this show? There are better things to do outside instead of sitting in front of the TV." My answer was, "Nah, I like watching this series because it's about the history of ancient Greece." Well, I know it wasn't 100% true, but nobody cared and I was afraid that if I told the truth, everything would change and people would look differently at me. Also, I wanted to keep my little perfect *Xena* world for myself so I could still hide in it. I grew with every episode and season a bit more as I learned lots of lessons from Xena and Gabrielle: people are equal no matter how they look, what they do or whom they love, women are strong and don't need to stand in anyone's shadow, everyone deserves second chances, you create your own life without depending on a male, and the most valuable lesson for me was that I need to trust myself, love myself, and have the courage to be myself.

I remember I was watching "Amphipolis Under Siege" and my sister came in and watched a little with me. She said that I was too old to keep watching a show about two gay women, and I said that you are never too old for *Xena* and that I am gay too! She looked at me in shock but I continued to watch the show. I didn't care anymore what people would think of me. I guess that was the start of my new life, or better said, the start of my real life. I was twenty-two years old.

After rewatching the show recently, I realized what a great impact it had on my whole life. I am so grateful to everyone involved—actors, producers, etc. *Xena* changed my world for the very best. I am especially thankful to Lucy Lawless and Renée O'Connor; without them, *Xena* wouldn't be what it is. Thank you, Ausxip, for letting us share our stories in this anniversary book.

Dave Mifsud
Country: Australia

It was 1996 and I saw a trailer for *Xena: Warrior Princess* coming soon to Channel 10 in Australia. The moment I saw it I fell in love and was so excited. The first episode, "Sins Of The Past," just blew my mind. I couldn't believe there was this amazing warrior woman in live action on my screen fighting for the greater good. Xena was strong and brave, and the fight scenes were so amazing. The mythology in the show was another thing which drew me to it, as I have loved mythology since I was a child.

A couple months after "Sins Of The Past" first aired, I went to high school and started to get bullied. I continued to watch *Xena*, but about three years later, when I couldn't take the bullying anymore, I left school. I had tried counselling, tried talking to the teachers and changing classes, but nothing helped; I even tried medication. I had to leave for my health. I suffered anxiety attacks, panic attacks, depression and eventually I didn't even want to leave the house or answer the phone. I couldn't sleep and would always run into my parents' room in the middle of the night and wake them up because of my panic attacks. My parents tried and were supportive, but nothing helped me. Leaving school was helpful because I didn't have to worry about going there every day to face the bullies, but what helped even more was *Xena*.

I was home alone for hours on end while my brother was at school and my parents were at work. That's when I completely fell into the Xenaverse. I would watch the latest episodes of *Xena* over and over, on repeat. If I wasn't watching *Xena*, I would be reading The Official Magazines, random magazine articles, comics, and anything I could get my hands on. I then got the internet, and wow, all the *Xena* news and information and images I found… I fell deeper into the Xenaverse.

Watching Xena being brave, standing up to the evil warlords, helped me day by day to fight my anxiety. Seeing Xena face her demons was so empowering. The more I fell in love with the show, the more I started to break out from my shell. I started to answer the home phone, I started to make phone calls, and slowly I started to leave the house without my mum, because if I did go out it was always if mum was with me.

Years went on and I just became more enthralled into the Xenaverse. I was chatting on the message boards and I even started my own little *Xena* fan group called Dave's Xena Fever. I had hundreds of fans sending me snail mail asking what latest *Xena* news there was and we would even share stories. I used to reply to every single letter, which kept me very busy. It all started when I wrote to the Official Xena Magazine published by Titan and they published two separate letters in two different issues.

The one which started my little fan club was when I wrote about sending a petition to Channel 10 for axing *Xena* during season 4. That's when the fans all started to write to me and I created Dave's Xena Fever. I started to leave the house more on my own to walk to the post box a few blocks away to send my letters. I started making more phone calls and even spoke to people at channel 10 about axing *Xena*.

These were all massive steps for me and it was all thanks to Lucy Lawless and her amazing acting in *Xena*.

I learned more about Lucy as well and admired her as a separate person from Xena. Lucy is so caring, so loving, so passionate about what she believes in, and that was a person I wanted to look up to.

Xena and Lucy both accepted and fought for gay rights and that helped me when I was trying to figure out my own sexuality. Having someone say it's ok and accepting you and fighting for your rights was a blessing for me and for many other people, I'm sure.

I came out to my family and friends and yes, some people were shocked, but I kept watching *Xena* and learned to be comfortable in my own skin.

Xena taught me that. Both Xena and Gabrielle taught me to accept who I am, they taught me to speak up for what I believe in and they taught me to love unconditionally.

This show is more than just an action show; it's a show that teaches you love. It can be love between best friends, love between soul mates or love between a same sex couple. It's such a strong and positive message, and more people in this day and age should take note.

Xena has helped me more than I could ever explain, and after being a part of this special fandom for nearly twenty-four years now, I still love it and will always be thankful for this show.

I love the action, I love the mythology, and I especially love the messages of love, acceptance, and forgiveness.

Lucy Lawless and Renée O'Connor are so inspiring and we need more people like them in the world.

I will always be thankful for this amazing and special show. It helped me through some of the darkest times of my life. When my depression was out of control *Xena* saved me. So thank you, *Xena*!

Gabe
Country: Peru

I started watching Xena as a junior in high school, through open TV. Right before college, I reported on the only Spanish speaking Xena webpage how the episodes were not aired in order. I submitted the report. My future ex read it and contacted me to let me know that I could see the episodes trough cable TV at the same time as they were aired in the US. I came out. My ex was an archaeologist and she showed me the love for this discipline. Now I am getting my Ph.D. in the US and married to my best friend, another archaeologist. I also met one of my closest friends through the series twenty years ago in Peru, and we are still very close.

Carmela Scalzo
Country: United States

October 21, 1996. I remember the night my friend Sandi called me on the landline yelling, "TURN ON CHANNEL 5! LESBIAN VAMPIRES!" I turned on my black and white TV (with the pliers I kept nearby) and adjusted the antenna, which were assisted by aluminum foil for reception. Sandi wasn't kidding. I beheld the head-shaved leather-wearing lesbian vampires circling a petite blonde-ish haired woman and stared, mouth agape, in joyous bewilderment at the screen.

This was my first formal introduction to Xena: Warrior Princess. I had heard it was a spin-off of Hercules, that show where sweaty Ancient Greeks seemed to have discovered hair mousse and push-up bras.

Apparently, though, Xena didn't get the memo, because when I first saw her I thought, "Oh, my god, her hair is SO FLAT! And bangs? Okay, fine, but look at that breastplate! I'm in!" I got used to the hair and became hooked on the fights, the leather, the campfire chats and side glances. Joined the fan club, bought the toys, wore the t-shirts, and went to Xena cons. Not since Diana Prince and Jaime Sommers had I been so enthralled with a show and a character. Every week my Saturday night was reserved for Xena and Gabrielle (and Joxer, whom I adore!)

At that point in my life, I spent my workdays as a courier, loudly practicing my war cry as my delivery van flew up and down the hills of Beverly and West Hollywood. Every now and then, I'd have to stop at the home or office of someone whose name I'd recognize from the show's credits, which was always a thrill. Once I had a delivery for Xena's music supervising editor, Phillip Tallman, at his studio in West L.A. I'm pretty sure he was working on "Kindred Spirits" at the time. He seemed pleased and pretty cool about my enthusiasm. I also went to the home of Brad Carpenter, a producer and actor on Hercules, whom I'd recognized after meeting him at an early convention. He was enthusiastic and spoke highly of Lucy, telling me they'd just had dinner together the week before. I resisted the urge to ask if I could touch him.

In 1997, I had a layover in Auckland, where a new friend took me for a quick ride to Piha Beach, and also innocently offered to ring up Lucy on the phone. Before I could object, he was telling his former employer, "Mr. Ryan, I have a friend visiting from America who is a fan of your daughter and I was wondering if Lucy was home?" She wasn't, but even if she had been, I'm sure she must have been frantically shaking her head at her dad to say, "No, no, no!" Looking back, and realizing I'd been in New Zealand during the years Xena was in production, I wish I'd taken the time to see more.

My first Hercules & Xena convention (back when they were combined) was in Pasadena in 1998, then to the cons in 1999 and 2001. I usually went alone. It was amazing. I wish it had occurred to me to get to know some of the other fans who were there. In the early days before high-priced photo ops, you could just walk up to the table, take a photo of an actor, and get their autograph. Eventually, as the show was coming to an end, the conventions became entirely devoted to Xena, and the convention audience had fewer children and more people who were like me.

In the years since the show ended, priorities changed and I lost track of what was happening in the fandom. I missed a LOT! But in early 2006, a night of insomnia combined with some internet surfing found me looking at Sharon Delaney's website, only to discover that Renée was going to be nearby at a benefit for a local charity. Bleary-eyed, I made my way to a fire station and met Renée, a friend who kept me informed of the local Xena-related goings-on.

Lucy was doing a lot of TV at that point, and in fall of 2006 I was thrilled to be in the studio audience for the live finale of the singing competition show, CELEBRITY DUETS. Lucy, all legs and huge hair flying all around her, sang the hell out of "Tell Mama." I was sat next to Rob and Daisy and a row in front of Sharon Delaney, and the whole joyous hour was completely invigorating. My hands were clapped raw. I still have a piece of confetti Lucy stepped on while signing autographs after the show right before she was pulled away.

Following Lucy's formal TV singing debut, I found my way back to the Burbank convention in 2007. It was magical. Meeting Jay Laga'aia (in an elevator and doing my best to be respectful, and NOT throw my arms around him), Steven Sears, and Brittney Powell were my highlights. But the #1 experience the entire weekend was Lucy's first concert at the Roxy in West Hollywood. She was phenomenal, and the room went into a frenzy when Renée joined her to dance on stage. It was there that I met some friends in line, one sparkly young Aussie in particular who would ultimately point my life in a happy new direction. If it hadn't been for that meeting with Jessica I might not be writing this today.

Even though I'd attended the 2008 convention, I had not yet gotten to know anyone else in the Xenite community, and I was lonely, uninspired, uninvolved. And when my life was upended by the end of my marriage in 2013, I received a random message from Jessica. We didn't know each other and hadn't exchanged messages before, even though we were both on Facebook. She excitedly mentioned that the 2014 Burbank convention was approaching and my enthusiasm was easily sparked. I went all out: photo ops, hotel room, plans to get to know everyone in the lobby! By the end of that sleepless weekend in Burbank I had made about 100 new friends!

It's no wonder that the fandom is one of the most loyal I've ever experienced. Thirteen years after the show went off the air, I again found myself among them at one of the final Xena cons in Burbank (the MOTHER of all cons) and discovered how amazing a group of people can be, whether they be fans or people who made the show. It's been one of the great privileges of my life to be involved with the people that went from throwing Xena con softball games and after-parties to hosting full blown weekend retreats in the mountains just North of Burbank.

Xenite Retreat is Xena con on drugs, power-boosted steroid multiplied by infinity. It is the magical glittery unicorn of all fan events. Lives have been changed there. I repeat: LIVES HAVE BEEN CHANGED THERE. Dreams realized. Lifelong international friendships solidified. Even if you have never seen Xena, a weekend at Xenite Retreat is still going to be the best time of your life.

We are so very fortunate as a fandom. It's always nice for a television show to feature strong characters we admire. But the actors on Xena who bring the characters to life are such extraordinary human beings that it is really something to be proud of! It isn't just that there is not a hint of scandal among those at the top of the cast list (which lately is remarkable when you think about it); it's that in their own lives they exemplify a way to be the best people we can be.

I've said this before: it isn't necessarily the show, or the actors—it's the fandom, the people, that make Xena so special. When Xena came into our lives, it was the philosophy of the show, the story-telling, the way it made girls and women (and me) feel capable, strong, courageous, empowered, visible, valid, valued, invincible... those things FEED the fandom. And it is my admiration and respect for those qualities that are motivation to live up to the things I love about Xena. *Xena: Warrior Princess* has definitely changed my world and made me want to be better.

Lynne Krause
Country: United States

The most wonderful part of the Xenaverse is the authentic engagement with the cast members. I met wonderful friends at the cons. We had no connection except Xena, and that built into a beautiful friendship, especially with my friends Ann and Nancy. Being part of the Xenaverse's greater good inspired me to be a better person and help those in need through charity work. I support a child in Uganda from World Vision because Lucy highlighted it at a con. Submitting videos to the cons reenergized my creative side and helped raise money for the James W. Ellis, Jr. Scholarship. Reading the fan fiction through AUSXIP, engaging with the Xenaverse bards and later supporting published authors is part of our shared experience. The Xenaverse is about more than just a television show; it's a community that is there for each other. The title of my video shown at the 10th Anniversary con was We Go On, and we do.

Macgrrl
Country: Scotland

When Xena finally aired in the UK, I was a closeted woman who hid her relationship from everyone. Watching Xena and the TV partnership that she and Gabrielle had started a change in me. Then I found the on-line fan community and that took my change to another level.

Apart from having to wait sometime hours for AOL to dial up and connect, the internet opened up a world of fan fiction, friendships, and eye opening to another world around female relationships and how to express yourself.

Websites such as Ausxip and writers such as Missy Good linked fans and allowed us to talk across continents. I also was lucky enough to attend conventions and met many members of the cast and made more fan friends.

When Xena ended it took me a long time to find another show that helped me move on in life—I'm not even sure if another show did that.

However, I am forever grateful for Xena, for Lucy, for Renée and for all the writers, fans, convention organizers and others.

This show really did change my world!

Luci Dreamer
Country: United States

Xena began to air during a seminal time for me. I had recently come out to my family, moved cities to be with my first girlfriend, and was just setting out to see what I wanted in the world.

My girlfriend at that time was already a big fan and introduced me to the show, and at first glance, I thought it to be too absurd and campy. But she convinced me to watch, and soon I was intrigued by the relationship between Xena and her intrepid sidekick Gabrielle. As the seasons unfolded, I found myself captivated by their love story, for it certainly was a love story, even if it was told and shown largely in subtext. To see two strong female characters so openly devoted to each other was a revelation and will live long in the hearts and minds of lesbians my age who yearned for representation and found an entire community in Xenites that carries on to this very day.

I'll always credit this show too for inspiring me to write. I'm pretty sure the modern-day lesbian romance novel owes quite a bit to the *Xena* fanfic community, as it inspired a generation of lesbian would-be writers to put their work out there, continuing the story of these timeless characters, and honing their craft along the way.

And even twenty-five years later, I'm still writing. I've moved through different fandoms, never feeling confident to submit my work for publication though, until someone who also got their start in *Xena* fanfic told me I should try. So, as of right now, I'm awaiting news to see if a dream, starting with my very first Uber-Xena story post, will become a reality. Even if it doesn't, I'll always think back on the show with great fondness. I know it had a part in shaping me as a writer, a mother, a wife, and a member of the LGBTQA+ community who will always appreciate the greater good of positive representation.

Claudia Haase
Country: Canada

There is something magical about Xena. Xena's character has helped me in times in my life when I needed her the most. I could call on the inner warrior to come out to carry me forward when I didn't think I had the strength to. One particular moment in my life was when I was first introduced to Xena back in 1996. I couldn't wait to see what this was all about. I remember it was the episode when Callisto first came on the scene and my Oma (who raised me) walked past and said, "Ach, Claudia, what are you watching?!?! It's so violent!" I replied, "Oma, it's Xena and its amazing!!!" In 1998 my Oma was in hospital and wasn't doing well. I came for a visit and she sat up in bed with such excitement and said, "Claudia, come quick—Xena is on!!!" It so happened it was the same episode that I first saw back in 1996. Xena for my Oma was a connection to me. It meant so much to me that my Oma had that because she was at the end of her life. My dear friend that introduced me to Xena sent me a card when Oma died and wrote, "A warrior princess once said, 'Remember that the dead can hear our thoughts.'" Reading that was so healing and helped me through one of the most difficult times in my life. Thank you, Xena!

1997

- Misty Marshall
- Santiago Harker
- Emma Wilson (Girl4Music)
- Regina Larson
- Angelina
- Bongo Bear

Misty Marshall
Country: United States

Xena was my gateway to sci-fi and women's history in the mid-90s when I watched the show as a 7th grader. I was a huge fan of STAR WARS too and so I would pretend that Xena and Gabrielle teamed up with Luke Skywalker's daughter to fight evil. She was the first female superhero that I admired, and to this day I quote the lessons of the show to friends and acquaintances. I was also fascinated with the portrayal of the Amazons: they were treated as a nation with laws and culture and so eventually, I studied Amazonian folklore and historical warrior women like Boudicca, Zenobia, and Artemisia of Caria. I also became a fan of Wonder Woman thanks to the show and I'm still waiting for that Wonder Woman/ Xena crossover comic.

Santiago Harker
Country: Colombia

The first time I watched Xena was in 1997, when I was three years old. My dad and I were at home. We both were watching TV and suddenly, in the local channel, Xena's episode "Chariots of War" came on the TV screen. He explained a little bit about how this strong and brave woman was fighting against injustice. Not understanding much about what he was telling me, many years later, I realized there were many reasons why this show became one of the most beloved parts of my life.

The first reason is that I have met the most incredible people who I now consider my global family. They embraced me since the first convention I attended by myself and made me feel loved, even though they didn't know me then. Many years later, they understood how emotional and meaningful was for me to meet Lucy Lawless and they did everything they could to make this moment special.

Secondly, during my childhood, I had to overcome difficulties with my health due to asthma and spine problems. I suffered from depression because I couldn't have a regular physical development like the other kids, and as consequence, I was bullied at school. However, Xena became my daily inspiration and pushed me to break out from that cycle of sadness and to have my mind focused on what I really wanted: to give and receive love unconditionally.

Thirdly, once I grew up, I made a deeper research through the internet about the show. I found where it was filmed and where the main actresses where from. Instead of continuing watching the episodes in Spanish on the VHS tapes my dad had recorded for me, I focused on my birthday's gift— the DVDs, so I could learn as much English as I could to meet Lucy. It took me about sixteen years to be ready and be able to travel by myself to a new country, not knowing anyone and with the only purpose of telling her that my biggest inspiration and dream was to talk to her and explain how the show has encouraged me all my life.

I want to say to all the Xenites out there who have made my life better and my heart smile—a big THANK YOU. Specially to my dear Jackie and dear Wanda, for their huge kindness and for always being willing to help me, and to Ann, whose beautiful spirit will always live with us.

Emma Wilson (Girl4Music)
Country: United Kingdom

The main reason why I love *Xena: Warrior Princess* has less to do with the action scenes and more to do with the characters' dialogue. There isn't a TV show (that I've seen) with such strong and substantial themes and messages integrated (to the depth this show has) within it today or even in the last decade. It's why I love it beyond anything I've ever seen and will never get tired of watching it for as long as I live.

The characters and writing in *Xena* keep me mindful and balanced in situations in my life where I want to be anything but. Have you ever known a TV show or movie that has set up the foundation and is the backbone behind your entire philosophy of life? Is it so important to you that you refer to it every time you feel yourself slipping off the edge of the Earth? Has it helped you discover your truest and highest self when all surrounding you has always pulled you away from that? *Xena* can teach some extremely important and valuable life lessons and will instill into you strong moral principles and values of what is right and wrong that I think is imperative to be aware of and understand going through reality's fluctuations. Particularly those of redemption, vengeance, love, forgiveness, and balance, which are the most reiterated themes throughout the course of the whole show that we can really take in and live by.

When you've watched it for as long as I have, you are shaped by it as a person, as a human. The lessons and philosophies it can teach you are the building blocks and constant reminders of who I am and what I care about in this world. What is most important to me in myself and in my reality. This show matters so much to me that I will never consider any other above it in terms of impact and influence. It's timeless to me! For me personally, it's the greatest show in history. I'm thankful for it being in my life and for teaching me how, and encouraging me, to live my own. It will forever be a part of me.

Twenty years is a long time to stick to a TV show for. For me, watching it and supporting it for two whole decades just exemplifies my loyalty to it, and I am so loyal to it because it's shown, taught, and given me so much that I am so very grateful for. It's taught me how to handle the most difficult of situations and circumstances in my life. It's taught me that there is always a reason for them happening when they do, whether I can see it or not in the moment. It's taught me that it's all an evolutionary process that only brings us to a higher consciousness. The character, Xena, taught me to embrace my darkness along with my light. She taught me that fighting for the 'Greater Good' is always the right thing to do no matter what. Her little blonde companion, Gabrielle, taught me that when in a dire situation, doing something is always better than doing nothing. She also taught me what it really means to put others before yourself.

The entire show has taught and shown me so much more than that. The meanings are endless, and 9,000 characters is just not enough to explain why it is so integral to my life. It's not just my favorite show of all-time. It's the reason I am who I am today. I would be a different person if I had never discovered it, never watched it, never grown up with it. I wouldn't be ME without it! I would have become someone else. Throughout childhood to adulthood, it has made me a person of sincerity and integrity. I'll never be able to fully explain or justify how much it means to me. It's literally and honestly my absolute EVERYTHING!

Happy 25th anniversary, *Xena: Warrior Princess*. You have changed the lives of so many people, and you will continue to teach and give your many themes and messages to generations of people to come. This is my tribute to you. It's been an incredible ride with you at my side and I'm not getting off any time soon. Thank you!

Regina Larson
Country: United States

I started watching *Xena* with my sister in 1997 and it was something we loved to do. She was my sister and my best friend. In 2011, she died very unexpectedly, and for a long time I could no longer watch the show because it was too painful. In the past few years though, my special needs daughter, who has autism, cranial surgery, type 1 diabetes, and seizures, became fascinated with the show and loves it so much. We both do and now once again I find healing, joy, comedy, and inspiration in it. Thank you for such an amazing show and the message it brings to women!

Angelina
Country: United States

The way that the show has changed my life is likely more subtle than others. I did not meet my soulmate at a *Xena* convention nor have I become a published bard out of writing fan fiction based off the show. No, my story is simple. I grew up watching *Xena* and *Hercules* with my mom. As a young girl, I was always more interested in watching *Xena*, and it wasn't until I got older that I realized why. *Xena: Warrior Princess* was the first show that I watched that had two strong female leads.

Xena and Gabrielle were the heroes of their own stories and saved themselves and each other countless times. I saw that I didn't just have to be a damsel in distress, but I could be the hero of my own story. As I was growing up, I lost track of the show only to rediscover it again as an adult with my girlfriend. We quickly fell down the *Xena* fandom rabbit hole with zero regrets. This whole new world was opened up to us where we were going to conventions, meeting the cast, and meeting other members of this beautiful fandom.

We call ourselves Xenites and make references that only other Xenites would understand. Xena and Gabrielle are household names and subtext is often discussed. The show has become a big part of our lives and rewatches happen often. The same episodes still make us laugh while others still make us cry. The ending still hurts deeply and the musical episodes still make us sing along. It's not just a favorite TV show; it's a part of us the way that Xena is a part of Gabrielle and will continue to be so.

Bongo Bear
Country: USA

I was a late comer to the fandom. I first became aware of the warrior princess and the bard back in early 1997. My participation in the fandom grew from passive to active when I started writing alternative fan fiction (AltFic). My personal story is really about the stories. This little hobby resulted in initially shaping the on-line fandom as it is today. Let's see.

There was a list of clichés in AltFic that made its way into a few Xenites' college dissertations and papers. Della Street (Towards the Sunset), Bat Morda (Is There a Doctor on the Dig), and I (The Hitchhiker) were the first bards to write what became broadly known as Uber fanfic. I also wrote in October 1999 an AltFic (Newsflash!) featuring cloned incarnations of our gals before "Send in the Clones" aired in April 2001. Stories written after the episode aired have since been dubbed a sub-category of Uber called Clone Fic. Uber in general eventually lit off a resurgence of lesbian romance that has blossomed into original commercial fiction over the last few decades.

Back in 2000, I noted in a Whoosh article, "Romantic Altfic is an adult fairy tale through which the bard expresses her own beliefs and ideals about loving relationships. One of these ideals is that lesbian lovers are as unremarkable as any heterosexual couple. This is an unspoken premise of almost all Altfic, romantic or not, and it is the significant differentiator from traditional heterosexual romance." Altfic bards who share this once radical premise were the driving force that morphed the collision of a rising technology — the Internet — with a fantasy TV series into an experience that transformed people's lives and in turn, transformed the TV series. In the twenty-five years hence, the transformation of people's lives has not diminished.

I left the fandom after 2001 and pulled my stories off the web when certain events set different priorities. After so many years, I rejoined the fandom in 2019 as an Amazon Elder and the stories are back along with some podcasts. Looking back fondly, I am honored to be a part of this Xenaverse story again.

1998

- Anthony De Bellis
- Ellixer
- Heather Van Gorder
- Sarah McKeithen
- Suzanne Flowers
- Virginia and Lourdes aka TwinXenas

Anthony De Bellis
Country: Italy

Xena Warrior Princess saved me. This is no exaggeration. She forged me to be the man I am today, she taught many lessons to me, and I'll always be grateful to this show. Xena is my HERO! I started watching *Xena* when it first aired in Italy, in January 1998. I was seven years old. I was a very shy kid, the one always hiding in a corner, afraid to speak up for himself, unable to defend himself from the bullies. Right after school, an Italian channel started to broadcast this new TV-show set in Ancient Greece. I was immediately fascinated by the lead character, a strong woman who was trying to redeem herself from her past, a woman who knew what she wanted and was determined to get exactly that. I loved the pilot and each day I waited to go back home so that I could watch the new episode. Xena was everything that I wasn't and everything that I always wanted to be—strong, independent, clever.

I started to feel the power I had in me. If I wanted something, I had to try and get it; if someone bullied me, I had to answer and not stay silent in my little corner. Nobody had to have power over my life except me.

One morning, on my way to school, I bought a notebook which featured an image of Xena on the cover—an infamous promo pic of her first appearance in *Hercules*. That was my most treasured possession. I showed that notebook to everyone with pride and when it ran out of sheets, I removed the cover with the picture and I hung it by my bed. Each morning when I woke up it was the first thing I saw: it reminded me to be strong, to look for the power I wanted in myself.

I was seven years old but I was very determined. I started to accept myself for who I was. I didn't need to play football if I didn't want to; I didn't have to hide my passions because someone might not understand them.

I was obsessed with the show. I carved many plastic chakrams, I made a sword out of a ruler and I convinced my classmates to play *Xena* all the time. Of course, I was Xena every single time.

I kept the notebook cover for many years, as a reminder: I was who I was thanks to that strong woman.

In 2014, when I was twenty-four, I had the immense privilege to meet Lucy Lawless in Paris at a *Xena* con. When I was in line to take my pic with her and Renée, my legs started to shake. She was my all-time hero, she had saved me, and she was there, right in front of me. As I approached them, I told them I was feeling uncomfortable because they were my childhood heroes and I didn't know what to do or how to handle the moment. Lucy greeted me with the biggest smile and she asked my where I was from. When I told her I was from Italy she started to speak in Italian, telling me that I was too thin and that I needed to eat more pasta. Then she looked at me and she said, "Darling, you're perfect the way you are." That's when I melted.

I wrote a letter to Lucy to tell her my story, to thank her, because it was because of her that I am who I am. The convention was packed, and there was no time to give her my letter on the first day. I was saddened, standing next to the stairs, knowing that I wouldn't be able to tell my hero my story, and why she and the show meant so much to me. Two minutes later, Lucy and her PA walked past by me. I was truly shocked! I asked Lucy for permission to give her my letter, and with the biggest smile she answered, "Give it to Sharon, darling." And that's what I did.

In that letter I wrote everything that you just read, and the moment I gave it to Lucy's PA, I thought that she would never read it, but still I was happy that I had tried. The following day, at the convention, I was in line to take my pic with Lucy and Renée. When my turn came, I approached them explaining how I wanted my pic taken, me hugging Xena while Gabby stepped aside with an angry face. Lucy grabbed me, hugged me, and said, "Ok, let's do this! Ren, this is Anthony, and you're going to be jealous of us."

I didn't pay attention to the fact that she had just called me by my name. How could she know my name? That's easy; she had read my letter!!!

During the autographs she told me indeed that she had read it, and that she was so touched by it. She told me that *Xena* was important to her because it touched/changed the lives of so many. I was so emotional and I just told her that she was my hero and that I was so grateful to her for what she had done for me, even if she didn't know. It's weird to say to a total stranger, "You're my hero; thank you for saving my life," but that's exactly what I told her. She looked at me and she said, "I may be your hero, but certainly you are mine," and she wrote that on the picture I had chosen for her autograph.

That's when I died. My hero told me I was her hero because of what I had been through.

This is my story, this is how *Xena Warrior Princess* saved me and shaped me, and this is why twenty-five years later it's still my fav TV-show. I'll always be grateful to the whole cast and crew, to everyone who worked on and for the show. *Xena* is and will always be such an important part of me! Thank you so much for allowing us to tell our stories.

Ellixer
Country: United States

I didn't start watching *Xena* until I was in high school. I was late to many a soccer game on Saturdays because I wanted to see the whole episode. When the last episode aired, I skipped soccer all together. I sat in front of my TV in my uniform and cleats and I just couldn't understand why the story had to end. Seeing this friendship and the relationship where no man was needed to rescue them opened something inside. This feeling you could see between them… I wanted that. I began to realize I was a lesbian. At this time I had been writing some fan fiction for other fandoms, but now I began writing fan fiction for *Xena* and I haven't stopped. The show drove me to write night and day for years and, as a result, I have grown into my own writing style. I am now hoping to write and publish an original work. All thanks to *Xena* showing me I can be strong for myself. And I have been through a lot of bad times in my life. I am very thankful to Lucy Lawless and Renée O'Connor for their portrayal of such strong women.

Heather Van Gorder
Country: United States

I had always heard about how generous Xenites were, but never experienced it until 2019. I have two stories that don't necessarily talk about the show itself, but about the many friends I have made because of this show.

Back in 2015, I had my best friend from middle school, Jaime Breazeal, find me again on Facebook. We found out that we lived only five minutes from each other. Over these last four years we have become even closer than we were back in middle school. Jaime has four children, and her oldest daughter, Adriann, has a condition where the fluid in her brain doesn't drain properly. This is called hydrocephalus. Adriann has what is called a shunt that starts in her brain and runs into her stomach, and it helps drain the fluid in her brain.

Every once in a while this shunt malfunctions, and Adriann needs to have surgery on her brain to replace the shunt. Between August 2018 and June of 2019, Adriann ended up needing around eleven surgeries. Usually, she will have the surgery and be able to go home the following day, but in April of 2019 she was in the hospital for a week and a half and needed five surgeries. Jaime was not working at this point, and her husband Phil had to take off multiple days to watch the other children. Missing work and making the trip to the hospital daily with the other children got kind of spendy, and this is where the story of Xenites come in. I made a GoFundMe page, so Jaime and Phil didn't need to worry about bills while taking care of Adriann. Xenites were so generous in their donations. They not only did not have to worry about the bills, but Jaime had enough money left over to purchase her security card, so she could start working with me as a security officer.

My second story also takes place in 2019. My father also had to have major surgery. In May and then again in November, my father had two very minor strokes. When he had his second stroke, the doctors had done an angioplasty on him, where they discovered that his carotid artery on his left side was 95% blocked. They also found his right carotid artery was 65% blocked. They had to cut out his artery, and they replaced it with a cow vein. My father and I are so close. I was such a nervous wreck when he had to have his surgery. I could not handle the fact that I could lose my father during this surgery, and the love and support that I got from of the Xenites were amazing.

I always knew that Xenites were an amazing group of people, and I am truly blessed to have become a part of this amazing family and tribe. I finally feel like I belong to something. And I wouldn't have if this show had never existed.

I just want to say a huge thank you to Rob Tapert for making this amazing show, Steven Sears for writing a beautiful love story, MaryD for making this book, and all the Xenites out there. I love you all.

Sarah McKeithen
Country: USA

At twelve years old I was becoming a fearful, hateful person. I envision the first time I saw *Xena* as a fork in the road. It changed the course of my life. A couple of years prior, another event set me on a different course. It was a random Monday in a stereotypical small town. I walked into school, and no one would talk to me. For hours I was left wondering why lifelong friends had literally turned their backs on me. At lunch, another kid finally told me: a rumor had spread that I was gay.

It is no coincidence that on May 11, 1998, I flipped channels while *Xena* was airing. I hit "record" on my VCR with no idea why—I was just drawn to it. I watched that half-episode over and over the entire week. I adored everything about the show, but especially how I felt watching: at peace.

I delighted in discovering the on-line Xenaverse, until I realized people thought Xena and Gabrielle were (gasp!) lovers. I agonized over that. I was so lonely and dying for what Xena and Gabrielle had–love and belonging. It felt like people tainted it with the thing that made my life impossible.

I told the Xenaverse what I thought. Imagine interacting with a kid like that today. Everyday people slam anonymous persons for their vile beliefs. You know what the 1998 Xenaverse did? They didn't tell me off or shun me. They told me they were gay, or had gay friends, and they showed me I was wrong.

I was not prepared for the people I hated to be kinder and more understanding than anyone I had ever been exposed to. I found love and belonging. My diaries chronicle the changes in me. It's a beautiful thing to witness. My mind opened and my heart no longer held hate. Thank God for that, considering the fact that I am SO GAY!!!

All these years later, I still watch and participate in fandom. How could I not? I am SO grateful, and I am absolutely at peace.

Suzanne Flowers
Country: USA

Intervals of Ten
I was a thirty-five-year-old musician and reading specialist working in a tough school in November of 1998 when I contracted the flu from a student the week before Thanksgiving. Blood tests identified the strain. The doctor advised me to rest at home until school resumed in January.

I sensed something was additionally wrong, but rationalized that I simply needed more time to sufficiently recover. However, my eyes would pop open around 1:15 every morning as if a volcano had erupted and awakened me. My body simply persisted in aching terribly to the very bone, my joints felt swollen but weren't, and the feverishness enveloping me never wanted to let up.

Unable to return to sleep, I began trudging to the guest bedroom I had turned into a cozy TV enclave. Thus, the wee hours of the morning twenty years ago marked the first time that the warrior princess and bard would keep me company when I was knocked down. Determined to get back to work, I did my best to cope with chronic pain in much the same way Xena forged on even while encountering reminders of her past deeds on a daily basis. It would be a year and a half before a rheumatologist diagnosed me with the fibromyalgia that had altered my good health so severely.

Exactly ten years later found me in another doctor's office receiving the news that I needed biopsies in both breasts due to the results of my most recent mammogram. So at the age of forty-five, I was scheduled for surgery right after Thanksgiving, followed by radiation treatments to begin in January. The surgeon readied his scalpel, I sharpened my sword of faith, and we went to medical war. And when radiation was scheduled to obliterate any remaining cancer cells, I found myself echoing Xena's powerfully blunt answer to her beleaguered troops when they asked what they would do about the Horde: "We're gonna kill'em all!"

Yet another ten year interval was marked this past spring at age fifty-five, as I was knocked down by the development of rheumatoid arthritis. Between the ages of forty-five and fifty-five, I had served as the caregiver for my elderly parents while continuing as a teacher and musician, but now I reminded myself more of Xena as she lay in a village barn suffering from the effects of Callisto's poisonous dart. Still, my faithful rheumatologist knew I did not intend to be sidelined for long if at all possible, so he began throwing his formidable skills into helping me overcome this newest health aggravation.

In response to this latest ten-year milestone, I resolved to change course and experience new avenues of adventure. I made the major decision of retiring from teaching and focusing on my music. During this time of transition, I also find myself once again coming full circle regarding the show, as these debilitating circumstances have afforded me the time to watch *Xena* again. This has given me pause to recognize the grit I've acquired over the years. I have some lines on my face now and plenty of scars in other places, but the starkly wonderful truth is that there's very little that can scare me anymore. Whatever the intervals of time may bring, I will battle on.

Virginia and Lourdes aka TwinXenas
Country: USA

Xena: Warrior Princess has definitely changed our lives for the better. We have never fallen in love with a TV show like we did with *Xena: Warrior Princess*.

The year was 1998 when stumbling on an episode one day and getting hooked gave our lives purpose. Through countless hours on the net, day and night, we immersed ourselves in finding, learning, and getting information about the show and its actors and actresses. After visiting *Xena* websites one after the other, joining mailing list after mailing list, our knowledge and curiosity were gradually satisfied. We first discovered Tom's Xena Page, but it was MaryD's AUSXIP page which caught our undivided attention and it became our go-to page for all-things *Xena*. Thank you, MaryD!

For being extremely shy, we were content to watch the show in our little own world, but there was something about the show that made us come out of our shells. So in 1999, we began attending *Xena* conventions and started meeting new friends. Up to "The Absolute Last Official *Xena* Convention: The Bitter Suite Finale - The 20th Anniversary Celebration," which was held in 2015, we were able to attend thirteen *Xena* conventions. Zeta, Deborah Abbott, Arlene Calandria, and Musetta have remained our close friends to this day. We also realized how we loved the costumes the talented Xenites wore at the *Xena* costume contests. Worldwidedeb Debbie (Deborah Abbott), in our opinions, is the most talented Xenite who created her own costumes. She has been our inspiration and our favorite Xena lookalike. She and Xena gave us the courage to dress up and so we started making our own costumes (some were store bought and we altered them) and entering the costume contests. We won once (3rd place), but we had fun every time we joined the costume contest, so we won either way! It was nice to be on stage making the audience laugh, getting applause, and having our pictures taken. Our enjoyment of dressing up has continued every Halloween.

Through a mutual friend, who is an inspiration herself, our family had an amazing experience—a healing experience under the passionate, dedicated, sincere and genuine healer, Musetta Vander, the actress who played Ilainus. We first heard of Medical Qigong when Musetta graced us with her presence at the 2010 Xena convention held in Los Angeles. As a former star of the show, Musetta updated the fans with her life after Xena. Little did we know then that months later, we would be under her care.

Seeing the stars of the show on stage and up close during autograph signing and photo ops was very memorable and surreal.

The show meant different and important things to many people. It affected people from around the world and from all walks of life, beliefs, religion, and sexual orientation. The show embraced everyone. We have never seen such a strong group of fans (Lucy Lawless herself described the fans as rabid) who helped each other, who helped others in need, who generously and endlessly gave to charities, etc. We were among strong women and we felt safe.

To sum it up, borrowing Xena's words: *Xena* is "the best thing that ever happened to us. It gave our lives meaning and joy. It will be a part of us forever." Although the show has already ended, *Xena* is very much a part of our everyday lives. There will always be a place for *Xena* in our lives, now and forever.

Never in our wildest dreams would we experience what we have with the things we did and the friends we made when we fell in love with a TV show. What an adventure! What a ride! What a great *Xena* journey!

1999

- Linda Kathleen E O'Connell
- C. E. Gray

Linda Kathleen E O'Connell
Country: Ireland

For me, *Xena* means life. I would have never discovered the real me without the show's examples which made me question myself, want to see me, and not just go through life living by rules and just fitting in.

Now I am different—an indigo. I embrace it and challenge people who want me to change. I like my individuality, weirdness to some, as it is who I am from my soul.

Xena taught me to fight to be an individual, to embrace my gifts, to not be a copy of others if that is not who I am inside, how history is important, to love ourselves even if others do not.

Do not pretend to be who you are not just to make others feel more comfortable, as it can scar you emotionally. Stand up for your beliefs. You need darkness and light to be whole. Bad things happen but we learn from them if we don't let them ruin us. Help others and love the world. See the world for what it is and how we could help it, even in a small way.

When we are down, sometimes we need help to get back up, so we should ask for help. If it is not given, know that even if it's hard, we still need to get up. It may take longer but can be done with belief (mine in God). Our life is ours.

We must trust our instincts, and if we find something that feels wrong or people try to make us do something wrong, we must have the courage to walk away from it even if it takes huge courage and any number of tries to achieve it.

Look out for your friends and do good. Try; trying is always a positive step. Most importantly, stand up for your beliefs. Stand up for yourself. If you fall, get back up.

Bad things happen to teach us lessons like these: love our friends, do not take life for granted or those we love, people, animals, or gifts we have, as you never know when they might go. Also, it reinforces the knowledge that women are strong and should always be equal to men. Women should not be downtrodden or not allowed in positions of power.

We are important, not second class citizens.

Forgiveness is key; without forgiving ourselves and others if we err, evil takes over. We betray our higher self, our teachers (who could be even a passing acquaintance in life with a glimmer of helpful knowledge or a word), but most of all we betray who we are inside.

Thanks, *Xena*, for teaching me so much and bringing the true me out from my hidden depths, and for helping me see the world from my own perspective, not just the ones I am told to see it from.

C. E. Gray
Country: United States

I stumbled across reruns of the first season my sophomore year of high school—specifically, "Hooves and Harlots." I did karate growing up, and practiced with the bo for one year, so seeing this strong female lead work with a staff immediately struck me. I was hooked. I got caught up over the summer and started watching the fourth season as it aired.

I'd always been interested in writing, but with *Xena*, I began writing fan fiction. General at first, but then I realized I was seeing myself in the relationship I saw on screen. I wrote Alt and then Uber and I loved it.

In 2002, I met someone on-line and we shared an interest in *Xena*, as well as reading and writing fan fiction. We became fast friends, and best friends. We began dating in 2006 and were married in 2012.

I never got the opportunity to go to a convention, but my wife and I have gone to every Xenite Retreat and don't plan to miss one. It's a family I never expected to find.

Xena helped me discover myself, my love, my tribe, and my happiness. Their courage became my courage. I am both warrior and bard. And I cannot thank this show and the cast and crew enough.

2000
- Martin Duggan
- Zazu80
- Emanoelle Soares dos Santos

Martin Duggan
Country: UK

I only caught two new seasons of *Xena* (5 and 6) and fell in love with the popular TV series. As a gay man, I always find strong female characters an inspiration to me, and Xena was no different. Xena taught me to stand up for myself and to be who I want to be. The right people will stay with you and be with you for who you are, so do good and be good. Lucy Lawless, thank you for bringing Xena to life and for entertaining me. That goes for all the cast, writers, and crew; thank you for making *Xena: Warrior Princess* the TV magic it was. Battle On!

Zazu80
Country: Germany

When I read about this book and that fans could submit stories, my first thought was, "Wow, I really want to add to that, but is my/our story interesting enough to read?" I still don't know; it could be boring for strangers. But to me, it is an important story of the friendships I made because of this show.

In the early 2000s, I got unemployed and had too much time on my hands, so I got into some TV shows to get my mind off it all. I discovered *XWP* on German TV. The show had something very unique about it, so I googled a bit and found my first German Xena board, which was run by Warrior Spirit at the time. People over there linked to YouTube videos, where I could see scenes from the show, and then I realized I had to watch the show in English. So I ordered the first DVD box and started watching the series. From this moment on, I watched every single episode and talked about them on-line and also joined a chatroom where I met some cool people I spent a lot of nights in chat with, talking about everything and nothing. But it also gave me some kind of strength to start over again, applying for new jobs, meeting new people, traveling etc.

When the old forums were not as busy as they had been before (and I think because she had time back then as well), Ellen (mono) from the chatroom created another German Xena board—the Xena24. I think it was fate that I found out very quickly that she was living only about thirty minutes away from me. We started meeting up and worked on the articles together. We also met Andy (Indy) on-line while we were all filling the forums with several thousand articles, posts, and stuff about *Xena, Hercules,* Greek gods (submitted by our friend Hera), and so much more. Today, I proudly call these people some of my best friends. Mono, Indy, and I became close as a little family back in the beginning days of the forums while we travelled to conventions around Europe, met amazing people, and arranged meetups and themed parties for birthdays, where we all dressed up. A few years later, we re-opened the forums as Teamtapert.de and also included the other shows produced by Rob Tapert and Sam Raimi. We also got our friend Steven (Xanderharris82) into writing stuff for the board and he will not stop until he's listed every old fantasy TV show he can find to the list. This forum is on-line today and will always be my safe place on-line to read and write stuff and watch pictures we took traveling and meeting up. It holds so many memories and posts, including silly stuff and games in one thread, and really deep, interesting conversations in others.

I always felt that the show was special because I think that it attracted people who believed in all the good things the series is about—love, friendship, justice, doing the right thing, fighting evil. I am still impressed how much money for charity Xenites have raised worldwide. I personally appreciated the show more and more as I've kept meeting cast, crew and awesome fans in this fandom. You can tell they are all so passionate about it, it is always a very special atmosphere and the "Fighting for the greater good" thing isn't just a phrase for most of them. The majority is really giving, inclusive, and open minded. In our little forums alone, we had people of all ages, genders, backgrounds, and cultures who bonded over the same interests and became friends and pals over time. I cannot list everyone here, but I am thankful for every single one of them.

It also was one of the first shows that attracted many LGBTQA+ fans all over the world because the subtext/relationship was so beautifully written and acted. That meant a lot to me personally, because I missed that on TV back then (still missing something like this today, to be honest).

I want to thank all the good friends, pals, and Xenites around the world I got to know during this time, and especially those I am still in contact with today. My friends Andy, Ellen, and Steven, the most active team members like Ducky and Doro, and many more.

Xena will always have a very special place in my heart because of the people I've met and the good times I've had with the board and in the Xenite fandom.

Emanoelle Soares dos Santos
Country: Brazil

In 2000, when I was five years old, I was channel surfing one day when I came upon a woman warrior, her blonde companion, and a breathtaking landscape. It was *Xena: Warrior Princess* and nothing would ever be the same from that day on.

I am adopted and that was the reason I was bullied all the time at school. In 2005, I moved to Gravatá, where I live today. On any given day, I would return home feeling sad and scared, and I desperately wished for help, for someone to come to my rescue. I used to watch *Hercules* in the afternoon and I loved that it was set in Ancient Greece. Then, after finding *Xena* and watching "Sins of the Past," I was so excited that I decided I wanted to learn martial arts and read everything I could about Greece and the Greek gods.

I liked writing my thoughts about each episode on a notebook. One day, my teacher saw it and read my latest entry out loud to the class. Although he said that he liked it, my classmates laughed at me and gave me the hurtful nickname 'Xena, the princess of the Macumba.'

My one friend at school, who watched *Xena* as well and had always supported me and got me through my worst moments, died of cancer, and I thought things couldn't get any worse, but then, in August 2008, on

Father's Day, my grandfather passed away. Another part of me died with him. *Xena* helped me cope with it all for years until, in December 2012, my father became ill and died. Shortly after, I was rushed to the hospital and was diagnosed with acute anemia, anxiety, and depression.

I missed my father and I was sad all the time. One night I dreamed that my father had enrolled me in a different school. I had wonderful friends and could talk about *Xena* with them! A friend called Nayara gave me a *Xena* notebook full of pictures, fun facts, stickers, and everything *Xena*. I was thrilled!

I turned twenty-three in December, and my mother gave me *Xena*'s first season on DVD, and I also got a magazine that came with a poster from 1999. I love it!

When I think of everything I have learned from *Xena*, I remember the show with warm affection: love, protection, respect, strength. The world needs Xena.

My niece Eduarda, whom I adore, has also become a huge fan of the show. She loves it when Xena gets into a fight and gets frustrated when Gabby gets her in trouble. Her brothers like playing with plastic horses imitating Xena and Hercules, and I am so proud!

I am still studying, I still keep up with news about the actors who were in the show, and I admire Lucy more and more. I will one day teach my future daughters to love her as I do. THANK YOU!

2003

Kat
Country: Sweden

At the end of 2007, my friend Caroline told me that there was going to be a Xena convention in London in May 2008. I had never been to a convention before, nor had I been to London. I was unsure if I could afford to go but decided that it would be worth it, with Xena herself attending the convention. When we were there standing in line for autographs, we realized that the two people ahead of us in line were Swedes too, so we figured we should take a photo. My friend turned to the first person behind us to ask her to take the photo. Her name was Helen. We ended up spending most of the weekend with her and her friend, as they became our tour guides and helped us find our way to the venue where Lucy had her concert. Today, ten years later, Helen is my wife. We have actual photos from the day we first met. My friend Caroline was one of our wedding witnesses and I will be forever grateful that I ended up going to the convention where I met the love of my life. That is how *Xena* changed my life.

2005

- Caly Ruffo AG
- Missilane de Lima

Caly Ruffo AG
Country: Brazil

(Translated from the submitted story in Portuguese)
Every time I start watching *Xena*, my childhood comes back to me. I loved to play catch with my middle sister and cousins among the trees and close to the river in the area where we lived. When someone ran after me, I remembered Xena running and doing flips, and when I jumped from a tree I always put my hands in front of me like she did. There was another game that we played—hide and seek. When it was my turn to look for the others, I used Xena's strategy of walking silently when approaching the enemy. Ah, how good it is to remember all this… This show has also taught me many valuable life lessons. I changed my point of view about a lot of things after watching *Xena*. She taught me to find my place in the world and to have a best friend who I blindly trust. I want to thank Mr. Rob Tapert and Lucy and Renée for this wonderful gift they gave us.

Missilane de Lima
Country: Brazil

(Translated from the submitted story in Portuguese)
I'm thirty years old, I'm Brazilian, and I live in Curitiba-PR, Brazil. When *Xena: Warrior Princess* started airing, I was only six years old, but I couldn't watch it because we lived in a remote area and my parents had no TV. Time went by and I grew up. I finished elementary school and I had to go to the city where my maternal grandparents lived to attend high school, because where my parents lived there was no high school. It was the first time I left home and stayed away from my parents. I was sixteen years old and I went to live with my aunt. It was 2005 and the series had already finished, but it was still being broadcast on Brazilian TV. I was a very shy girl; I didn't like going out because I was always afraid of what people might think or say about me.

The first time I watched *Xena*, I saw her courage, her strength, her fight for the greater good in defense of the weakest or those who could not fight for their rights. I saw Gabrielle, whose sweetness, innocence, peaceful heart, and courage led her to fight with Xena to become a better person through difficulties and challenges. All this motivated me, taught me that life must be lived intensely, helping each other, and that difficulties exist so that we can improve and be better, so that we inspire peace, joy, and courage to those who see us and seek a light in us. I found it in Xena and Gabrielle, and also in Lucy and Renée. They push us to move forward with our heads held high, and to never give up on our dreams.

I have every season of *Xena: Warrior Princess*, and I always watch it, because it shows us women's strength and courage, and teaches us that we should not bow our heads, but instead say to ourselves, "I can; I'm capable." Xena and Gabrielle taught me how to be a better, happier person, and I can say I have a lot of friends for being this way. I am and always will be proud to say that I am a fan of Xena and Gabrielle, and even more so of Lucy Lawless and Renée O'Connor. Thank you to the entire cast for giving us such joy. Thank you, Lucy and Renée, for your existence and being part of my life and many other people's lives, for changing our lives forever by teaching us to be strong and courageous. I love you very much!

2006

- **Cheyne Curry**
- **Ana Carolina Félix**
- **Sam Paedae**

Cheyne Curry
Country: United States

I had been writing fan fiction (*SVU*/*Cold Case*/*China Beach*) when another FF writer friend (The Raven) suggested that I write Uber. I had no idea what that meant so she explained to me about Xena Uber. I knew about the show as all my friends had raved about it; mostly about Xena and Gabrielle's relationship.

I remember seeing bits and pieces of the show when it originally aired (my first thoughts were, "Damn, those women are gorgeous, and what's up with that saddle horn?"). But I never sat through an actual episode except "Fallen Angel," which was the first full and only episode I saw. Not knowing ANY of the background, I was not impressed (except that the women were still gorgeous).

Fast forward to late 2005. I had just started writing Renegade with *SVU* characters Olivia and Alex in mind. It was not flowing and my muse was being stubborn. On Raven's recommendation, I began reading Xena Uber (my first was Road To Kilimanjaro by KG MacGregor). That opened up a whole new world to me. I couldn't get enough of Uber stories. Then I began reading *XWP* fan fiction, noting that there was so much of it that the show HAD to have had something special that I must have missed.

I searched for the show on-line to see who might be showing reruns and found it on one cable channel at 6:30 AM. It was in early 2006 and after the first three episodes, I was hooked, thinking, "Why am I always late to the party?"

Sometime along viewing the third season (which in reality was, with the show being on every day, maybe three months later), I started working on Renegade again. I couldn't get the Lucy - Renée chemistry out of my head, so I rewrote Trace and Rachel with that in mind, and from then on, the words just flowed. Renegade was my first published book.

I went on to write several stories using the Lucy - Renée chemistry, and one day, in 2007, I got a fan letter regarding The Tropic of Hunter, which was on-line before it was published. The letter writer and I had a lot in common (including being US Army Military Police veterans, which is not a common thing for me. Female MPs from old were rare). We started corresponding, and in June 2007, when I went on a cross-country adventure, we met briefly for drinks and to say hi. We both felt the spark. We had our first date in September (which included watching episodes of *Xena*) after I had returned from my trip. The spark was still there but we lived in two different states—she in the midwest and I am in New England. We continued corresponding, and in 2008, we went to our first *Xena* con together and I attended my first Bard's Dinner, which was the most sense of belonging I had felt in years.

In June of 2008, I left Vermont and moved in with her, and in 2014, we married. We started a small film company together, where we made several short films (her producing, me writing, scoring, and occasionally acting), mostly for local contests.

Also, two of my five published books are co-written by Roselle Graskey. Roselle is also another former MP - what are the odds? Maybe because we gravitate toward a character who is unapologetically strong, smart, and takes no crap from anybody. Ro and I met because I wrote her a fan letter in 2006 regarding her book, Life's Little Edge, which I initially found on-line on Royal Academy of Bards. Ro pointed me in the direction of PD Publishing, who invited us to a writing retreat in Montana (part of my 2007 cross-country trip). Roselle and I became good friends and we are writing the 3rd book of our dystopian trilogy, The Sanctuary Series.

I am still good friends with The Raven, even though we've never met in person. This is how *Xena* changed my life. Not only did I meet my wife because of it, but I wrote several stories and novels motivated by it and co-wrote two novels with another product of a Xenaverse friendship. Because of *Xena*, I was able to fulfill childhood dreams of becoming a published author and a filmmaker.

Inspiration of *Xena: Warrior Princess* continues to influence my artistic side and I believe it always will. I raise a glass to honor the *Xena* powers that be, especially Lucy and Renée for their genius of breathing such realistic life and allure into two characters; Xena and Gabrielle will clearly live forever. Sláinte and thank you.

Ana Carolina Félix
Country: Brazil

Xena is part of my life to this day. I started watching the show as a child, and even though I didn't quite understand the message of the series, I loved it madly. When I reached adulthood I felt the need to re-watch the show, and it was then that I understood the important mission of two women warriors of different personalities, but who could defeat even the gods of Olympus if they worked together. *Xena: Warrior Princess* taught me to be strong, not to give up on my dreams, and to never lose hope in what I believe. I can only be grateful to everyone involved in this series, which has changed my reality by turning every dream of mine into a battle for success. Thank you very much.

From: Sam Paedae
Country: United States

I was sitting in the audience at my first-ever Xena con amongst newbies, Amazon Elders, Xena lovers all. I was talking to my seat neighbor, a stranger I'd met just a few minutes prior, about other TV shows we liked. "I like the X-Files," she said, "and the actress that plays Scully..." She shrugged. "I mean, I don't know if you're gay, but I have a huge crush on her." What I said next came as easily as breathing, "I totally get it; I'm gay too." It was the first time I said that out loud. To anyone, even myself. But I'd felt so comfortable at the con, so surrounded by love and acceptance that it was easy, effortless. And it lifted a crushing weight from my shoulders. My seat neighbor and I kept talking; she didn't realize the momentous, sonic boom moment that had passed for me, lost in the hum of excited conversation. But I did, and that moment paved the way for me to come out to my friends, my family, and everyone else. First Xena, and then the Xenaverse helped me to become proud of who I am. It gave me friends and a community I craved. For that I am forever grateful.

2010

- **Rosa Alonso**
- **Serena**

Rosa Alonso
Country: Spain

The first thing I got from *Xena: Warrior Princess* was a burn. Go figure. It was the morning of one summer day in 2010. I stood in the doorway to my living room eyeing a pile of clothes on the couch. I hate ironing, and it was stifling hot. I couldn't think of any new excuses to put it off again, so I sighed and plugged in the iron. I turned the TV on thinking it might help distract my mind from the tedious task. I'm not a TV person, which probably explains why it took me so long to know of the existence of *Xena*, so I didn't have much faith. Halfway through my favorite shirt, I happened to look up for a second and the world stopped turning. Xena's eyes filled my TV screen and I dropped the iron on my wrist. It was that scene in "One Against An Army" in which she's looking out through the boards covering a window in the armory where she and Gabrielle are getting ready to fight the entire Persian army. I binge-watched the whole show in a matter of days and never looked back. I wear that scar on my wrist proudly too.

Since then, *Xena* has been the gift that keeps on giving. I discovered fan fiction and devoted all of my free time to devouring hundreds upon hundreds of stories. I read everything I could find and lived in a state of permanent bliss. Then I won a bunch of bids at one of AUSXIP's Charity Auctions. I was happy to be the owner of some really cool *Xena* related stuff, but what I got out of that auction was a million times better—I got a friend for life, a true mate. MaryD took a huge chance on me and allowed me the pleasure of editing her books, and to this day, there are very few things I enjoy more than our regular Skype chats about plots, and characters, and life, and train trips.

At my first con, in 2014, I found my tribe—my family of choice. The sense of belonging I experienced then was exhilarating. I sat in that crowded room while they dimmed the lights and played the *Xena: Warrior Princess* opening theme...and I knew I was home.

The Xenite Retreat was born two years later, thanks to the force of nature that is Penny Cavanaugh, to make sure the spirit of the show lived on even after the conventions ended, and oh boy, is it alive and kicking indeed. It's a different setting, a different structure, a different concept, but the same phenomenal display of generosity, acceptance, fun, and encouragement that the show first inspired in all of us.

Their courage did certainly change our world, and it does have that power still. Just gather a bunch of Xenites and you'll see them change the world for the better today.

Serena
Country: Germany

Watching *Xena* had, and still has, a huge impact on my life because of the great wisdom, philosophy, and all the life-lessons it contains: lessons of love and forgiveness (also towards yourself!); wisdom before weapons; the balance between light and darkness; life paths and karma/destiny/etc.; faith; selflessness; the greater good; all the little quirks of being human... and so many more!

I have a forty-page collection of quotes that are so true and meaningful and significant. I could tell you how each of them has impacted my world view/belief system/ideology...or how they helped me through a really hard, rough and dark time of my life...

But even more than that, it corroborated (and maybe even helped shape?!) my view and values of friendship. Yes, I choose to see Xena and Gabrielle as the best of friends there ever could be, rather than as a couple, although I also don't object to that viewpoint and enjoy reading the fan fiction depicting them as lovers.

There's simply NOTHING these two wouldn't do or give for each other, and that's how I've always felt and thought towards my friends as well. This made it so easy to relate to and empathize with the characters, so, while I was watching the show for the very first time, I sometimes knew exactly what they were going to say or do, because even though the story or situation originating the emotions and (re-)actions is totally different (because, let's face it, WE are not living in a time of ancient gods, warlords, and kings), they themselves are the same. This happened quite often, even to the heart-wrenching point where it seems surreal and you wonder how the writers could possibly know you so well and marvel at the actresses for the amazing job they did, expressing and conveying them.

Seeing a friendship embodying my own ideals always work out just fine in the end (even knowing it was only fictional and not real) gave me the reassurance that, even if it was hard to bear, sticking with those ideals was the right thing to do. It helped me be the bigger person instead of giving in to my dark side/base motives/ego-driven wants and encouraged me to keep striving to be a better person in general.

On some accounts though, despite the alikeness of perspective at large, *Xena* also made me reconsider my own code of conduct, because it got me thinking about which way of behaving was truly more beneficial for your friends. The most notable example would be the immense difference between following a friend blindly, just accepting whatever they do and, alternatively, stepping in, intervening when the friend is about to make a mistake or do something they will regret later. Even though in our world, fortunately, the stakes will rarely be someone's purity of soul or the like.

To put it in a nutshell, I guess the show made me an even bigger idealist than I already was, taught me important life lessons, and gave me much food for thought, thus fueling my philosophical reflections and thereby influencing my attitude, moral compass, and mindset – all for the better.

2011

Nehir Ceren Uygun
Country: Turkey

I was five when I discovered *Xena: Warrior Princess*. I was a student in my mother's kindergarten at the time. We were going to play Snow White as an end-of-year show and I wanted to be Snow White so bad. I loved her fluffy dress and the fact that the prince fell in love with her, but my drama teacher chose another girl for the role of the princess.

How could she do that?

I went to my mother crying, sure that she would fix it. She could have told the teacher to make me princess. After all, she owned the school. I walked into her room without even knocking.

"Mom, I want to be a princess, but my teacher chose another girl."

My mother took me in her lap and wiped away my tears. "If your teacher made a decision, we should respect it," she said.

"But I want to be a princess!" I yelled.

"So you want to be a princess... A princess who lets someone she doesn't know enter her house? A princess who eats food that someone she doesn't know gives her? You want to be a princess who marries a prince just because he kissed her?"

"I never thought of that. I think you are right."

"If you want to be a princess, there's only one princess you can be."

My mother showed me a photo of a tall woman in black leather on her computer.

"There's a real princess—strong, smart, and free. If you're going to be a princess, you have to be a warrior princess," she said. She then had me watch the adventures of Xena and Gabrielle. That year, on my birthday, she gave me a warrior princess costume, and I spent the day fighting the bad guys with my sword. Xena was my mother's idol. When I was nine, I went to Australia with my mother and met Lucy. I'm thirteen now. I know now that I can do whatever I want in life. I know that when I grow up I will be a strong warrior princess and make my own destiny, just like my mother.

2013

Crystal Mertes
Country: United States

XWP helped me rediscover my true aspirations in life in a time when I was struggling to find my own calling. Throughout the series, I noticed how I could relate in different ways to Xena and Gabrielle's stories in comparison to my own life situations. I can say *XWP* helped me unravel my own hidden truths, some I thought I had hidden way down deep never to be expressed. I felt inspired to take a stand and fight for others. I continued to show up, to keep fighting, but was just short of getting where I wanted to be. Many would say they'd understand if I gave up and tried something else, but I couldn't. I never wanted anything easy in life; I just wanted the possibility to make a difference if I could. I have struggled coming out while trying to discover the right career, while at the same time breaking out of my comfort zone.

XWP came back in my life again in my college years and forever changed my mindset by reminding me to be the best version of myself that I could be. After watching the episode "The Greater Good," all my perspectives started to change and I discovered how I'd rather protect others above all else. I wanted to be a warrior, so I acquired a career in criminal justice. Later on it developed into becoming a peace officer with the department of corrections. A few years down the road, I started struggling, not afraid of the job itself, but more of what was becoming of me when I thought I had to do what it takes to be successful.

In the beginning of my career, several people told me that the job can change you, and I was naive to think I was an exception to this warning. The environment inside a prison is not something to take lightly; it's a vast negative place with its own dangers around the corner.

After some time, I was not so concerned about the job but about what I was becoming. I could not shake the harsh, blunt, negative, stand-offish attitude. I thought I had to be this way in order to be successful in this career, but not at the expense of no longer recognizing myself. I was not in the greatest mindset and chose the one show that always seemed to lift my spirit—*XWP*. Unbeknown to me, my perspective would be forever altered.

Xena and Gabrielle both had taught me several things through the years, but maybe not as pronounced as when I watched the series this time. Xena taught us that we have dark sides we try to forget but they also make us who we are. Gabrielle, on the other hand, is the heart, but also so willing to be her own warrior and stand and fight. "Having a soft heart in a cruel world is courage, not weakness." I needed the chance to remember why I chose this career, why I wanted to do my part for the greater good. *Xena Warrior*

Princess not only helped me discover my calling for the greater good, but also gave me many new friends that share the love of Xena and Gabrielle!

2016

- **Anna Weatherspoon**
- **Filippo Polverini**
- **Heather Parker**

Anna Weatherspoon
Country: United States

When I was a senior in high school, I had a hard time figuring out what to do next till my dad and I saw the first episode of *Xena* together. I knew that I was hooked. Each episode tells a story. I love to write and take pictures. When my uncle Steve was alive, he gave me two Xena figures and I kept them after he passed away. My first cat, Princess, passed away two years ago and I watched *Xena* and Lucy Lawless videos to cheer me up. Whenever I get an update from Lucy, I felt that I finally belong in a fanbase. I have a poster of Lucy as Xena and I took a picture of it. I posted it on Twitter and guess who liked it…Lucy Lawless! I was so happy and thankful. I would love to meet her someday.

Xena has played a big part in my life and it still does today. I will never forget the moments I get from a beautiful, strong woman like Lucy. When I feel sick, I watch some *Xena* to cheer me up. You know that you can learn a thing or two from the series and the cast. My parents got married in May the same year as Lucy and Rob. I have seen many different sides of our characters like Xena, Gabrielle, Joxer, and Ares. It is like each character tells me a story. I have a disability and I learn differently, but I feel that there is a warrior princess inside of me. I fight hard to get what I want. I am a buddy director and being a leader is tough, but I do what I can and I show my best buddies what I am made of.

I can always count on *Xena* for making me smile and feel loved again. When my aunt Barb passed away, I listened to Lucy Lawless's songs and I literally cried when I heard her sing so beautifully. I also dreamed that I was working with Lucy. It would be cool to have her as a boss. A girl can dream, can she? As a woman, I was picked on a lot just because I am different, but that doesn't mean that I can't be a strong woman who wants to become a photographer someday.

The best part of being a Xenite is building a fanbase with other Xenites around the world. 2016 was a tough year for me, but I know that deep inside I am a warrior princess. I love to write stories, being a leader, a friend, a girlfriend, a sister, a daughter, a granddaughter, a niece, a cousin, a photographer, and a tough woman who is ready to conquer the world. I learned to be myself and be a leader.

Anyone can be a Xenite who has that warrior princess or bard inside of them. Life is tough and there is a lot of hate in the world. I know that there is love also and that is the Xenite family. No matter where we go, no matter where we are from, we have each other. We will always be there no matter what.

It was my dad who got me into *Xena*. Since I was born in 1996, I didn't get into *Xena* till I was a senior in high school. Back then, it was on Netflix and my dad talked to me about a show that I might like. I watched that first episode and I was hooked. I love it! I have overcome a lot of things in life but I have my friends and family by my side. *Xena* has shown me that no matter what you do, you always have someone by your side.

I remember the first Lucy Lawless video I ever saw. I was on YouTube and I was watching Lucy Lawless singing I'll Stand By You. It was so beautiful and smooth. Lucy has a beautiful voice and I loved it.

The first *Xena* artwork I did was a pillow, and I added the three letters of XWP to the fabric. It was my back pillow. My second artwork was my best one; I made a poster of Lucy as Xena and I have different pics of her as the queen of the battlefield. I finally got it done on her birthday. That's the one Lucy liked on Twitter. If I do have a chance to meet her, I would give her my poster as a thank you for being an inspiration to me.

I do have a few favorite episodes, but each episode is different and they all tell me a story. I am not a huge fan of "Past Imperfect" or "Ides of March." As for villains, I have a few favorites. I like Ares, Alti, Callisto, Caesar. They all gave Xena a hard time, poor girl.

When I was sick, I watched a *Xena* episode and Joxer appeared and he did something funny and I was laughing so hard. Joxer was my favorite character who made me smile and laugh. Everyone has their favorite celebrity to follow on social media, but my favorite celebrity to follow is Lucy Lawless. She loves her fans even though we bug her sometimes. I usually send a message to check in on her but I know that she is busy. I learned a lot of new facts with every episode and I can actually relate to some of the characters. I am stubborn but I am also a leader. My favorite is Aphrodite. She is so lovey-dovey, feisty, and so unique.

If there was a meet and greet in Kettering about *Xena*, I would go in a heartbeat. I never give up on what I want to do in my life; I will never give up on finding that perfect job and college that is right for me. I will always be a Xenite and I will pass it down to my children. My aunt, my first cat, my uncle, and my grandma will always be my angels. I am so thankful and blessed to be in an amazing fanbase army like the Xenites.

Xena: Warrior Princess played many different parts in our lives and I will always be a Xenite. Being a Xenite is the best gift and I can't imagine my life without my Xenite brothers and sisters. Xenites, I love you all and I am blessed to be one of you.

Filippo Polverini
Country: Italy

My story doesn't start in 1996, when I started watching *Xena*; my story begins in 2016, when I decided to rewatch the show after watching *Ash vs Evil Dead*, which featured a lot of actors I had seen in *Xena*, like Lucy Lawless, for example. The rewatch of the warrior princess's adventures brought me back to my childhood when I watched the show for the first time. I guess I was unconsciously influenced by *Xena,* and that's why, for example, twenty years later I feel attracted to brave, strong women. This appeal probably has its roots in *Xena*.

Rewatching this show made me get absorbed in the plot and enthralled by some characters too. Joxer is my favorite because of his motivation. In fact, one of the conversations between Joxer and Xena changed my life. There's an episode where Joxer is sad because he think he's a fool, and Xena tries to comfort him saying that what we know of ourselves is probably what we believe to be true, but not what we really are (and we probably are better than what we think). Xena's wisdom was important for me because I also think I'm a fool, and so weak and prone to anger that my destiny is probably to live like a villain or die an unloved man. I'm even scared by demons and hell because I think that is the world for me after death.

Xena's words made me change the way I saw myself and realized I was wrong. I live better now, but I still think that life can be very hard and there's no room for what is right and good. I hope to see something new in *Xena* to change my views again and find the way to live a better life. I also dream of writing episodes for a reboot or revival of *Xena*. I know it is too ambitious, but I want to give something back to Xena because she' given me a lot. Writing my story for this book is a start!

Heather Parker
Country: USA

Brynn, my eight year old daughter, started watching *Xena* shortly after I did in 2016. She became obsessed with "The Bitter Suite," and it took me forever to get her to watch "A Day in the Life." Those two episodes became her go-to episodes, and she would watch them, or parts of them, on a daily basis during the summer. Finally last year she started watching more. She went as Xena last year for Halloween and began talking about the show with me more. So, when my partner, Shawna, and I started discussing going to FanX, we decided that we had to take the kids with us. It would be a once in a life time experience for them to meet Renée and Lucy. Little did we know that it would be so much more than we expected.

Brynn and Garrison (five years old) were excited but didn't quite know what to expect. They met both Renée and Lucy in the autograph lines, and were so excited already. Then the most amazing thing happened. There were several problems with the photo-ops, and when we went to take their picture with Renée, no one came behind us and moved us out. I was walking out and I turned around to make sure they were both with me, and there was Renée, with my sais, giving Brynn a lesson!! This was such an incredible moment, and I fumbled to get anything to document it. Luckily, the wonderful agent that was with Renée was on top of it and got them before I did! We must have gotten to spend a solid five minutes with Renée. And I will be forever grateful to my friend Raychal Ashton who held up the line a bit because of her words, "There was no way I was going to interrupt the Battling Bard's weapon lesson!!"

Obviously after that, Brynn was on cloud nine, and so was I! My kid can talk, she is my kid after all, but she was without words. We came out and she was so excited she was crying. All I could do was pull her to me and help her process the moment. I will never forget the caring and wonderful way Renée treated my child. I will never forget the sparkle in her eye when we walked out.

By the time we got back to the hotel, MaryD had posted the photos on AUSXIP from the agent's Instagram and Penny Cavanaugh tagged me. I was floored. Brynn was excited that Penny had noticed (because for some reason, she kinda digs Penny), and then to know that Mary was a world away and posting this, she was overwhelmed. She took a ten-minute shower to calm down and was still crying. She sat on the bed with me and said, "Mommy, Ms. Renée was so nice to me. I just can't believe this happened!" By the time she went to bed that night, she was a bard for life, just like her mommy.

On a side note. About two weeks later we were talking about it and she looked at Shawna and me and said, "It's been a few weeks, so I figure in the next 7-10 days people will start recognizing me on the street." LOL!

Shawna was an introverted internet badass. In person she was quiet and kept a lot to herself, but when she got on-line to chat with Xenites or to promote Artemis Motion Pictures, she was her truest self. Thankfully, that is where I met her, in a Xenite chat room. Shawna was an OXG (Original Xenite Gangsta). She watched the show from the beginning and had a love for Lucy Lawless that was pure and loyal. At first I did not get it, but when she talked about Lucy she smiled, and when Lucy tweeted Shawna was there. It was like Lucy was a long-time friend that she had just not had the chance to meet up with yet. And I have to say, after meeting Lucy, I now understand, but I am getting ahead of myself.

In 2016, I started watching *Xena* when I was going through some major losses. Between January and June four people in my inner circle passed away. The only way I was drawing much strength was by watching *Xena*, because the relationship between Xena and Gabrielle reminded me so much of my best friend, and a person I consider a soul mate, Wendy.

When I was sad I would watch the show and I would feel like she was with me, or I would laugh or cry because of something that was so similar to Wen. But the biggest part of the show that I loved was the ending. I know this is not a very popular opinion, but it gave me comfort and peace seeing the pain that Gabrielle endured for Xena. Seeing Xena fade and then reappear on the boat, kiss Gabrielle's head, and know that she was with her from there on out. That changed me somehow and gave me a knowing that Wen would always be with me.

In June, my mom's cancer finally got the best of her and we spent a month nursing her through her final days. It was one of the longest and hardest experiences of my life. When I got home I told my husband that I needed to get more involved with this show and possibly try to meet Renée, because Gabrielle is my heart. To my utterly crushing disappointment, I had just missed the last convention. But then, I found Xenite Retreat! I started talking to people going to Retreat and one of them introduced me to the chatroom that Shawna (also known as Shadow) was in. That was it. It was instant friendship and we all talked all the time. I got educated on *Xena*, we had gif wars, we just had fun. Our friendship grew from there, and when my husband of twenty-six years and I decided to divorce, Shawna was there; not just there—she carried me. She was my sounding board and my best friend! I was in a relationship and so was she. I had no idea that she was developing feelings for me and I was in my natural state of ignorant naiveté.

Eventually, my relationship showed that it was not going to work out, and after a few weeks of doing the honorable thing of not trying to interfere with a relationship, Shawna finally told me how she felt, and that was it. I let myself feel everything and I fell deeply and passionately in love with my best friend. Shawna was my grounding, she was the string that kept me safe while I flew, because I am a bard that has a hard time keeping my feet on the ground. Through all the doubts, through all the pushing away, my warrior stood steady and strong. She never wavered in her love for me or her commitment to me.

We had an amazing summer where we drove all over the country, meeting friends, seeing new things, and healing my heart from my mom and my divorce. Eventually, through lots of talking and multiple trips to make sure we both fit with each other's kids, I asked her to please come live with me. Actually, I don't know if I ever even asked; I just said I was ready for her to be here and that was it—we started planning. Shawna gave up everything for me. She left her home in St. Louis to move to Denver. She left her family, her life-long friends, and most incredibly, she left her godson Blaize, who was just like her own child. We had almost a year, an amazing year (not that there were not bumps, since I'm pretty neurotic, but for being together 24/7 for nine months, we did pretty amazing). Shawna loved my kids. Man, did she love my kids and do they love her!

Then on September 7, 2018, it happened. I took Shawna to meet Lucy! She was so incredibly happy. And Lucy was so generous and gracious. Shawna also had to concede Renée's greatness after she saw the time Renée took to show Brynn, our eight year old, how to use the sais after a photo op. You see…we had this fun rivalry. I adore Xena, but my heart is with Gabrielle, and Shawna was the tough warrior who loved her bard, but had to remain loyal to Lucy (Xena) over Gabrielle (Renée). That weekend in Salt Lake was one of the best of my life. Meeting Renée and Lucy, seeing Shawna's long-time dream come true, and having the chance for her to meet even more Xenites from Retreat was incredible, and I will forever be even more grateful now than I was then that we went.

About two weeks after Salt Lake we went to Colorado Springs to meet a new friend, a Xenite named Juniper who belongs to our tribe and had just not met anyone yet. It was a great night, one that will stay in my heart forever too. Then the next day we went to see one of Shawna's other passions—our oldest daughter Maddie, who had just gone back to school a few weeks earlier. Shawna missed her as much, maybe even more, than I did. We had lunch with Maddie and came home. I don't really want to talk about the process of Shawna's death, but by Sunday night we were in the ER and she passed away early that Monday morning, September 24, 2018.

I will forever be thankful for this show. For the people it attracts and the bonds we forge because of it. My love, my soul mate, my Shadow, will always be with us. In spirit, in memories, in pieces of her that we will always keep around the house, and in *Xena*. I know that I can always turn on this show and feel her presence. I am so grateful that our youngest ones, Brynn and Garrison, will always have *Xena* too.

They will always have memories and pictures of Shawna with them and with her hero, smiling the biggest smiles, and glowing with love, for Lucy and for us! So thank you to everyone who has ever had anything to do with this show. It will always, always hold a special place in my heart and in my children's hearts. There are now two warriors standing beside this bard on that boat, and I am one lucky woman because of them. *(Publisher's note: More of Heather's story can be found in Part 9 Friends In Need: The Xenaverse Code, Chapter 57: I Will Always Be With You,)*

2017

Lola Lucena
Country: Brazil

The series brought me spiritual, moral, and intellectual liberation. I had depression, and one fine day I started watching the show on YouTube out of nowhere. The series taught me to love me as I am, to accept myself, and to respect myself and others. *Xena* taught me to face all the difficult problems of everyday life. I saw that many of these problems are not out in the world, but inside me, and Xena showed me that we can get better by working on ourselves!

2018

Teresa Griffin
Country: United States

Xena changed my life... More than that... I had cancer, four surgeries, got divorced, lost my home and job because of cancer, and raised my four girls on my own by working seventy-two hours a week. It took a major toll on my body and I gained an awful lot of weight... but I was alive!

Just this year, 2018, I watched *Xena* (I know... It took me long enough, right?). I have seen in Xena's character the strength and determination I needed to overcome my battle with cancer, weight, and fitness—my battle with life. I became determined to have that same warrior spirit, and Xena being beautiful was just an added feature! I wanted to be beautiful too. I began my journey and seven months later I had lost over 100 lbs, and I am in great shape. I wanted to be better this year than I have ever been. I'M ALIVE, and BEAUTIFUL! Someday my hope is to tell Lucy face to face what *Xena* and the character she portrayed have done for me.

PART 11

THE XENITE MEMORIAL –
IN MEMORY OF OUR FALLEN WARRIORS

Chapter Sixty-Two

Becky Calvert's Legacy – The Xenite Memorial

by MaryD

THE SADDEST PART of AUSXIP is a place I don't want to go into. It's the saddest place because I recognize names of the friends I have known for twenty-four years. The Xenite Memorial is a special place for the friends we have lost. I know that when I update it and add another name, my eye will drift down the long list of names of my fallen friends and the sorrow I felt when they passed will be with me again.

In June 1999, Xenite Becky Calvert created a section on her site called "The Xenite Memorial" to honor the fans who had passed away. This was a beautiful way to remember those that are no longer with us.

This place was created around a need to have a safe place to show our feelings, our serious sides. I have very mixed emotions about this area of the site. I am glad to pioneer this page, but the reason it was done now is due to a terrible tragedy. On June 4, 1999, the world lost the sweet voice of another Xenite, Evie Lamberth. I would, therefore, like to dedicate this page to her, her soulmate, and all the others she left behind. God willing, this page will not have to be dedicated to others, but if this is to be, we will honor their memories also.

I feel we have long neglected this side of our personas. Many times we do not want to talk about the deeper, more raw emotions we experience. The pains, the losses, the hurts, and that terrible grief that goes with those feelings. But there comes a time when we just have to let them out. We may not know what to do or how to handle these emotions. Writing out your feelings can be helpful. I want to offer you a safe place to put them.

This section of the site is for more than grief and pain. There is a second side to those emotions. There is joy, elation, love, and friendship. What is behind these emotions is every bit as strong and powerful as the ones we might consider negative, and sometimes they can be just as scary. This is a place for those emotions, feelings, and accompanying doubts as well.

One of the most important things we have and seldom acknowledge sincerely are our friends and family, and many times our friends are our family. If I can

Xena: Their Courage Changed Our World   499

do nothing else in my life, I hope that I can help remind you, and myself as well, of how important these relationships can be.

Acknowledge the people around you. Tell someone that you care. Tell your friends you love them, because they might not be there the next time you turn around. Remember that a friend is not limited to those people you may 'actually know.' A friend on-line is just as important as the friend down the street, however it is much easier to forget to acknowledge an on-line friendship, or for some others to believe in the depths that these friendships can reach.

To all my friends (on and off line), my partner, and my family: know I love you always. And know also that I will always do my best to be there in your hour of need. I am much stronger with you than without you, and "even in death, I will never leave you."

Becky Calvert,
Commander in Chief, The NutBread Brigade/SSPA
June 5, 1999

Unfortunately, on May 10, 2007, Becky herself passed away. That left the memorial without someone to take care of it. I was asked if I could step in and maintain it. Of course, I agreed because this was part of our history and we needed to remember our fallen. On April 8, 2008. Becky's Xenite Memorial was incorporated into AUSXIP. It continues the work Becky did to remember our friends that have passed.

As the years have come and gone, more names are added, and the list gets longer. The names still bring tears to my eyes. We have been blessed with extraordinary friends. It's Becky Calvert's legacy that this memorial was started and it has continued long after she has passed.

In Remembrance of Becky

On May 10, 2007, a good friend and original Flawless member, Becky Calvert died after a 10 year battle with her body. She was a true original, a dear friend to many, and is survived by her family and her partner, Shirley Landon. – Lida

Becky was one of the good ones, and beloved by many of those Xenites it was my best privilege to know. So, even though we didn't know each other well directly, I feel her loss. May you who survive her rest in the memory of her good soul, and in the warmth of each other's company. – alwayslooking

I didn't know Becky, but was amazed at the medical hardships that she battled with grace and humor. Her account of the XWP set visit and the testimony I have heard from her friends show a warm, wonderful person. She will be missed in the Xenaverse, no doubt. Peace and good thoughts to the survivors … – KT

I dunno what to say… I've been part of the nutbreaders for over 10 years…

and her occasional posts were always something to look forward to...i met her for the first time in person only 10 days ago...and she was cheerful and upbeat and just full of this incredible energy that seemed to fill the room... she will definitely be missed... – Downtown Robot

Becky was a great Lady, with a big heart. She was passionate about Xena a passion that was very contagious when you were around her. She and Shirl guided me to the Nutbreaders where I met a lot of really great people. I would always be very grateful for her friendship she would be very missed -- Beboman

I've known Becky and Shirl for quite a while, and Becky "The Commander" was always a blast on the SonofaBacchae list. Her humor and wit and love of Xena will always be remembered by those of us from the SoB. Battle On Becky! Our thoughts and prayers go out to Shirl and Becky's loved ones. – LeatherQueen

Becky you will always have a place in my heart. You and Shirl sent me love and prayers when I was ill and I will never forget that great kindness. The Xenaverse has lost a good person but her soul will shine on. Shirl I send you my love and know you will always have a friend. – Buffy

I will always remember Becky as the person that "drafted" me into the Nutbread Brigade. My 'Chief' showed me a wonderful world I had been unaware of most of my life. Her warmth, compassion and wacky humor set her apart as a very special and unique person. There will always be a special place in my memory and heart for Becky. Irreplaceable, irrepressible, and wonderful beyond my poor words to express, she was a wonder to anyone fortunate enough to know her. Battle on Becky, for I know you will, where ever you are – Bardy (Becky's name for me)

I knew Becky through the Flawless list and then she and I set up the Nutbread list with a bunch of wonderful (a bit wacky) women. She and I corresponded enough that I learned that she was an always positive, caring, funny person, and a devoted Xenite. She helped me through some difficult personal times and I will always be grateful to her. I introduced her to her current wife and I was there at their wedding. I will remember her with love and I promise you Shirl, she went peacefully and thinking of you... – SB the CoCic

I'm from Houston, lived with Becky for 3 years as a special friend. It's such a shocker even though I knew she was sick. Met her in 1985 and remember her days as a DJ and my radiology supervisor. She got me into radiology and very thankful. Shirl and her family, I send my prayers. I Will miss you Beck! – Anonymous

It was my privilege to know Becky, she is a special friend, staying with me for a year while she was in New Zealand. My thoughts are with Shirl and Becky's families and loved ones – Nikki

Chapter Sixty-Three

A Real Life Xena – Aleida Santiago

by Cat Crimins

I FIRST MET Aleida Santiago at a one-day seminar at CSUN, a local Southern California college, in September of 2002. The name of the seminar was something to the effect of "*Xena* and Its Influence on Pop Culture," and it was being presented by an honest-to-god professor for actual college credit. I had heard about it in one of the many on-line *Xena* forums I belonged to and of course I had to go!

Our beloved show had been off the air for over a year by this point and I was a full-fledged Xenite; attending conventions by myself, reading fanfic, rewatching episodes over and over, going to AUSXIP everyday looking for new *Xena* updates. But something was missing. I didn't have any Xenite friends. I didn't have a tribe. Being an introvert with social anxiety, I was really bad at making new friends. I kept to myself at conventions, never taking the terrifying first step of introducing myself to other fans. I had no intention of actually talking to anyone at this seminar. The plan was to go in, enjoy the nerdiness, and then get the hell out of there.

I arrived a little early so I would be able to find a good seat. As I walked into the large college auditorium, I quickly realized finding a seat would not be a problem. Besides myself and the professor, five other people showed up: Adam, a young college student; Alana, a very successful attorney; Sarah, an aspiring actress; Kelly, a television editor; and finally, Aleida Santiago. She was a diminutive Cuban woman in her early 60s. As a twenty-four-year-old, befriending someone my father's age wasn't exactly something I was seeking out, but as fate would have it, meeting Aleida that day would change my life for the better, forever.

The six of us lingered after the seminar finished, not ready to go back out to face the real world quite yet. We chatted awkwardly about the seminar and about our favorite show. Finally, with her Cuban accent and leadership-prone personality, Aleida suggested, "Why don't we all go have lunch?" And so our little *Xena* tribe was born. That afternoon we sat in a mediocre Mexican restaurant for hours, chatting about our favorite episodes, least favorite episodes, convention experiences, and the awesomeness that were Lucy and Renée. Of the small group of Xenites sitting at that table (some of whom are my most cherished friends to this day), Aleida was by far the most interesting (sorry, ladies). She was a retired teacher, a community activist, and a former Cuban counter-revolutionary. This small woman was fascinating and funny and I wanted to be her friend. By the time we parted ways, we had all exchanged email addresses and phone numbers with plans to meet up again.

Marathons, Meet-Ups, and Memorabilia

Aleida volunteered to host the first of our many Xena marathons. Our small group piled into the Venice Canal home she shared with her partner, Grace, who always made herself scarce on Xena marathon day. We sat in their small living room, feasted on a variety of snack foods, and watched all of our favorite episodes. The highlight of that first marathon was by far the Xena Room, as it will forever be known. You see, Aleida Santiago had many passions. She loved watching professional tennis, she was very active in her community, and she loved to travel. But her biggest passion by far was being a collector of all things Xena. And I do mean all things.

Once all of the attendees of that first marathon had arrived, with a mischievous smile and a glint in her eye, Aleida announced that she wanted to show us something. She led us into a small spare bedroom-turned-museum of her extensive collection of *Xena* memorabilia. Everything from action figures and posters to actual costumes and props used on the show. A full set of Lucy-worn Xena leathers, THE ring from "The Ring" trilogy, Xena's urn from "A Friend In Need," and that's just the tip of the *Xena* iceberg. This was a serious collection. I'm sure she was the scourge of many a Xenite Ebay-er in the early 2000s. The Red Baron of *Xena* auctions. And she had kept it all neatly tucked away and out of sight until she could show it all to people who would truly appreciate it. Until she had a tribe. As our tribe grew (we slowly collected more Xenites over the years), she took great delight in introducing new members to the *Xena* Room. The look on people's faces when being introduced to the collection for the first time was always a fun way to start a marathon.

A Warrior With A Dark Past

As Xenites, we all have our own very personal reasons for why we were (and still are) drawn to this show. For me, at its core, *Xena: Warrior Princess* is a show about redemption. Our hero has a dark past that she is trying to atone for every day by devoting herself to the greater good.

While Aleida was neither a conqueror of nations nor a warlord, to hear her tell her life's story, it's not hard to see some parallels between our fiery Cuban friend and the Warrior Princess herself.

Less than a year before she passed away (she would not be diagnosed with cancer for another two or so months) she agreed to sit down with myself and Kelly one Sunday afternoon to talk about her experiences in Cuba before fleeing to the US in exile.

Aleida was born in Havana, Cuba on October 27th, 1940. She was the eldest of four children born into the upper-middle class Santiago family. Her father worked (and did very well) in the tobacco industry, and by all intents and purposes she had an idyllic, privileged childhood. Her parents instilled a belief of justice and charity in their children at an early age. As a young woman, Aleida devoted a lot of her time, ironically, as a volunteer for a national cancer patient charity.

She also was not afraid to speak her mind (that never went away either, by the way). When girls her age were having elaborate quinceañeras - which in her words 'was a wedding without the groom' - she told her parents, "don't even think about it." She was not the 'put on make-up, a big dress and dance with boys' kind of girl. She was more of the 'wear trousers, ride a horse and play sports' kind of girl (very progressive for the 1950s).

Aleida was twelve years old when Fidel Castro's revolution against the Batista dictatorship started in July of 1953. She was eighteen when she celebrated Castro's victory with her family on New Year's Eve, 1958, and she was nineteen years old when she, along with the rest of the country, was betrayed by Castro and his self-imposed dictatorship.

She took what she learned during Castro's revolution (she was involved mostly in a support capacity) and used it against the newly declared dictatorship in the counter-revolution.

The counter-revolution movement was born at the University of Havana, the school Aleida was attending. She was close to the leaders of the group and was heavily involved in the hiding and transportation of people, information, and weapons.

One of the stories she loved to tell involved her smuggling explosives. She received a call one day, communicated entirely in code, that she needed to drive her car to a certain address to pick up a package before Castro's men arrived to search for it. That package ended up being nitroglycerin. She arrived at a home where the highly explosive compound was being hidden. The canister of glycerin was loaded into her back seat and an envelope of nitro pills was stuffed into her underwear moments before Castro's men appeared. In Aleida's words, "I drove past and waved at them and went on my way."

Aleida and her father both knew the other was also involved in the counter-revolution, but they didn't discuss it until after they had both left

Cuba. Because tobacco was one of the only exports Cuba had to offer the world, her father was given the freedom to travel back and forth to the United States as needed. She would eventually learn that her father was recruited by the CIA during one of these trips. He supplied the US government with information from within the island, including troop movements and Russia's support of Castro.

The Santiago family home also became a safe house during this time. People would come and go, no questions asked, smuggled in and out from the underground garage so as not to alert the neighborhood spies of any strange activity.

Another close call involved a truck full of guns being hidden in her family's garage. Aleida recalled watching from her bedroom window as a military truck full of soldiers rolled through her neighborhood conducting random searches. The military truck made it halfway down her driveway before being waved off by another truck full of soldiers, having chosen a different house to search across the street. The Santiagos were mere feet away from being exposed and possibly executed for their support of the rebellion against Castro. All of this while Aleida was just nineteen years old.

Finally in 1961, when the Bay of Pigs invasion (a US supported/Cuban exile lead operation) failed and all hope of Castro being thwarted was gone, Aleida's father decided it was time to seek political asylum for himself and his family in the United States. Aleida didn't want to leave. It meant leaving her beloved country, her home, and leaving the men and women she had been fighting side by side with for a better Cuba. Her father insisted she join the rest of her family in Miami and secured her passage on the last ferry boat off the island before all transportation for Cuban citizens ceased. As a last act of defiance, she smuggled her mother's jewelry off the island instead of surrendering it over to Castro's treasury, as was required of all Cubans. Standing on the deck of the ferry, with necklaces, rings and bracelets stitched to the inside of her dress, Aleida Santiago watched as her island home disappeared into the horizon. She was twenty years old.

She would stay in Miami for the next three years. She described that time as very dark. Angry. Filled with survivor's guilt, feeling like a traitor. It was not only the guilt she felt for abandoning her fellow revolutionaries that stayed with her. The guns and explosives she had transported for the rebels were used by guerrilla warfare to kill people - sometimes innocent bystanders - and that was not lost on her. Therapy helped. So did the passage of time. Aleida never shied away from her complicated history. Once in her classroom, while discussing her revolutionary background with her students, the question of 'was I a solider in a war or a terrorist responsible for murder' was raised. She decided to let her 6th grade students put her on trial and decide for themselves. It was no stretch to see why some thirty-five years later Aleida could relate to a television show about a warrior atoning for past sins.

A Different Battle

By the time 2006 came around, Aleida had been feeling off for a while. Her body was telling her something was wrong but doctors were having a hard time finding the source. On a positive note, because of her frequent attendance at *Xena*-themed events and volunteering to help with the *Xena* fan club, Aleida befriended her beloved Xena, Lucy Lawless herself. It didn't take long for Lucy to become a fan of Aleida's, listening intently to all the stories that had enthralled us years before.

It was toward the end of March 2006 that Aleida was diagnosed with esophageal cancer. When she called to tell me the horrible news it was like a punch in the gut, but she was trying to stay positive. It was never a thought in my mind that she wouldn't beat it. It wasn't possible.

On April 4th, she sent out an email to family and friends, Xenites and otherwise, updating everyone on her diagnosis in true Aleida 'good news, bad news' fashion. Yes, it's cancer but it's treatable. Yes, the news was a shock but no reason to dwell on the why or how. It was time to fight with the help of her family and friends; she'd take it one day at a time and keep living her life.

"All of this will help me beat this and, hopefully at paella time next year, it will all be just a bad memory." And she kept her word—she lived her life like she wasn't sick. Traveling to tennis tournaments, frequent trips to the movies, and even some epic days at Disneyland. She didn't want to be a victim. She wanted to live.

We continued our *Xena* marathons, just not as frequently and not always at her house. Our tribe's unofficial matriarch was ill, so we sprang into action, helping in any way we could: accompanying her to chemo treatments (she'd watch *Xena* episodes on a portable DVD player during treatments) and making her house more walker-friendly when she was having a hard time getting around. Several of us would head over once a week, not always on the same day, to make sure her house was still a place of laughter and good stories.

During her illness, she would send out a weekly email updating everyone on her health. Some emails were more promising than others, but she never failed to approach each milestone or setback with the same 'good news, bad news' mentality.

Six months and twelve days after sending out the first email announcing her diagnosis, she dictated her last email update to Kelly, being too weak to type it herself. Her liver was shutting down and she was in a lot of pain. The doctors were stopping the chemo treatment. Grace was seeking a second opinion. Aleida needed to use a walker to get around but wouldn't be taking off the tags yet so she could return it when she started her marathon training the next week.

Things weren't looking good. They were looking terrible, actually. It was finally sinking in that Aleida might not win this battle. And there was one friend who wasn't on that last email but needed to know that Aleida was slipping away from us.

Aleida was fiercely protective of Lucy and their friendship. She never asked Lucy for anything; she was just happy to have her in her life. She didn't want to burden her with the news of her dying, so we did what a loyal tribe does; we did it for her.

Kelly found Aleida's address book and left a message on Lucy's voicemail: "Aleida's not doing well. If you want to say goodbye it should be soon." To Lucy's credit, she showed up the next day. And she brought Renée. And Aleida got to show them the *Xena* Room, her museum dedicated to their beloved characters. They didn't leave that room until every last thing was autographed, a huge smile never leaving Aleida's face.

When Aleida ultimately lost consciousness, she was watching old home movies from her happy childhood in Cuba surrounded by Grace, her partner of over twenty-five years, Lucy, and a few Xenites. From that moment until the moment she died, she was never alone. Her final hours on this earth were surrounded by laughter, love, and shared memories of our own little warrior.

Aleida Estela Santiago passed away at 6:54AM on October 20th, 2006. She was buried four days later. Her two brothers, nephew, and four of her tribe members were her pallbearers. Lucy sang Xena's funeral dirge as Aleida's casket was being lowered into the ground. A sendoff fit for a warrior.

Remembering Aleida

"Aleida once told me she had no regrets. She was a fiercely loyal friend and would not stand for injustice, great or small. She would never give unsolicited advice, but if you did ask for her opinion she would give it to you, honestly and with your best interest in mind. I loved making her laugh. I think about her every day." - Cat C.

"Aleida was a quiet force. She wasn't pushy or abrasive, but if she wanted something, she got it. She waited patiently for people to come into her life, slowly drawn by her will and resolve not to let the good ones get away. She brought passion and joy to the things she did and it spilled out over to those lucky enough to be around her." - Kelly D.

Xena changed my life by giving me a cadre of incredible friends. We shared Xena marathons, holidays, moving parties, heated disagreements about Xena plots and the value of various characters, and we shared the loss of Aleida, who could have put the whole world right if she had had a larger power base. She was staunch, opinionated, philosophical, and the kindest, most generous friend. When I thanked her for her help one day, she said, "That's what friends do." She did not like George Bush." - Alana B.

"Aleida Santiago was a beautiful human and a great spirit. I will always be touched by her courage and strength in the face of adversity. Her life in her birth country of Cuba is the stuff of legends. The recollections of her time there during the revolution will forever stay in my memory. She still inspires me with the way she faced her terminal diagnosis and helped us to accept it as well. She was the quintessential Xena fan and her famous Xenathons gave us all a place to celebrate the show and form friendships that continue to this day. She was a huge fan of Lucy and supported her in all her endeavors. I miss her every day and believe that she is watching over us and smiling at all that is being done to celebrate the 25th Anniversary of her favorite show." - Nora M.

"I remember her to be a kind person with a big heart. She always did for others and she deeply loved Xena and Lucy Lawless. The one thing that she told me that I will never forget was, 'Deb, don't give up on your art; you have talent there.' She is missed." - Deb A.

"Aleida was a very humble and unassuming lady. Underneath her gentle kind appearance was a woman whose life was far from your average person's. I only knew her later on in her life, but the short time I knew her she made a big impression on me. When we first met she welcomed me with open arms and heart and made me feel like I had known her a lifetime. She made me smile, laugh, and love her more, the time I spent in her company. She will always be in my heart and mind and I feel blessed to have known her." - Jo M.

"I met Aleida as part of a Xena Meetup group and was intrigued with the stories she would tell. Her spirit seemed to carry the same fire that we as a group loved so much in the character of Xena. Aleida was smart, funny, and very sharp...but more than that, she was giving of heart. From telling us daring stories of her youth in Cuba to defying the expectations of her local school to do what was right, Aleida represented a figure that I couldn't help but liken to Xena herself." - Adam B.

Chapter Sixty-Four

Our Fallen God of War –
In Memory of Kevin Smith

by MaryD

ARES, GOD OF WAR, was a fearsome (at times cheeky, and then back to evil) character among the Olympian gods and goddesses as depicted on *Xena: Warrior Princess*. Kevin Tod Smith, who played Ares, was so far removed from his character. The actors who worked with him loved him. The fans adored him. He was an actor on the rise and destined for stardom. Until tragedy struck.

On February 15, 2002, it was announced that Kevin had passed away from a fall he sustained in China. The Xenaverse was shocked to its core. The Official *Xena* convention in Pasadena was starting on Friday and the news would shock the entire Xenaverse. I remember the morning of the 15th when I opened my email to see the tragic news. I couldn't believe it. All the *Xena* webmasters held an urgent on-line meeting to decide how we were going to report the news. Those at the convention would not have heard the news (unless they went on-line first thing in the morning).

We all decided to report it at the same time. Creation Entertainment, who was holding the convention, decided to add a note on every chair letting the fans know of Kevin's passing. What a shock it was for them to see that message.

It was a somber convention. Renée O'Connor, Ted Raimi, Hudson Leick, Victoria Pratt, Alexandra Tydings, Alexis Arquette, Bruce Campbell, Steve Sears, and Lucy Lawless (live telephone call from New Zealand – Lucy did not attend because she was pregnant with her third child, Judah) all paid tribute to Kevin.

Lucy paid tribute to Kevin on New Zealand TV and summed up the man she knew and the actor that he was; she talked about his intellect and rapier wit, how he was without malice nor was he mean or vindictive. Kevin truly was a passionate, compassionate man. A trust fund was set up to help Kevin's wife and children

Watch Lucy's eulogy to Kevin on the Paul Holmes Show in New Zealand https://www.youtube.com/watch?v=SIfsCtKN5EE

Chapter Sixty-Five

The Xenite Memorial – Our Fallen Warriors

by MaryD

"You are the best thing that ever happened to me.
You give my life meaning and joy; you will be a part of me forever."
– Xena: Warrior Princess, S4 E01

2020

- Pat Deihl – August 5, 2020. Age 80. Lost her battle with cancer. Beloved in the Xenaverse and by her (now deceased) life-partner, Mary Lee. They were together for 36 years. Together again forevermore.
- Wannetta M. Wilson – June 6, 2020. Age 64. Amazon Elder and beloved friend.
- Julian Sears, Warrior Puppy, passed away on April 25, 2020. Age: 11 and a true Xenite. Julian's human was Steven L Sears. Julian was a beloved Xenite who captured the hearts of all the fans during conventions.

2019

- Lee McQuaid – October 1, 2019. Age: 73. Beloved brother to Pat Vowles and Xenite.
- Jaroslav Verner (Lida Verner's father) – He passed away unexpectedly on July 12, 2019.
- Capt Skip – He passed away on July 11, 2019 from a long illness. He was a long serving Xenite and friend to many in our community but especially the Merwolf pup list.
- Lisa Annette Scoggins – May 12, 2019. Age: 50. Lisa passed away after she lost her battle with cancer. She was a beloved sister and friend.
- Susanne M. Beck (SwordnQuill / Blade) – April 20, 2019. Age: 55. Sue passed away in her sleep over the Easter weekend. She was a beloved sister, friend, bard, and Xenite to the core.

2018

- Shawna Headrick – September 24, 2018. Shawna was a beautiful soul with a generous heart who was taken way too soon.
- Baermer – September 4, 2018. Baermer was a beloved bard and friend to many in the Xenaverse. We will miss her greatly!
- Pany LL – June 17, 2018. She was a beloved friend to many in the Xenaverse and passed away from brain cancer. She was such a glorious personality—larger than life and a fun person to be around.
- Karen M. Nielsen – April 17, 2018. Age 76. Beloved mother to Angie and Amazon Elder.

2016

- Ann Pilichowski – September 13, 2016 – She passed away at age 54 from an aggressive form of ovarian cancer. Beloved friend in the Xenaverse.
- Alexis Arquette – September 11, 2016. She was an actress and played Caligula in Xena Season 6 Episode 12: "The God You Know."
- Theresa Geis – July 25, 2016. Age: 75. She was a beloved Xenite and mother to Susan Geis.
- Heather Spurlin – May 22, 2016. A generous soul and a big heart.

2015

- Kim Rosell – October 19, 2015. Age: 51. She was a beloved friend
- Nene Adams – October 3, 2015. She was a talented bard, a Xenaverse Amazon Elder, and a beloved friend and wife (to Corrie Kuipers).

2014

- Patricia L. Givens (Dax) – February 9, 2014. Age: 44. She was a beloved bard, wife to Rita, and Xenite to the core.

2011

- Lisa Smith-Cruz – November 25, 2011. She was an active community member and fundraiser for many very worthy causes.
- Karen "Nightgal" – October 7, 2011. Age: 53. Karen was a Civilian Crime Scene Investigator and a huge Xena fan. She was always there for her friends despite the long hours she worked, and she was an all-around sweet person.
- Cinthie (Ciegra) – May 14, 2011. She was a gifted artist and friend to many on Merwolfpack list.
- Cathy Liddicoat (CathBard) – March 20, 2011. She passed away from a long battle with lung cancer.

- Julie Sanges – March 12, 2011. She passed away from a long illness. No memorial was planned as was her wish.
- Diane Norris (Didah, dinars) – February 20, 2011. She was a hardcore Xenite and a great Kevin Smith fan. Diane was also a great photographer

2010

- Liz Staub (Cousin Liz) – October 10, 2010. She was a beloved friend, an avid collector, and a webmaster (Soulmates).
- Marjanka Oudshoorn – June 25, 2010. Age: 39. Lost her battle with cancer.

2008

- Regina Ward (Queenfor4) – July 13, 2008. She was a wonderful bard, author of Snowbound, Gabrielle's Gift, and A Day in the Con.
- Elisa Lynn Hissong (Gila) – June 22, 2008.
- Mr Richard Wood (Priestess Charis father) – May 2008.
- Suzie Solares – April 9, 2008. She was "Gabrielle" to CindyT, a beloved friend and soulmate.
- Atara – March 21, 2008. She was a bard, a mother, and a true Xenite.

2007

- Mrs. Joan Wood (Priestess Charis' mother) – September 2007.
- Michelle De La Rosa – July 19, 2007. She was a beloved friend, artist, and webmaster.
- Becky Calvert – May 0, 2007. Becky created this memorial page, and she was a beloved friend and a true warrior.

2006

- Aleida Santiago – October 2006. She was a beloved friend, an activist, and a Xenite to the core.
- Linda (Lynka) – August 8, 2006. Bard, webmaster, extraordinary artist.
- Dr. Susan Barnes (Alaska) – August 5, 2006. Beloved friend.

2005

- LJ Maas – October 29, 2005. Beloved friend, extraordinary bard, artist and webmaster.

2003

- Robert S. Kenney II (Meleaguer) – April 21, 2003.
- Susan Mullarky – February 3, 2003. Beloved friend.

2002

- Kevin Tod Smith – February 15, 2002. Ares on *Xena: Warrior Princess*. Beloved father, husband, actor.
- Carolyn "Diamonddog" Cason – February 10, 2002. Bard and beloved friend.

2001

- Tonya Muir – January 25, 2001. Beloved bard and wife of Clive.
- Laura (Galdriel) January 2001. TX Member.

1999

- Rebekah (a.k.a. WebHermit) – October 29, 1999 Beloved bard and friend.
- PD Lamberth – August 1999.
- Evie Lamberth – June 4, 1999.
- Kellie Ann Stec – May 28, 1999. Bonnie Fitzpatrick's sister.
- Shirl Landon's Dad *(Date not known)*
- Kristian S. Fisher *(Date not known)*
- Vanessa Ma. Dan's Mother *(Date not known)*

These names were listed but without a date but they passed during1999 to 2000

- "Monnie" Huffman. Frances's (Lyric369) mom.
- Ralph Singer. Shirl's Dad.
- Nancy. Di's (Asklipius) mom.
- John. Di's (Asklipius) dad.
- W. Frank Baum. Frances's (aka MizNick/alwayslooking) father.
- Baby Cora. Daughter of Jennifer, aka Proud Warrioress.
- Unco. Loving mother to Morgan and Meghan, wife to Charles, and best friend/soulmate to Cheryl.
- Inez Gray. Jules's mother.
- Frances McIntyre. Mother of Ellen Pate.
- Nicole Sutherlund.
- Gayle Baker (irishgayle).
- Susan Lafalgio (ares_bard).
- Agnes (Szalkiria).
- Svet (Hybridstar).
- Amy Goodwin (Leslaureat).
- Marlo Jean M. Leon Guerrero (Yakkut The Amazon 72).
- Olivia Lassance Cabral.
- Frances Spinella.
- Ron Murillo

PART 12

TO INFINITY AND BEYOND...

Chapter Sixty-Six

Xena Reboot and Movie Campaign

by Ariel Wetzel

IT MAY SURPRISE those outside of the *Xena: Warrior Princess* fandom that there has never been a *Xena* movie. After all, it was both the top–rated syndicated TV series in the United States and a global hit airing in over 100 countries. Even Xenites—members of the *Xena* fandom—may be unclear why there has not been a *Xena* movie in the two decades since the massively popular series ended. Xenites have campaigned for a *Xena* movie since the series ended in 2001. For a short period, from 2016–2017, a rebooted *Xena* series almost came to fruition.

In 2016, the *Xena* fandom erupted at the news NBCUniversal was developing a *Xena: Warrior Princess* reboot in collaboration with *Xena* producers Rob Tapert and Sam Raimi, under their production company Ghost House Pictures. Soon, *Lost* writer–and–producer Javier Grillo-Marxuach was attached and completed a pilot script the following year. After a decade and a half of *Xena* fans (known as Xenites) campaigning for a *Xena* movie, a continuation of *Xena* was finally happening. However, this news was controversial among Xenites. What was in development was a rebooted TV series with a new cast, not a movie starring Lucy Lawless and Renée O'Connor, which was the desire of most Xenites. Still, others argued, more *Xena* was sure to bring new fans and renewed interest in a crossover with Lawless and O'Connor reprising their roles as Xena and Gabrielle.

However, these debates about the best way to revive *Xena* would be short-lived. The reboot went the way of 96% of proposed TV shows: it died before the pilot was cast or shot. By 2017, Grillo-Marxuach left the project and the reboot was put on hold indefinitely. The following year, Rob Tapert stated that he himself was the wrong person to be at the helm of a *Xena* reboot. https://christopherming.com/2018/05/how-many-tv-pilots-ordered/

The story of the *Xena* reboot is an emotional one for Xenites. On the one hand, this news represented the power of what fans could accomplish. On the other hand, it meant there would potentially be even more years until another attempt was made at a *Xena* revival. With each passing year, the likelihood decreased of the one thing the majority of fans wanted out of a new *Xena* series or movie: Lawless and O'Connor as Xena and Gabrielle.

How did we get to the point where NBCUniversal ordered the pilot for a *Xena* revival? I believe it is through the renewed efforts of fans during the new modes of media engagement enabled by social media. We cried out for our heroes, and we were briefly heard. This chapter will give an overview of the history of fan campaigns through the lens of the Xena Movie Campaign (XMC), one of the prominent fan campaigns of the 2010s. Full disclosure: I write as an insider, as I am one of the administrators of the XMC and a member of the Netflix generation of fans active on social media at the beginning of the streaming era.

2001-2010: Recovering from "A Friend in Need"

However, Xenites felt about "A Friend In Need" (2001), the polarizing but mostly derided conclusion to *Xena: Warrior Princess*, they largely clamored for more. Many were heartbroken that Xena was dead and Gabrielle alone. Others wished to see Gabrielle's warrior journey continue as the new "girl with a chakram." As fanlore has it, Rob Tapert never intended for "Friend in Need" to be the end of *Xena*, as there was interest in four TV movies. Katherine Fugate, who penned the beloved "When Fates Collide," even wrote a film treatment.

However, a *Xena* movie, at least in the aughts, wasn't meant to be. For years after the series ended, Xenites believed a rights dispute was the reason a *Xena* movie had not been made. Who owned *Xena*? Tapert's own production company, Renaissance Pictures, or Universal? Lucy Lawless may have been the origin of this perception. In interviews during this decade, she reported that the rights to the franchise were in dispute.

"Nobody can agree who owns the rights, and it's a big fat pain in the ass," she reported to SciFi Wire in 2005. NBC and Universal's 2004 merger did not help clarify the matter. http://ausxip.com/xena-movie/xenamovie-news.php

Without comment on the rights issue, Rob Tapert offered some insight into why his own desire to immediately follow up the series with a number of TV movies did not come to fruition. "Unfortunately, based on Lucy's and Renée's sentiment at the time, I called and said NO to the TV movie offer when I should have said Yes," Tapert wrote in a Question & Answer session on AUSXIP's *Talking Xena* message board in 2007. https://www.tapatalk.com/groups/talkingxena/20-answers-from-rob-tapert-t754.html

As he elaborates: "I tried at the last minute to get Renée and Lucy to do four TV movies. Lucy was kind of game, but, at the time, Renée was pregnant [...]. She had no interest in doing any more Gabrielle at that time.

As it was, at the end of six solid years, Lucy and Renée wanted to hang up their outfits."

In this Q&A, Tapert noted that by the mid-aughts, the changing media terrain made it difficult to fund such a project: "Something tells me that a Renée and Lucy movie that hinted of *Xena* would work for the 200,000 people who bought the season box sets. By studio calculations (200,000 x $9.00 per DVD) that would justify a budget of around 1.8M with TV as the potential profit center. That isn't much money." He noted that the media terrain was changing, and the market for DVDs was shrinking, though "A movie or miniseries or a DVD series would freshen up the library on the 134 episodes they have that continue to play around the world. There just isn't a division that sees a huge profit center from doing a one-off. However, from an overall corporate strategy, freshening up the series with new material would increase the value of the assets they already have.**"**

During this decade, fans continued to cry out for more *Xena*. In 2006, a fan held up the sign, "We want a *Xena* movie," in the background of Lawless's appearance on the reality TV series *Celebrity Duets*. There were a few petitions and small letter-writing campaigns over the years. However, the franchise seemed to be winding down. With no new officially licensed comics, novels, or toys being published, all was quiet on the *Xena* front for the rest of the decade. *Xena* only lived on at the annual conventions, in fan fiction, reruns, and most significantly, the rise of streaming services.

Not everyone wanted a *Xena* movie. At my first convention, in 2012, I asked Xenites why they wanted a *Xena* movie. I recall one Amazon Elder—the nomenclature for the senior-most Xenites—patiently explaining why she didn't. It was the same concern started by Lawless and Tapert themselves: the actresses (then in their early 40s) were "too old" and would be recast as conventional Hollywood babes, and, even worse, given boyfriends. But beyond fear of a remake sullying Xena and Gabrielle's legacy, fans had been promised more *Xena* throughout the aughts and were wary of what it could become.

The 2010s: Social Media, Netflix, and Xena Movie Campaign

Netflix, then known as the internet-based DVD rental company, would introduce video streaming in 2007, and *Xena* was one of the early inclusions. Though we may never know the viewing numbers on Netflix, Xenites saw an influx of new fans who discovered the series through streaming. Meanwhile, those who had watched *Xena* as children were coming of age, rediscovering the series, and joining the fandom.

New fans converged on old platforms such as the forums Talking Xena and Xena On-line Community, and new Web 2.0 social media platforms like

Tumblr, Facebook, and Twitter. At the annual *Xena* conventions, when the cast and crew asked, "who here is a [con] virgin?" hundreds of hands would shoot up.

In the 2010s, new fans and old would work together to revive the efforts for a *Xena* movie using social media platforms. One such movement was the Xena Movie Campaign (XMC), which began as a Facebook page in 2011 and soon grew to nearly 100,000 followers. Much of what we did was build the fandom's presence on social media, primarily Facebook but also Twitter, Tumblr, and Instagram. Social activities included the weekly "Cheeky Tuesday" photo captions, trivia contests, downloadable wallpapers and calendars, and prize giveaways. We took advantage of Google hangouts new live-streaming capabilities to host a *Xena* broadcast talk show. We sent Xenites in massive numbers to vote for *Xena* in any and every on-line "battle of the fandoms" contest, demolishing the competition. We attended the annual *Xena* conventions in Burbank, California, from 2012-2015, interviewed Xenites, and shared daily video recaps.

The social efforts built community. Our primary efforts were campaigns on social media, posting on Universal's Facebook page, tweeting #XenaMovieNow, and throwing our support behind warrior women franchises, such as *Wonder Woman* and *Terminator*, to show that a *Xena* revival would be profitable. Letter-writing campaigns were updated with a tri-annual mail-in of movie tickets to Universal in a campaign called "Fistful of Tickets," where we printed faux "*Xena* Movie" ticket stubs and mailed them to NBCUniversal. We also supported parallel campaigns such as the "*Xena* Movie Fans" petition to Universal, an older campaign method used alongside the new.

XMC began campaigning with Netflix under the hashtag #NetfliXena, asking the streaming giant to pick up a *Xena* season 7. The 1990s revivals were in. Classics ranging from *Twin Peaks* and *X-Files* to *Will & Grace* and *Full House* were getting new seasons, some on network television and others on streaming services. This wave of revivals followed the ground-breaking success of the fan-funded *Veronica Mars* Kickstarter in 2012 and the return of *Arrested Development* on Netflix in 2013.

The fans' biggest success was getting #Xena to trend on Twitter and Facebook at several points beginning in 2012. It helped that Lucy Lawless was the biggest public supporter of a *Xena* movie in interviews, convention appearances, and tweets. Her efforts paid off. #Xena trended in 2013 when Lucy tweeted, "Had an interesting call from a chap who wants to re-invigorate the #Xena brand. You guys may have started something."

The support from our leading lady was invigorating. However, campaign efforts sometimes left us wondering if we were tweeting into an abyss. Were we being heard by anyone beyond NBCUniversal's social media team?

Then, finally, Hollywood Reporter broke the news of the *Xena* reboot described above. In August 2016, The Hollywood Reporter reported that, "Sources tell *THR* that the new, modern Xena would have to have the charisma and charm of Lawless and the smarts of *The Hunger Games*' Katniss as producers are said to be looking for a sophisticated and smart superhero for a new generation."

https://www.hollywoodreporter.com/live-feed/xena-reboot-nbc-confirms-search-815073

Xena was trending again and the broader community of fantasy fans expressed excitement about a genre series featuring an iconic warrior woman. However, many fans were concerned. In the same article, NBC Entertainment President Bob Greenblatt told *THR*, "I don't think it's just a continuation, but we haven't gotten that far. I think it's a great character, and we should try to figure out how to revive it somehow." If the reboot featured Lucy Lawless, it would be difficult to find a way to include her on screen. "We'd love to have Lucy be a part of it — if we felt that her presence didn't overshadow the direction we take with it," Greenblatt told *THR*. "I'm not sure how she could be part of it if she wasn't playing Xena, and I don't know if that's a direction we'll ever go."

By December 2015, The Hollywood Reporter announced that Javier Grillo-Marxuach would be the writer and producer. Grillo-Marxuach's list of fantasy and science fiction credentials was impressive, including the popular series *Charmed* and *Lost*, and the cult classic comic and TV series *The Middleman*.

https://www.hollywoodreporter.com/live-feed/nbcs-xena-reboot-finds-writer-848493

Xenites, as the core group of fans who were actively engaging with the series and each other, were divided. Fans had initially campaigned for a movie with the original cast. Most took little issue with a new *Xena* property taking the form of a TV series rather than a movie, but those who supported a recast of the characters were in the minority in the fandom. Lucy Lawless and Renée O'Connor were in their mid-to-late 40s at the time, and many fans were struck by the contradiction that these actresses were "too old" when male action stars like Arnold Schwarzenegger and Sylvester Stallone were reprising their iconic *Terminator* and *Rocky* characters in their 60s and 70s.

Xena Movie Campaign took the following position: while a reboot was not our first choice, it was likely necessary to bring in new fans who would then rediscover the old series and join the efforts for a reprisal by the original cast. In other words, the reboot was a path towards a revival. Grillo-Marxuach, who was accessible to fans on social media, reassured fans in early 2016 that "there is no reason to bring back *[X]ena* if it is not there for the purpose of fully exploring a relationship that could only be shown sub-textually in first-run syndication in the 1990s." We were further reassured that Rob Tapert was attached and that the show would be filmed through his and Raimi's production company, Ghost House Pictures.

https://okbjgm.tumblr.com/post/140591060316/do-you-think-the-fans-reaction-to-lexas-death

Then, reboot news went quiet for several months. Early in 2017, Grillo-Marxuach quietly announced that he'd left the reboot due to "insurmountable creative differences." By August 2017, The Hollywood Reporter confirmed that the project was dead.

https://www.hollywoodreporter.com/live-feed/xena-warrior-princess-reboot-dead-at-nbc-1031380

We learned later from an interview with Grillo-Marxuach on the *Xena Warrior Business podcast* that the reboot pilot script, *Xena: Destroyer of Nations*, made some key changes. The tone would have been *"somewhere between Gladiator and [Mad Max] Fury Road."* While he found that the campy style of the original played well on 90s first-run syndication show, he "really wanted the show to be a little more… grounded is the wrong word. I just wanted it to live in a world where the stakes felt really high, where there was violence." Plot-wise, in this pilot, Xena aided Hercules in completing his infamous twelve labors, but he took credit for what was largely her accomplishments. After this show's version of the gauntlet, Xena's heart was unchained not by a kiss with Hercules (like in the original) but by Gabrielle nursing her back to health. Gabrielle, in this incarnation, was a tattooed Scythian, a member of the nomadic people believed to be a basis for the myth of the Amazons.

https://www.tor.com/2018/09/28/gladiator-meets-fury-road-the-xena-reboot-that-could-have-been/

We may never learn what creative differences led to the cancelation of the *Xena* reboot. Some fans speculated it was homophobia. Grillo-Marxuach countered this rumor on social media, noting that all parties were supportive of Xena and Gabrielle having an explicitly romantic relationship in the reboot.

Rob Tapert did not speak publicly on the *Xena* reboot until his appearance with Lucy Lawless at the Motor City Comic Con in 2018. He considered himself *"the wrong person to be at the helm of doing Xena"* and *"I feel like we told a lot of really good stories and we captured lightning in a bottle with Xena."* Tapert had not seen a *Xena* script that "reached the next potential."

http://xena2.ausxip.com/rob-tapert-xena-reboot/

Unfortunately, since Tapert's comments in 2018, there has been no news of movement towards a *Xena* reboot. Lucy Lawless has continued to express public support for a continuation of *Xena*. In 2019, she responded to the *Terminator Dark Fate* trailer with new enthusiasm for returning to her iconic character: *"I was like, why are they not doing that with Xena? Bring back me and Renée [O'Connor] at the ages we are now and hand the baton over. I'm not signing a six-year [TV] contract to play Xena, but as a movie? Great!"*

It only takes a comment like Lawless's to set #Xena trending once again. This indicates there is still massive interest in more *Xena: Warrior Princess*, especially starring the original cast. However, fan campaigns have died down for the time being. Xena Movie Campaign is currently on hiatus, waiting for the next generation of fans in the 2020s to revive new interest in the franchise and campaign.

Will the 2020s be the decade we finally see more *Xena*? As Lucy Lawless and Rob Tapert say, it is only a matter of time before someone brings the character back.

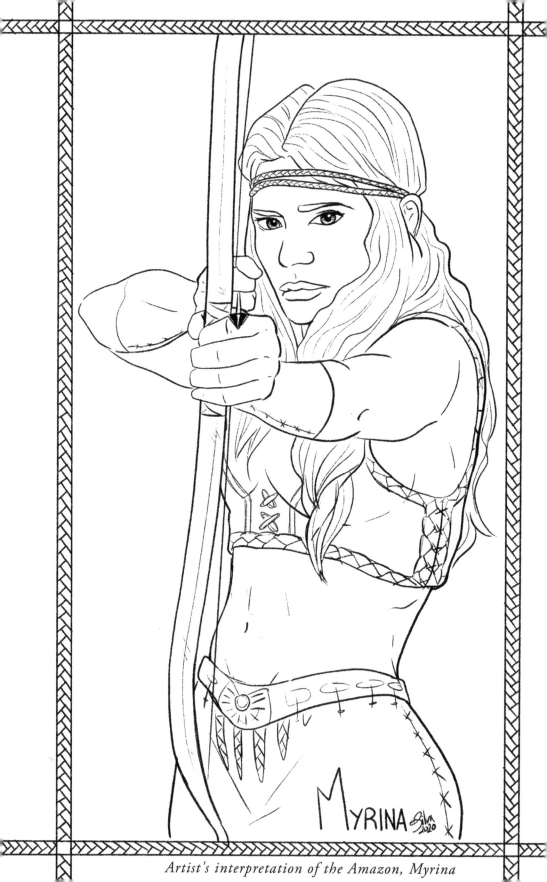

Artist's interpretation of the Amazon, Myrina

Chapter Sixty-Seven

Xena: Warrior Musical, The Lost Scroll – The Xena Musical of the Next Generation

by S.C. Lucier and Meghan Rose

XENA: WARRIOR MUSICAL, The Lost Scroll is a full length musical with more than twenty original songs —plus a few epic battle scores!— that pay tribute to the show we know and love. On their way to the Amazon village to celebrate the naming ceremony of a promising new junior regent, Xena and Gabrielle learn of a Roman warlord's plot to steal a valuable and very powerful item from the tribe. With Joxer's help, Xena uncovers the details of the scheme, but not before our villain Kāko attacks the Amazons and kidnaps leader-in-training Myrina. With Ephiny injured and Myrina missing, Gabrielle has no choice but to promise to remain in the village, leading Xena down a path of traveling alone. Aphrodite and Ares manage to narrate the tale despite engaging in their signature battle of wits. Will the Amazons prevail in the face of devastating and endless greed? Will their new leader, Myrina, live to restore strength to the Amazon Nation? Will Xena and Gabrielle ever express their feelings for one another, or will they go their separate ways? This action-packed show is an exciting new way to experience the timeless characters of the Xenaverse. New songs. New story. Same hero!

***

Writing this musical was a thoroughly rewarding process that took nearly two years to complete from conception. It began as an idea to combine our work in Broadway-style shows and our love for the Warrior Princess. It was a beautiful challenge to both pay tribute to and add layers to a world as vast as the Xenaverse, all while bringing it to life in only about two hours of performance. And don't get us started on timeline anomalies! There were, however, a few things that we were considering as a "given" right from the start. We knew we needed the musical to have the same feel as the series did: a heavy amount of camp but with a genuine heart. The result of this is an eclectic soundtrack in which each character's song takes on a style that is most true to them. We wanted the story to reach the larger-than-life scale of live theatre and touch on struggles that we are currently experiencing in our world. We definitely needed fight scenes and some killer battle scores to match. Oh yeah, and it's Xena, so of course, it had to rock!

We also felt it was important to write for a new generation of fans, especially because the piece was scheduled to premiere in none other than the 25th anniversary year. To accomplish this need, we created a character named Myrina who exudes a fierce hope for the future of the Amazons and inspires the best from her people. She is representative of what can be, even today, the often-overlooked qualities in female-presenting characters: she lifts others up around her, she inspires community responsibility, and she is an excellent leader. It is fitting to the show's legacy that there is so much potential for good that we know will come from the future Xenas of the world. Myrina is our contribution to this future.

We strived for the show to utilize the depth of knowledge that long-time fans would be bringing as an audience by including as many references as possible and pulling from associations that were already developed in their relationship to the show. There will also be, hopefully, people who listen to our work that have never seen the series before, who might be inspired to become true fans. In the end, of course, every fan we can reach with our music is really a testament to the original series. For a group of people to come together and create characters, storylines, and themes that are still just as powerful decades later is astonishing. It is truly an honor to contribute to such a legendary fandom.

The Lost Scroll Credits
by Lucier & Rose

Xena: Warrior Musical is an unauthorized musical theatre show and concept album inspired by the TV series Xena: Warrior Princess.

Cast:
Xena: Melissa Rose Hirsch
Gabrielle: Hannah Ripp-Dieter
Amazons: Joyah Love Spangler
Kāko: Andrew Swackhammer
Myrina: Kristian Espiritu
Joxer, Vlakas: Angelo McDonough
Ephiny: Zia
Aphrodite: Kristin Dausch
Ares: Sean Quinn Hanley

Watch the Trailer on YouTube:
https://youtu.be/EssR95Fp7o4

Chapter Sixty-Eight

Passing the Chakram to a New Generation

by MaryD

WE HAVE ARRIVED at the last chapter of this book about this groundbreaking fandom. You have read how this fandom was born and what it has accomplished. With that in mind, please remember that with grit and determination, people prevail through the darkest of times. I'm writing this chapter, while the COVID-19 pandemic has ravaged the world. So much pain and sorrow… But amid the pain, there is hope. You have to have faith that tomorrow will be a better day. It will be brutal, and it will be a test, but one thing that Xena has taught us is that we will prevail if we reach out (social distancing when possible) and help those in need. The Greater Good is activated all the time but especially crucial at this time and, as we have found out in the last twenty-five years, in a time of crisis, our community bands together and fights.

What's next for the Xenaverse? I will predict that this fandom will continue to grow (all that time in self-isolation will give new fans a chance to discover the Warrior Princess and her Bard). I was finalizing this extraordinary book when I received a message that was just astonishing. I was given an extraordinary gift; the Xenaverse is chockers (Aussie speak for 'filled') with truly amazing and talented people (no big surprise there). That message changed the course of this final chapter.

Two extraordinarily gifted Xenites have been working on Xena: Warrior Musical, The Lost Scroll. Chapter Sixty-Seven goes into detail about the show and how it was created. I was so impressed, I had to include it in the book. I wanted S.C. Lucier and Meghan Rose, the creators of the musical, to tell you about it. They sent me the full soundtrack to listen to (yes, I'm thrilled to bits and extraordinarily blessed).

I'm writing this while I'm listening to the next generation produce a future Xenaverse Classic. They are astonishingly gifted. The future of the Xenaverse belongs to the next generation, and if this is the caliber of creativity from them, the future is bright.

There will come a time when Universal decides to resurrect Xena, and a new generation of actors will fill the iconic roles. We will see an influx of new Xenites and the old guard, the Amazon Elders, who will pass the chakram to the new generation. Until that day comes, the Elders and new fans will continue to express their love for the show and will close ranks when needed to help others.

The Xenaverse is a family that we have chosen. That's the message of *Xena*. We strive to make our community the best it can be and be there for people in need. Once you help others, you help yourself.

If you are reading the print edition (hardback or paperback), you will find that at the end of this book, there are some blank pages. They were left empty because James Gottfried from the Xenaversity of Minnesota had a great idea. He asked me to leave a few pages blank so that you can all get your friends to sign it (similar to a school yearbook) or have the Xena cast/crew sign it at the next convention.

I hope you have enjoyed this love letter to the Xenaverse. What an extraordinary fandom. It's been a huge honor and a pleasure in putting this book together. It's been a labor of love. It would not have been possible if not for the support, encouragement and help from friends I have known for over twenty years.

I had a definite idea of how I wanted to end this book. The only problem was that I am not an illustrator. I asked my friend, Hayriye Makas Uygun, to create an illustration of what I had envisaged being the final image. I wanted everyone represented in the Xenaverse; to have fans walking towards their new adventures with Xena and Gabrielle looking on in approval. Hayriye gave me precisely what I wanted, and it's a fantastic final image.

Xena: Their Courage Changed Our World will be updated and republished in a few years time for the 30th Anniversary and hopefully for decades to come. Eventually, this too will be passed on to the next generation just like the Amazons of old, preserving our history and traditions.

In the meantime, be strong, be safe until we meet again!

Before I end this final chapter, I would certainly be remiss if I didn't continue the Xena tradition of putting in a disclaimer to end this body of work...

No writers, artists, beta readers, or an overworked editor were
harmed during production of this book. However,
a lot of black jelly beans were consumed by the publisher.

TO A STRONG AMAZON NATION!

BATTLE ON!

CONTRIBUTOR INDEX

XENITE STORY INDEX

PHOTO & ILLUSTRATION CREDITS